D0175250

AMERICAN ARSENAL

PATRICK COFFEY

AMERICAN ARSENAL

A Century of Waging War

OXFORD
UNIVERSITY PRESS

OXFORD
UNIVERSITY PRESS

Oxford University Press is a department of the University of Oxford.
It furthers the University's objective of excellence in research,
scholarship, and education by publishing worldwide.

Oxford   New York
Auckland   Cape Town   Dar es Salaam   Hong Kong   Karachi
Kuala Lumpur   Madrid   Melbourne   Mexico City   Nairobi
New Delhi   Shanghai   Taipei   Toronto

With offices in
Argentina   Austria   Brazil   Chile   Czech Republic   France   Greece
Guatemala   Hungary   Italy   Japan   Poland   Portugal   Singapore
South Korea   Switzerland   Thailand   Turkey   Ukraine   Vietnam

Oxford is a registered trade mark of Oxford University Press
in the UK and certain other countries.

Published in the United States of America by
Oxford University Press
198 Madison Avenue, New York, NY 10016

© Patrick Coffey 2014

All rights reserved. No part of this publication may be reproduced,
stored in a retrieval system, or transmitted, in any form or by any means, without the
prior permission in writing of Oxford University Press, or as expressly permitted by law,
by license, or under terms agreed with the appropriate reproduction rights organization.
Inquiries concerning reproduction outside the scope of the above should be sent
to the Rights Department, Oxford University Press, at the address above.

You must not circulate this work in any other form
and you must impose this same condition on any acquirer.

Library of Congress Cataloging-in-Publication Data
Coffey, Patrick.
American arsenal : a century of waging war / Patrick Coffey.
pages   cm
Includes bibliographical references and index.
ISBN 978-0-19-995974-7
1. Military weapons—Research—United States—History.
2. Military weapons—United States—History—20th century.
3. Weapons systems—United States—Technological innovations—History.
4. Inventors—United States—History—20th century.
5. Military research—United States—Case studies.
6. History, Military—United States—20th century. I. Title.
U393.C545   2014
355.80973—dc23   2013015070

1 3 5 7 9 8 6 4 2

Printed in the United States of America
on acid-free paper

To Ellen

CONTENTS

Introduction 3

1 Edison at War 12

2 Gassing the Senator 26

3 Mitchell's War in Three Dimensions 43

4 The Bombsight 61

5 Precision Bombing Tested 73

6 Napalm 90

7 The Switch 105

8 The Atomic Bomb 121

9 The Weapon Not Used 145

10 The Cold War and the Hydrogen Bomb 169

11 Missiles 189

12 War Games 209

13 Four Lessons from Vietnam 233

14 Star Wars 255

15 Smart Bombs and Drones 272

Epilogue 285

Sources and Acknowledgments 291

Notes 294

Index 316

AMERICAN ARSENAL

Introduction

I began to think about this book while writing a book on the history of science, a book that described the intersection of science and war including chemical warfare, submarine detection, and the atomic bomb.[1] C. P. Snow spoke of a divide between scientists and nonscientists, and that has certainly been evident in weapons development. But America's defense efforts are divided in other ways as well, and the rifts have become more evident in the limited wars America has fought since World War II. Both nonscientists and scientists put too much faith in technology, politicians did not understand the military's commitment to victory, military officers saw politicians as hacks worried about reelection, and everyone blamed defense contractors for inflated budgets. All participants were driven by both higher motives (patriotism, loyalty to their service branches, saving lives, and the advancement of human knowledge) and baser motives (career advancement, glory, and profit). Military officers, scientists, politicians, and businessmen have often spoken past one another, and the results have been usually inefficient and sometimes fatal.

Military technology has always been important, but the outcome of nineteenth-century wars did not depend on new weapons being developed while the war was under way. World War I was different. Scientists and inventors were active participants, developing new poison gases, airplanes, tanks, and submarine detectors that influenced the course of the conflict. That trend accentuated in World War II, where the Germans introduced rockets, jet propulsion, and nerve gas, and the Americans and British invented radar, napalm, and the atomic bomb. In that war, technology determined the outcome—if Hitler had possessed an atomic bomb in 1942, the war would have ended on his terms.

America's military focus changed with the twentieth century. Before 1917, the United States had limited its foreign wars to the Western Hemisphere and the Pacific, and the United States had followed Thomas Jefferson's advice to avoid "entangling alliances" in Europe. That changed when Wilson sided with England and France after World War I had been deadlocked for more than two years. America had a good navy and almost no army at all, but in less than eighteen months, its citizen-soldiers and industrial might tipped the balance against Germany and Austria. Then, for twenty years, the United States returned to isolation. America demobilized and ignored the rise of Nazism, Fascism, and Japanese militarism until shortly before Pearl Harbor, when President Roosevelt began to prepare for United States entry on the side of England and the Soviet Union. After that war, America has remained entangled abroad in ways that might have appalled its founding fathers.

The transformation—from isolationist state to superpower—has been unplanned, undesired by many, and enormously expensive. It was also inevitable. The change is too large for a comprehensive history, and this book describes it selectively. It begins in 1917, when Progressivism was the political movement of the day. Progressivism was neither isolationist nor expansionist, neither Democratic nor Republican: Woodrow Wilson, Theodore Roosevelt, Robert La Follette, Josephus Daniels, and William Jennings Bryan—very different in their ideologies and politics—all claimed the label "progressive." They favored regulations of railroads and banks, child labor laws, and workplace safety regulations, and they brought those same high-minded attitudes to war. When America entered World War I, many claimed that it did so with only good intentions, and that the nation's

Progressive ideals would save lives because the United States, fighting on the side of democracy, would shorten the war.

America's academic scientists were not up to European standards in 1917, but the nation was proud of its inventors, such as Thomas Edison and Henry Ford. They made practical things that people wanted—telephones, electric lights, motion pictures, and automobiles. America's inventiveness, combined with its Progressivism, meant that the nation's weapons should be both innovative and lifesaving, and the century would see repeated claims along those lines. America's use of poison gas was humane, because gassed soldiers died from its effects less often than did soldiers who suffered wounds from high explosives or shrapnel; the Norden bombsight was so accurate that bombers could destroy factories and rail yards without hitting workers' homes; atomic bombing of Hiroshima and Nagasaki made an invasion of Japan's home islands unnecessary and saved a million American casualties; the Strategic Defense Initiative would shield America from nuclear attack; "smart" bombs would find the ventilator shaft of an enemy's command center and leave a hospital across the street undamaged; and the operator of a drone aircraft could sit in a cubicle, hovering, watching terrorists, striking only when no civilians would be hurt. As will be seen, some claims proved more accurate than others.

Each of this book's chapters illustrates the unplanned nature and the unintended consequences of America's military transformation. All history is selective, this book more than most. I have emphasized weapons and strategy over foreign policy, and have chosen stories that have, in my view, been undertold—the plan for all-out nuclear attack against the Soviet Union, for example, rather than the Cuban missile crisis. Subjects include submarines, chemical weapons, strategic bombing, atomic and hydrogen bombs, the nuclear standoff with the Soviet Union, the missile race, the Reagan-era Strategic Defense Initiative, "smart" bombs, the M-16 rifle, handheld anti-aircraft missiles, and unmanned aerial vehicles. Some patterns emerge, and I go into most detail about chemical weapons, strategic air power, and nuclear weapons.

The book has its principal characters, figures who appear in more than one chapter and who marked the century. James Bryant Conant, a Harvard chemist who managed development of the poison gas Lewisite in World War I, was civilian head of the Manhattan Project in World War II, and unsuccessfully opposed development of the hydrogen bomb in the Cold War. Curtis LeMay, the youngest American lieutenant general since Ulysses Grant, was World War II's most influential air commander, and led the Strategic Air Command and then the Air Force in the Cold War. Edward Teller, a nuclear physicist in the Manhattan Project, was known as the "father of the hydrogen bomb" and was a proponent of unrealistic projects in Ronald Reagan's "Star Wars" Strategic Defense Initiative. And Robert McNamara, secretary of defense during the Kennedy and Johnson administrations, was an architect of the Vietnam War and of America's nuclear strategy. Conant and Teller were scientists, LeMay was a soldier, and McNamara was a business executive turned military strategist. They shared qualities—intelligence, persistence, and, perhaps most significant, arrogance. They believed that they knew what America needed, and they were impatient with dissent.

Clausewitz, the nineteenth-century Prussian author of *On War*, famously said that war is politics continued through other means. American politics means presidential elections every four years, which gives presidents an incentive either to delay hard choices or to make them impulsively. Eisenhower, Kennedy, Johnson, and Nixon all pursued Vietnam policies in which they had little confidence, but none of them wanted the defeat to occur on his watch. Nixon would have tried to continue the war to the end of his second term but, brought down by Watergate, passed Gerald Ford a failed South Vietnam. Reagan promised to shield America against nuclear missiles, and his successors—George H. W. Bush, Bill Clinton, George W. Bush, and Barack Obama—have spent billions rather than admit the promise's impossibility.

The political problems are embedded in America's very structure. Who is to run a war? America's Constitution mandates civilian control of the military, yet generals and admirals have long known that they can outlast a particular secretary or administration, and they lobby their congressional supporters directly. And although the president is the nation's commander in chief, presidents often tolerate insubordinate military officers because they fear the political consequences of firing them. Calvin Coolidge court-martialed the Army Air Corps' General Billy Mitchell only when Mitchell accused his superiors of "almost treasonable" behavior in the press. Many generals who had supported Roosevelt's demand for unconditional surrender in World War II objected to the political limitations that presidents imposed on the wars in Korea and Vietnam: Truman dismissed Douglas MacArthur in Korea, but only after he made his insubordination public, and Kennedy detested Curtis LeMay (who did not make his policy objections public) but kept him as Air Force chief of staff in order to silence him.

The idea that a president can direct or control nuclear war is an illusion. First, if it ever comes to that, the president would very likely be dead or incommunicado. Second, the plans for nuclear war are so complex and intertwined that there are very few options—in 1961, there was only one: unleash every American weapon in what Air Force generals called a "Sunday punch." Most presidents have shown little interest in nuclear strategy (Carter, trained as a nuclear engineer, was the exception). Months after Kennedy took office, he asked for a demonstration of the "red telephone" from which he was to respond to a Soviet attack. No one could find it—it had been in Eisenhower's desk drawer, but Jackie Kennedy had swapped desks when she redecorated the White House.[2] And the military certainly did not believe in civilian micromanagement. LeMay angrily told Assistant Secretary of Defense John Rubel, "Who needs the president if there's a war? All we need *him* for is to tell us there *is* a war. We're professional soldiers. We'll take care of the rest."[3] Before the Cold War's nuclear standoff, a president had time to remove incompetent, insubordinate, or unstable commanders, as Lincoln and Roosevelt had done earlier. But a war with the Soviet Union in the 1960s would have lasted only a few hours, and a "Dr. Strangelove" scenario, in which a rogue general launched a nuclear attack, was entirely possible. General Tommy Power, in charge of the Strategic Air Command (SAC) from 1957 to 1964, was generally seen as the most likely to do so. He gleefully presented SAC's plans to launch thirty-two hundred warheads to Secretary McNamara; even his superior LeMay called him a sadist, and his subordinate General Horace Wade said of him, "I used to worry that General Power was not stable. I used to worry about the fact that he had control over so many weapons and weapon systems and could, under certain conditions, launch the force. . . . SAC had the power to do a lot of things, and it was in his hands and he knew it."[4]

Political control is further complicated by each military service's "doctrine," the set of principles that guide both its strategic and tactical decisions. The Navy's doctrine in World War I, for example, was to keep the fleet concentrated and ready for a great naval battle. Technological changes, including the submarine and the aircraft carrier, forced doctrinal modifications in World War II. Doctrines are persistent, and they are often poorly understood by civilians—even presidents—who underestimate their importance.

Services will twist language rather than admit that they are acting contrary to their doctrines. The Army Air Corps had little practical experience prior to World War II, and it constructed a precision bombing doctrine that was untested and unrelated to any mission it had been assigned. By the end of the war, the Army Air Forces (AAF, the successor to the Air Corps) had all but abandoned precision bombing. The AAF bombed city centers in Germany, bombed sixty-six Japanese cities with napalm incendiaries, and dropped atomic bombs on Hiroshima and Nagasaki. Yet it refused to admit that its doctrine had changed—it simply redefined the terms "precision bombing" and "military target."

Inter- and intraservice rivalry is a repeated motif throughout the book. The most egregious cases: the Navy refused to release Norden bombsights, for which it had little use, to the Army Air Forces, who were attempting precision bombing of Germany in World War II; and the Army and the Air Force engaged in a wasteful missile race in the 1950s—not with the Soviet Union, but with each other. It sometimes seemed that the enemy was not a foreign power but an American wearing a different service uniform.

Service traditions have often impeded the replacement of old weapons with new. The Navy hung on to its battleships even after they were shown to be vulnerable to bomber attack, because its battleship tradition went back to John Paul Jones and the *Bonhomme Richard*. The Air Force, whose generals rose from the ranks of combat pilots, resisted developing missiles because they threatened its bombers, and it still resists unmanned aerial vehicles because they threaten to make pilots obsolete altogether. As a result, weapons can persist long after they have been proven to be useless or obsolete. Chemical weapons lasted for eighty years after World War I, and nuclear weapons, which have proven to be militarily useless, persist today. Barack Obama, George Shultz, Henry Kissinger, Sam Nunn, and William Perry have all called for the elimination of nuclear weapons, but there has been little movement in that direction.

In an ideal world, military doctrine would drive strategy, and strategy would in turn drive weapons development. When the Air Corps developed its precision bombing doctrine in the 1930s, it had neither the bomber nor the bombsight to support it. But by the beginning of World War II, it had acquired a few B-17 heavy bombers, and they were equipped with Norden bombsights it had wrested from the Navy. By the war's end, the United States had produced more than thirty thousand heavy bombers and spent more than half as much on Norden bombsights as it did on the entire Manhattan Project.

Sometimes, however, the technology that is necessary to support a strategy is not only unavailable but impossible. In 1983, President Reagan announced that America would develop a shield to protect America against nuclear attack. Edward Teller used his reputation as a scientist and his success in developing the hydrogen bomb to convince the president, Congress, and the American public to support hugely expensive weapons programs called "Excalibur" and "Brilliant Pebbles" that would never be deployed.

Effective weapons demand to be used, even if they are unsupported by doctrine. Napalm is an example. Developed by Harvard chemist Louis Fieser in 1942, it made the firebombing of Tokyo and other Japanese cities an option, although attacking civilians was contrary to the Army Air Forces' precision-bombing doctrine. And the atomic bomb did not fit within any service's doctrine. Neither President Truman nor Secretary of State James Byrnes concerned themselves with military strategy, an international arms race, or the threat of global annihilation before bombing Hiroshima and Nagasaki. As Truman said, "Having found the bomb, we used it." After the war, the Air Force formed the RAND Corporation to help answer the question "What do we do with the bomb?" Was an atomic bomb just bigger, to be used in the same way as any other bomb? That was Curtis LeMay's opinion. RAND's analysts—Bernard Brodie, Albert Wohlstetter, William

Kaufmann, and Herman Kahn among them—and others, including Henry Kissinger, spent years searching for some rational way to fight a war with nuclear weapons. They never found one.

Rationality assumes the availability and use of good data. It is often in someone's political interest to distort the data, as in the 2003 claims that Saddam Hussein had weapons of mass destruction in Iraq. In the 1950s, the Air Force justified its enormous budgets by inflating estimates of Soviet strength, warning first of a "bomber gap" and then of a "missile gap" with the Russians.

Ethical questions have usually been considered very late, if at all, and groupthink has allowed workers to enjoy collaborating on a weapon's development while ignoring its eventual use. The physicist Hans Bethe said of the Manhattan Project scientists, "Only when our labors were finally completed, only when the bomb dropped on Japan, only then or a little bit before then, maybe, did we start thinking about the moral implications."

Some, such as LeMay, saw morality in terms of patriotism and duty; LeMay never seemed to question his actions as a soldier. Some, such as Harold Urey, who managed uranium separation in the Manhattan Project, turned from away from weapons and toward advocating disarmament. Some, such as Glenn Seaborg, who managed the production of plutonium for the Manhattan Project, seemed not to concern themselves with ethics at all: Seaborg's diary showed that he was more interested in plutonium's effects on his career than on its effects on Nagasaki. Some, such as Robert Oppenheimer, talked about moral responsibility without evident effect on their actions. Oppenheimer supported Conant's suggestion to drop the atomic bomb on Japan without prior warning but then melodramatically told Truman, "Mr. President, I have blood on my hands." Later, Oppenheimer tried to block development of the hydrogen bomb because it represented a policy of "exterminating populations." That, however, was when the bomb seemed technologically impossible. Eight months later, when Edward Teller showed him the solution, he became excited and said it was "so sweet" that it had to be done.

Films and magazines have dehumanized the enemy and shielded the American public from knowledge of how its weapons are used. Walt Disney's film *Victory Through Air Power* portrayed bombing German cities in animated cartoons, and James Agee said of it, "I have the feeling I was sold something under pretty high pressure. . . . I noticed, uneasily, that there were no suffering and dying enemy civilians under all those proud promises of bombs; no civilians at all, in fact." In a *Fortune* magazine survey shortly after World War II's end, almost a quarter of the respondents said that the United States should have quickly used *more* atomic bombs on the Japanese before they had a chance to surrender. The media could turn villains into heroes. Wernher von Braun was a Nazi and an SS officer, and he built the German V-2 missile using concentration camp laborers, thousands of whom died in the process. At the end of the war, the Army's "Operation Paperclip" brought von Braun, his fellow rocket scientists, and the German nerve-gas chemists and their families to the United States. Ten years later, von Braun was talking about America's space program on Walt Disney's television show. It was a remarkable transformation.

America's passage from isolationist state to superpower is still under way, and a historical assessment will need to wait. But it is not too soon to begin to examine the processes embodied in that transformation—American exceptionalism and reliance on technology (which both minimizes American casualties and detaches individual soldiers from war), as well as the attempts to control public opinion in ways that hide the reality of weapons and strategy. We may be seeing change on this last point. In 1982, the Reagan administration reluctantly gave a nuclear missile the still-euphemistic name "Peacekeeper" when its original choice, "Peacemaker," was too much for the public to swallow. Given that, there is something refreshing about calling a drone aircraft "Predator."

Edison begins this book, and his work reverberated throughout the century. In the waning days of World War I, two members of Edison's Naval Consulting Board developed a prototype "aerial torpedo"—a radio-controlled, explosive-packed unmanned airplane meant to be aimed at an enemy ship. It did not see action in that war, but its successors—drone aircraft and smart bombs—have transformed today's battlefield. They are the subject of this book's last chapter, on America's new way of waging war.

Edison at War

O n May 2, 2011, President Barack Obama and his defense team gathered in the White House Situation Room and waited for the assault operation to begin. Live video links connected them to the operation's commander, Vice Adm. William McRaven, in Afghanistan; to CIA director Leon Panetta in Langley, Virginia; and to a camera in a drone aircraft that hovered over a Pakistani compound. Seventy-nine Navy SEALs flew into Pakistan in six silenced, radar-evading Black Hawk helicopters. The SEALs, equipped with night-vision goggles, rappelled from the helicopters, stormed the building, shot and killed Osama bin Laden, and carried off his body. American technology made it possible—the attack itself, its command from afar, and its display to the commander in chief, who sat in the White House, on the other side of the world.

On March 20, 1917, President Woodrow Wilson and his advisers gathered in the White House Cabinet Room, one floor up from the room where Obama and his team would sit almost a century later. They met to consider United States entry in the "Great War." The European powers had spent almost three years locked in a stalemate of infantry trench assaults, naval blockade, and submarine attacks. Millions had died already, and no end was in sight. Since the war's beginning, Wilson had tried to follow the counsel of Washington and Jefferson, who had warned against becoming involved in European conflicts. Wilson had won reelection a few months earlier, when he had led the Democratic ticket on the slogan "He kept us out of war." Now, only weeks after his inauguration, he was about to take the nation into the conflict on the side of England and France.

Secretary of the Navy Josephus Daniels remembered Wilson telling him, "I can't keep the country out of war. They talk of me as though I were a god. Any little German lieutenant can put us into the war at any time by some calculated outrage."[1] German submarines sank American merchant ships in February and March, causing the deaths of American sailors and passengers. Wilson asked his cabinet members for advice, and they were unanimously for war, including Daniels. In the end, however, it was Wilson's decision.

When Wilson asked Congress for a declaration of war, the U.S. Army had only two hundred thousand men under arms, a twentieth of the German army's strength. It had no gas masks, no airplanes that could match Germany's, and only a few days' inventory of artillery shells, given the rate at which the guns were firing on the Western Front. Brass bands played "Over There," crowds cheered, and mothers and sweethearts kissed their boys goodbye.

America had no idea what it was in for. It would nonetheless prepare as best it could, starting at the individual level. That included America's archetypical inventor, Thomas Edison, who offered to direct the U.S. Navy's weapons development. Edison assumed that the Navy would welcome his control, but the Navy had its own service traditions, for which Edison— who had never served in the military—had no understanding or sympathy. The result is an unhappy story compounded by greed, ambition, and politics.

When Europe had descended into war in 1914, Edison was sixty-seven years old. He was the inventor of an incandescent light bulb, the phonograph, a multiplexed telegraph, and a motion picture system—he had been issued more than a thousand patents and was universally considered a genius. He was also difficult. Almost completely deaf, he was a tobacco-spitting, slovenly curmudgeon who scorned theoretical science and claimed that a school ed-ucation would have ruined him as an inventor. His publicity department and a friendly press had manufactured his image as a grandfatherly wizard. He advocated animal rights, but during his battle over the standards for electri-cal current transmission, his employees demonstrated the danger of alternat-ing current by publicly electrocuting dogs. And if dogs were not enough to convince the public, Edison used his movie theaters to show a film of the electrocution of Topsy the elephant. He cheated the inventor Nikola Tesla out of a promised $50,000, telling him, "When you become a full-fledged American, you will appreciate an American joke," and he stole and exhibited without payment a copy of *A Trip to the Moon*, thereby contributing to the bankruptcy of the French filmmaker Georges Méliès. Nonetheless, America had canonized him.

Learning about the outbreak of war, Edison told the *New York Times* that it made him "sick at heart." But not too sick to take a dig at an old rival in the lighting business, Hiram Maxim, who had invented the recoil-driven machine gun: "Making things which kill men is against my fiber. I leave that death-dealing work to my friends the Maxim brothers."[2] Edison did not make or sell guns, but he was nonetheless a military supplier. A week after his interview on the war, the *New York Times* ran another article: "Tests of storage batteries designed by Thomas A. Edison for use in submarine craft have been entirely satisfactory. . . . If the final tests are equally so, new sub-marines will be equipped with the Edison battery."[3]

Edison had been working on batteries for years. In 1900, he had become convinced that the electric car represented the next big opportunity. The lead-acid battery (the same battery now used to start automobiles) had been in common use for twenty years, but it was heavy and contained cor-rosive sulfuric acid. Electric cars would need a lighter, noncorrosive power source, and Edison formed the Edison Electric Storage Battery Company to develop one.

He announced his new alkaline nickel-iron battery to great fanfare in 1903, and he and his son Charles drove off in a shiny red electric car at the end of the press conference. The battery, however, was a disaster. It leaked, and its storage power fell off quickly.

Edison offered returns on all the defective automobile batteries and released a new version in 1909. By then, however, he had missed the automobile market—Ford had shipped his first gasoline-powered Model T the year before. Nonetheless, Edison's battery sold well for uses in which connection to the electric grid was not available—in miners' helmets, in railroad trains, and in boats.[4] And another opportunity looked promising: as of September 1910, the Navy had nineteen submarines in service,[5] all of which used lead-acid batteries as a power source while submerged.

The commercial face of the Edison submarine battery would be Miller Reese Hutchison—a handsome, ambitious man and a flashy dresser. He was an inventor in his own right (the Klaxon auto horn and the Acousticon hearing aid, among other inventions; some joked that he had invented the auto horn to drum up business for his hearing aid). Hutchison, a master at promotion, convinced Edison that his battery was ideally suited for the submarine. Should the sulfuric acid in submarines' lead-acid batteries leak and come into contact with seawater, poisonous chlorine gas would be produced, while Edison's alkaline batteries were safe in that regard. By November 1910, Hutchison and Edison had come to an agreement: Hutchison would work on developing a submarine version of the Edison battery and would receive a 10 percent commission on battery sales to any government, with the exception of Germany and Austria-Hungary. (When their agreement was signed in 1910, that exception had nothing to do with American foreign policy or politics. The German rights to the Edison battery patents were held by an Edison subsidiary, which had its own sales arm. Edison sold the subsidiary to a German firm in 1913. Anti-German feeling was on the rise by autumn 1914, and both Edison and Hutchison would be careful to conceal the German navy's tests of the Edison battery in its submarines.)

After he had come to an agreement with Edison, Hutchison immediately went to work on three fronts: developing the submarine version of the battery, contacting sales prospects, and cultivating Thomas Edison's approval. Hutchison moved right into Edison's laboratory. In a New Year's Eve diary entry at the end of 1911, Hutchison wrote, "I have no regrets as to advancement. Am e[n]sconced here, right next to the greatest living inventor and

■ Miller Reese Hutchison, Edison's chief engineer and the salesman for his submarine batteries. *National Park Service.*

apt to step into his shoes when he passes away."[6] In August 1912, Edison fired his chief engineer and named Hutchison to the job, and Hutchison had his letterhead printed with the tag "Chief Engineer and Personal Representative to Mr. Edison."

At the top of Hutchison's list of sales prospects for the submarine battery was Josephus Daniels, who had been appointed secretary of the Navy in 1913 by President Wilson. Daniels, who always looked as if he had slept in his suit, asked Wilson to appoint the patrician Franklin D. Roosevelt, then 30 years old, as Assistant Secretary. Daniels and Roosevelt were an odd pair. Roosevelt later said of Daniels, "When I first knew him, he was the funniest looking hillbilly I had ever seen."[7]

Daniels had a troubling, even sordid history, at least by today's standards. As editor of the *Raleigh News and Observer*, he had been an instigator of

the Wilmington, North Carolina, race riot of 1898, in which a city government that included African American officials was violently and successfully overthrown by a white supremacist mob, killing somewhere between
eleven and one hundred people—the actual number is unknown, as many
bodies were never found. Daniels boasted forty years later that the insurrection had been due to the joint work of "men who could write, men who
could speak, and men who could ride—the last by no means least important."[8] By "writers" he meant newspaper editors (such as himself) who created white supremacist and anti-black propaganda; by "speakers" he meant
politicians who inflamed crowds; and by "riders" he meant thugs who in-
timidated and murdered.

Daniels was one of the most effective of the "men who could write." His
newspaper published racist cartoons on a daily basis and ran front-page articles with inflammatory headlines, including "Red Shirts to be Worn" (the
standard dress for vigilantes), "Whites Are Justified," "Riotous Negroes,"
and "Negro Rule Doomed." On the morning of the Wilmington riot, his
headline was "A Noose for Him"; on the day following, it was "A Day of
Blood in Wilmington; Negroes Precipitate Conflict by Firing on Whites."
Adjacent to that story, Daniels placed an ink portrait of Col. Alfred Moore
Waddell, the mob's leader and the new Wilmington mayor, who gazed se-
renely into the future. The portrait's workmanship suggests that Daniels
had prepared it long before the riot.

By 1912, Daniels had moderated his racial positions somewhat (he had
no need to be so aggressively anti-black, as North Carolina was by then
completely in the control of white supremacists), and he was ready to step
onto the national stage. He had been an early and effective supporter of
Woodrow Wilson, who appointed him secretary of the Navy.

To sell Secretary Daniels on the Edison battery, Hutchison played on
their shared southern heritage. He would write to Daniels using his idea of
slave dialect, addressing him as "Marse Josephus" and referring to "Marse
Franklin" (Franklin Roosevelt). He began a later letter, "Hit sho am good
fer sore eyes ter see yer hanriten ergin."[9] He flattered Daniels, writing to
Daniels's aide that Edison had walked into the laboratory that morning
and said, "I guess we are getting near the home stake, with a man at the

head of the Navy that has the brains to appreciate a good piece of apparatus and the courage of his convictions."[10] The Navy ordered a set of submarine batteries in February 1915, with the promise of additional orders if things worked out.

On March 25, 1915, the Navy submarine F-4, equipped with lead-acid batteries, sank with the loss of all hands. Months later, a court of inquiry would conclude that chlorine gas was the probable cause.[11] Edison did not wait to see the evidence. Certain that a lead-acid battery had caused the accident, he weighed in immediately: "The only remedy is an alkaline battery," he announced, adding that it was more expensive but lasted longer and was "better in every respect."[12]

In April 1915, the New York Times published a multipage article about the Edison submarine battery, and it read like an Edison press release: "Edison, the man opposed to war and its implements, has perfected a battery which will not only make the submarine habitable by preventing asphyxiation of the crew . . . but will practically double the strategic efficiency of the submarine craft." The article went on to relate that the commander of the Navy's E-2 submarine had detected chlorine leaks the previous November. The boat had surfaced immediately, but two sailors' lungs hemorrhaged from breathing chlorine, and the sub had to be towed into port. The reporter quoted Secretary Daniels on the problems with lead-acid batteries: "The lead casings around the battery are liable to be eaten out by the sulphuric acid in the batteries," he said. "Mr. Edison proposes to use an alkaline solution in the cells of his battery and thus eliminate the danger to the lead casings and the steel partitions," the article continued.[13]

The Edison name seemed to inspire unquestioning confidence in Americans. His batteries were to be tested in the E-2, the very submarine that had reported chlorine leaks near Honolulu.

On May 7, 1915, a German submarine torpedoed and sank the British passenger liner Lusitania, killing 1,198 people, including 128 Americans. Secretary Daniels ordered an accelerated buildup of the Navy. Hutchison expected large commissions on submarine battery orders, and he was convinced that those orders would increase if he could bring Edison and the Navy closer. He found a way—the Naval Consulting Board, which was

■ Thomas Edison inspecting the E-2 submarine. *Edward N. Jackson.*

announced in the *New York Times* on July 13: "Edison Will Head Navy Test Board . . . Got Idea from the Times." The newspaper reported that Edison had accepted Secretary Daniels's request to head a "department of invention and development."[14] The *Times* bragged that the idea for the department came from an interview it had published with Edison on May 30, when he had said, "I believe that . . . the Government should maintain a great research laboratory, jointly under military and naval and civilian control."[15]

In a letter to Daniels, written twenty years later, Hutchison would claim that the board had been entirely his idea. Not only had he conceived it, he had "drummed it into Mr. Edison's head," set up a *New York Times* reporter to interview Edison, and then paid the reporter's expenses to travel to Washington to see Daniels. His letter to Daniels went on: "You wrote to Edison you would form such a Board. He wrote, on the margin of the letter, 'Hutch: What do you think?' . . . I hopped the [train] to Washington, called on you at your home, and said Mr. Edison would be glad to head such a Board."[16]

From Daniels's point of view, he had brought America's greatest genius into the Wilson administration. Daniels named Edison as chairman of the board and Hutchison as a member (Hutchison would sit by the deaf Edison during meetings and tap what was said onto Edison's knee in Morse code). Edison asked the leading scientific and engineering organizations to nominate two members each, but he indulged his prejudices against ivory tower science: when a board member protested to Edison during a meeting that he had selected no physicists, Hutchison broke in to speak for Edison, "It was because of his desire to have the Board composed of *practical* men who are accustomed to *doing* things and not *talking*."[17]

Edison used the Naval Consulting Board to lobby for what would eventually be the Naval Research Laboratory, for which he drew up detailed plans. Secretary Daniels and the Navy's admirals were enthusiastic. They saw little prospect of congressional approval for the laboratory without Edison's advocacy, but thought that his voice would change things.[18] However, their enthusiasm hid an unstated disagreement about the laboratory's control: the Navy admitted it did not have the personnel to staff the lab, but it was not willing to cede control to civilians, and while Edison had said in his *Times* interview that the laboratory should be held "jointly under . . . Naval and civilian control," he would privately say, "No Naval officer should have anything to do with it."[19]

Then disaster. From the *New York Times*, January 16, 1916: "Hydrogen Leak Suspected; Interior of E-2 Wrecked; . . . Daniels Orders Inquiry." The E-2 submarine had been rocked by an explosion while it was in dry dock in the Brooklyn Navy Yard. It had been testing the Edison battery. Four men were killed immediately, and another would die a few days later. Ten others were injured. As Hutchison and Edison claimed, the alkaline Edison battery could not emit chlorine. But if a cell of an Edison battery was reversed (that is, after full discharge, it was subjected to an external current in the direction of discharge), the cell's water would decompose into hydrogen and oxygen—an explosive mixture, especially in the confines of a submarine.

The Navy formed a board of investigation to determine the cause of the E-2 explosion. Lt. Charles Cooke, the submarine's commander, testified that the Edison staff had requested a rapid full discharge of the submarines batteries at 2,100 amperes, that that test that was under way at the time of the explosion, that he had warned the Navy of the danger of hydrogen and had asked for hydrogen-detecting equipment, and that he had asked for individual voltmeters for each of the battery cells. (He had worried that some cells would fully discharge before others and then emit hydrogen when they were reversed by current generated by the still-charged cells, all of which were connected in series; this is apparently what caused the explosion.) Cooke said that his requests had been denied by both the Navy and the Edison Storage Battery Company.[20]

Edison maintained that he was too busy with experiments to talk to the press and that he "awaited the findings of the Board of Investigation with perfect confidence in the ability and impartiality of the officers conducting it."[21] Had Hutchison done the same, he might have been all right. Instead he quickly made several statements to the press that would haunt him: he said that the Edison battery had been safely used in (unnamed) European submarines for years without any problems. This caused surprise, as it was generally assumed that the battery had been reserved for the American Navy. He also said that he had inspected the batteries in the E-2 after the explosion and found them undamaged, implying that the batteries were not the cause of the explosion. Finally, he maintained that the small amount of hydrogen emitted by the battery could not be possibly be explosive.[22]

The next morning, the Board of Investigation's president instructed Hutchison that the Edison Storage Battery Company was an "interested party"—given that the company might be found at fault—and that he should therefore stop making comments that might prejudice public opinion.[23] Hutchison was called before the Board of Investigation two days later, and it was clear that the Navy had taken offense at his comments to the press. A *New York Times* article reported his testimony: "Knew of E-2 Danger but Warned No One; Edison Chief Admits He Knew That Battery Was Likely to Generate Gas; Blames Lieutenant Cooke."[24] The Board of Investigation's president grilled Hutchison:

"Did the Edison Company know that large quantities [of hydrogen] might be given off in a very short time?"

"No, what happened was in many respects a new phenomenon."

"In other words, when you find out things about something you did not know about before, it becomes a new phenomenon?"

"Yes."

Hutchison admitted that the Edison Company had not sent a representative to the battery test and that he had not informed Lt. Cooke of the condition of the batteries because, as he put it, "I would no more think of giving such information to men like Lieutenant Cooke, who know their business, than I would of telling an engineer that he must keep water in his boilers while his fires are going." His implication was that the accident was due to Cooke's incompetence.

Edison, Daniels, and Hutchison all wanted the Edison battery cleared, but for different reasons; they had overlapping but not identical objectives. Edison had put seventeen years of work into his battery and saw it as a linchpin of his electrical empire—a way to provide electrical power to devices disconnected from the grid. If the battery was blamed for the E-2 explosion, his reputation and business would suffer. Daniels, for his part, wanted Edison's support for Wilson's 1916 reelection campaign, and he delayed delivering bad news to Edison until six weeks after the election, when he wrote to tell him that the Navy had rejected his request that the Naval Research Laboratory be located near his offices in New Jersey. Daniels soft-soaped Edison, telling him how much the country needed him,[25] and while Edison threatened to quit the Naval Consulting Board, in the end he did not resign.[26] Finally, Hutchison was paid on government sales of the Edison battery, and his customers were canceling their orders after the E-2 explosion. He saw his future as Edison's successor, and that, in turn, depended on the battery's success. As things fell apart, Hutchison tried to pressure Daniels, writing that "Mr. Edison made a lot of enemies in [the Navy] by coming out as he did for the Democratic Party."[27]

But the Navy had had enough of the battery, of Edison, and of Hutchison (and likely of Daniels too, though there was nothing to be done about him but wait for a change in administration). The Navy was well aware of the risks of gases in submarines—the F-4 disaster, which likely had been caused by a lead-acid battery, had been much worse than the E-2 explosion. The Navy would have accepted the E-2 casualties had they been the sacrifice necessary to develop a better submarine battery. But Edison's grab to control the Navy's future weapons and Hutchison's attempts to blame a Navy officer for the explosion mattered more than any technical arguments. Edison might have been beyond attack, but Hutchison was not, and the Navy focused on him.

Edison and Daniels kept their distance from Hutchison and supported each other. Edison endorsed Wilson's 1916 reelection, although he had previously called himself an independent Republican.[28] It was a very close election. Wilson would win California by a margin of only 0.3 percent, and that state decided the election. And Daniels supported Edison against the uniformed Navy. When the E-2 Board of Investigation sent him its report in February, Daniels refused to release it. Furthermore, he refused press comment on a rumor that the board had concluded that "responsibility rested on someone outside of the United States Naval Service." He did say that the board recommended that the E-2 should continue to be used for tests of the Edison battery.[29] (This did not happen; the E-2 would sit in the Brooklyn Navy Yard's dry dock until March 1918, when it was refitted with lead-acid batteries and returned to active service.)[30]

Unwilling to release the Board of Investigation's damning report, Daniels called for a formal court of inquiry (which included Lt. Chester Nimitz, later fleet admiral). Daniels delayed releasing that court's report until December 30, 1916, almost a year after the accident, possibly hoping that it would receive little notice during the holiday season. By a three-to-one majority, the court of inquiry recommended "that no Edison battery be installed in any of our submarines until further tests show that their disadvantages have been overcome."[31] Hutchison later wrote to Daniels that the report made Edison so angry that he "ordered all tools and dies, fabricated at enormous expense, for the manufacture of Submarine Batteries, to be broken up with a sledge hammer."[32]

By then there was no way for Edison to make a graceful exit from the Navy, even had he wanted to do so. In December 1916, before the release of the court's report, Daniels had visited Edison in New Jersey and told him that the Allies were at risk of defeat by German submarines. He asked Edison to work on the submarine menace, and Edison announced that he would dedicate his laboratory full-time to naval research.[33] On April 6, 1917, the United States declared war on Germany.

Working from his own laboratories in New Jersey, Edison sent the Navy one invention after another: sea anchors that would swivel a ship away from a torpedo's path; small depth bombs (about the size of shotgun shells) to determine whether there was sufficient safe water under a vessel; gyroscope-mounted signaling lights with louvered shutters for secure communication between ships in a convoy; a shell that would not "skip" when it struck the sea's surface and could be fired at a submerged submarine; a passive-sonar listening device that was based upon his new Dictaphone; and a network of sonar- and radio-equipped submarine-detection buoys to be placed along the U.S. coast. He spent months at sea on rented yachts testing his ideas.[34]

The Navy was not listening to him. Edison later told a reporter, "I made about forty-five inventions during the war, all perfectly good ones, and they pigeon-holed every one of them." He would send an idea to Daniels, Daniels would send it to someone in the Navy, and nothing would happen. Edison could not get the Navy to even explain what was needed. He complained that he was "pulling ideas out of the air" and wrote Daniels, "I am still without adequate information about submarine warfare in actual practice as no one . . . has given me any data of real value. Until I get some kind of data, I will have to depend on my imagination."

Edison's greatest contribution was not his inventions but his common-sense analysis. He asked for information about submarine attacks, for example, and when he was told the data had not been compiled, he put his own analysis team together. In November 1917 he sent Daniels and the British Admiralty a report with graphs, charts, and forty-five maps. The conclusions he drew were straightforward. Most German submarine attacks were near French and British ports; if ships operated there only at night, they would be much less vulnerable. German subs also seemed to be lying in wait in prewar shipping lanes and near lighthouses, so those areas should be avoided. Merchant ships should be equipped with radios so that they could call for help from destroyers if attacked. Moreover, merchant ships' old (and useless) sailing masts could be sighted by enemy subs from a great distance and should be removed. Smokeless anthracite coal should be burned in danger zones in order to reduce visibility, and lookouts should be stationed not on deck but at portholes near the water's surface, where they could spot a sub's periscope in profile against the sky. The Navy proved willing to listen to these, perhaps because Edison had given them to the British as well.

Congress did not fund the Naval Research Laboratory until 1920, after the war's end. When Daniels told Edison of the final plans for the laboratory, Edison testified before Congress in an attempt to get the site and management changed. Even his fellow members of the Naval Consulting Board would not back him on that, and Edison lost on all counts: the laboratory was to be situated in Washington, D.C., and it would be under Navy control.[35]

Concerning the E-2 explosion, the Navy was right: Hutchison had negligently ordered a procedure—the deep and rapid discharge of 240 battery cells in series, half the submarine's complement—that was almost certain to emit hydrogen. Hutchison was right too: the Edison battery was safer than the lead-acid battery and not specifically to blame for the explosion, as a lead-acid battery (or any other wet-cell battery) subjected to that procedure would have emitted hydrogen and exploded in the same fashion. But Hutchison and Edison never seemed to understand that the technical cause of the E-2 explosion was immaterial, at least as far as the Navy was concerned. The Navy knew that Edison considered its officers to be ignorant martinets—he said so often enough. And when Hutchison blamed the explosion on the incompetence of the E-2's captain, the Navy, which prided itself on its traditions and autonomy, closed ranks. Its officers saw Edison as an irrelevant meddler, Hutchison as a snake, and Daniels as a political hack. Edison was perhaps America's greatest inventor, but he was woefully ignorant of the ways of the military. The twentieth century would see this sort of misunderstanding repeated many times.

2

Gassing the Senator

By the time the United States entered World War I, the Europeans had been gassing one another on the battlefield for two years. The American Army had no experience of chemical weapons. It should have worried about defense against gas attacks—training officers and individual soldiers, providing masks and decontamination gear, and familiarizing its medical staff with treatment of gas casualties— but it did not, and American soldiers would suffer as a result. Rather than concentrate on defense, the Army began a crash program to develop its own poison gas, a secret weapon that would force Kaiser Bill to his knees.

———

Gas was a horror, beginning with the first attack at Ypres in April 1915, when the Germans released chlorine gas from six thousand cylinders. When chlorine comes into contact with unprotected human tissue, it reacts immediately, burning the skin or the eyes if the exposure is prolonged or concentrated. When chlorine is inhaled, it corrodes the lungs, which fill with fluid. There is no antidote to chlorine poisoning—with moderate exposure, the body may heal itself, but if the exposure is severe, the victim drowns in his own fluid. One soldier described it as "an equivalent death to drowning only on dry land. The effects are these—a splitting headache and terrific thirst (to drink water is instant death), a knife-edge of pain in the lungs and the coughing up of a greenish froth off the stomach and the lungs, ending finally in insensibility and death. The color of the skin from white turns a greenish black and yellow, the color protrudes and the eyes assume a glassy stare. It is a fiendish death to die."[1]

A leading German physical chemist, Fritz Haber, had proposed the use of chlorine. The gas had several advantages: it was commonly available in cylinders as an industrial chemical, it was quite poisonous, and it was heavier than air, so it would creep into trenches and foxholes. Haber watched as the first chlorine cloud approached Algerian soldiers in the French lines at Ypres. Those who did not succumb to the gas ran in terror. When the chlorine had dissipated sufficiently, the German soldiers (who had not been issued protective masks and had only wet cloths to hold over their faces) advanced tentatively for four miles into the abandoned French positions. They were almost as surprised by the effects of the gas attack as were the French, and they stopped at that point to regroup. Night was falling and they had accomplished their immediate objective. For the rest of his life, Haber would claim that this had been the missed opportunity for Germany to win the war. Had the generals had only listened to him and advanced in force, he believed, they could have shattered the Allied lines and forced a negotiated peace.

Haber took charge of the German poison gas effort and developed gases that were even more lethal. Phosgene, sixteen times as deadly as the same amount of chlorine, was first used by the Germans and then quickly deployed by both sides. About the time that America entered the war in 1917, Haber developed dichlorodiethylsulfide, which was to become known as "mustard gas" because of its slight mustard-like odor. Unlike chlorine and phosgene, which had their principal effects upon the lungs, mustard was a blistering agent that caused skin burns, blindness, and internal and external bleeding. Soldiers often took four to five weeks to recover or die, putting a further load on the enemy's medical services, and the pain was so bad that soldiers had to be strapped to their beds. Here was a far more terrifying weapon than chlorine. Because mustard attacked the skin, soldiers had to cover every inch of the body in a poncho during an attack. And mustard had another advantage—whereas phosgene and chlorine dissipated quickly, mustard was actually not a gas but a liquid that was sprayed as an aerosol. It was persistent, poisoning grass, plants, and the earth for days. It could be used to deny territory to the enemy, to support the flanks in an infantry advance, and to cover a retreat. Mustard was by far the most deadly agent used in the Great War.

Haber saw gas as a psychological weapon that could "turn soldiers from a sword in the hand of their leader into a heap of helpless people."[2] The gas mask, especially the heavy British single-box respirator, was one more burden for the soldier to carry into battle. Soldiers in the trenches found themselves constantly sniffing for gas, and a soldier in a gas mask, even if it was functioning, was half blinded, unable to aim properly or to see peripherally. When a gas attack occurred and the concentration of gas became so high that it began to overcome the filter and to be felt in the throat, the desire to rip the mask off and breathe deeply became almost irresistible, and some did succumb to the urge.

Haber believed that chemical weapons were a natural stage in the evolution of warfare. Advances in the technology of artillery and machine guns had led armies to burrow into trenches; the next step was to develop chemical weapons, which would make those trenches uninhabitable. The tactical use of gas was becoming increasingly complex, and, as usual, the Germans led the way. Lt. Col. Georg Bruchmüller, nicknamed "Breakthrough," developed an entire system of tactical gas employment, saturating enemy troop concentrations using surprise, pinpoint targeting. He varied the timing and the agents used based on temperature and wind speed.[3]

Haber believed that gas was of greatest advantage to the most industrialized nations—the Germans were best at it, the British better than the French, and the Russians hopeless. He saw conventional warfare as a game like checkers, but gas warfare like chess—gas shells might contain two or even three agents, and that forced the combatant armies to develop a new gas mask filter to block each new combination.[4]

The Americans, as they entered the war, were novices at the game of chemical warfare. When the first U.S. troops arrived in Europe in July 1917, the American public knew little about poison gas. The British Royal Navy had cut the German transatlantic cable in 1914, two days after the start of hostilities, and almost all war news that came to America came via the Allies. While the French and British deplored the Germans' gas attacks in their propaganda, they were vague about the effects of gas because they did not want to scare the Americans off. By the spring of 1917, the Allies imposed a total news blackout on gas warfare because, in the words of the British assistant secretary of war, it might result in an "unreasonable dread of gases on the part of the American nation and its soldiers."[5]

The American public's ignorance of chemical warfare was more understandable than the American military's failure to prepare for it. During a 1916 congressional hearing, a senator asked a colonel on the Army's General Staff whether the Europeans were using poison gas. He replied, "The papers say so, but we have not had any actual reports from our observers."[6] Not until February 1917—two months before the United States entered the war—did the Army quartermaster general ask who would supply gas masks should the need arise. The Bureau of Mines was assigned the task.[7] In May, the Army General Staff ordered twenty-five thousand gas masks using the British box respirator mask as a model. When the masks were shipped overseas, the British immediately found them to be so poorly manufactured as to be useless.

Even had masks been available, no one in the military knew enough to construct a training program for their use. By mid-July twelve thousand United States troops were thirty miles from the front with no defensive gas training and no gas masks, even though Gen. Pershing had on July 5 established a Gas Service section within the American Expeditionary Force. He appointed Amos Fries, a combat engineer who held only the rank of lieutenant colonel, as its chief. By September, Pershing realized the urgency. He cabled Washington: "Send at once chemical laboratory, complete equipment and personnel, including physiological and pathological sections, for extensive investigation of gases and powders."[8]

The majority of the United States troops entered the European fight during and after the German spring offensive of 1918. The Germans had a field day gassing the green American soldiers, whose casualty rate was extremely high.

An Indiana soldier wrote in his diary, "A doughboy who was under fire for the first time Thursday . . . told me that half of his company was wiped out by gas attack. Those fellows, without actual battle experience, didn't detect gas in time, and their officers gave no order to put on gas masks. By the time they got their masks on, if indeed they got them on at all, half of them were casualties, many of them dead."[9]

An American infantry officer described the confusion and terror that gas caused on the battlefield: "Some one gave a false gas alarm. . . . The men put on their masks needlessly, and the two rear platoons got confused and went up the wrong road. Men kept yelling, 'Gas! Gas!' I found myself with only two platoons, out on an earthen causeway, heading toward an unknown woods across gas-smelling fields, with shells falling ahead. I got the sergeants to go down the line to stop the men calling 'gas!' and got the masks off." When the gas was real, things were of course much worse: "We got back into the woods just in time to get into a gas bombardment. . . . Our first platoon got the worst dose and the men suffered intensely. . . . One of the greatest trials was having to march gassed men when there was nothing else to be done, although sometimes it was fatal."[10]

More than a year after the United States' declaration of war, the American Expeditionary Force at last required that gas officers be assigned to each unit. The officers were responsible for training the troops in the use of gas masks and shelters, inspection of equipment, and knowledge of enemy tactics and material.

Gas defense was not the whole of the American story. The United States employed gas offensively in the same way as did its allies and enemies—firing artillery and mortar shells that were loaded with chlorine, phosgene, and mustard, all gases that had been developed by German chemists. But back in Washington, the Army's chemists were preparing an American surprise for the Germans.

Immediately after the United States entered World War I, American University in Washington dedicated its campus to the war effort. The Army had no experience in chemical warfare, so the Bureau of Mines, which knew about poisonous gases in coal mines, planned to use the campus for research and pilot production of chemical weapons. The campus consisted of only a single building at the beginning of the war; by its end, twelve hundred scientists would occupy 153 buildings on American University's 509 acres. No one seemed to question whether the nation needed to pursue its own poison gas development or whether Washington was a suitable site for such research.

On Saturday, August 3, 1918, Senator Nathan Bay Scott was taking the morning air on his back porch with his wife and sister-in-law. Scott had represented West Virginia for two terms. After his electoral defeat in 1910, he had remained in Washington, and things had worked out well. He had gone into banking and grown rich. Sipping his coffee, he looked out over the American University campus, which adjoined his house. He had watched sixty-five buildings go up in the last sixteen months, including barracks, mess halls, and training facilities for forty-four hundred troops.[11] The construction noise and dust had no doubt been annoying, but the senator likely accepted the sacrifices as necessary in wartime.

Washington in August is often unbearably hot, but the weather was pleasant that morning—seventy degrees, a clear sky, and a breeze from the east. That breeze, the senator noticed, was pushing a yellow cloud toward his house. Perhaps, the senator thought, someone was burning brush. Then he and his family choked as the cloud attacked their throats and eyes and burned their faces. They stumbled inside and closed the house as best they could. It was a narrow escape.

The *Washington Post* ran a story the next morning: "While experimenting with what is said to be German mustard gas, . . . [soldiers] came very near killing Senator Nathan B. Scott and several of the women members of his family. . . . A number of chickens, birds, and some small animals were killed by the fumes."[12] That was the Army's cover story; in fact, the gas was not German mustard but a secret American weapon, Lewisite.

A pipe had backed up at the pilot plant that was manufacturing the poison, spilling about eight pounds. Two years later, after the end of the war, the *New York Times* would call Lewisite "the deadliest poison ever known," a substance so deadly that a "drop poured in the palm of the hand would penetrate to the blood, reach the heart and kill the victim in agony."[13]

Lewisite's origins are unclear. The substance was likely first synthesized by the Rev. Julius Nieuwland, a Catholic priest at the University of Notre Dame, in 1904. But Captain Winford Lee Lewis, an Army chemist, is the undisputed father of Lewisite as a weapon. While mustard gas had proven to be an extremely effective blistering agent, it was considered too persistent to be used on the offensive—it hung around so long that it would poison the attacker's own troops as they moved into territory that the enemy had abandoned. It had another disadvantage: its physiological action is delayed for hours, like a particularly hellish poison ivy, so enemy troops were often not immediately aware they had been gassed and would continue fighting. Captain Lewis was asked to find a poison gas that would outdo mustard, one that was "(1) effective in small concentrations; (2) difficult to protect against; (3) capable of injuring all parts of the body; (4) easily manufactured in large quantities; (5) cheap to produce; (6) composed of raw materials that were readily available in the United States; (7) easy and safe to transport; (8) stable and hard to detect; and, most importantly, (9) deadly."[14] A colleague suggested that Lewis take a look at Father Nieuwland's doctoral dissertation, in which the chemist-priest had described combining arsenic trichloride and acetylene. The result had made him deathly ill. When Lewis repeated Nieuwland's experiment, he found that the results matched his goal—immediately painful, more toxic than mustard, and less persistent than mustard because it decomposed in water.[15] But he insisted that his compound, a yellow liquid, was not the same as whatever Nieuwland had made, which Nieuwland had described as a black, gummy mass.[16] Lewis was adamant that he deserved credit for the weapon's discovery, and he was successful in gaining recognition. "Lewisite" was the name that would be used, perhaps because "Nieuwlandite" was just too difficult.

Once he had established Lewisite's properties, Lewis passed the compound to his supervisor, Captain James Bryant Conant. Conant had been a twenty-four-year-old Harvard organic chemistry instructor when he had offered his research skills to the country during the war; he worked as a civilian for the Bureau of Mines at first and was later commissioned in the Army Sanitary Corps.

Conant was a thin, bespectacled Yankee from Dorchester, a working-class suburb of Boston. He had been awarded a scholarship to Harvard, where he had majored in chemistry and graduated Phi Beta Kappa in 1914. He was both secretive and ambitious; his son would say, "Anything that he wrote or he said he always weighed the political consequences."[17] When Conant's autobiography appeared in 1970, John Leonard reviewed it in the *New York Times* and commented that it seemed "to have been written in an airless room on some other planet." "Mr. Conant doesn't examine his life," Leonard continued, "he reports it as might an obituary writer."[18]

As an undergraduate, Conant had not limited himself to science. He had survived intense competition to become an editor of the *Harvard Crimson*, the student newspaper, and had been invited to join the Signet, an exclusive Harvard literary club. Despite hailing from Dorchester, he had broken into the circle of the Harvard elite, making contacts that would serve him in later life—as president of Harvard, civilian head of the Manhattan Project, and high commissioner in Germany after World War II.

Conant had continued in Harvard's graduate program and received his Ph.D. in organic chemistry in 1917, just as the United States entered the war. He and two chemist friends could see that many organic chemicals were selling at very high prices because of the war. They decided to manufacture benzoic acid, but they found that producing chemicals in large batches was not the same thing as working in laboratory flasks: they burned down one building and used the insurance settlement to move the business to a second.

When Roger Adams, an instructor in organic chemistry at Harvard, moved to the University of Illinois, Harvard offered Conant the open faculty position.* He accepted, and the move to Harvard was timely, as the benzoic acid business ended in catastrophe with a second fire two months later. In his autobiography, Conant says, "The laboratory work on which the new process was based (and which yielded a patent eventually) proved to

---

*Roger Adams was also involved in chemical weapons research. He would develop Adamsite, a gas unused during World War I but the cause of death for several veterans' children when cavalry troops, led by Maj. George Patton under the command of Gen. Douglas MacArthur, used it against protestors during the 1932 Bonus March on Washington.

■ James Bryant Conant in the laboratory. *Photo courtesy of Harvard Archives.*

be incomplete.... A fire demolished all but the concrete walls of the plant. Stanley Pennock [one of Conant's partners] and a plumber ... who was repairing the piping were killed almost at once. Loomis [the other partner] escaped with minor injuries."[19] Conant did not mention the plumber's name (Max Stein), nor did he remember that a mechanic, Samuel Welte, also died.[20]

When Congress declared war in 1917, Conant considered enlisting, but an MIT professor convinced him that he could best contribute by offering his chemistry skills to the government.[21] He was put in charge of a research group at American University in Washington. In September 1917 he was given the task of devising an industrial process for the synthesis of mustard gas, which the Germans had begun using only two months earlier. His efforts resulted in a process that yielded thirty tons of mustard a day.[22]

In May 1918, a year after the American entry into the war, Conant was assigned the task of turning Lewisite into a weapon, a job that included both developing an industrial process for its production and determining its toxic qualities on animals and human volunteers. One of the test volunteers, Sgt. Temple, later said that after a small drop of Lewisite was applied to his forearm, extremely painful inch-high silver blisters formed that didn't heal for eight weeks; his forearm was still scarred when he was interviewed almost fifty years later. The animal test subjects were not treated as gently as Sgt. Temple. Dogs and goats were attached to stakes in nearby fields, exposed to Lewisite bombs, and observed as they struggled and died. "Their nostrils clogged and they coughed excessively. Many died at this stage. If the dogs continued to live, they sneezed violently with a continuous flow of watery fluid from their nostrils. More dogs died during this period."[23]

The government had difficulty convincing chemical companies to produce poison gases. The work was dangerous, and the only customer—the government—would immediately discontinue purchases whenever the war ended. The Army constructed its own plants at Edgewood Arsenal in Maryland for chlorine, phosgene, and mustard (using Conant's process).[24] The accident rate among the plant's employees was appalling; at one point mustard gas production had to be shut down for lack of workers.[25] After the war, the editor of the *Journal of Industrial and Engineering Chemistry* paid tribute to those "who were killed, not in the thrill of battle, not under the glory of a charge, but back here in the steady grind of preparing material for the men at the front."[26]

In the spring of 1918, the Army pushed to take control of all chemical warfare operations, including research and production within the United States. On June 28, President Wilson established the Chemical Warfare Service (CWS). Although Gen. Pershing had earlier removed Gen. William Sibert from command of the 1st Infantry Division before it was deployed in combat, he recommended him to command the CWS, with Gen. Amos Fries reporting to him and running things in France. Because Lewisite was to be America's secret weapon, it was not produced at Edgewood but assigned its own production site in Willoughby, Ohio, about thirty miles from Cleveland. The similarities between Willoughby in World War I

■ Soldiers loading mortar shells filled with gas at Edgewood Arsenal. *U.S. Army photograph.*

and Los Alamos in World War II are striking: Willoughby was called "the mousetrap," because soldiers could get in but not out—no one assigned to Willoughby was transferred until after the armistice, and soldiers were told they would be court-martialed if they revealed what was being manufactured or even where they were stationed. The plant's mailing address was a post office box in Cleveland, and all mail was censored.[27]

If Willoughby was the Los Alamos of World War I, Conant was its Oppenheimer. By late July 1918, Conant, working at American University before the project moved to Willoughby, had devised a five-step industrial synthesis for Lewisite. He dreamed that this would be the weapon that would win the war.[28] By that time, the Army had taken over the poison gas effort, and Conant had been commissioned as a captain. He was promoted to major and sent to Willoughby to produce Lewisite in quantity—three thousand tons would be needed for an offensive planned for spring 1919.[29] His departure for Willoughby was as timely as his earlier departure from the benzoic acid business: two weeks later, the exploding pipe in his American University pilot plant released the Lewisite that gassed Senator Scott and his family.

Conant asked for a thousand men at Willoughby, and by November 1918 a total of 542 enlisted men and twenty-two officers were stationed there.[30] They worked to repair an old automobile plant on the site, lay railroad sidings, and build the production facilities. It is uncertain how much Lewisite Willoughby produced before the Armistice on November 11; Winford Lewis claimed that three thousand tons were synthesized, while Conant said that only pilot production runs were accomplished, although he gave no figures. Other accounts mention 150 tons produced with peak production of ten tons per day. The disposal of the Lewisite is equally hazy. According to one account, the material had been loaded into shells and was halfway across the Atlantic when the order came to dump it at sea; according to another, 364 fifty-five-gallon drums of Lewisite were shipped by train after the war's end from Willoughby to Baltimore, where they were loaded onto barges and sunk fifty miles off the coast.[31]

The armistice ended work at Willoughby, and America's secret weapon was not used. Winford Lewis said that the joy the soldiers at Willoughby felt at the Allies' victory was mixed with disappointment: "We of the Chemical Warfare Service felt strangely punctured, depressed and irritable next morning after the celebration."[32]

For the rest of his life, Conant would be defensive about his work on poison gas. He wrote in his autobiography, "To me, the development of new and more effective gases seemed no more immoral than the manufacture of explosives and guns. . . . I . . . do not see . . . why tearing a man's guts out by a high-explosive shell is to be preferred to maiming him by attacking his lungs or skin." He had the foresight not to name any poison gases "Conantite," and his memoir is silent on his work on the synthesis of mustard gas, skims over his work on Lewisite in a paragraph, and does not mention Senator Scott at all.[33]

Chemists were the celebrated scientists of the early twentieth century, much as molecular biologists are today. Membership in the American Chemical Society increased from 1,715 in 1900 to 15,582 in 1920, with the majority working in industry.[34] As did most of the rest of America, the chemists responded patriotically when war was declared. Some enlisted in the Army and went to Europe with the troops, and others, such as Conant, served within the United States, initially as civilians working for the Bureau of Mines.

America's war lasted only eighteen months, and the armistice went into effect less than five months after the formation of the Chemical Warfare Service. Gas was not as successful as its proponents, including its originator, the German chemist Fritz Haber, had hoped. In 1921 Haber said that, "looking back, [gas] wasn't such a godsend to the Germans."[35] Gas had not broken the deadlock of trench warfare, and against a properly trained force equipped with masks and skin protection, it was not a wonder weapon. For all the war's combatants, less than 5 percent of casualties were due to gas. For all but the Russians, who never developed a satisfactory mask, less than 5 percent of the gas casualties were fatal.

The American experience with gas was different from that of the British or French. Americans troops were first deployed at the front in July 1917, just when—as we have seen—the Germans began to use mustard, which was far more effective than the other gases; 23 percent of American casualties were from gas, although only 2 percent of these were fatal.[36] While the high casualty rate was certainly due in part to inadequate American preparation, the British gas rate spiked at the same time: of the 188,000 British gas casualties inflicted after Haber's first chlorine attack on April 22, 1915, about 161,000 occurred after July 1917. Most were from mustard.

The CWS, like the rest of the Army, rapidly demobilized after the war's end. The regular Army officers detested gas and, along with the general public, wanted gas warfare abolished. Gen. Peyton March, the Army chief of staff, testified before the Senate: "When I was in France I saw 195 small children brought in from about ten miles from the rear of the trenches, who were suffering from gas in their lungs, innocent little children who had nothing to do with this game at all."[37] A congressional bill, supported by the War Department, proposed placing a greatly diminished CWS under the Corps of Engineers.

But the chemists fought back. In the spring of 1919, the American Chemical Society (ACS) urged its members to support the "continuance, in an intensive form and under a distinct organization, of chemical work affecting the Army."[38] Gen. Fries addressed local groups of chemists and gave interviews to newspapers, saying, "Gas is too deadly, too dangerous, too easy to develop and produce in secret for any nation to give it up."[39] A twelve-part series on the Chemical Warfare Service appeared in the *Journal of Industrial Engineering and Chemistry*, which all ACS members received. Against the wishes of his superiors, Gen. Sibert appeared before Senate and House committees to testify against the War Department's plans to subordinate the CWS to the Corps of Engineers. He argued that that it should be maintained as a "distinct and independent part of the Army."

Gen. Sibert and the chemists prevailed, and Congress preserved the status of the Chemical Warfare Service. Sibert's congressional efforts did not go unpunished: he was summarily removed from command of the CWS and appointed commander of Camp Gordon in Georgia, which the *New York Times* called "a comparatively unimportant post."[40] Fries replaced Sibert as head of the CWS.

The reorganization of the Army was too arcane to interest most Americans, but revulsion at chemical warfare had not diminished. Many knew someone who had been gassed, or saw veterans sitting in the street, wheezing and holding a tin cup. Germany, the country that had introduced chemical warfare, had been defeated and disarmed, so there seemed no reason to continue developing chemical weapons. In 1922, an international Conference on the Limitation of Armaments was convened in Washington, and a ban on first use of chemical weapons was on the table. A group of technical advisors to the conference included two Americans who were firmly opposed to any limits—Gen. Fries, by this time head of the CWS, and Edgar Fahs Smith, president of the ACS, whose magazine had been celebrating the accomplishments of the CWS. President Harding had established an advisory committee to represent the American public, and that committee conducted a survey of public opinion: by a count of 385,170 to 169, the public favored abolition of gas warfare. The American delegation to the conference introduced a resolution opposing use of poisonous gases or liquids, which was incorporated in the treaty submitted to Congress. Seven weeks after its signing, the Senate voted 72 to 0 to ratify, and the ACS and the CWS did not have time to mobilize public opinion.[41]

The treaty never went into effect—France refused ratification because it opposed a clause on submarine warfare. In 1925, a second disarmament conference was convened in Geneva. A similar resolution, banning first use of poisonous gases or liquids, including bacteriological weapons, was signed by the U.S. delegation, again over the objection of a CWS officer whom Gen. Fries had sent unasked to advise the delegation.[42] This time, however, eighteen months elapsed between the American signing of the treaty and the start of Senate debate, and the CWS and ACS had time to lobby individual senators and to speak to the public as technical experts. Many veterans of the CWS were by this time in senior positions in industry and were able to mobilize their colleagues and subordinates.

A new group, the United States Chemical Warfare Association, included chemists, industrial leaders, and regular and reserve Army officers. Its founder and secretary, a Department of Commerce chemist named Frank Gorin, was a former CWS officer and DuPont chemist. The association's board included ACS officers and chemical company presidents. Gorin kept a Washington office next door to the editorial offices of the ACS, and he sent a weekly newsletter to all members of Congress. Winford Lewis, the father of Lewisite, stated that the association's purpose was "to convey to the public through lectures and articles correct information on chemical warfare, as to its humanity, efficiency, and economy."[43]

James Norris, the president of the ACS, organized a committee to call on President Coolidge. The editor of the *Journal of Industrial and Engineering Chemistry* ran repeated editorials asking, "Why are not representatives or our chemical industry consulted by statesmen?" and urging members that it was "your duty as a chemist to spread the truth about chemical warfare."[44] Just as Edward Teller would later claim that his knowledge of nuclear physics gave him standing to speak on the need for the hydrogen bomb, the ACS argued that it took a chemist to understand the need for chemical weapons. None of the local sections of the ACS opposed the national position, and no individual member publicly supported the treaty (although Conant, among others, kept silent and did not attach his name to any of the petitions that were circulating, pro or con). In a foreshadowing of the Red scares of the 1950s, Gen. Fries called some of the treaty's proponents traitors and Communists: "They have fine words for murderous Soviet Russia . . . but never a word for America and her wonderful traditions and ideas."[45]

The motives of the officers of the CWS, whose Army careers were at stake, are understandable, as are the motives of those who would profit from supplying chemical weapons. It is not as obvious, however, why the ACS and chemists in general were opposed to the treaty, especially given the strong sentiment of the general public against chemical weapons. Perhaps it was group solidarity. More than 10 percent of America's chemists had served in the CWS during the war, and more than five hundred chemists remained as reserve officers of the CWS in 1925; they were proud of their service and may have resented the implication that they had been engaged in something dirty.[46] Chemists may also have feared that controls would be placed on the manufacture of chemicals if the treaty was enacted.[47]

Gen. Fries and the ACS succeeded in blocking the treaty, which was ratified by all of World War I's belligerents except the United States and Japan. It was sent back to the Senate Committee on Foreign Relations, not to reappear until 1975. Fifty years after the Geneva Conference, President Ford resubmitted it, and the U.S. Senate ratified it.

Today, the area around the American University site is an affluent Washington neighborhood called Spring Valley. In 1990, construction workers dug up laboratory equipment and a fifty-five-gallon drum there, and then headed for the emergency room complaining of burning skin and eyes. In 1993, utility workers uncovered rusted bombs, and the Army Corps of Engineers excavated and removed forty-three shells suspected of containing poison gas. The Corps then announced that the site was safe.

In 1996, workers who were planting a tree were overcome by odors and suffered severe eye burning. They dug up broken bottles and glassware containing liquids, and an environmental firm assayed the soil and found arsenic, a component of Lewisite. The Army ignored that finding, but in 1999 agreed to test the South Korean ambassador's residence, where it found high levels of arsenic. Shortly after that, another excavation unearthed 380 shells, several fifty-gallon drums, and forty bottles, most of which contained mustard gas and Lewisite.[48] In 2004, the Army estimated that another four years would be required to fully decontaminate the American University site.

As of 2012, the work continued: the Army Corps of Engineers was demolishing a house that may sit on top of a disposal pit that Sgt. Charles Maurer, stationed there in World War I, photographed.[49] On the back of one photo, he wrote: "The most feared and respected place in the grounds . . . Death Valley. The hole called Hades." Late in life, he would not go near the spot.[50]

3

Mitchell's War in Three Dimensions

On the battlefields of World War I, no one seemed quite sure what to make of the airplane, but every military commander knew it was changing warfare. The airplane could spot positions and activity behind enemy lines, harass an enemy's advance or retreat, and attack railroad trains, trucks, or ships. A few officers, including Brig. Gen. Billy Mitchell, revered by many U.S. Air Force officers today as their service's founder, were thinking ahead to the next war. They predicted that bombs from airplanes would destroy an enemy's industrial fabric—its power plants, chemical factories, rail hubs, munitions plants—and that after a few months of such bombardment, the enemy, unable to supply its troops or feed its civilians, would surrender. The airplane would make both armies and navies irrelevant.

America's airpower doctrine was shaped by early twentieth-century Progressivism—a belief that the country's technological ingenuity and moral stature placed it apart from other nations.[1] While European air theorists saw the bomber as a weapon of terror that would destroy cities and break morale,

Mitchell and his protégés (who would command the Army Air Forces in World War II) advocated focusing on military targets and avoiding infliction of civilian casualties. Despite lapses in practice, that principle remains the basis of U.S. Air Force doctrine today.

East of Verdun at the La Cheppe aerodrome, three weeks after America entered World War I, Mitchell strapped himself into a French reconnaissance plane. He was then only a lieutenant colonel, and his mission was to spot targets for the French artillery. Mitchell, acting as the observer, sat in front with a machine gun, a compass, and a map; the pilot sat behind him, and a gunner, equipped with two machine guns, took the rear seat. The French supported the brief flight with several squadrons of pursuit (fighter) planes. Mitchell would be the first American to fly over enemy lines, and it would not have encouraged the American public had he died from his experience.[2] Mitchell marveled at the airplane's ability to rise above the battle, to move in three dimensions: "We could cross the lines of these contending armies in a few minutes, whereas the armies had been locked in the struggle, immovable, powerless to advance in three years."[3]

Mitchell's military career was one of privilege and flash. He enlisted as a private in the Spanish-American War at age eighteen, and his father, a senator, quickly arranged for him to be commissioned in the Signal Corps. Even in the squalor and mud of World War I, Mitchell demanded perquisites, establishing his headquarters in châteaux, where he entertained lavishly. He had the looks of a movie star playing an officer, and he dressed for the part. When he first met Gen. Hugh Trenchard, the field commander of Britain's air forces in Europe, he appeared in an elaborate uniform that he had designed himself, and he attached his personal insignia—a silver eagle on a scarlet field surrounded by a gold band—to his airplane.[4] He played to the American public and Congress. His image was that of a combat pilot, but he had paid a private instructor for flying lessons only two years before the war, and he required a second pilot whenever he took to the air.[5]

His superiors gave him mixed reviews as an Army officer. He was daring and innovative in his use of American pilots, and he was meticulous in his preparation for combat and in evaluation of the results. He wrote clear battle plans—and made the slowest officer on his staff review each order, figuring that if that man could understand it, anyone could.[6] But he also argued that air forces should not be subject to commanders of ground troops, and his conduct often bordered on insubordination. Although Gen. Pershing, the commander of the American Expeditionary Forces, valued Mitchell's combat leadership, he brought in a series of higher-ranking heads of what would become the Air Service above him. Mitchell clashed with one of his chiefs, Brig. Gen. Benjamin Foulois, and Pershing replaced Foulois with Maj. Gen. Mason Patrick—Pershing was not about to lose Mitchell's combat leadership. Mitchell inspired subordinates (among them Henry "Hap" Arnold, Carl "Tooey" Spaatz, and Ira Eaker) who would refine his ideas and lead the Army Air Forces in World War II, but he also made lasting enemies among the Army brass, Foulois among them, and that would cost both him and the Air Service after the war.

When World War I began, the United States was as unprepared for air warfare as it was for ground warfare. The Aviation Section was part of the Signal Corps, and its assigned role was observation. Although the Wright brothers had been the first to achieve heavier-than-air flight only a few years earlier, two years of air combat had spurred the development of European aviation, and American pilots would be flying European planes in combat. They finished ground school and initial flight training in the United States, but the latest airplanes and the experienced instructors were all overseas. The rookie pilots were therefore shipped to Europe for combat training (called "finishing school") in pursuit, bombing, or observation flying and then sent to frontline squadrons. Congress appropriated $640 million for air operations.* That money would be mostly wasted: at the end of the war the government would sell new airplanes, some still packed in their crates for transport to the front, as surplus for pennies on the dollar.

Compared to later military airplanes, World War I aircraft were limited in range and capability. Their primary function, either directly or in support, was to provide targeting information for the most fearful weapon of the

---

* Adjusted for inflation, $640 million in 1917 dollars is the equivalent of $11.5 billion in 2013 dollars, but that understates the magnitude of the expenditure: $640 million was about 1 percent of the United States' 1917 GDP, and the same fraction of its 2013 GDP is $160 billion.

war—artillery. The trenches of the Western Front stretched in an unbroken line from the North Sea to the Swiss border, and airplanes offered a way to see what the enemy was doing behind his lines. They could be used to spot enemy troop movements and concentrations, which could then be targeted by long-range artillery. In order to stop observation flights, one force's pursuit planes attacked its opponent's observation planes, and they were in turn attacked by the opponent's pursuit planes. This became a struggle for what became known as "command of the air," the ability to fly one's own planes and to deny the enemy's planes the ability to do the same. Whoever had command of the air had a monopoly on information above the battlefield. Aerial combat between pursuit planes often degenerated into disorganized dogfights whose outcome depended on the skills of individual aviators.[†] Gen. Giulio Douhet, who directed the Italian air forces, argued, "This aerial knight-errantry ought to be supplanted by a real cavalry of the air—the Independent Air Force."[7]

In May 1918, the Aviation Section was detached from the Army Signal Corps and given the name "Air Service," but it remained part of the U.S. Army. Two months after that, Mitchell began lobbying for an independent air arm. He proposed dividing the air forces into "tactical" forces responsible for observation and support of ground troops and "strategic" forces consisting of "bombardment and pursuit formations [with] an independent mission very much as independent cavalry used to have." These latter, he maintained, "would be used to carry the war well into the enemy's country."[8] He did not get all that he asked for. Pershing agreed to a separate "GHQ [General Headquarters] reserve"—he refused to use the term "strategic"—but he did not assign its command to Mitchell's boss Gen. Mason Patrick, the chief of the Air Service, instead keeping it under the Army General Staff. It was this GHQ reserve, greatly augmented by Allied planes, that Mitchell would command in battle.

On September 12, 1918, Mitchell led the largest concentration of aircraft that had yet operated under a single commander: 1,481 pursuit planes, observation planes, bombers, and balloons, mostly provided by America's

---

[†] The term "dogfight" for aerial combat came into use in the latter days of World War I.

French, Italian, and British allies. They would support an attack on the German trenches at Saint-Mihiel in northeast France. Pershing was in command of the assault, leading the American Expeditionary Forces and forty-eight thousand French troops. He hoped to squeeze the salient that protruded from the German lines and then break through to capture the fortified city of Metz.

Mitchell planned four stages for air operations on Saint-Mihiel: in the days before the attack, he would establish air superiority and observe enemy troop concentrations and movements; the night before the attack, he would bomb behind enemy lines, destroying airfields and bridges; on the day of the attack, he would interfere with enemy reinforcements and counterattacks; and finally, in the drive to Metz, he would attack the enemy's retreating troops and support the Allied tanks.

As in most battles on the Western Front, the advance did not succeed. The Germans retreated from their salient at Saint-Mihiel but stabilized their new lines and prevented a breakthrough to Metz. The air battle was also inconclusive. The weather was bad for the first two or three days, limiting Mitchell's ability to execute his battle plan. Maj. Tooey Spaatz, who would serve as commander of air operations in Europe and then Asia in World War II, flew in combat at Saint-Mihiel for the first time. He had convinced Mitchell to allow him to fly a pursuit plane, and he claimed to have downed one German plane on the last day of the battle.[9] By the end of the war, he would receive credit for three kills.

The war ended two months after the Battle of Saint-Mihiel, and Mitchell and others began reviewing what could be learned and considering the future of military aviation. Compared with an artillery barrage, strafing or bombing by airplanes was only an irritant, although airplanes did have greater range than artillery. In a foretaste of the terror bombing of World War II, the Germans had bombed London and East Anglia with squadrons of zeppelins (dirigibles), beginning in 1915. They attacked at night in the dark of the moon, because the zeppelins were vulnerable to both anti-aircraft fire and airplane attack when they flew at altitudes low enough to target industrial sites. Using fighter planes, artillery, and searchlights, the British destroyed five of eleven zeppelins during an attack on October 19, 1917.[10] In May 1917, the Germans began attacking Britain using the twin-engine Gotha bomber, which was enormous for its time: a 78-foot wingspan, a 15,000-foot ceiling, an 800-mile range, and a 1,100-pound bomb-load. By the standards of destruction of World War II, the effects of bombing were minimal, but seeing zeppelins and bombers flying over England rattled the British, who had long relied on the Channel and their navy to protect them from attack.

Mitchell had begun developing his ideas of "strategic bombing"— attacking the enemy's industrial base—during the war, but he did not press Pershing at the time. He knew that Pershing saw the Air Service's mission as limited to artillery spotting and infantry support, and because he wanted command of the air forces, Mitchell did not rock the boat (although after the war he would criticize Pershing's staff for "trying to handle aviation as an auxiliary . . . instead of an independent fighting arm").[11] Instead of trying openly to convince Pershing, Mitchell worked behind the scenes. The secretary of war had appointed Maj. Raynal Bolling, a peacetime leader in civil aeronautics, to head a commission to chart a strategy to spend the $640 million that Congress had authorized. When the so-called Bolling Commission visited Europe in June 1917, it met with Mitchell, who worked closely with it to shape its conclusions. The commission recommended a large air force that would operate "independently of U.S. military forces, of which 25 percent would be day bombers and 37.5 percent night bombers." (Day bombers needed to be fast enough to elude enemy pursuit planes; night bombers could be larger and slower and therefore carry a bigger payload.) "There seems good reason to believe that [night bombing] might determine the whole outcome of military operations," Bolling announced.[12] The commission recommended that the United States manufacture adaptations of the Italian Caproni bomber. Pershing disagreed and recommended production of the newer British Handley-Page bomber, which appeared in the war in increasing numbers only after the commission's report.[13] In the end, parts for both were ordered, complicating what was already a bureaucratic quagmire. When Howard Coffin, head of the Bureau of Aircraft Production, boasted that he would have forty thousand aircraft ready by June 1918, Col.

Arnold asked him how many spare parts he had ordered. Coffin replied, "What do you need spare parts for?"[14] In the end, the United States sent one Caproni bomber and twenty-four Handley-Page bombers to England before the armistice was declared. None of them made it to the front.

After the war, the Air Service needed a peacetime head. Mitchell had the backing of the men he had led, but he had made enemies among the senior officers in Europe. Pershing no longer needed Mitchell's skills as a combat commander and chose Gen. Charles Menoher, an artilleryman, as chief; Mitchell was appointed his deputy and chief of the Training and Operations Group, where he was to develop training programs and war plans. Mitchell began independently lobbying Congress and the American public, expressing ideas that were clearly contrary to those of the War Department and of Menoher in particular. Mitchell advocated an independent cabinet-level Department of Aviation, with separate military, naval, and civil divisions.

Once air fighting had stopped, those who had commanded air campaigns began to propound ideas for the next war. The two Europeans who had the greatest effect on Mitchell were Giulio Douhet of Italy and Hugh Trenchard of Britain. Both favored an independent air force, something Trenchard had achieved with the Royal Air Force (RAF), which was formed in Britain on April 1, 1918. Douhet proposed a grand thesis, that airpower in future wars would take the battle beyond the trenches, destroying the enemy's industrial base and with it the will to resist. The bomber and biological or chemical weapons would complement each other: "One need only imagine what power of destruction that nation would possess whose bacteriologists should discover the means of spreading epidemics in the enemy's county"[15] Douhet was not the only one with plans to combine chemical weapons and airplanes; shortly after the war's end, the *New York Times* quoted an unidentified American military source: "Ten airplanes carrying 'Lewisite' would have wiped out . . . every vestige of life—animal and vegetable—in Berlin."[16] Mitchell had planned an assault using incendiary bombs and poison gas on the interior of Germany for 1919. But because the first American night bombers did not arrive at the front before the armistice, his ideas remained untested.

The Western Front had locked in trench warfare because of the defensive power of the machine gun, against which frontal charges proved suicidal. Douhet argued that the object of war was not to defeat the enemy's army but to destroy the enemy's will and ability to resist, and that this could best be done by striking *behind* the front. He saw the airplane as the ultimate offensive weapon; it could soar over the trenches and attack anywhere with great rapidity. This was before the invention of radar, so he saw no defense against an enemy bomber attack. The attacker knew his target, but the defender would need to protect every potential target with a fleet the size of the attacker's. Douhet saw anti-aircraft fire as useless, like using muskets to shoot at swallows. The only defense against the enemy's airpower was to achieve command of the air, and this could not be done in air battles, as there would be no way to force a weaker enemy to engage in combat; rather, it would be accomplished by going after the enemy's airfields and aircraft industry—"destroying the eggs in their nest."

Once command of the air was achieved, Douhet wrote, the enemy's ground and naval forces would be unable to resist the power of the bomber. The enemy's homeland would be subjected to such horrors as to force surrender. Douhet saw pursuit aircraft as of little use—mass attacks by fleets of bombers could not be stopped. The bombing need not be particularly accurate, since the goal was to demoralize the enemy's civilians. He prescribed a mixture of high-explosive bombs, incendiaries, and chemical or biological weapons.[17]

After the British RAF separated from the British army in 1918, Trenchard was put in charge of the "Independent Force" (that is, independent of the army field commanders), whose mandate was to retaliate for the cross-Channel raids by German zeppelins and Gotha bombers. He immediately began to develop his ideas on strategic bombing. Like Douhet, Trenchard saw the bomber as the ultimate offensive weapon. Shortly after the war's end, Winston Churchill, who was the civilian leader of the new RAF, appointed Trenchard the RAF's chief. He demonstrated to Churchill's satisfaction that airpower could be used more cheaply than infantry to suppress insurrections in Somaliland, Iraq, Transjordan, Egypt, and Sudan.[18]

Trenchard was more circumspect than Douhet, perhaps because he was responsible for heading Britain's postwar air service, while Douhet was a disgruntled outsider. Trenchard did not deny the importance of using airpower to support ground troops, but he emphasized the offensive nature of the bomber and the need to obtain command of the air. Like Douhet, he spoke of the devastating effect of bombers on enemy morale, but the training manuals that he supervised mandated targeting the enemy's systems of production, supply, communications, and transportation rather than indiscriminately spraying poison gas.

Mitchell had met both Douhet and Trenchard during World War I, and he was influenced by both. He had kept his postwar criticism of the American air force command structure low-key at first, but he eventually began lobbying Congress, giving speeches, and writing articles in newspapers, where he was less than politic. Trenchard said of Mitchell that he "tried to convert his opponents by killing them first."[19]

Mitchell had a number of backers in Congress, but the Army Reorganization Act of 1920 left the Air Service where it was—as part of the Army, still headed by Pershing. Mitchell did prevail on one key point: over the objections of both the war and Navy secretaries, Congress decided at his urging that all aerial operations from land bases, including coastal defense, would be the job of the Air Service. If an enemy fleet attacked American soil, Army bombers would be the defenders.

Pershing was angry at Mitchell's independent voice but was unwilling to upset Mitchell's congressional supporters by dismissing him. Instead, Pershing transferred him to a job with no duties. This proved unfortunate from Pershing's point of view, as it gave Mitchell even more time to lobby Congress and make speeches. When the Navy exploded a nine-hundred-pound bomb on the deck of an obsolete battleship last used in the Spanish-American War, Secretary of the Navy Josephus Daniels announced that the ship had not been seriously damaged and that the test demonstrated its invulnerability to aerial attack. Daniels tried to keep the photographs of the bombing test secret, but somehow they leaked and provided enough evidence for Mitchell to publicly disagree with Daniels's conclusion. In congressional testimony in early 1921, Mitchell challenged the Navy to permit a live bombing test, saying that one bomber, which cost $100,000, could sink a battleship, which cost $10 million. The Navy reluctantly allowed Mitchell to command an Army air brigade as part of its own tests for aerial bombing of the *Ostfriesland*, a modern battleship that it had acquired from the German navy after its surrender. Newspaper reporters said that Daniels was so confident of the battleship's invulnerability that he offered to stand bareheaded on the deck and let Mitchell take his best shot.[20]

Daniels did not stand on the deck, and Mitchell's planes sank the battleship on the second day. After the *Ostfriesland* went down, Mitchell waved as his plane buzzed the Navy's observer ship, where reporters, admirals, and politicians who supported the Navy's battleship program had lined up at the rail to watch. No one spoke, and some of the admirals reportedly wept.

There are two versions of what had happened that day. Mitchell's version was that the Navy was using its control of the test to make sure the ship was not sunk. The Navy insisted that after each hit, its inspectors would board the battleship and assess the damage. Mitchell's Air Service planes complied during the first day, circling above the battleship while their fuel ran low. On the second day, Mitchell had had enough. He radioed that the Navy airplanes should not interfere as his Air Corps Brigade bombed and sank the ship, conclusively demonstrating that bombers could sink battleships. The Navy's version of the test was that Mitchell had proved nothing more than that an entire fleet of bombers, flying at low altitude, could sink a ship that was dead in the water with no fighter support or anti-aircraft defense. Conditions in actual battle, the Navy said, would be entirely different.

The *Ostfriesland*'s sinking marked a turning point in American naval doctrine. The aircraft carrier, not the battleship, would have the key role in future naval battles, and some Navy airmen quietly thanked Mitchell for what he had done. The Navy's report on the *Ostfriesland*'s sinking was a secret document, but Mitchell leaked it, and Menoher attempted to fire him for it. Pershing was still unwilling to offend Mitchell's congressional backers, so he transferred Menoher to the infantry and put Mason Patrick, who had headed the Air Service in wartime, back in charge. Mitchell sent Patrick a memo on what he thought his duties should be—running everything, with Patrick a figurehead—and Patrick responded that he "proposed to be chief of the Air Service in fact as well as name." Mitchell threatened to resign but backed down when he was told his resignation would be accepted. Patrick sent Mitchell on an extended tour of airbases to keep him out of Washington.

Mitchell's next few years included a messy divorce from his wife, Caroline, who suffered an unexplained bullet wound from Mitchell's .38 revolver. (She claimed he had shot her while drunk; he claimed the wound was self-inflicted.) She said he was mentally ill, and the Army insisted on giving him an examination, which he passed. Soon after divorcing Caroline, he married a young Detroit socialite. Mitchell continued to lobby for an independent air force in articles in the *Saturday Evening Post*. In August 1925, he published *Winged Defense*, a book that attacked the Army and Navy leaders and included unflattering cartoons of the secretary of war. When the Navy dirigible *Shenandoah* crashed in Ohio during a thunderstorm, killing fourteen men, Mitchell publicly said that it was "the direct result of the incompetency, criminal negligence, and almost treasonable administration of the national defense by the Navy and War Departments."

Mitchell thought that his statement would spur a congressional investigation.[21] Instead, it got him a court-martial proffered directly by President Coolidge, who called him a "God-damned disturbing liar."[22] Giulio Douhet had also been court-martialed for criticizing his superiors; after a brief jail term, he had been brought back to run the Italian air service. Mitchell may have had a similar redemption in mind. In letters to his sister, he bragged that he would use the trial to advance his agenda and to make money from book sales and magazine articles.[23] Although the newspapers followed his trial in detail, Mitchell's book sold only forty-five hundred copies during the peak of the publicity. It was peacetime, and Hap Arnold later said that the public did not care about the organization of the air force—its enthusiasm "was for Billy."[24] Mitchell's defense counsel was inept, and the prosecution accused him of plagiarizing part of his book from a classified speech made by an Army captain. Newspaper accounts substantiated this accusation. Although the court did not admit the plagiarism as relevant to the charges, it was clearly damaging to Mitchell's case, and Mitchell may have plagiarized Douhet as well, although the evidence for that is less clear.[25]

Mitchell's closest supporters within the Air Service—Hap Arnold, Tooey Spaatz, and Ira Eaker—testified in his defense, as did Amos Fries, the head of the Chemical Warfare Service, who felt that his own service also had been neglected by the Army General Staff. None of it helped. Mitchell was convicted of insubordination and resigned his commission.

Mitchell attempted to continue lobbying for airpower as a civilian, but without his military platform he was far less effective. In 1926, the Air Service was renamed the Air Corps with a large authorized increase in force. The change was mostly semantic, however, as the Air Corps remained part of the Army. And although Congress authorized additional planes and staffing, it did not fund the expansion.

Mitchell was gone, but his ideas were developed by his fellow airmen. He had been instrumental in founding the Air Corps Tactical School (ACTS) in Langley, Virginia, through which virtually every future Air Force leader would pass. The school stressed the primacy of the bomber as a war-winning weapon, and it used Mitchell's bombing manual until 1939.[26] Bombing would win a war, the school taught, not by directly attacking enemy forces but by destroying the enemy's ability and will to resist. Because a modern society was so complex, removing a few key components of its industrial

■ Billy Mitchell (far right) at his court-martial. *Library of Congress Prints and Photographs Division.*

web—rubber, oil, transportation hubs, steel mills, chemical plants, ball-bearing factories—would result in a breakdown of industrial production, an inability to supply troops, and a collapse of civilian and military morale. In World War I, the ACTS taught, Germany's surrender had come not from defeat on the battlefield but from the naval blockade, which destroyed the country's ability to supply its troops and starved the populace. The bomber could do the same job more quickly and efficiently.

The ACTS's airpower doctrine was not the same as Douhet's or even Trenchard's, which focused directly on the morale of the civilian population. The ACTS position was that attacking cities directly would be both inefficient (in that most bombs would not fall on parts of the industrial web) and—reiterating the Progressive philosophy of World War I—immoral. Bombing was to be used as a precision tool, with targets carefully selected. The ACTS used the American economy as its model (most likely because foreign officers attended the school, and it would have been impolitic to use Germany or Japan as examples). If America lost its Northeast industrial quarter in a hypothetical war, the ACTS argument went, America's web would be so damaged that it would have no choice but to surrender.

The ACTS argument that bombing could win a war was almost entirely theoretical, and events in World War II in Europe would prove it wrong; Britain would survive the Blitz, Germany would maintain war production while under intense and sustained bombing attack, and the Soviet Union would reorganize its economy after abandoning its European industrial base and retreating thousands of miles. In none of these countries did a collapse of either the industrial web or of civilian morale force a surrender or even negotiation.

The ACTS's precision-bombing doctrine was based on unfounded assumptions, and it ignored problems. First, precision bombing would require visual sighting of targets and would need to be conducted during daytime. But in daylight, bombers would be more vulnerable to enemy fighters. Long-range escort fighters capable of matching the bombers' range were not seen as technologically feasible, and the Air Corps leadership saw no possibility of getting Congress to simultaneously fund both new bombers and new fighters. So the problem was simply denied: the ACTS assumed that armed bombers flying in tight formation would be able to defend themselves against enemy fighters. Second, daylight precision bombing would require clear weather for targets to be identified. In fact, cloud cover in Europe could last for weeks, as would be seen during World War II. Third, at low altitude, bombers would be vulnerable to enemy anti-aircraft fire. The ACTS solution was to bomb from high altitude. That would admittedly make precision bombing more difficult, but the ACTS instructors assumed that this was a technological problem that could be solved—that an accurate bombsight capable of correcting for aircraft instability, headwinds, tailwinds, and crosswinds—would be developed. Fourth, a long-range, high-altitude, high-payload bomber with multiple defensive guns would be required. The Air Corps assumed that it would eventually get such a plane, although it was unlikely that the War Department or Congress would approve purchase even if one were offered, as it did not fit either of the Air Corps' defined missions of coastal defense and combat support.[27]

Much of the Mitchell-based doctrine was self-delusion. Maj. Gen. Haywood Hansell Jr., who had been a bombardment instructor at the ACTS, admitted in 1951 that Air Corps leaders "had a tendency to build our doctrines around the drawing board designs of aircraft still in the design stage," believing that bombers in proper formation could conduct running firefights and defend themselves against fighter attacks. "Unquestionably this was based on hope and not on existing fact. . . . In the period before the war our lack of experience led us to be far too optimistic in gauging the number of bombs and the number of trials it would take to destroy a target."[28]

In 1935, the Air Corps announced a competition for a multiengine bomber. The Air Corps had two assigned missions: support of troops in combat, and coastal defense. For combat support, low-altitude dive-bombers would likely be preferred. Range would be relatively unimportant for these planes, as they would operate from bases close to the front lines. For coastal defense, extended range would also be relatively unimportant, as the planes would operate close to coastal bases. Escort fighters would defend the bombers, so they would need little in the way of defensive guns. And because the planes could quickly return to base to load more bombs, payload would not be a deciding factor. What would be important was the cost of the bombers—they would need to be purchased in quantity and distributed to airbases along the coasts, ensuring that a rapid response could be mounted against an attack anywhere, and that bombers from other bases could swarm to the attack site to provide quick reinforcements. A two-engine medium bomber would have fit the bill for both coastal defense and combat support. What the Air Corps wanted, however, was a bomber that fit its unapproved mission—long-range, large-payload, high-altitude strategic bombing, operating without fighter support.

Three aircraft manufacturers submitted planes for the competition: Douglas and Martin both offered two-engine bombers, and Boeing, knowing the importance of the unapproved mission, came up with a four-engine plane—the Model 299, the prototype of what would be called the B-17. The 299 could reach 250 miles per hour at 14,000 feet, operate at 30,000 feet, and carry 2,500 pounds of bombs; it had a maximum range of 2,260 miles with a reduced bomb load. Although it cost almost twice what its two-engine competitors did, it was the Air Corps' dream plane. The newspapers dubbed it the "Flying Fortress" because of its menacing Plexiglas machine-gun blisters. Boeing immediately trademarked the name.

The Air Corps wanted to purchase sixty-five B-17s, but the prototype Boeing 299 crashed during the competition after the pilot took off with the controls locked (one reason why today's pilots go through a checklist before takeoff). The crash disqualified the B-17 from the competition, and the Air Force was forced to order the Douglas B-18 instead.

By 1935, the Air Corps had been reorganized, with all combat planes under a "GHQ Air Force." The Army chief of staff, Gen. Douglas MacArthur, appointed Brig. Gen. Frank Andrews to run the combat arm. Andrews was a strong advocate of Mitchell's doctrine of strategic bombing. He managed to purchase thirteen B-17s on an experimental basis, enough to equip a single squadron, suggesting that there was at least some support within the Army General Staff for long-range bombing. That support went only so far: the Army's deputy chief of staff, Hugh Drum, said he saw no reason that an airplane's range should exceed three days' march by the infantry.[29]

The year 1935 was not good for the Air Corps. Gen. Malin Craig replaced MacArthur as chief of staff, and he did not share Andrews's plans

■ The Boeing 299, the prototype of the B-17 heavy bomber. The 299 crashed during flight tests. *U.S. Air Force photograph.*

for strategic bombing or for the B-17. By the time that Germany attacked Poland in September 1939, four years later, the Air Corps had added a net of only one B-17 to its inventory of thirteen, although it had requested 206 more. Drum's successor as Army deputy chief of staff, Maj. Gen. Stanley Embick, laid down a blanket ban on additional purchases of four-engine bombers, insisting that they did not fit any Army mission. He refused to even consider a planned bomber with an eight-thousand-mile range, calling it a "weapon of aggression."[30]

As Mitchell had done, Andrews operated outside the Army command, lobbying congressional supporters and giving radio addresses on the importance of airpower. And like Mitchell, he made enemies in the Navy. In 1937, the Air Corps participated in a joint Army-Navy simulated bombing of the battleship *Utah*, and seven of its bombers were successful while flying under a heavy fog. The Navy complained that the overcast let the bombers operate at low altitude. The Air Corps bombers scored again, this time in clear weather from up to eighteen thousand feet, surpassing the scores the Navy bombers had achieved from lower altitudes.[31] After Andrews sent six B-17s on a publicity flight to Buenos Aires, Gen. Craig refused to allow flights from the West Coast to Hawaii.

In May 1938, Andrews—now fully channeling Billy Mitchell— organized another publicity stunt. As a demonstration of the ability of the B-17 to defend the coast, the Air Force announced that B-17s would inter- cept the Italian passenger liner *Rex*, bound for New York, at a substantial distance from America's seaboard. Lt. Col. Ira Eaker, one of Billy Mitchell's supporters at his court-martial, was chief of the Air Corps' Information Di- vision, and he loaded the B-17s with a live NBC radio crew and reporters from the *New York Times* and *New York Herald Tribune*. The lead navigator on the exercise was a first lieutenant named Curtis LeMay, who later said he had been terrified at the prospect of failing to find the ship. But his cal- culations were spot-on. When the bombers broke out of a squall line 620 miles east of Sandy Hook, New Jersey, they immediately spotted the *Rex*. The B-17s flew past the liner at low altitude while the passengers waved from the decks.

The Navy and Army brass were furious, and Gen. Craig ordered Andrews to restrict all flights to within one hundred nautical miles of the coast, an order that Andrews believed came at the urging of the Navy. When An- drews's term as chief of the Air Corps GHQ expired, Craig reduced him to his permanent rank of colonel and sent him to command an air base in Texas. But in 1939, Craig was succeeded by Gen. George Marshall, whom Andrews had converted to advocacy for strategic bombing in 1938. Mar- shall appointed Gen. "Hap" Arnold to lead the Air Corps and recalled An- drews from his exile in Texas.[32]

By 1940, belief that airpower would be decisive went to the top. Presi- dent Roosevelt had watched what the Germans were doing with airplanes in the Battle of Britain and in Europe, and he ordered an enormous buildup of the bomber fleet, telling Secretary of War Henry L. Stimson, "I know of no single item of our defense today that is more important than a larger four-engine bomber capacity." On May 6, 1941, he ordered the production of five hundred heavy bombers a month.[33]

In June 1941, the Air Corps was reorganized as the Army Air Forces (AAF) with Hap Arnold at its helm. It was still part of the Army, however; Arnold reported to the Army chief of staff, George Marshall. In August 1941, months before Pearl Harbor, the AAF delivered Marshall its plan for the war that seemed destined to come: 63,467 airplanes would be required. Marshall signed off, "Okay, G.C.M."[34] Propelled by that one word and those initials, the Air Corps would soon be given the chance to test precision daylight bombing and to vindicate Billy Mitchell.

The Bombsight

The B-17 bomber gave the Air Corps a test vehicle for strategic bombing, and other heavy bombers, the B-24 and B-29, would follow. But the Air Corps needed more than a long-range bomber—its doctrine was predicated upon being able to reliably hit a rail yard, a factory, or a bridge. That would require an aiming device, a bombsight.

Dropping a bomb from a moving airplane and hitting a target is a complicated business, even when a bombardier can see the target and has instruments to measure altitude and airspeed. The bombardier's job is to calculate both the path that the airplane must fly and the bomb's point of release along that path. If there were no atmosphere, the calculation would require only high school physics and trigonometry, and Galileo could have done it in the early 1600s. But an airplane flies in air. Each type of bomb has its own aerodynamic properties, and the air pushes against a bomb as it falls, changing its speed and direction. Air density and wind speed can be measured at the point at which the bomb exits the airplane's bomb bay, but they will vary unpredictably as the bomb descends. Exact solutions of the equations describing the bomb's arc are therefore impossible, and even approximate solutions were difficult before the invention of digital computers. But solving those equations was the job of the bombardier, and his calculator was the bombsight.

THE BOMBSIGHT'S CALCULATIONS

Briefly, here is what a bombsight must calculate. Start with the simplest case: a bomber flying straight and level toward the target at a constant speed in a vacuum. With no atmosphere, a dropped bomb will not be slowed by the air's drag. It will follow a parabolic arc, staying under the airplane for the entire drop, striking the ground while the airplane is still directly overhead. Thus the bomb should be dropped at the moment when the time remaining before the airplane passes over the target exactly matches the time for the bomb to fall from the airplane to the ground.

The bombardier sights on the target using the bombsight's eyepiece. As the plane flies toward the target, he keeps the target centered in the eyepiece by turning a rate knob that changes the eyepiece's angle to the vertical, called the sighting angle. The sighting angle will decrease as the bomber approaches the target, and it would reach 0 degrees if the bombardier continued sighting until he was directly above it. Given altitude, airspeed, the acceleration of gravity, and Galileo's law of falling bodies, the bombsight can exactly calculate both the time to target and the bomb's drop time, and it can solve for the sighting angle that will be observed when those two times are equal. That is the dropping angle. The bombardier waits patiently as the plane flies straight and level on its bombing run, sighting through the eyepiece on the target, rotating the rate knob, until the sighting angle matches the dropping angle. Then he drops the bomb.

Even in a vacuum, precision is important. If the values for altitude and airspeed are off, if the airplane (and therefore the bombsight) is unwittingly tilted from level flight, or if the bombardier releases a second too early or too late, the hit will turn into a miss.

The atmosphere complicates the bombing problem. The air's drag slows the bomb's vertical descent, so the bomb's drop time is longer, sometimes much longer, than Galileo's law predicts. Drag increases as the air becomes denser during the bomb's descent, and it depends on temperature and humidity as well as altitude. As the bomb descends, it may reach a high terminal velocity in the thin upper air, for example, and then slow as it falls into denser air. Drag varies approximately as the square of the bomb's velocity, and it depends on the aerodynamic characteristics of the bomb. The bombsight must account for drag and calculate the actual drop time.

The bomb begins falling with the same horizontal velocity as that of the airplane, but drag slows the bomb's forward motion in the same way that it slows its vertical descent. The airplane, powered by its engines, continues to fly at a constant speed above, but the unpowered bomb lags behind, and its point of impact will be behind the airplane's position. The lag distance is called "range trail," which the bombsight must determine before it calculates the dropping angle.

Wind complicates things further. An airplane's instruments measure airspeed, but the bombing equations are based on groundspeed, which is the airspeed corrected by the effects of headwind or tailwind. The bombardier can measure groundspeed by sighting on a point in the distance through

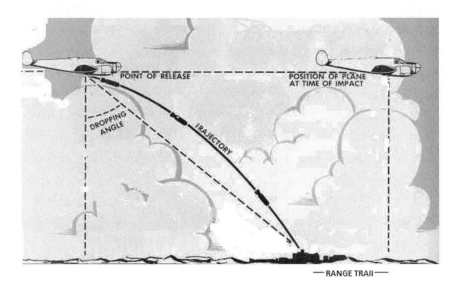

▪ The bombsight must account for the range trail (the distance the bomb lags behind the airplane at point of impact). *Diagram modified from figure in* Bombing Student's Manual *(Midland, TX: Army Air Forces Training Command, 1944).*

his eyepiece, calculating the distance to the point using the sighting angle and the measured altitude, and then clocking the time to pass over that point. The bombardier had to do just that with early bombsights, but it took time and concentration, things that are not always easy to come by in battle. Later bombsights automatically calculated groundspeed, based on the rate at which the bombardier rotated the sighting angle knob while keeping a distant object in the eyepiece.

Crosswind causes even more difficulties. As the bomb leaves the aircraft, any crosswind pushes it to one side. Even if the crosswind were to disappear at all lower altitudes, this initial push would still impart a cross velocity to the bomb throughout its descent (although drag would gradually reduce this cross velocity during the bomb's fall). If no correction for crosswind is made, the bomb will land left or right of the target, and just changing the dropping angle cannot correct for crosswind. If the bomb is to hit the target, it must be dropped from a crabbed flight path upwind of the direct path toward the target, and the bombsight must indicate that path to the pilot or, better still, control the airplane.

Headwinds, tailwinds, and crosswinds continue to affect the path of the bomb after its release. They vary with altitude, changing both direction and speed. These changes are all unknowns, especially in the enemy's territory where bombers operate, and no bombsight could compensate for them. Higher altitudes (and the Air Corps doctrine espoused high-altitude bombing) meant greater uncertainty.

Finally, the problem is complicated by aircraft stability. Straight and level flight, assumed in all the bombsight's calculations, is difficult to maintain even in the best of circumstances. Bad weather, enemy fighters, and anti-aircraft fire could make it nearly impossible.

HOW CLOSE IS CLOSE ENOUGH?

There is an old joke that closeness only counts in horseshoes and dancing. In strategic bombing, closeness is not worth much at all. A five-hundred-pound bomb, an American standard for World War II, left a crater only twenty-two feet in diameter.[1] If it fell a hundred feet from an airplane factory, for example, it would likely do little more than break windows and scar the facade.

In 1932, the Air Corps owned twelve thousand Wimperis bombsights that had been purchased during World War I for airplanes that were never built. They were all but useless. The Wimperis bombsight was not stabilized against turbulence, could not measure groundspeed, could only be used if the plane was flying directly with or against the wind, and had an average margin of error of 790 feet from an altitude of eight thousand feet, which was only half the altitude that the Air Corps specified in its bombing plans.[2] And even that error was measured on a test range on a clear day. The Air Corps continued to test bombsights from the Sperry, Seversky, Estoppey, and Inglis companies into the early 1930s but saw little progress toward meeting the standards demanded by its doctrine of high-altitude precision bombing.

The Navy was doing better, although it was trying to keep that information from the Army. In 1932, Army 1st Lt. Clarence Thorpe and Navy Lt. Malcolm Schoeffel compared notes, and Thorpe learned how much better the Navy's new Norden Mark XV bombsight was than anything that the Army had. (Schoeffel was later promoted to rear admiral despite his indiscretion.) Communication between the Army and the Navy was at such a low state that the Navy had kept the Mark XV entirely secret from the Army until a few months earlier, although Norden had been a Navy bombsight contractor and supplier since 1920.[3] Benjamin Foulois, the Air Corps' chief, immediately devoted the entire 1933 Air Corps budget for bombsights to the new Norden model.

As the Air Corps would discover, Carl Norden was not an easy man with whom to work. To the Navy, he was known as "Old Man Dynamite." He was a Dutch citizen, born in 1880. His father had been born in Germany, however, and his wife was Austrian German. He preferred to hire German American draftsmen, machinists, and watchmakers, which would cause the FBI no end of concern during World War II. But he hated the German nation, and he also refused to work with the British, saying no respectable Dutchman would do so. He was a domineering, often abusive perfectionist who worked sixteen-hour days. Norden insisted on taking long working trips to Switzerland, from where he shipped his drawings and papers back to the Navy via United States diplomatic bag.[4] He saw the world in rigid moral terms—he despised Franklin Roosevelt because he had repudiated U.S. gold certificates in 1933, thereby breaking the nation's word. Norden had promised the Navy that he would take no other customers, and he meant to stick to that. As far as Norden was concerned, if the Army Air Corps wanted his bombsights, it could buy them from the Navy.

The Norden Mark XV bombsight was nothing like the old Wimperis. It was an analog (electromechanical) computer that used discs, cams, screws, and gears to solve the necessary equations. Before the start of a bomb run, while the plane was flying straight and level, the pilot engaged stabilizing gyroscopes that kept the bombsight fixed even if the plane pitched or rolled; the bombardier then used dials to enter the altitude, bomb type, airspeed, temperature, and barometric pressure, giving the bombsight the information it needed to calculate the time for the bomb to drop to the ground. The bombardier next located the target in the eyepiece and "killed

■ The bombardier's view from the nose of a B-17. The Norden bombsight is center bottom. Note the bombardier's .50-caliber machine gun on the left, its controller on the right, and the chin turret controller at top. *Photo Telstar Logistics.*

drift"—drift being the sideways effect of wind—by adjusting a wind knob and a drift knob until the target stopped moving left or right in his eyepiece; he then "killed rate" by adjusting a rate knob until the target stopped moving forward or back. Finally he adjusted a displacement knob until the target was dead center in the crosshairs. The bombsight did the rest—calculated the groundspeed based on how fast the bombardier had turned the rate knob, calculated the proper dropping angle to the target, and dropped the bombs at the right time. In earlier Norden models, the bombsight sent a signal to an indicator that showed the pilot the drift-killing course, but in later wartime versions the bombsight took over completely, flying the plane during the bombing run. The Army Air Corps had found the bombsight it needed, but it was the property of the ungenerous Navy, and, like the B-17, it appeared only *after* the Air Corps' precision-bombing doctrine had been promulgated.

Though a vast improvement, the Norden bombsight was far from perfect. Everything was mechanical, so friction and dust degraded its accuracy. It was not mass-produced—bombsights were built one at a time, and Carl Norden insisted that all parts, including ball bearings, be "machined to fit," which meant that every bombsight differed slightly from any other. Maintenance would be a constant problem because replacement parts could not just be pulled off the shelf and dropped in. The bombsight required visual sighting, so it would not work at night, in overcast weather, or if smoke obscured the target. It required straight and level flight for several minutes, which would terrify bomber crews under anti-aircraft fire and fighter attack. And the Norden could not compensate for what it did not know, such as the changes in wind conditions between the airplane and the ground. But if the Air Corps' precision bombing doctrine had any hope of working, it lay with the Norden bombsight.

The Norden was billed as being able to drop a bomb into a pickle barrel from twenty thousand feet. Between 1936 and 1940, in clear weather, the Air Corps dropped 115,000 practice bombs from an altitude of fifteen thousand feet. After arbitrarily excluding misses of more than a thousand feet, the average miss was still well over three hundred feet.[5] The Air Corps' answer was more bombers dropping more bombs—if one bomber could not hit the target, perhaps forty could. Hap Arnold, in charge of the Air Corps' combat arm, organized his teams into forty-plane formations that would drop their bombs simultaneously. Accuracy improved, but not by enough. One of the founders of the strategic bombing doctrine, Laurence Kuter, began to lose faith. He calculated that destroying the Sault Ste. Marie locks, one of his Air Corps Tactical School textbook examples, would require 120 bombers and a thousand bombs, which would yield the nine hits that would do the job.

Although the Navy had taken the lead on the development of the Norden Mark XV, its own bombing doctrine was in a state of flux. It had three different approaches to bombing from its carriers: high-altitude bombing using the Norden bombsight; torpedo bombing, in which a bomber drops an underwater torpedo while flying horizontally at low altitude toward an enemy ship; and dive-bombing, in which a bomber dives at a ship at a steep angle, releasing its bombs at low altitude. By 1931, the Navy was beginning to doubt that torpedo bombers would survive concentrated enemy anti-aircraft fire. (This proved to be the case; American torpedo bombers suffered terrible losses in World War II.) At the urging of its aviators, the Navy began moving away from high-altitude bombing and torpedo bombing and toward dive-bombing. For the Navy, dive-bombing had a number of advantages over high-altitude bombing. An enemy ship was a moving target that would try to elude a bomber, which meant that low-altitude dive bombing left less time for a ship to dodge a bomb; in addition, cloud cover and smoke were not as great an impediment for dive bombers. So at about the same time that the Navy agreed to sell Norden Mark XVs to the Army, it began to lose interest in the bombsight. Rather than continuing to fund improvements to the Norden, the Navy invested its money in a dive-bombing sight, first with Sperry and then with Norden. Both of these projects were unsuccessful, and when Germany invaded Poland in 1939, Navy dive-bombers were equipped with a simple line-of-sight pointing device.

The Navy continued to waffle. It was unwilling to commit to dive-bombing to the exclusion of torpedo and high-altitude bombing, so it refused to relinquish control of the Norden Mark XV to the Air Corps. At the same time, it refused to fund improvements to the Norden that would enable it to be manufactured on an assembly line. By the time that the Germans invaded France, President Roosevelt had become a convert to the Air Corps' strategic bombing doctrine and ordered a massive increase in heavy bomber (and therefore bombsight) production. From 1931 to 1938, Norden had produced an average of only 108 bombsights a year, one at a time, and Carl Norden had inspected every part and every bombsight personally. The Air Corps knew that he would not be able to meet its demand.

In 1934, the Norden Mark XV bombsight had such a high security classification that Air Corps crews were not permitted to see its instructional manuals. After eighteen months of trying, the Air Corps managed to get the security classification reduced to "confidential," and its bombardiers could at last read Norden's instructions. The security anxiety was not due to fear of foreign espionage—Carl Norden was worried that information on the bombsight would wind up in the hands of his competitor Sperry. Meanwhile, he continued to spend months in Switzerland, which shares a border with Germany, and he continued to hire German American machinists and watchmakers in its New York plant. The Army secretly assigned Lt. Col. Herbert Drague to spy on Norden in Switzerland, and FBI director J. Edgar Hoover planted twenty-six informers in the Norden plant and examined its mail.[6]

Throughout the war, the United States and Norden made a fetish of security. The bombsight was removed from each bomber as it landed, and the bombardier then carried the bombsight in a locked case, under armed guard, to a secure Norden locker. Bombardiers swore an oath: "Mindful of the fact that I am to become a guardian of one of my country's most priceless military assets, the American bombsight . . . I do here, in the presence of Almighty God, swear by the Bombardier's Code of Honor to keep inviolate the secrecy of any and all confidential information revealed to me, and further to uphold the honor and integrity of the Army Air Forces, if need be, with my life itself."[7] When a bombardier was forced to bail out or ditch, he was supposed to destroy the bombsight with three rounds from his .45 pistol—something like a cowboy shooting a lame horse—or, better yet, melt it with a thermite-packed incendiary device. Of course, when the first B-17s began crashing over occupied Europe in 1942, the Germans had as many bombsights as they could want, and in any case, Germany had acquired the plans to the Norden Mark XV in 1938 through a spy who worked for Norden as a draftsman. But the bombsight was of little use to the Luftwaffe. Germany had forgone developing heavy bombers in favor of the medium bombers and dive-bombers that supported its blitzkrieg strategy; it occupied virtually all of Europe, so it had few bombing targets; and it had not trained its pilots for precision bombing.

Claiming security concerns, the Navy, with Norden's cooperation, prohibited any direct contact between Norden and the Army Air Corps, which wanted to integrate its Norden bombsights with the A-2 autopilots that it was purchasing from Sperry. Because the two systems used different electrical systems, a direct hookup of the devices was not possible, and the Air Corps began developing an adaptor that would sit between them. When Carl Norden heard that the Army planned to attach his bombsight to an instrument from Sperry, a company that he despised because of its attempts to control technology through patents, he began work on his own stabilizing device for control of the airplane during a bomb run. He called it the Stabilizing Bomb Approach Equipment, or SBAE. It was heavy and did not work very well, and the Navy and Norden refused to let the Air Corps have a production version for two years.

The Air Corps was not successful in its attempts to integrate the Norden bombsight with the Sperry A-2 autopilot. It was able to tie Sperry bombsights to the A-2, but the Sperry bombsights did not perform as well as the Norden. So the Air Corps accepted the Norden SBAE, although it added 126 pounds to the airplane and performed abysmally. Finally, in October 1941, shortly before Pearl Harbor, the Minneapolis-Honeywell Regulator Company came through with its C-1 adaptor, which linked the Norden and the newer Sperry A-3 autopilot. It worked beautifully. The Navy tried to claim the right to be the C-1's sole customer, but the Air Corps was not about to allow the Navy to control another of its critical components.

The Air Corps requested more improvements to the Norden, including automatic leveling at the start of the run. Leveling the bombsight manually was no small task, especially in turbulent air. The Navy resisted funding all such changes. Norden did attempt to build an automatic leveling device using its own money, but the Air Corps judged the result to be too complicated for combat use.[8]

As war approached, bombers were rolling off the assembly lines, but without bombsights. Carl Norden was still building bombsights one at a time, although he had at least subcontracted parts manufacture. The Navy promised to share Norden's production equally with the Air Corps, but instead took as many as it wanted (most of which ended up on the shelf as spares) before releasing the remainder. When President Roosevelt announced his plan for fifty thousand new aircraft, Norden, on the Navy's instructions, was planning to produce only one hundred bombsights a month. The Navy held up the Air Corps' paperwork when it placed orders for bombsights, sometimes for months.[9]

In June 1941, the Air Corps became the Army Air Forces (AAF), with Hap Arnold its chief. After Pearl Harbor, he was given a seat on the Joint Chiefs of Staff, and the AAF was largely independent of the Army. That, however, did not fix its problems with the Navy, which still controlled access to the Norden bombsight. As a stopgap, the AAF equipped both its own bombers and those shipped to American allies with obsolete bombsights from other suppliers.

The Navy did agree to have Norden set up a separate subsidiary, Cardaniac, which would manufacture sights for the AAF and would subcontract manufacture to other suppliers. Nonetheless, the Navy continued to control all paperwork and to arbitrarily delay AAF purchase orders when it thought that they might threaten fulfillment of Navy orders. The Army needed its own supplier, and it contracted directly with the Victor Adding Machine Company (a manufacturer of mechanical calculators) to build copies of the Norden sights. Norden was less than helpful in supplying engineering help to Victor, and a shortage of parts and machine tools impeded Victor's production.[10]

In the first year after Pearl Harbor, the Navy grabbed 75 percent of Norden's production of sixty-nine hundred bombsights.[11] The AAF therefore turned to Sperry, which had developed a new S-1 bombsight that was coupled to its A-5 autopilot. The S-1 included autoleveling and was ergonomically easier to use—in the Norden, all knobs were on the right-hand side, while the Sperry allowed the bombardier to use both hands—but the AAF wanted the Norden.

The AAF's growing relationship with Sperry convinced Norden to be more cooperative. The champion of the AAF-Sperry relationship, Maj. Gen. Frank Andrews, died in a crash over Iceland in early 1943.[12] By May the bombsight shortage was turning into a surplus (partly as a result of a new AAF strategy of having only the lead bombardier in a formation use the bombsight, with other bombardiers dropping on his command), and the AAF cancelled all Sperry orders and contracts. Sperry production ended in February 1944. Two thousand Sperry bombsights and tens of thousands of Sperry autopilots were scrapped or put into storage.[13]

In July 1944, the Navy finally conceded that it did not need the Norden for its dive-bombers, and it removed almost all Norden sights from its planes in March 1945. In January 1945 it offered to turn the production from the Norden factory over to the AAF, which refused it—by then the AAF had its own factories and wanted nothing further to do with Carl Norden.

Although the various Norden bombsight manufacturers were eventually able to meet production demands, the AAF judged the quality of mass-produced bombsights to be poor when compared with Norden's earlier hand-tooled models.[14] In total, about ninety thousand Norden bombsights were purchased at a total cost of $1.1 billion. To put that into perspective, it was more than half the cost of the Manhattan Project and about three times the cost of all the M1 Garand rifles produced before the war's end. The bombsight was a key to the AAF's plan to win the war with precision strategic bombing of military and industrial targets; how well that strategy worked is another story, described in the next chapter.

5

Precision Bombing Tested

Born in Columbus, Ohio, Curtis LeMay was the eldest of six children of a French Canadian father and a mother of English ancestry. His father beat him regularly, and his family moved every few months, traversing the country while his father found and lost jobs. By the time he was eight, LeMay was the family's provider, fishing in midwinter Montana while his father sat by the fire. The family made the circuit of the country and returned to Columbus.

From early childhood, LeMay wanted to be an airman. He was not confident enough to apply for a congressional appointment to West Point, so he enrolled in Ohio State's ROTC program, where he supported himself by working six night shifts a week at a local foundry. In 1928, he accepted a second lieutenant's commission in the Ohio National Guard, applied for flight school in the Air Corps, and was accepted.[1]

By 1941 he had been promoted to major in the prewar military expansion. As operations officer for the 34th Bomb Group, he always worked weekends, and he was driving between Westover Air Force Base and his home in Holyoke, Massachusetts, when he heard that the Japanese had bombed Pearl Harbor. LeMay later wrote that he experienced the same emotion that he had felt when his B-17 broke through the clouds and he had seen the Italian liner *Rex* in the 1938 test run—a feeling of relief: "There wasn't anything very pretty in the spectacle of our sailors and soldiers lying burned or drowned out there in Hawaii; but . . . [n]ow we knew where we were going. We were going to war."[2] LeMay would take the tools he was given—the B-17 and other heavy bombers, the Norden bombsight, high-explosive and incendiary bombs, and young, untrained air crews—and apply them to the task of wrecking first Germany and then Japan. He was not much concerned with the AAF's doctrine. If high-altitude daylight pre-cision bombing worked, fine. If not, he would find another way to get the job done. By the end of the war, he would be a thirty-eight-year-old major general. Robert McNamara, later secretary of defense during the Kennedy and Johnson administrations, served under LeMay in the Pacific and called him "the finest combat commander of any service I came across in war."[3]

When Germany invaded Poland on September 1, 1939, President Roos-evelt appealed to the governments of Germany, Italy, Poland, France, and Britain to "under no circumstances undertake the bombardment from the air of civilian populations or of unfortified cities."[4] Roosevelt was ignored, and not only by the Germans, who were then bombing Poland. Both the British and the Germans promised that they would not target civilians but soon engaged in an escalating series of attacks on each other's cities. After the Luftwaffe bombed London, Churchill called for an "absolutely devas-tating exterminating attack by very heavy bombers from this country upon the Nazi homeland."[5] Hitler responded with the Blitz, saying in a speech on September 4, 1940, "If they attack our cities, we will eradicate their cities."[6]

At first, the British attempted precision daylight bombing. Their losses were very high, and the British bombsights did not approach the accuracy of the American Norden. By late 1940 they were targeting German towns and industrial centers. Cities were easy to hit. Hugh Trenchard, the "father of the RAF," argued that ninety-nine out of a hundred bombs aimed at pre-cision targets would miss, but that if dropped on a city, every one would do damage.[7] Once the RAF decided to target cities, it moved to night bomb-ing, which made things more difficult for German fighter and anti-aircraft defenses. Eight days before Sir Arthur Harris took over Bomber Command, Britain's secretary of state for air said, "The primary objective should now be focused on the morale of the enemy civil population." A later British history said that the British bombing effort was based on the "principle that in order to destroy anything it is necessary to destroy everything."[8] The polite name for the British approach was "area bombing," less polite was "morale bombing," and most accurate was "terror bombing."

The Americans entered the war with a plan, AWPD/1 (Air War Plans Division/1), thrown together in nine days in July 1941 at the direction of the AAF's commander, Hap Arnold. Based on input from civilian advisors, AWPD/1 targeted specific electrical power plants, transportation networks, oil refineries, aircraft assembly factories, aluminum plants, and magnesium sources. The plan estimated the ordnance needed and the loss rates in aircraft and crews; its predicted requirements for the AAF were 63,000 airplanes and two million men. These numbers, then perceived as outlandish, would prove accurate as far as manpower but too conservative where airplanes were concerned: by the end of the war, 231,000 aircraft were produced, including 35,000 heavy bombers.[9] AWPD/1 was based on the AAF's central tenet—that strategic bombing could defeat an enemy without a land invasion. It assumed that a bombing attack was unstoppable, despite immediate evidence to the contrary—Germany's bombers had lost the Battle of Britain. But Arnold's dream of an independent air force depended on proving that assumption.

In 1943, Walt Disney made *Victory Through Air Power*, a film based on the best-selling book of the same name by Alexander de Seversky. Seversky, an ace aviator for the Russian navy in World War I, had been an assistant to Billy Mitchell after the war and had embraced his ideas on airpower and strategic bombing. He had invented an air-to-air refueling system and bombsights, and was the founder of Seversky Aircraft, from which he had been pushed out by his investors in 1939. When Disney read Seversky's 1942 book, he offered to use his own funds to produce a film version that combined animated sequences with interviews with Seversky. The animation is primitive by Disney standards—showing unending streams of bombers destroying German cities—but the film begins with an archived interview with Mitchell (who had died in 1936) and a paean to his struggle for an independent air force. *Victory Through Air Power* received mixed reviews, even in wartime. James Agee said, "I only hope Major de Seversky and Walt Disney know what they are talking about, for I suspect an awful lot of people who see 'Victory Through Air Power' are going to think they do."[10] The film was not a commercial success, but Disney sent a print to Churchill and Roosevelt for nighttime screening at their Quebec conference in August 1943, where it reportedly strengthened Roosevelt's commitment to strategic bombing.[11]

In June 1942, Arnold sent Maj. Gen. Carl Spaatz to Britain to command the Eighth Air Force. The RAF's Air Marshal Harris tried to convince Spaatz to join the British in night bombing of German cities, but Spaatz declined. AWPD/1 was based on daylight, high-altitude precision bombing of military targets, and Spaatz meant to follow the plan. "It wasn't for religious reasons or moral reasons that I didn't go along with urban area bombing," he later said, but because precision attacks "would win the war more quickly."[12] After the first American bombing raid on August 17, 1942, on a rail-marshaling yard near Rouen, France, Spaatz told Arnold that he could defeat Germany with only fifteen hundred bombers and eight hundred fighters—many fewer planes than AWPD/1 predicted. Spaatz was too optimistic, and in any case, his airplanes and crews did not arrive even according to that diminished plan. LeMay, for example, when he was appointed commander of the 305th Bomb Group, was supposed to have forty-eight B-17s; in fact, he had three, and his pilots, bombardiers, and gunners came to the group almost untrained. It was not until November 1942, almost a year after Pearl Harbor, that LeMay's 305th flew to England with thirty-five B-17s to join the heavy bomber command of Spaatz's Eighth Air Force. And even when planes did arrive, the Army brass diverted them from what Arnold and Spaatz saw as their primary task—the destruction of the German industrial network—to supporting the invasion of North Africa.

The B-17 was not the only American heavy bomber in Europe. The Air Force was uncomfortable with a single supplier for heavy bombers, and it asked Consolidated Aircraft to license B-17 production from Boeing. Consolidated instead proposed its own plane, which would become the B-24, officially designated the "Liberator" but called by its crews the "Flying Coffin." The B-24 was a high-wing, four-engine plane that could fly faster than the B-17 with a larger payload. It had a lower ceiling, however, making it more vulnerable to flak (bursting anti-aircraft shells that sprayed steel fragments) and fighters. It also had a tendency to come apart or catch fire in a crash landing, and it had only one exit—through the rear, at the end of a nine-inch-wide catwalk the crew had to traverse if it became necessary to bail out. Aircrews customarily named their planes, famously "Memphis Belle" and "Magnetic Maggie." One B-24 crew named its plane "A Tisket, A Tasket, a GI Casket."[13] Consolidated delivered eighteen thousand B-24s to the Army over the course of the war, but most groups in the Eighth Air Force flew the B-17.

When LeMay arrived in England, he found that bombing as conducted had nothing to do with the training manuals or official plans. Losses were heavy; the average life of a B-17 crew in the early days of the AAF in Europe was eleven missions. It did not take the crews long to figure that their prospects were dim. As LeMay put it, "In the end everybody was going to be shot down."[14] He quoted an anonymous song that his aircrews sang:

> Take down your service flag, Mother,
> And turn the blue star into gold.
> Your son is an aerial gunner;
> He'll die when he's nineteen years old.[15]

B-17s were unheated, and temperatures at altitude dropped to forty degrees below zero, against which the only protection was sheepskin and a heated flightsuit. The missions were up to ten hours of freezing boredom with interludes of terror. The poet Randall Jarrell, who served in the Army Air Forces, wrote "The Death of the Ball-Turret Gunner":

> From my mother's sleep I fell into the State,
> And I hunched in its belly till my wet fur froze.
> Six miles from earth, loosed from its dream of life,
> I woke to black flak and the nightmare fighters.
> When I died they washed me out of the turret with a hose.[16]

LeMay had Ulysses Grant's attitude toward war—hurt the enemy badly enough and he will stop fighting. He was personally brave, and he was matter-of-fact about the losses his crews took: "People who were burned up in the air or on the ground, were burned up; and people buried by the Germans when there was anything left to bury, were buried; and people who were alive were carted off to Stalag Luft-something-or-other. The ones who drowned in the ocean were drowned, and the ones who were picked up by Air-Sea Rescue were picked up. The crews who were in Switzerland sat and ate Swiss chocolate, far as I know."[17]

In an attempt to offer at least some hope of survival, Eighth Air Force crews were promised a return to the United States after flying a "tour" of twenty-five missions.* Making it through a tour was a long shot. Of the B-17 Eighth Air Force bomber crewmen who flew in 1942–43, only 35 percent survived.[18] In 1944, the crew of the "Memphis Belle," the first B-17 to complete twenty-five missions, was the subject of a gripping documentary, directed by William Wyler: it provides live footage, from morning briefing to return, of a raid on the submarine pens on Wilhelmshaven.[19]

American pilots were sure that they would be shot out of the sky if they flew straight and level through enemy flak, so they broke formation and took evasive action during bombing runs. LeMay said, "I went around making a nuisance of myself, hunting for photographs of bomb damage. Couldn't find much." Photos were not available for many of the missions, but LeMay plotted the data that he had. "These people didn't know where half the bombs fell," he wrote. "And most of the bombs didn't hit the target anyway. . . . [Even the best bombardiers] couldn't hit a target with a ten-second bomb run. Purely impossible. . . . [I]f we were going to get some bombs on target, we had to go straight in, and for a lot longer than ten seconds."[20]

The bombers could not count on fighter escorts in 1942 and 1943—the fighters did not have sufficient range for missions over Germany, and they were not always available even for shorter missions over France or Holland.

---

* Required missions for the Eighth Air Force were increased to thirty in 1944 and to thirty-five in 1945. Such increasing targets were the subject of running commentary in Joseph Heller's novel *Catch-22* (New York: Simon and Schuster, 1955). Heller was a B-25 bombardier in Italy, where he flew sixty missions.

With its ball, waist, and tail guns, the B-17 was supposed to be able to defend itself, but German fighters found a single B-17 an easy target. While standing in the top turret of a B-17 during a mission, LeMay designed a tight formation that gave the machine gunners interlocking fields of fire for mutual defense. Tight formations required careful flying. "Once in a while some muttonhead wouldn't be on the ball, and we would have a mid-air collision," LeMay said.[21] The Americans called LeMay's formation the "combat box," but the German pilots called it *der Pulk* (the herd), and it became the standard for the entire Eighth Air Force.

Using an old artillery manual, LeMay calculated that a German anti-aircraft gun had little chance of successfully aiming at a bomber at twenty thousand feet—flak was effective because the Germans threw up a blanket of it, so evasive action was not improving the crews' chances of survival. In a November 23, 1942, attack on Saint-Nazaire, he insisted that his crews fly straight on a seven-minute bomb run, and he piloted the lead crew. Not one

■ On May 19, 1944, a B-17 over Berlin drifted below a bomber above it. The stream of thousand-pound bombs destroyed the lower plane's left horizontal stabilizer. The plane went into an uncontrollable spin, and all eleven crewmen were killed. Impact, *September 1944, 37.*

aircraft was shot down by flak, and the 305th put twice as many bombs on target as did any other group flying that day.

LeMay introduced the concept of "lead crews," to which he would assign his best pilots, bombardiers, and navigators. Lead crews would study reconnaissance photos of a potential target and its surroundings. When that target was later selected, the responsible crew would be less likely to be disoriented by clouds or smoke. The bombardiers of other crews in formation would not use their bombsights but would drop upon a signal from the lead bombardier. As noted in the previous chapter, this had the added advantage of alleviating the shortage of Norden bombsights, and LeMay removed the bombsights from the nose turret of most B-17s and replaced the bombardier, a trained officer, with an enlisted bomb "toggler" who would release the bombs on command.

In January 1943, Roosevelt and Churchill met at Casablanca to plan Germany's defeat. They concluded with a statement that they would accept only Germany's unconditional surrender—that, unlike World War I, this war would not end without an acknowledgment that the German nation had been defeated on the battlefield. At Arnold's urging, Eisenhower summoned Ira Eaker, then commanding the Eighth Air Force after Spaatz had been sent to command the Twelfth Air Force in North Africa, to come to Casablanca. Churchill was pushing the RAF's strategy of night area bombing, and Arnold wanted Eaker to defend the AAF's daylight precision-bombing plan. Eaker succeeded in convincing Churchill that round-the-clock bombing would allow the Germans no relief from an Allied offensive. The British and the Americans set up a Combined Bombing Offensive (CBO). For the most part, there was little cooperation between the RAF and the AAF, each of which pursued its own strategy. Arnold believed in the AAF's strategic bombing plan, and he formed a Committee of Operations Analysts (COA), consisting for the most part of civilian economists and industry experts, to advise Eaker on target selection. The COA emphasized bombing aircraft, electric power, oil, rubber, transportation, and electric equipment.[22]

Gen. George Marshall had agreed that target selection would be controlled by the British until the AAF's strength surpassed that of the RAF, and the British insisted that the bombers attack the German submarine pens in France and the Low Countries. Those targets were heavily fortified, small, and difficult to damage, but they had the advantage of being near enough to Britain to allow fighter support. The first American attacks against Germany proper began in January 1943, but against naval facilities at Wilhelmshaven rather than the targets selected by the COA. And when the AAF was allowed to attack strategic targets, it found that dense cloud banks made precision visual bombing impossible. Eaker found it all discouraging. His replacement bombers were diverted to support the North African invasion, and his losses increased because of lack of fighter support.

Arnold, back in Washington, suffered his first heart attack (of which Eaker was not informed). Roosevelt allowed Arnold to stay on as commander of the AAF, against regulations, and Arnold promised the president that Eaker's strategic bombing could end the war by destroying only fifty or sixty targets. As an example, he said that "a stoppage, or a marked curtailment, of the production of ball bearings would probably wreck all German industry."[23] That was much too optimistic. Ball bearings were easy to stockpile and were available for German purchase from Sweden, but they nonetheless became an obsession for the AAF's target selectors.

Eaker needed to show Arnold results, and he had little time and not much to work with; desperate to keep his command, Eaker promised that if he were given twenty-seven hundred bombers, he would repeatedly hit a list of seventy-six targets that would produce the desired effect, shutting down the German war effort in six months. It was a fantasy, predicated upon perfect weather, ineffective German fighter and anti-aircraft defenses, and an unrealistic view of the accuracy of the bombsight; in any case, Eaker never came close to receiving that number of bombers.[24]

The British were meanwhile bombing cities by night, and Churchill had convinced Roosevelt that the destruction of German cities would accelerate the acceptance of unconditional surrender by the German population. At the end of July 1943, the RAF bombed Hamburg for more than a week. The Americans joined in for two days, attempting to hit military targets there, but found them obscured by smoke, so many of the American bombs fell on the city center. More than 43,000 civilians died in Hamburg, and

750,000 were made homeless ("de-housed," to use the British euphemism). Roosevelt was impressed with the results, and Arnold endorsed the use of incendiary attacks on German cities "when the occasion warrants."[25] But at the same time, he wanted to preserve the AAF's image. He instructed Eaker that in any press release he should stress the industrial or military target rather than the city or town. With Hamburg, the hypocrisy began. Arnold insisted that there had been no change in doctrine or practice, but he now permitted bombing civilian housing if it was labeled a "military target." This would become the AAF standard in Europe and especially in the Pacific, although individual officers would protest and resist.

In August 1943, strategic bombing got its first big test with massive attacks on the Axis industrial web. On August 1, Eaker and Spaatz, who was then commanding the AAF in North Africa, jointly targeted the oil refineries at Ploesti, Romania. For the most dangerous parts of the journey, the bombers had no fighter support. After a series of navigational blunders, the bombers arrived in disarray over the target. More than 30 percent of them were lost in the attack, and another 30 percent were heavily damaged. Within weeks, the Ploesti refinery was producing more oil than before the raid. On August 17, 139 B-17s attacked the German Messerschmitt aircraft factories at Regensburg, and 227 attacked the ball-bearing plants at Schweinfurt. The two attacks suffered from poor planning, dense fog, and three hundred German fighters. More than 40 percent of the attacking bombers were lost or heavily damaged, and 22 percent of the crews were lost.

Eaker continued to be plagued by cloud cover. The British had developed a radar system for high-altitude navigation that could provide some information through clouds. It was useful in distinguishing land from water but could not provide detailed images of ground features. Even when it worked perfectly, the system's inherent inaccuracies added half a mile to the already unsatisfactory error of the Norden bombsight. The British devices were not radar bombsights, but Eaker used them as such. With visual sighting, bombardiers dropped a third of their bombs within a thousand feet of the target in 1944; with radar bombing, accuracy fell to two or three miles from the target.[26] Radar bombing was a daylight version of the RAF's

■ B-17s flying in formation to bomb ball-bearing factories in Schweinfurt, August 17, 1943. The mission was a disaster. *U.S. Air Force photograph.*

area bombing, although Arnold instructed Eaker to maintain the pretense of precision, calling it "bombing through overcast" and banning the terminology "blind bombing."

At Eisenhower's request, Arnold transferred Eaker to North Africa at the end of 1943, replacing him with Spaatz. Although Eisenhower had no complaints about Eaker, he had a high opinion of Spaatz and wanted his help in preparing for D-Day. Eisenhower's highest priority was not strategic bombing but achieving air superiority over Europe in preparation for the 1944 invasion.

The bombers and crews that had been promised to Eaker began to arrive as Spaatz took over. And the bombers finally had fighter support. The P-47 "Thunderbolt" and P-51 "Mustang" fighters were equipped with drop tanks, which gave them the range to fly from England to Berlin. Despite taking heavy losses, Eaker had decimated the German fighter force in the autumn of 1943, and Eisenhower and Spaatz now focused on gaining air superiority—Eisenhower wanted German fighters and bombers suppressed to the point that they could not attack the Normandy beachheads. Spaatz of course did as he was told, but he would have preferred to continue bombing Germany's industrial heart. He still believed that the bombers could win the war without a ground invasion, which he viewed "as a necessary temporary diversion of the strategic air forces."[27] Spaatz bombed airfields, and he used bomber missions as a lure to draw German fighters so that they could be eliminated. With a steady supply of fighters and bombers arriving from the States, he was willing to fight a war of attrition, one that would give Eisenhower the air superiority he demanded.

The weather was not conducive to precision bombing in any case. Spaatz bombed Frankfurt at the end of January using "overcast bombing techniques"—indiscriminate bombing of the city center. The weather cleared in early February, and Spaatz began "Big Week," an extensive series of attacks directed against the German aircraft industry. Big Week was expensive—three hundred aircraft lost and twenty-five hundred casualties—but Spaatz believed that the damage it inflicted on the German fighter force, both in lost production capability and in fighters and pilots lost in combat, was worth the cost. In March he began attacks on Berlin. Their forces so diminished, the Luftwaffe refused to send fighters to oppose the American bombers. Spaatz had gained air superiority, although at great cost.

On April 1, 1944, Eisenhower took operational control of both the AAF and the RAF bomber commands in preparation for D-Day, and he would keep control until September. He bombed transportation hubs, bridges, and roads that the Germans might use to move troops or supplies. He had no interest in long-term strategic attacks on oil refineries or ball-bearing plants. Arnold and Eaker complained to each other that the Army had no idea of how to use the air forces, that they would be used merely as "flying artillery," "plowing up . . . terrain in front of the ground forces."[28] Spaatz pressed Eisenhower, arguing that attacks on oil refineries would slow the German resupply during the invasion. Eisenhower relented, and when a decoded message indicated that the Germans were so concerned with defense of the refineries that they had canceled the movement of flak batteries to France, Eisenhower gave Arnold and Spaatz more freedom in target selection.

As the Allies pushed through France and the Low Countries after the invasion, the RAF proposed Operation Thunderclap, a massive attack on military and government centers in Berlin, with the aim of forcing either surrender or a military coup that would lead to surrender. The targets would be offices in the city center, and 275,000 civilians were predicted to die or be seriously injured. Eisenhower was tempted by Thunderclap, saying the project would be a "good one" and that they would no longer need to focus on "strictly military targets." Spaatz argued that Thunderclap ran counter to the AAF's bombing policy. "We are prepared to participate in an operation against Berlin," he countered, but would "select targets for attack of military importance." Eisenhower had no attachment to the AAF's strategic bombing doctrines and no compunctions about bombing city centers. He waffled about attacking Berlin, but he kept the Thunderclap option open and ordered Spaatz to be ready. Spaatz in turn ordered Jimmy Doolittle, then Eighth Air Force commander, to prepare for "bombing indiscriminately on the town" if Eisenhower so ordered.[29] Spaatz continued to attack oil and transportation targets, but the bad weather continued, preventing follow-up raids, and German oil production was quickly restored to pre-attack levels.

The Ardennes offensive in December 1944 proved that the Germans were far from finished, and Arnold and Spaatz began to attack the population centers of Berlin, Dresden, and Leipzig. In theory, nothing had changed—the official targets were military. But when Doolittle asked for clarification before the Berlin attack as to what he should do if the oil installations were obscured by clouds, Spaatz told him, "Hit oil if visual assured; otherwise Berlin—center of City."[30] The Americans insisted that they bombed civilians only incidentally. From the civilians' point of view, of course, distinctions based on intention were meaningless. The RAF bombed Dresden by night, and the AAF bombed it by day; when the smoke from the previous night's fires obscured the rail-marshaling yards that were the B-17s' targets, the American bombers used their inaccurate radar bombing devices to drop their loads, hitting Dresden's center yet again. The RAF's commander, C. M. Grierson, announced that bombing the Dresden population contributed "greatly to the break up of the German economic system."[31] Howard Cowan, an Associated Press reporter, wrote in the *Washington Star* on February 18, 1945, "The Allied Air Commanders have made the long awaited decision to adopt the deliberate terror bombing of great German population centers." Hap Arnold, recovering from his fourth heart attack, demanded an AAF statement that there had been no change in policy: "Our attacks have been in all cases against military objectives," Spaatz's deputy commander stated. But by that time, just about anything in Germany constituted a military objective.[32]

In early 1945, the AAF and RAF began Operation Clarion, designed to take the air war into Germany's small towns in an effort to shatter morale. Rail lines and bridges were by definition military targets, so almost nothing was off-limits. Eaker protested to Spaatz, "[Clarion] will absolutely convince the Germans that we are the barbarians they say we are." He predicted that 95 percent of the casualties would be civilians. According to the AAF's official history, Clarion had no perceptible effect on breaking German morale.[33]

By the European war's end, the AAF's strategic bombing campaign left much of Germany's industrial base and its cities in ruins. At the war's beginning, the AAF had scrupulously held to military targets; near the end it joined the British in bombing city centers. But its language did not change, only its definitions of "precision" and of "military target." The AAF would not admit it, but precision bombing had failed, and area bombing had worked.

In November 1944, Secretary of War Henry Stimson organized the United States Strategic Bombing Survey in an attempt to assess the effectiveness of America's strategic bombing in both the European and Pacific theaters. Its mission was to consider not only physical destruction but bombing's effect on the enemy's ability to fight. The survey's leadership was assigned to civilian economists and industry specialists, many of whom had been involved in the COA, which had selected targets for bombing. George Ball, Paul Nitze, Walt Rostow, and John Kenneth Galbraith, all of whom were to serve prominently in postwar government positions during the Vietnam War period, played leading roles. The AAF leadership supported the survey because it wanted validation for its strategic bombing doctrine and support for a postwar independent air force. The survey was in theory impartial and independent of the AAF, but by the time the survey began its work, the AAF had defined and limited the structure. Comparison of the effectiveness of bombing of civilian populations versus military installations was not to be considered, and a British request to conduct a joint RAF/AAF survey (which would have opened that question) was denied. The question of air force independence was also off the table—while Arnold wanted the survey's conclusions to support his arguments for independence, he did not want to risk directly asking civilians for their opinions. Historians, who would have brought a wider political and sociological perspective, were not asked to participate because Arnold had been unhappy with an earlier 1943 Committee of Historians that had delivered a report concluding that airpower alone would not defeat Germany.[34] The survey was to concentrate purely on how effectively strategic bombing had impaired Germany's industrial web.

Secretary Stimson had a great deal of difficulty in finding anyone willing to accept leadership of the survey. James Conant, then president of Harvard and chair of the National Defense Research Committee, turned him down, as did thirteen others, until Franklin D'Olier, the president of Prudential Life Insurance and the national commander of the American Legion, accepted; Galbraith described D'Olier as an "amiable figurehead."[35] Some of those who declined the leadership role may have doubted that they would have the promised independence.

After the German surrender in May 1945, survey officials were able to move freely and to interview Nazi leaders, including Albert Speer, who had been Hitler's economic minister. George Ball reported that Speer spoke of the disastrous effect on German morale of the 1943 raids on Hamburg, saying that if the Allies had continued their concentrated city attacks, German morale would have been undone. Ball noted that he found Speer's

comments "curious," and in any case neither he nor the other survey analysts pursued the question of the effectiveness of area bombing. That omis-
sion might have been due to the inability to fit such information into the
survey's quantitative structure, or to a disinclination to encourage bombing of civilians in Japan, where the war was continuing.[36]

George Ball made a distinction between the "mode" of an attack (for
example, precision visual bombing of military targets versus area bombing of a city center) and the "objective" of an attack (destroying military
targets versus killing civilians and thereby degrading enemy morale). An
area attack on a city center that included a military target was permissible,
even if hundreds of thousands of civilians died in what would later be
called "collateral damage." According to Ball (and the AAF leadership),
it all depended on intention. Area bombing as practiced by the Americans, by Ball's reasoning, was nothing like area bombing as practiced by
the British.

The survey's overall conclusions were mixed: strategic bombing had not
broken enemy morale, due at least in part to the regimentation and control of the Nazi state. But strategic bombing did have a "decisive effect"
on winning the war through damage done to the German industrial web.
The survey did not define "decisive," however, and strategic bombing certainly would not have ended the European war without a land invasion, as
the prophets of airpower had claimed. But the AAF was not interested in
looking back to compare the results against its prewar doctrine of precision daylight bombing, which was supposed to have made ground forces
irrelevant. Its goal was to use the survey to justify its independence from
the Army.

In fact, precision daylight bombing of military targets in Europe did
not work, at least not as advertised—the Norden bombsight was not accurate enough, and the German defenses were too formidable. "Smart"
bombs with sufficient precision to make the AAF doctrine workable—
the subject of this book's last chapter—would not become available for
another generation. What did work were massed attacks, first against military targets and then against city centers. And that was achieved at tremendous cost: the Eighth Air Force had the highest mortality rate of any

American unit—fifty-one hundred aircraft lost, more than forty-seven thousand casualties (almost half of all AAF casualties in the war), and twenty-six thousand killed (probably about a fifth of those who flew in combat, although the death rate among those who flew early in the war was much higher).[†]

[†] I have been unable to find direct evidence for the estimate that a fifth were killed, but the following calculations give it support. A total of 350,000 soldiers served in the Eighth Air Force, but most of these were support troops—mechanics, drivers, armorers, cooks, clerks, bomb loaders, quartermasters, bombing analysts, chaplains, electricians, medics, nurses, firemen, supply personnel, and so forth—who backed up each bomber crew. In mid-1944, the Eighth had a total strength of two hundred thousand (see "Eighth Air Force History," U.S. Air Force, www.8af.af.mil/library/fact-sheets/factsheet.asp?id=4632) and had at most four thousand 10-man heavy bomber crews on hand (see www.303rdbg.com/8af-bombers-crews.html, a table taken from Roger H. Freeman, *The U.S. Strategic Bomber.* [London: McDonald and Jane's, 1975]). This indicates an approximate four-to-one ratio of support personnel (including fighter pilots) to bomber crews at a particular time. The calculations get rougher at this point, but my estimate is that about ninety thousand served in bomber crews over the course of the war, including about twenty thousand killed and twenty thousand wounded or captured who were replaced.

6

Napalm

On October 23, 1940, Roger Adams's living room in Urbana, Illinois, was crowded with chemists, all summoned by James Bryant Conant. As we saw in Chapter 2, Conant and Adams were old friends—Adams had left Harvard for the University of Illinois in 1916, creating a faculty opening for Conant, and during World War I they had both worked on chemical weapons at American University in Washington, D.C. After the war, Conant had returned to Harvard's chemistry department, where he had become the most influential of the early physical organic chemists.[1] In 1933, when he was only forty years old, the Harvard Corporation—the board that manages the university—had called him to be president.

The chemists in Adams's living room were not strangers—they all knew one another from scientific meetings they had attended over the years. They conversed easily before the meeting began, falling silent when the thin, bespectacled Conant stood and read his list of defense projects, asking for volunteers to take them on. With the approach of war, Conant had been asked to head the chemistry section of the National Defense Research Committee (NDRC), where he was put in charge of civilian research on bombs, fuels, poison gases, and anything else that needed chemical expertise. Vannevar Bush, the powerful NDRC chairman, had told Conant that the line between civilian and military research would be less defined in this war than in the last, when soldier-chemists had been inducted into government arsenals and laboratories. Rather than put chemists in the Army uniform of the Chemical Warfare Service, the NDRC would for the most part keep them as civilians.* It would be less expensive and more efficient to issue government contracts that would leave them working in their existing academic and industrial laboratories.[2]

As Conant stepped through his project list, he looked to Louis Fieser, a Harvard professor whose doctoral research Conant had directed in 1924. He asked Fieser to take on the synthesis of new nitro explosives, compounds like TNT.[3] Though little known to the general public—certainly less so than Conant—Fieser was one of the twentieth century's important synthetic organic chemists. Much of his work had direct physiological significance, including blood-clotting agents, vitamin K, anti-malarial drugs, and steroids such as cortisone. He is best remembered, however, for work that was not useful to humanity or chemically demanding: he is the man who invented napalm.

Fieser's memoir shows his enthusiasm for military work, and more than half of it concerns his inventions of explosives, shells, grenades, and bombs.[4] He was physically unimpressive—bald, with a Charlie Chaplin mustache—but he loved to wear uniforms and visit military bases. Yet he showed at least some self-awareness. When he visited Germany in 1945 before the war's end, he posed for a photo in his field officer's hat and overcoat: "I felt a little silly as an unarmed consultant to the army with the assimilated rank

---

* The National Defense Research Committee and the Chemical Warfare Service had overlapping responsibilities. The NDRC's Chemistry Division was a civilian organization responsible for directing research through industrial and academic contracts. The CWS was a uniformed branch of the Army responsible for the production, stockpiling, and deployment of offensive and defensive chemical weapons and devices—for example, poison gases, incendiary bombs, gas masks, smoke screens, and flamethrowers. The CWS conducted its own research and awarded its own contracts.

of Colonel," he wrote in his memoir, "which meant that I had this rank at Officers Clubs and in case of capture by the enemy."[5] Jack Couffer, who worked with him, said that when Fieser chose images for his memoirs, he selected photos of himself "taken from low angles with strong crosslight, the photographer's device to portray a heroic image."[6]

A few months after the meeting in Urbana, Conant asked Fieser to look into explosions that had damaged a DuPont plant that manufactured divinylacetylene, a chemical used in coatings and in the manufacture of neoprene rubber; if the stuff could blow up a chemical plant, there might be a military use for it. Fieser enlisted E. B. Hershberg, a member of his research group who was a reserve Army officer in the CWS. The two of them poked at different batches of divinylacetylene as it dried, and they watched the batches turn from liquids to gels. At the end of each day, they burned the gels and watched them spark and sputter. Even as they burned, however, the gels did not turn liquid but stayed sticky and viscous. This suggested that a bomb composed of the material might scatter globs of burning gel. Hershberg filled tin cans with black powder and divinylacetylene and set them off in deserted areas in the nearby town of Everett. The results, he reported, were promising.[7]

■ Louis Fieser in his office (left) and at Carlsbad Air Force Base. *Photo at left courtesy of Michigan State University.*

During the summer of 1941, nine months after the Urbana meeting, the NDRC was reorganized (with Conant now as chairman) as part of the new Office for Scientific Research and Development, which Vannevar Bush would head. Conant was given responsibility for the atomic bomb, and as a result had less time to manage chemistry projects. Someone in NDRC management told Fieser to stop research on explosives and to begin work on poison gases similar to mustard and Lewisite. That made Fieser unhappy—not because he had moral objections to poison gas, but because he thought that his research would not be used in the war.[8] While waiting for his new assignment, he visited the CWS arsenal at Edgewood, Maryland, where he took a look at the Army's projects on incendiary bombs—bombs whose function was to start fires rather than to blow things up. The Army had two incendiaries under development, a thermite (aluminum and iron oxide) bomb and a magnesium bomb. Fieser thought that the thermite bomb was likely to be a flop, because its ignition seemed to yield only a puddle of molten iron. Magnesium incendiary bombs certainly worked—the British had been using them for two years—but magnesium was in short supply. When he returned to Harvard, Fieser asked for permission to switch his research area from poison gas to improved incendiaries, and the NDRC approved.[†] He gave up both his teaching and his ordinary research at Harvard and started work.[9]

Fieser and Hershberg tested gels made from gasoline that had been thickened with rubber, and they found that they burned wooden test structures more effectively than did the divinylacetylene that had blown up the DuPont plant. The CWS shipped him M-47 bomb cases, which had been designed to hold mustard gas, and Fieser's Harvard team loaded the bombs with the rubber-gasoline gels and exploded them behind Harvard Stadium.

[†] Another of Conant's former students, Paul D. Bartlett, may have taken over Fieser's poison gas research at Harvard. Bartlett, one of the century's most prominent physical organic chemists, waited until after the war to patent a preparation of Lewisite (Paul D. Bartlett, Hyp Joseph Dauben Jr., and Leonard J. Rosen. Preparation of Lewisite. Patent 2,465,384. United States, 1949) and to publish his wartime work on reactions of mustard gas (Paul D. Bartlett and C. G. Swain, "Kinetics of Hydrolysis and Displacement Reactions of B,B'-Dichlorodiethyl Sulfide [Mustard Gas] and of B-Chloro-B"-Hydroxydiethyl Sulfide [Mustard Chlorohydrin]," *Journal of the American Chemical Society* 71 [1949]: 1406–15).

They stood on top of the stadium taking photos and movies. In his memoir, Fieser notes that "a film to be shown to the military had to be edited carefully for the removal of an occasional small-boy spectator."[10] The results convinced the Army to begin production. On November 27, 1941, the CWS filled ten thousand M-47 bomb cases with Fieser's rubber-gasoline gels and shipped them to Manila.

The bombs never made it to the Philippines. The Japanese attacked Pearl Harbor on December 7, and the ship carrying the incendiary bombs was sunk while under way. All sources of natural rubber in Southeast Asia were suddenly unavailable, so Fieser had to look for a new incendiary recipe.[11] He tried the known synthetic rubbers, but none of them worked, and the Army's specifications were demanding: "The gel must not thin out at 150°F. (operations in the tropics), or become brittle at -40°F. (or C.), the temperature usually reached in a bomb bay; it must be tough enough to withstand the blast of an explosive charge and not shatter; it must not deteriorate in storage; it must be adaptable to a simple field operation."[12] Three other groups were working on incendiaries for the NDRC: Standard Oil Development, DuPont, and Arthur D. Little, which reported that it had tested aluminum napthenate, a black sticky by-product of petroleum refining, but that it could not be stirred into gasoline to form a gel. Fieser took a look at the substance and found in February 1942 that combining aluminum *nap*thenate with another compound, aluminum *palm*itate, *did* yield a gel when mixed with gasoline—hence the name "napalm." He later replaced palmitic acid with coconut oil, but by that time the name "napalm" had stuck.[13]

Using M-47 bomb cases, Fieser and Hershberg tested napalm on the soccer field behind the Harvard Business School, a practice that they discontinued only when the Navy, which was using the field for drilling, complained that its ROTC students were sickened by the fumes.[14]

The M-47, a standard hundred-pound bomb, was not the ideal package for napalm—for many missions, it was too big. The goal of an incendiary bomb is to start fires, and because a fire can spread on its own, many small incendiaries are often more efficient than one large one. Standard Oil Development had developed an M-69 "bomblet" that weighed only 6.2 pounds and had only about 6 percent the volume of the M-47. It consisted of a tube twenty inches in length and three inches in diameter that could be loaded with an incendiary gel. In combat, thirty-eight M-69s would be encased in a five-hundred-pound cluster bomb that would disperse the bomblets mid-air. The M-69 was equipped with a three-foot cloth streamer that kept it from tumbling—the bomb needed to strike nose down. When an M-69 struck a roof, it would punch its way through and drop into the building. If it missed a roof, it would drop into a road, yard, or field and lie on its side. The impact would trigger the fuse, and a few seconds later, a white phosphorus charge would ignite the loaded gel and propel it from the end of the bomb's tube. The burning gel would stick to whatever it hit—a building's interior or external wall, a vehicle, furniture, or skin.[15] When Fieser received the new M-69 bombs, he filled them with napalm and returned to the field behind Harvard Stadium for further tests.[16]

The Army was satisfied with the M-69 bomb, but which incendiary gel would fill it was still an open question. Standard Oil Development had its own candidate gel (nicknamed "applesauce"), Fieser and Harvard had napalm, and DuPont had a gel called IM. NDRC ran a series of competitive tests in May and June 1942: Standard Oil's applesauce performed poorly, but both napalm and DuPont's IM did well, and IM was declared the winner in a close contest. Several million M-69 bombs were filled with IM and sent to England, where they failed. Investigation showed that IM had broken down under vibration in shipment. The NDRC quickly dropped IM in favor of napalm and refilled the bombs.[17]

Incendiary bombs had been orphans within the Army in the years after World War I. The CWS had been responsible only for filling the bombs, which were designed, purchased, and stored by the Army's Ordnance Corps. Maj. Gen. William Porter, chief of the CWS, had been liaison officer to different Army Air Forces groups. He was convinced that incendiaries would be an indispensable weapon in the air war, and he wanted complete control for the CWS. (His enthusiasm may have been partly motivated by his concern that poison gases, the historical focus of the CWS's research, would not be utilized in the coming war. Incendiaries might be the CWS's only way to contribute.) At Porter's request, and at the urging of Brig. Gen. Tooey Spaatz, then chief of staff of the AAF, George Marshall—the Army chief of staff—assigned complete responsibility for incendiary bombs to the CWS in September 1941.[18]

As we have seen in previous chapters, the AAF's strategic-bombing doctrine opposed targeting civilian housing. In a 1939 lecture at the Air Corps Tactical School, Maj. Muir Fairchild (later chief of plans for the AAF in World War II) argued against attacking civilians,[19] and Maj. Gen. Haywood Hansell (who would be one of the authors of the AAF's initial plan for World War II and would initially lead the XXI Bomber Command in bombing Japan) rejected "direct air attack of urban populations . . . except as a last resort."[20] That may have been AAF doctrine, but it meant nothing to the CWS, who had been assigned full control of incendiaries. The CWS wanted to test and fine-tune its napalm-filled bombs against what it saw as their logical targets—German and Japanese housing.[21] Its tests, for which the AAF provided bomber support, began *before* the July 1943 joint British-American bombing of Hamburg that resulted in the first destruction of a city by a firestorm. The firebombing of Hamburg, Dresden, Tokyo, and other cities was not accidental but was planned by the CWS from the beginning.

The CWS's official history notes that "supplies of M-69 bombs were becoming available in 1943, when the AAF was giving thought to the strategic bombing of Japan. . . . What was the best incendiary for the new mission?" That question was answered by experiment, by simulating Japanese (and German) housing as closely as possible. At Dugway Proving Grounds in Utah, the NDRC employed Standard Oil Development as the principal contractor in the construction of a "German-Japanese Village" that was repeatedly bombed, burned, and rebuilt.[22] Nothing was overlooked in the village's design. Brick, wood, and tile structures were outfitted with authentic furniture, bedspreads, rugs, draperies, children's toys, and clothing hanging in closets.[23]

Standard Oil hired the best consultants: for German housing, it enlisted two expatriate modernist German architects, Eric Mendelsohn and Konrad Wachsmann, who were then working at Harvard with Walter Gropius, the founder of the Bauhaus School. Mendelsohn advised on construction, and Wachsmann advised on materials. Mendelsohn, a Jew, had left Germany in

1933 after being expelled from the Union of German Architects; he had designed a number of prize-winning buildings, including Essen's Jewish Youth Center, which the Nazis had burned in 1938 in Germany's Kristallnacht. For Japanese housing, Standard Oil hired the Czech architect Antonin Raymond, who had assisted Frank Lloyd Wright in 1920 in the construction of Tokyo's Imperial Hotel. Raymond had lived and practiced in Japan for almost twenty years.

Penetrating a roof was critical for incendiaries—to be effective, they needed to get inside and ignite something flammable. Standard Oil built simulated German tenements with both slate-on-sheathing roofs (found mostly in the Rhineland) and tile-on-batten roofs (found mostly in central Germany). Ideally, a bomb would smash through the roof and stop in the attic, where it would ignite the wooden beam and joists. If it dropped further, the typical German interior was plaster and brick—not particularly flammable—so the best chance of starting a fire would be through the furniture. Standard Oil hired two set designers from the Authenticity Division of RKO Studios, which had built replicas of German houses for the 1943 American propaganda film *Hitler's Children*. They were familiar with the typical arrangement of the furniture in a dining room or bedroom, the wooden furniture, the rugs and draperies, the bedclothes, and the stuffing and fabric in upholstered pieces.

Standard Oil built two types of Japanese roofs as well—tile-on-sheathing and sheet-metal-on-sheathing. To ignite Japanese homes, the tatami mat—the rice-straw mat that was used in flooring nearly every Japanese home—would be key. Ideally, a bomb that had punctured the roof would stop on the mat. If the bomb went through the floor and embedded itself in the earth, a fire would be less likely than if it sprayed burning gel across the tatami, which would yield impressive results: the mat, the paper-and-wood walls, and the futon and zabuton cushions would all quickly ignite. Standard Oil acquired authentic rice-straw tatami mats from Hawaii and the West Coast.[24] When the sources of authentic mats (perhaps left behind by interned Japanese families) ran out, Standard Oil used thistle to construct imitation tatami mats that were "shown by test to approach the original mats in both bomb penetration and flammability."[25]

Standard Oil built six German tenements and twelve Japanese two-family dwellings at Dugway, all modeled on worker housing. A local sub-contractor used prison labor to put up the buildings in only forty-four days and then stood by to repair and rebuild after every fire. A comprehensive series of photos of the Japanese Village is available online, as are the NDRC's summary report[26] and Standard Oil's detailed report on its work.

From May through September 1943, four different incendiary bombs were tested on the German-Japanese Village. The napalm-filled M-69 proved most successful. The British worried that conditions at Dugway were drier than those in Japan, although Standard Oil had been careful to hose down the Dugway wooden structures between bombings. The Army agreed that further tests in a humid environment would be useful, and in April 1944, B-17s bombed simulated Japanese housing at Eglin Field in Florida.[27] The M-69 bombs started fires at Eglin that could only have been handled by a

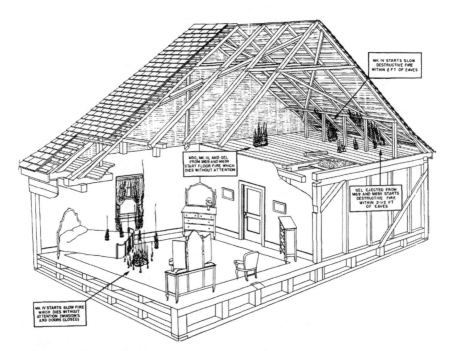

■ Diagram of tests of different incendiaries on German housing in the German-Japanese Village. *Office of Scientific Research and Development and National Defense Research Committee, "Fire Warfare: Incendiaries and Flame Throwers,"* Summary Technical Report of Division 11 *(Washington, DC, 1946), 3:70.*

major city's fire department, and all the simulated housing units were destroyed.[28]

Everyone involved in the design, the construction, and the repeated destruction and reconstruction of the German-Japanese Village knew exactly what he was doing, and yet no one expressed ethical objections. Euphemisms such as "de-housing" could not disguise what was being done at great expense and effort. The CWS, with the direct support of the AAF, designed and tested a very effective weapon to do precisely what AAF doctrine precluded: to burn civilians in their homes.

For all the thought behind its design, the M-69 bomb was a weapon without intelligence of its own; it simply fell where it landed and then sprayed burning napalm gel. What if a bomb could orient itself, find an attic, go there, and *then* detonate? Lytle S. Adams, a Los Angeles dentist, had a plan for such a bomb, and he enlisted both President Roosevelt and Louis Fieser in his project. It involved bats.

In January 1942, Adams sent his idea directly to FDR. "[The] lowly . . . bat," he wrote, "is capable of carrying in flight a sufficient quantity of incendiary material to ignite a fire."[29] Adams's plan was to attach small firebombs to millions of bats and to release them over Japanese cities, where they would roost in every attic. After a suitable delay, the bombs would detonate, igniting all of urban Japan. Adams had thought it all out: bats hibernate during the winter, so they could be easily collected, equipped with bombs, and warmed up just before release. "An important consideration is that a bat weighs less than one-half ounce, . . . which means that approximately 200,000 bats could be transported in one . . . airplane."[30]

Adams's proposal might have been expected to go straight to the White House wastebasket, but it got President Roosevelt's attention, most likely because Adams knew the First Lady. Eleanor Roosevelt had earlier become interested in a device Adams had invented that allowed an airplane to pick up a mailbag without actually landing, and Adams had flown her around the country as he demonstrated the device. The president wrote a note about Adams to his aide and former law school classmate William "Wild Bill" Donovan, who would soon be head of the Office of Strategic Services, the precursor of the CIA: "This man is *not* a nut. It sounds like a perfectly wild idea but is worth looking into."[31]

Adams had a copy of Roosevelt's letter, which he flashed whenever he met resistance. He knew only a little about bats, so he went to Harvard to consult experts. They in turn sent him to Jack von Bloeker Jr., a mammologist and bat specialist in California. Von Bloeker's assistant was seventeen-year old Jack Couffer, who, as an eyewitness to all that transpired with the bat bomb project, has written the definitive book on the subject.[32] Von Bloeker formulated the questions that would need to be answered before Adams's ideas could be realized: Could an incendiary bomb be made that was small enough for a bat to carry? How could millions of bombs be attached to bats? Could bats be brought in and out of hibernation at will? How would the time-delay fuses work? What would keep them from triggering early and incinerating the bomber carrying the bats? How would two hundred thousand bat firebombs be stored and then dropped? No one asked any questions about the ethics of capturing millions of bats, stapling firebombs to their chests, dropping them from bombers, and incinerating them.[33]

The competition among napalm, DuPont's IM, and SOD's applesauce was still under way in July 1942 when the Army asked Fieser to comment on Adams's plan. Fieser's response was not positive, and his was the first of many attempts to stop the project; the Army and its consultants repeatedly tried to kill the bat bomb.[34] Given that it had Roosevelt's endorsement, that was not an easy thing to do. In March 1943, after napalm had proved itself to be the incendiary of choice, the CWS called Fieser to Edgewood Arsenal and told him that he should devise small incendiaries that could be carried by bats.[35] Fieser took a trip to Adams's laboratory, where his personality and bluster (according to young Couffer, who despised Fieser), set everyone's teeth on edge.[36] Von Bloeker volunteered to test the load-carrying capability of a bat; to everyone's surprise, healthy Mexican free-tail bats, which could be found in the millions in Carlsbad Caverns, could each carry fifteen to eighteen grams—more than their own weight—and still fly. That set an upper limit on the weight of the incendiary. Fieser and his team constructed a small, pencil-like napalm bomb with a delayed chemical trigger that could be set by a syringe injection. It would not be possible to set two hundred thousand triggers in that way, but Fieser's injection device would allow tests.

The first tests were scheduled for May 1943 at Muroc Army Air Base (now Edwards Air Force Base) near Los Angeles. The goal was to test bats' load-carrying capacity and the altitude at which they would come out of hibernation. The plan was to capture three thousand bats at Carlsbad, fly them in a B-25 bomber to Muroc, keep them in a hibernated state in refrigerated trucks overnight, attach dummy bombs to their chests, and drop them at a series of different altitudes the next morning. Fieser's report of the test:

> Everything went off on schedule, and shortly after dinner the bomber flew in loaded with kicking, shrieking bats. . . . The crates were loaded onto the truck and the refrigeration turned on full tilt. But the howling went on without abate for a couple of hours, and it became evident that the refrigeration unit was not adequate to cope with such a large amount of body heat all of a sudden. So we mounted a series of fans in position to blow air in over cakes of ice. Finally, about midnight, the noise ceased; hibernation had been accomplished. . . . A first batch of bats in hibernation with weights attached was dumped out of the bomber [the next morning] at low altitude. . . . Other batches were released from higher and higher altitudes. . . . Eventually it was clear that the bats were not in hibernation but dead. Our cooling had been too efficient.[37]

The next test was at a new auxiliary airfield at Carlsbad Army Air Base, which was much closer to the source of the bats. Because the test was top-secret, even the colonel who commanded the base was banned from the site, and the CWS ran the test behind locked gates. The bats were packed like eggs in specially designed crates, stacked for release by the bomber. It all went like clockwork. After the bats dropped, they came out of hibernation and flew.

If the test had ended then, it would have been a success. The story according to Couffer:

Then Fieser said he wanted the photographic record of bat bombs going off in various realistic situations, "with complete verisimilitude," as he put it. . . . [H]e also asked the photographers to shoot some pictures of himself with the bats and their attached bombs. . . . We attached . . . unarmed capsules of napalm to half a dozen [hibernating] bats for Fieser to have his fun. Fieser [injected] one capsule after another until all the bats were armed. . . . Once injected, the capsule became a ticking bomb, a firecracker with a short fuse. Then . . . all the bats simultaneously came to life. "Hey!" I heard Fieser shout. "'Hey! They're becoming hyperactive. Somebody! Quick! Bring a net!" By the time I got there with a hand net, Fieser and the two photographers were staring into the sky. . . . Exactly fifteen minutes after arming, a barracks burst into flames, minutes later the tall tower erupted into a huge candle visible for miles. Offices and hangars followed in order corresponding to the intervals between Fieser's chemical injections."[38]

Because the bat-drop bombing tests had been run with dummy bombs, no one had ordered firefighting equipment. The air base's commanding colonel, who had been shut out from the tests, saw the smoke and appeared with three fire engines at the field's padlocked gates, where he was told to go away. Couffer again: "'That's my Goddamned field,' the colonel roared. 'What the hell do you mean, 'go away?'"[39]

Fieser's account of the same incident differs:

The photographer made ready to shoot and the rest of us were crouched around the sagebrush. Then someone glanced over his shoulder and saw smoke. The administration building was on fire. We saved the refrigerated truck parked alongside, but nothing else. The building, all our supplies, and some valuable photographic equipment, went up in smoke. The observation tower was a mesh of twisted steel girders. . . . I had the unpleasant duty, in thanking the C.O. [the colonel commanding the base] for his hospitality, and of reporting the accident. The C.O. was not greatly concerned; after all, it was a secret project.

Probably what had happened in the confusion was that one operator placed an activated and armed bomb on a rail outside the building and another, unknowingly, picked it up and placed it indoors."[40]

Perhaps from embarrassment at the Carlsbad fiasco, Fieser tried to get the project killed. The AAF had had enough of bats. Nonetheless, the CWS persisted and managed to get the bat bomb transferred to the Navy, where it was renamed Project X-Ray.[41]

Burning down the airfield at Carlsbad should have been sufficient demonstration of the bat bomb's effectiveness, but further tests were scheduled for the German-Japanese Village at Dugway. Couffer remembered walking through the simulated housing, and imagining it "crowded with life . . . People coming and going to the factories; hawkers, shoppers, kids playing games." Couffer said he was grateful that he "could watch our little incendiaries do their dirty work without hearing the screams, the cries of pain, the yells of hysteria, the clanging of fire carts, the roar of burning paper and wood, the sobs of mothers and fathers and sons and daughters."[42]

The Dugway tests were successful, and the NDRC reported that "X-Ray is an effective weapon."[43] Two months later, however, the Navy put the project into hibernation and eventually killed it, saying that the project could not be implemented before the end of the war.[44]

Although Fieser had at first resisted the bat bomb, in his memoirs he mourned the cancellation of Project X-ray. He imagined a silent night attack on Tokyo, each plane delivering thousands of bats—no explosions to give warning. Four hours later, "bombs in strategic and not easily detectable locations would start popping all over the city at 4 a.m.," he wrote. "An attractive picture? All those working on the project thought so." But he was philosophical. Although the bats weren't used, "the job was done very effectively by M-69s."[45]

World War II saw napalm used in firebombing Japan and Europe, and in flamethrowers and incendiary shells as well. Fieser was proud of napalm; his memoirs feature it prominently. But he wrote his book in 1964, just as the American involvement in Vietnam was escalating. A year or so later, the antiwar movement seized on napalm as a symbol of the war's brutality: one of the iconic photos of the war is Nick Ut's Pulitzer Prize–winning picture of a naked nine-year-old girl, Phan Thị Kim Phúc, running with other screaming children after a napalm attack.[46] During the war, Harvard students shouted "Baby killer!" at Fieser and spat upon him as he crossed the campus. In 1965, the *Harvard Crimson*, the student newspaper, awarded Fieser a facetious honorary degree: "A special L.H.D. (hon.) will be awarded to Louis Frederick Fieser, Sheldon Emery Professor of Organic Chemistry and Father of Napalm. Fieser's citation, engraved in burning letters, will read: 'You have brought new light to darkest jungles.'"[47]

Napalm subsumed everything else that Fieser had done. When questioned about it, he became defensive. "I have no right to judge the morality of Napalm just because I invented it." He refused to debate the Vietnam War. "I don't know enough about the situation. . . . I was working on a technical problem that was considered pressing. I'd do it again, if called upon, in defense of the country."[48] He was frustrated. Many scientists had worked on military research in wartime, and many of his chemist friends had worked on poison gases or on the Manhattan Project. After the war, he had received letters from soldiers thanking him for inventing napalm, saying it had saved their lives. Yet he was suddenly demonized.

Fieser died in 1977, a member of the National Academy of Sciences, America's most prestigious scientific society. When a member of the National Academy dies, a fellow scientist, usually a friend or a former student, is asked to write an obituary that describes his scientific achievements, and publication usually occurs within a few years after the scientist's death. Often the scientist, keen to present his scientific legacy in the best light, involves himself before his death both in selecting his obituary's author and in summarizing his own research. Marshall Gates, a chemist who had received his Ph.D. at Harvard under Fieser's direction, wrote Fieser's obituary. It did not appear until 1994, seventeen years after Fieser's death and twenty years after the Vietnam War's conclusion. It does not mention the word "napalm."[49]

The Switch

Noon, November 1, 1944. The air raid sirens sounded, and Tokyo's citizens stopped in the streets or stepped from their doorways, shielding their eyes as they scanned the sky. They had heard rumors of a new American bomber, but that day a single plane flew so high that it was only a tiny silver speck, so high that the anti-aircraft guns could not reach it. Another single bomber followed the next day, and another the day after. Then several came at a time, but still no bombs. The bombs would come later; these airplanes, as Tokyo's citizens knew, were photographing their city.

Tokyo's schoolboys helped the fire crews to prepare, demolishing houses to build firebreaks that might limit destruction. Tokyo had almost no public shelters—each family was to defend its own home. When the sirens sounded, people were to crouch in slit trenches in their gardens and then run to quickly smother or douse fires using stockpiled sand, wet mats, and buckets of water.

In August 1944, the American forces had captured the Marianas—the islands of Guam, Saipan, and Tinian—at a cost of 9,500 dead. For the first time, the large cities of the Japanese homeland were within range of the B-29 Super-fortress, the war's most advanced bomber. Despite the plane's many problems, the Army Air Forces commander, General Henry "Hap" Arnold, had rushed it into production for the campaign against Japan. By the end of October, B-29s were operating from an airfield on Saipan, where General Haywood "Possum" Hansell commanded the Twenty-First Bomber Command of the Twentieth Air Force. By the war's end, 900 B-29s would operate from five airfields on the three islands. Japanese civilians would call the plane "B-san"—Mister B.

The B-29s began bombing Tokyo before the end of November. The skies were quiet for a time in January, while the Americans concentrated on the invasion of the Philippines. Then the bombers returned, and the pace accelerated. But it was not only high-altitude B-29s that hit Tokyo—low-altitude U.S. Navy planes, launched from aircraft carriers, bombed airfields and factories and then strafed the city's streets. The Japanese navy, so powerful three years earlier at Pearl Harbor, could not keep the American carriers from Japan's coasts. Shattered at Midway and later battles, and starved of fuel, the Japanese navy no longer existed as a fighting force.

A steady high wind blew in Tokyo on the night of March 9, 1945. About eleven o'clock, the B-29s came, and in force. Robert Guillain, a French newspaper correspondent who lived in Tokyo throughout the war, gave an eyewitness report:

> For the first time, they flew low or middling high in staggered levels. Their long, glinting wings, sharp as blades, could be seen through the oblique columns of smoke rising from the city, suddenly reflecting the fire from the furnace below. . . . There was no question in such a raid of huddling blindly underground; you could be roasted alive before you knew what was happening. All the Japanese in the gardens near mine were out of doors or peering up out of their holes, uttering cries of admiration—this was typically Japanese—at this grandiose, almost theatrical spectacle.[1]

The center of the attack hit the Tokyo flatlands, where the Sumida River passed through thousands of wooden workers' houses. "Around midnight," Guillain wrote, "the first Superfortresses dropped clusters of the incendiary cylinders the people called 'Molotov flower baskets.'" These were cluster bombs dispersing M-69 bomblets filled with napalm, and large fires immediately erupted. "The planes that followed, flying lower, circled and criss-crossed the area, leaving great rings of fire behind them. Soon other waves came in to drop their incendiaries inside the 'marker' circles. Hell could be no hotter." The high winds made fighting the fires impossible when a house could be hit by ten or even more of the M-69s, which "were raining down by the thousands." As they fell, Guillain noted, the cylinders scattered "a kind of flaming dew that skittered along the roofs, setting fire to everything it splashed." The "flaming dew," of course, was napalm. Almost immediately the houses, which were made of wood and paper, caught fire, "lighted from inside like paper lanterns." The results were nightmarish:

The hurricane-force winds puffed up great clots of flame and sent burning planks planing through the air to fell people and set fire to what they touched. . . . In the dense smoke, where the wind was so hot it seared the lungs, people struggled, then burst into flames where they stood. . . . [I]t was often the refugees' feet that began burning first: the men's puttees and the women's trousers caught fire and ignited the rest of their clothing. Proper air-raid clothing as recommended by the government consisted of a heavily padded hood . . . to protect people's ears from bomb blasts. . . . The hoods flamed under the rain of sparks; people who did not burn from the feet up burned from the head down. Mothers who carried their babies on their backs, Japanese style, would discover too late that the padding that enveloped the infant had caught fire. . . . Wherever there was a canal, people hurled themselves into the water; in shallow places, people waited, mouths just above the surface of the water. Hundreds of them were later found dead; not drowned, but asphyxiated by the burning air and smoke. . . . In other places, the water got so hot that the luckless bathers were simply boiled alive.[2]

It was often impossible to put a cause to an individual's death—the fire sucked up the available oxygen, so there was none left to breathe; smoke choked, carbon monoxide poisoned, flames incinerated, superheated air roasted, falling debris crushed, water boiled or drowned, and crowds trampled. Nonetheless, the United States Strategic Bombing Survey later noted that many of Tokyo's dead were found in positions that indicated that they had "died peacefully and without evidence of a struggle."[3]*

In Europe, the British had pressed the Americans to join them in their night raids on German cities—Cologne, Hamburg, Dresden. While the Army Air Forces participated in some of those attacks, it at least tried to adhere to its strategic bombing principles: the British might bomb city centers in indiscriminate night raids, but, when possible, the Americans would use their Norden bombsights for precision daylight strikes on military targets. Most AAF leaders continued to believe in this doctrine, either for moral reasons or because they thought it more effective. As we have seen, when the RAF had in August 1944 proposed a massive area attack on the center of Berlin code-named Operation Thunderclap, Carl Spaatz, the Eighth Air Force commander, had said, "We are prepared to participate, . . . but in doing so will select targets for attack of military importance." Gen. Laurence Kuter, Hap Arnold's chief for plans and combat operations, had said that it was "contrary to our national ideals to wage war against civilians."[4] The AAF had certainly fudged in the European air campaign—its shifting definition of a "military target" and its use of euphemisms such as "bombing through overcast" rather than "blind bombing"—but it had at least kept up a pretense of following its doctrine. Japan would be another story.

The B-29, America's most advanced bomber, was designed with precision bombing in mind. The plane was pressurized so that it could fly at

---

* Kurt Vonnegut tells a similar story of his time as a prisoner of war in Germany, when he removed the dead from the shelters of Dresden after the firestorm: "When we went into them, a typical shelter, an ordinary basement usually, looked like a streetcar full of people who'd simultaneously had heart failure. Just people sitting there in their chairs, all dead." Kurt Vonnegut and William Rodney Allen, *Conversations with Kurt Vonnegut* (Oxford: University of Mississippi Press, 1988), 173.

thirty-five thousand feet, far above the enemy's fighter and anti-aircraft defenses as it dropped its payloads on aircraft factories, power plants, and rail hubs. The bombardier sat at the very front of the Plexiglas nose bubble, between the pilot and copilot, hunched over his Norden bombsight.

The B-29 raid on Tokyo had nothing to do with precision. The bombers attacked at night, at low altitude, their target Tokyo's sprawling working-class residential districts rather than the aircraft factory, and their primary weapon the M-69 incendiary bomb. Fifteen square miles of Tokyo disappeared that night, and more civilians died in Tokyo than would perish in either Hiroshima or Nagasaki a few months later. The Tokyo bombing of March 9–10, 1945, remains the most devastating air raid in history. How had the AAF come to this?

Curtis LeMay, whom we have seen as the Eighth Air Force's most successful commander in Europe, planned and directed the Tokyo attack. In August 1944, Arnold had transferred him to the Pacific theater, in command of the Twentieth Bomber Command in China. In one of the most poorly planned operations of the war, the Twentieth was attempting to use Chinese air bases in territory controlled by Chiang Kai-shek to bomb Japanese targets in Kyushu, Manchuria, and Formosa. Claire Chennault, then the de facto commander of Chiang's air force, had written Arnold in 1940 that, were he given five hundred aircraft staffed and maintained by Americans, he could "burn out the industrial heart of the Empire with fire-bomb attacks on the teeming bamboo ant heaps of Kyushu and Honshu." Arnold rejected the idea, but FDR was delighted and ordered his cabinet to get it done—all this more than a year before Pearl Harbor, while the United States was still at peace. The War Department managed to block the plan's execution, but it came up for discussion again in 1942. Roosevelt and Chiang wanted the first combat B-29s to be assigned to Chennault's Fourteenth Air Force—the successor to the American Volunteer Group, known as the "Flying Tigers," which had been incorporated into the AAF in July 1942 only after the Army threatened to cut off all its supplies. George Marshall said of Chennault's plans for using the B-29s that it was "just nonsense, not strategy, just nonsense."[5] The Joint Chiefs recommended against the mission, but

Roosevelt insisted that Chiang must be supported. Arnold prevailed in keeping the bombers under his direct control, but Roosevelt's enthusiasm meant that he had to give bombing from Chinese bases a try.

The Chinese bases were so far from Japan that even the B-29s, with their fifteen-hundred-mile radius of operation, could target only Kyushu, Japan's southernmost island. Because the Japanese controlled all sea access to the air bases, fuel and supplies had to be flown in over the Himalayas from British bases in India. The B-29s themselves were used as tankers and cargo planes. A B-29 would land in China, off-load fuel and supplies, and then return empty to India. It took seven shuttle trips between India and China to enable one bomber's attack. Robert McNamara was a lieutenant colonel on LeMay's staff at the time; he recalls that on some occasions the incoming B-29s had to be given additional fuel so that they could make the return trip.[6] Chiang used the operation to extract money from America—the Chinese constructed the runways by hand, crushing rock with hammers and dragging enormous rollers with teams of coolies.[7]

In the end, the Twentieth Bomber Command dropped only eight hundred tons of bombs on Japan from the Chinese bases.[†] Still, LeMay used the assignment to shake some of the bugs out of the B-29, which Arnold had rushed into production, and to train his crews in formation flying and targeting. LeMay later said that "there can be no sustained and intensive effort by any bombers who have to feed their own fuel to themselves."[8] The problematic B-29 and the mountainous route through the Himalayas resulted in a very high loss rate, and more than 70 percent of the Twentieth Bomber Command's losses were from causes other than combat.[9]

The Allies had no effective strategy for the Pacific theater. In Europe, the need for cooperation among the Americans, the British, and to some degree the Russians had forced coordinated planning. In the Pacific, however, the Americans had by far the largest forces, and Roosevelt did not

---

[†] Three of the B-29s made emergency landings in the Soviet Union after suffering mechanical problems; the Soviets, who were at that time not at war with Japan, interned the American bombers, flight-tested them, disassembled them, and reverse-engineered an exact copy, which they named the Tupolev-4. It was a mainstay in their bomber fleet and in the Chinese Communist fleet through the mid-1960s.

set clear lines. There was no supreme commander like Eisenhower in Europe; the American command was divided between Adm. Nimitz and Gen. MacArthur, with Lord Mountbatten commanding the British forces and Chiang an uncooperative ally. Each had his own plans. Arnold, who was by then a member of the Joint Chiefs of Staff (although still, as a member of the U.S. Army, subordinate to Gen. Marshall) kept direct control of the AAF in the Pacific to make sure that its planes were not dispersed among the disputatious chiefs.

Arnold wanted to prove that strategic bombing could defeat Japan, and he knew that bombing from China was not going to do the job. He would have liked to use Russian bases, but the Soviet Union was not at war with Japan. It had its hands full with Germany, and it refused to allow the AAF to set up Siberian air bases (or even weather stations) within short range of Japan, despite repeated requests by the Americans that began even before Pearl Harbor. But by the end of 1944, the capture of the Marianas put Japan's principal cities just within range of new air bases in Guam, Tinian, and Saipan.

Arnold had two aims. The first was to shatter the Japanese economy and make its defeat inevitable, a goal he was confident he could achieve. Japan's defenses were far weaker than Germany's had been, and new B-29s and escort fighters, which would soon be able to provide support from Iwo Jima, were arriving with crews every month. And if those resources were not enough, the war in Europe would end soon, and the European bombers and crews could be shifted to Japan. Arnold was less sure of his second aim: to turn Japanese defeat into Japanese surrender without the necessity of an invasion by the Army. If the AAF could do that, its postwar independence—the dream of airmen since Billy Mitchell—would follow inevitably. Despite Arnold's hopes, the AAF had not been able to end the European war without a land invasion. The failure, he believed, had been due to the interruptions in the strategic bombing campaign by demands from Roosevelt and Churchill to support invasions of North Africa, Sicily, Italy, and France. Arnold now had more material and a weaker opponent, and Japan would be AAF's last chance to prove its claims. Arnold's nickname was "Hap," but he was not known for making his subordinates happy—he harassed and insulted them, and one officer suffered a heart attack and died on the carpet in front of Arnold's desk. Arnold was a doer, not a strategist. He had no particular attachment to *how* the AAF was going to win the war—if daylight precision bombing worked, fine, but if not, it was up to his subordinates to find a better way.[10]

At the Casablanca conference in January 1943, the Allies had proclaimed that the Axis powers must surrender unconditionally—that no terms would be offered to any German or Japanese governments, even to possible successors of the Nazi or militaristic Japanese regimes. There were two reasons for this policy. First, it allayed Soviet fears that Britain and America might negotiate a separate peace with Germany. Second, the Allies regretted that in World War I they had allowed a German surrender without an occupation that might have rooted out German militarism. They were determined not to repeat that mistake. Both Germany and Japan would be reconstructed as disarmed democracies. Some historians believe that this demand prolonged the war unnecessarily. For the Japanese, whose divine emperor was the essence of their national self-image, unconditional surrender seemed to imply not only defeat but national suicide. Converting Japanese defeat into Japanese surrender would not be easy (and Germany too would fight long after its defeat was a fact).

American military commanders disagreed on what forcing "unconditional surrender" would require. Each of the services wanted to be responsible for winning the war. Arnold of the AAF and Adm. Ernest King, the Navy's chief of staff, respectively argued that bombing or naval blockade would force Japan to surrender without an invasion, while Marshall and MacArthur insisted that a land invasion by the Army would be necessary. Arnold, who was still a member of the Army and on good terms with Marshall, was unwilling to press his views and form an open alliance with King.[11] By mid-1944, the Joint Chiefs had agreed to plan and prepare for a land invasion, although not until May 1945 did they specify invasion dates: November 1, 1945, for the invasion of Kyushu, Japan's southernmost island, and March 1, 1946, for the main island of Honshu. That gave Arnold very little time for the AAF and strategic bombing to win the war.[12]

Arnold appointed his chief of staff, Haywood Hansell, to command the Twenty-First Bomber Command, whose mission was attacking Japan from the Marianas. Hansell had been an instructor at the Air Corps Tactical School, and he had been one of the authors of AWPD/1, the prewar plan for organizing America's air effort. He was a firm believer in precision strategic bombing, and he mistakenly believed that Arnold shared his commitment to the doctrine. Hansell began bombing Japan by the book—a daylight raid on Tokyo's Nakajima aircraft engine factory on November 24, 1944, using the information garnered from the photographic flights initiated on November 1. But the bombers hit a problem that no one had anticipated—the B-29s were flying above thirty thousand feet, and the Norden bombsight had not been designed for jet-stream winds of 150 miles per hour. LeMay and two other AAF generals discussed the problem after the war: "The bombsight couldn't handle it. . . . If you bombed crosswind to the Jetstream the bombsight wouldn't take the drift that you needed; it was too great. If you went upwind . . . you sat there forever. You would be there until you ran out of fuel. If you came downwind the bombardier had a hard time getting synchronized. You were doing 500 to 525 knots."[13] Only twenty-four of Hansell's 111 B-29s bombed the aircraft factory, and only forty-eight bombs fell within the factory's boundaries. The rest of the planes dropped their loads on the city or the docks.[14]

The raids that followed did not go much better, and Hansell wrote to Arnold, describing his problem and reiterating his commitment to daylight precision attacks. Arnold, who was recuperating from the fourth of his wartime heart attacks, turned the matter over to his chief of staff, Gen. Lauris Norstad. Norstad had been attending meetings of the civilian Committee of Analysts, which did not share the AAF's and Hansell's commitment to precision bombing. The COA recommended incendiary bombing of Japan's industrial areas: "We have been intrigued with the possibilities . . . of complete chaos in six cities killing 584,000 people."[15] On December 18, Norstad ordered Hansell to use a hundred B-29s to hit the main residential district of Nagoya with M-69 napalm bombs. Hansell protested directly to Arnold, writing that "our mission is the destruction of primary targets by sustained attacks using precision bombing methods." Arnold replied only through Norstad, who explained that Nagoya was a "special mission resulting from the necessity of future planning." Hansell was either misreading or ignoring Arnold's signals. Years later, Hansell wrote in his memoirs, "Future planning? Was the switch to area bombing already underway?"[16] Hansell complied with Arnold's and Norstad's order, but he used only forty-nine planes, bombed the Nagoya aircraft factory rather than the residential neighborhoods, and used five-hundred-pound M-76 napalm bombs, designed to break through steel and concrete, rather than the lightweight M-69s designed for housing.[17]

Hansell had indeed missed the "switch" to area bombing, which Arnold and Norstad had implemented after Hansell's departure from Arnold's staff.[18] He had not been given new plans because his superiors—Arnold, the Joint Chiefs of Staff, and President Roosevelt—did not want their names on any such orders or policy statements. Arnold kept his distance by refusing to reply personally to Hansell's cables, continuing to use Norstad as a cutout. He wanted a commander who would take hints and act on his own, which Hansell was not willing to do. Arnold found that commander in LeMay, who began incendiary area bombing the same day that Hansell balked at Norstad's orders to bomb Nagoya. On December 18, 1944, at the request of the commander of American forces in China, LeMay's B-29s burned down half the Chinese city of Hankow using incendiaries; the fires lasted three days. Arnold saw Hansell as dogmatic and LeMay as flexible. On January 20, 1945, Arnold fired Hansell and put LeMay in charge of the Twenty-First Bomber Command.

LeMay was the commander Arnold wanted and needed. He planned his missions, thoroughly trained and prepared his crews, and was never happier than when he was actively commanding.[19] Like William Tecumseh Sherman in his Civil War march to the sea, he saw his job as destroying the enemy's ability to resist—"bomb and burn them until they quit"—while expending as few of his own soldiers' lives as possible.[20] He was not motivated by politics or racial prejudice—despite his later anti-Communism, he had a good working relationship with Mao during the war, and in retirement he would drive a Honda.[21] Like Arnold, he had no dogmatic or moral attachment to the AAF doctrine of precision daylight bombing. Were he instructed to bomb in that fashion, he would do so; were he permitted to find a better way, he would do that.

When LeMay attempted to use standard precision bombing tactics, he ran into the same problems Hansell had—B-29 failures, overcast weather, jet-stream winds. Norstad suggested firebombing Kobe's residential districts, and LeMay complied on February 4. Norstad next ordered LeMay to "prepare a conflagration that is beyond the capacity of fire-fighting control" in Nagoya. He told LeMay that aircraft engine plants would remain his primary target, but that "selected urban areas for test incendiary attack" would be secondary targets.

The AAF had repeatedly failed to damage Tokyo's Nakajima aircraft factory; when the Navy hit it, LeMay felt even more pressure. Norstad told LeMay that he was coming to the Marianas for discussions of a "personal" nature, and LeMay knew what personal discussions had led to for his predecessor Hansell. High-altitude daylight bombing was not working, and if he wanted to keep his job, he needed to do something else.[22] He planned the low-altitude night March 9 attack on Tokyo, essentially turning the AAF's strategic doctrine on its head.

Years later, LeMay recalled his thinking. He had reviewed the photos of Tokyo, where he saw few emplacements of low-altitude anti-aircraft guns. Furthermore, he believed there were only two squadrons of Japanese night fighters in Tokyo. A low-altitude night attack might therefore surprise the Japanese. If so, he could remove the guns, gunners, and ammunition from the planes and carry more bombs. And a low-altitude raid would save fuel, so the B-29s could carry still more bombs—overall, double the normal load. He considered clearing his plans with Arnold and Norstad but decided that they would not want their fingerprints on the raid if it failed.

"Drafts from the Tokyo fires bounced our airplanes into the sky like ping-pong balls," LeMay later wrote. "According to the Tokyo fire chief, the situation was out of control within minutes. It was like an explosive forest fire in dry pine woods. The racing flames engulfed ninety-five fire engines and killed one hundred and twenty-five firemen. . . . About one-fourth of the city went up in smoke that night anyway. More than two hundred and sixty-seven thousand buildings." He quoted the Air Force history of the war, and he italicized the quote: *"No other air attack of the war, either in Japan or Europe, was so destructive of life and property."*[23]

■ B-29s pass Mount Fuji at night. *U.S. Air Force photograph.*

Afterward, Arnold wired him, "Congratulations. The mission shows your crews have got the guts for anything."[24] LeMay said later, "In any case it was my decision and my order which sent the B-29s to the task in the manner described. I was glad that I had not consulted General Arnold."[25] LeMay was fooling himself. He was given the freedom to make the tactical decisions (altitude, defensive armament), but the decision to firebomb Japan had been made much higher up. Arnold surely would have fired LeMay had he not taken the initiative to move to area bombing, just as he had fired Hansell. Norstad likely would have been Arnold's next choice as commander, and Norstad would have had no compunctions about incendiary bombing.

Tokyo may have been the greatest of the incendiary air raids, but it was far from the last. LeMay wanted to repeat the experience with an attack on Nagoya the next night, but his wing commanders needed a day to recover. They attacked Nagoya on March 11. From LeMay's point of view, they were less successful: "This time we tried to step up the [the interval between bombs] to one hundred feet. It seemed to me that perhaps we had been concentrating our detonations at Tokyo more tightly that we actually needed to, and by scattering bombs more widely we could achieve the same results, but over a larger area. Nagoya showed how wrong I was. . . . Still there was a lot of blaze."[26]

The bomber commanders and crews could see that their whole approach had changed. The AAF denied it. St. Clair McKelway, LeMay's press officer, was ordered to counteract "editorial comments . . . about blanket incendiary attacks against cities . . . Guard against anyone saying this is area bombing."[27] At a press conference in Washington, Norstad bragged about the damage to Japan's economy but refused to estimate civilian casualties and denied any general switch from explosives to incendiaries. McKelway, who had been a *New Yorker* editor before the war, wrote four articles for the *New Yorker* saying that "the incendiaries were dropped with precision" and that it was "pin-point, incendiary bombing."[28] Not everyone bought it. A *New York Times* reporter who had flown on the Tokyo attack wrote, "I not only saw Tokyo burning, . . . I smelled it." He called it "a holocaust."[29]

On March 13, Osaka; March 16, Kobe; March 18, Nagoya again. Five raids in nine days, thirty-two square miles destroyed in Japan's four most populous cities—41 percent of the area the AAF destroyed in all of Germany during the entire war, and at a total cost of only twenty-two B-29s and their crews.[30] LeMay quit there, at least for a time—he had run out of napalm.

The Americans had finally learned what the British had tried to explain to them three years earlier: firebombing city centers was more effective than high-altitude precision bombing. But the AAF would not admit the change, even to itself. An internal AAF report says that "the object of these attacks was *not* to bomb indiscriminately civilian populations. The object was to destroy the *industrial and strategic targets* concentrated in the urban areas of those four cities" (italics in the original).[31]

The idea of destroying Japan with incendiaries was not invented by Curtis LeMay or by Hap Arnold. It had many fathers. Gen. Billy Mitchell had suggested the possibility of burning Japan's "paper and wood" cities as early as 1924.[32] In November 1941, George Marshall threatened to "set the paper cities of Japan on fire" if war came.[33] Immediately after Pearl Harbor, Churchill recommended "the burning of Japanese cities with incendiary bombs."[34] President Roosevelt saw in the RAF's 1943 destruction of Hamburg in an incendiary firestorm "an impressive demonstration" of what might be done to Japan. For the Americans, however, it was important that bombing civilians have the appearance of bombing military targets. A May 1943 request for a bombing plan noted, "It is desired that the areas selected include, or be in the immediate vicinity of, legitimate military targets."[35]

In November 1943, two months after the tests of napalm bombs on the German-Japanese Village at Dugway, the Committee of Analysts reported that firebombing Japan would ignite "uncontrollable conflagrations," and it ramped up the production requirements for incendiaries.[36] Vannevar Bush recommended that incendiaries be used against Japan, sending Arnold a report in October 1944 that estimated that they were five times as effective as high explosives by weight. Bush did say that switching to incendiaries would require a decision at a high level, but this did not bother Arnold, who already knew that he had the president's backing.[37] Arnold kept both Marshall and the president informed about firebombing. While they might not explicitly endorse his actions, they did not raise objections.[38]

Historian Stephan McFarland has written, "B-29s were the greatest and most expensive expressions of the doctrine of daylight precision bombing," but that, ironically, they symbolized its failure. "Doctrine makers of the 1930s looked to strategic bombing to avoid the horrors of World War I trench warfare. What they found in the skies over Japan avoided the trenches but was equally horrible."[39]

Americans found the deaths of Japanese civilians less disturbing than those of European civilians. This was in part motivated by desire for revenge against an enemy who was seen as waging war in an inhuman fashion. Americans today generally see the inventors of the Nazi death camps as more evil than the Japanese. But during the war, Americans saw Germans as more like themselves and the Japanese as fanatical killers. The Japanese had mounted a sneak attack on Pearl Harbor; they had bayoneted and starved American POWs in the Philippines; they had refused to surrender despite hopeless positions at Iwo Jima, Okinawa, and other islands, inflicting terrible casualties as they fought to almost the last man; they had used poison gas against Chinese troops; and their Kamikaze fighters were sinking American ships in suicide attacks. Burning their cities was simply what they deserved. But revenge was not the whole story—much of it was simple racism. When the Allies bombed Rotterdam in occupied Europe, they did everything possible to mitigate Dutch civilian casualties. Things were different for Chinese civilians in Japanese-occupied Asia, where LeMay burned half of Hankow in China before his attack on Tokyo. Other bomber commanders used incendiaries without much concern in Formosa and China, resulting in thousands of civilian casualties. Asian lives were simply worth less than European lives.

LeMay returned to high-altitude precision bombing while he waited for his incendiaries to be restocked. On May 14, 1945, he restarted firebombing and began targeting Japan's smaller cities with five-hundred-plane raids. Bombing Japan was relatively painless for America—Japan's defenses had never been what Germany's had been, and now even less so. Cities were bombed and then rebombed. On June 18, LeMay told Arnold and the Joint Chiefs that by October 1, he would run out of industrial targets.[40] Meanwhile, the Navy had completed its blockade of Japanese shipping, so that many of the factories that LeMay bombed were empty, having been idled by material or power shortages.

Even the atomic bomb did not end the incendiary attacks, which continued between Hiroshima and Nagasaki and then after Nagasaki until the Japanese surrender. The AAF wanted to win its independence by defeating Japan without a land invasion (a hope that was "not for public consumption," as LeMay wrote to Arnold and Norstad),[41] but it had no plans beyond running its bombing machine, which worked so smoothly that it had its own momentum. It would have required a decision by President Truman to stop it, and he seemed oblivious; his memoirs indicate that he believed that the bombing began to do real damage to Japan only in midsummer 1945.[42]

The meaning of "military target" continued to erode. One of the justifications for area bombing of Japanese cities was that Japanese industry, unlike German industry, was dispersed among small machine shops and factories within residential neighborhoods. LeMay wrote after the war that he would never forget the drill presses in Yokohama. "There they were, like a forest of scorched trees and stumps, growing up throughout that residential area."[43] But the United States Strategic Bombing Survey later concluded that by 1944, the cottage industries were no longer a significant part of the Japanese war economy.[44] In July 1945, the Japanese called up all men between fifteen and sixty and all women between seventeen and forty. The Fifth Air Force's intelligence officer declared that "the entire population of Japan is a military target. . . . THERE ARE NO CIVILIANS IN JAPAN."[45]

The AAF exulted in the destruction. One press release crowed that a "fiery perfection" of "jellied fire attacks" had "literally burned Japan out of the war," that the "vaunted Twentieth" had "killed outright 310,000 Japanese, injured 412,000 more, and rendered 9,200,000 homeless." For "five flaming months . . . a thousand All-American planes and 20,000 American men brought homelessness, terror, and death to an arrogant foe, and left him practically a nomad in an almost cityless land."[46] In his final war dispatch, Arnold found a way to make Americans feel the terror of firebombing. He included a map of Japan, with the name of each of the sixty-six firebombed cities paired with the name of an American city of the same size.[‡] So much for Roosevelt's prewar condemnation that bombing civilians "sickened the hearts of every civilized man and woman."[47]

By the summer 1945, it no longer made sense to speak of Japan's "industrial web." Whatever that had been, it was gone. Japan was defeated. Defeat, however, was not the same as surrender, and the Allies' demand for unconditional surrender meant that negotiations were not possible. The invasion of Japan's home islands was scheduled, and the atomic bomb was almost ready.

[‡] Errol Morris repeated this device in his film *The Fog of War: Eleven Lessons from the Life of Robert S. McNamara*, in which he had McNamara read the name and the percentage destroyed of several firebombed cities and compared them to American cities of the same size. Unlike Arnold, however, Morris was not gloating.

8

The Atomic Bomb

THE MEN

Two physicists, both Hungarian Jewish refugees from Hitler's Third
Reich, drove from Columbia University in Manhattan to Peconic Bay,
at the end of Long Island—Edward Teller behind the wheel and Leo
Szilard in the passenger seat. It was Sunday, July 30, 1939. Szilard and
another physicist, Eugene Wigner, had made the same trip two weeks
earlier, but Wigner was out of town that day, and Szilard had asked Teller
to drive. They pulled into the driveway of a house on the bay, where
Albert Einstein appeared in old clothes and slippers to invite them to the
porch for tea. Szilard reached into his briefcase for his draft of a letter to
Franklin Roosevelt that he wanted Einstein to sign. While Szilard and
Einstein discussed the letter—Einstein thought it was too long—Teller
was likely silent. Despite his brilliance at physics, his role that day was
as Szilard's chauffer and secretary. Szilard's draft warned Roosevelt that
German scientists had recently split uranium atoms, which, according to
Einstein's famous formula $E = mc^2$, released a large amount of energy;
that it had been determined that splitting uranium atoms could support

a nuclear chain reaction; that such a chain reaction might be used as a power source or as a bomb; and that the Germans were likely working on uranium, as they had stopped its sale from the mines they controlled in Czechoslovakia.

Five years earlier, before anyone knew that the atom could be split, Szilard had filed for a patent on a nuclear chain reaction—the idea that if one atom was changed due to a collision with a neutron in a way that released energy, and if that change then resulted in the release of two or more neutrons, the effect would be multiplicative.[1] One change would release its energy and cause two more changes, which would cause four more, then eight more ... While the energy released from any one atom's change would be small— splitting a single uranium atom, for example, releases just enough energy to make a grain of sand twitch—a few thousand cycles in the chain would unleash the energy in an enormous number of atoms. And given enough material and left uncontrolled, those thousands of cycles would take only a fraction of a second, leading to a huge pressure increase and an explosion that would dwarf anything seen from chemical explosives such as TNT. It would be an atomic bomb.

In Berlin in 1938, Otto Hahn, Lise Meitner, and Fritz Strassmann had bombarded uranium atoms with neutrons in an attempt to form a new, heavier element. No such element appeared. It took the scientists some time to understand what they had done, but they eventually determined that they had split some of the uranium atoms into two smaller atoms, barium and kryptonite. When Szilard heard of their experiment, he immediately realized that the particular isotopes of barium and kryptonite formed by splitting uranium would be unstable, and that two or more neutrons would be released. Uranium would support his idea of a chain reaction: one neutron in, a uranium atom split, two neutrons out.[2]

Ordinary uranium would not support a chain reaction. The Danish physicist Niels Bohr pointed out that naturally occurring uranium was a mixture of different isotopes—uranium atoms whose nuclei contained different numbers of neutrons.[3] Only one of the isotopes, uranium-235, could be split, and that accounted for less than 1 percent of the natural uranium. A chain reaction would occur only in the presence of some (then unknown) "critical mass" of uranium-235. Uranium-235 would need to be separated from the other uranium isotopes and piled up until that critical mass was met. All the uranium isotopes are identical in their chemical properties, so separating isotopes could not be achieved by the simple chemical processes used to purify and concentrate most substances—precipitation, distillation, fractionation, selective reactions with other substances. Isotope separation would prove to be the central problem in developing nuclear energy.

Szilard was an expert in nuclear physics, and Einstein was not. But no one knew Szilard, and everyone, including Roosevelt, knew Einstein, the world's most famous scientist. Alexander Sachs, an adviser to Roosevelt, told Szilard that a letter from Einstein would carry weight. Convincing Einstein, a lifelong pacifist, to sign a letter recommending development of an atomic bomb was probably out of the question, so Szilard simply asked Einstein to warn the president of the possibility that the Germans were developing an atomic bomb. Although Einstein likely knew that this might lead to development of an American atomic weapon, he agreed to write a letter. While he hated war, he hated the Nazis even more. He knew the state of nuclear research in Germany, and he was not willing to leave Hitler in sole possession of such a weapon, so he dictated a revised version of the letter to Teller. After the exchange of a few drafts, Einstein signed a letter on August 2, and Szilard gave it to Sachs for Roosevelt. On September 1, Germany invaded Poland, and World War II began. When Sachs finally managed to meet with the president on October 11, Roosevelt was uninterested in the details (and may not have even read the letter), but he got the message: "Alex, what you are after is to see that the Nazis don't blow us up," he told Sachs. He instructed his secretary to take action, which had the usual Washington result—the formation of a committee. Lyman Briggs, the head of the National Bureau of Standards, was appointed to head it.[4]

FDR did not fund the Briggs Committee, so his scientific adviser Vannevar Bush had the Carnegie Foundation, of which he was director, provide funding for the first few months. Briggs eventually scrounged up enough money from the Naval Research Laboratory to buy Szilard and Italian physicist Enrico Fermi some uranium and graphite, and he then waited for further direction from the president, which was not forthcoming. Sachs,

Szilard, and Einstein pressed for action, but there seemed to be no urgency. The United States was not yet at war, and many scientists viewed the whole idea of atomic energy as a pipe dream. The required critical mass of uranium-235 might be tons, and other priorities—a peacetime draft, bombers and their bombsights, Navy ships, radar—were more pressing.

The British, who were at war with Germany, viewed the bomb as urgent. In February 1940, Otto Frisch and Rudolf Peierls, German Jewish physicists who had taken refuge at the University of Birmingham, did some calculations. They concluded that the critical mass of uranium-235 was not tons, but rather about one kilogram—a little over two pounds. This would later be shown to be too low (the actual value is about fifteen kilograms, or thirty-seven pounds), but it suddenly made a bomb seem feasible. The Frisch-Peierls memorandum impelled the British government to establish its own committee to investigate separation of uranium-235 and the construction of a weapon. In January 1941, the British committee concluded that "the work [in the United States] appeared to be several months behind that carried out in this country and further, it would not appear to be proceeding as fast as ours."[5]

With the fall of France in June 1940, defense work acquired a new urgency for Roosevelt, and Vannevar Bush convinced the president to centralize weapons research and development. Roosevelt authorized formation of the National Defense Research Committee, with Bush at its head and the Briggs Uranium Committee reporting to him. Bush recruited Harvard's president, James Conant, as an NDRC member and put him in charge of all chemical projects, including explosives and poison gas.

The Briggs Committee was getting a bad reputation. Karl Compton, the president of MIT and an NDRC member, sent Bush a letter complaining of Briggs's incompetence in managing atomic research, pointing out that "our English friends are apparently farther ahead than we are, despite the fact that we have the most in number and the best in quality of the nuclear physicists in the world." He complained that the Briggs Committee "practically never meets."[6] Bush convened a National Academy of Sciences panel to consider Briggs's fate. When the panel learned that the British thought they might have a bomb in two years, it recommended "that it would be advisable to have [the Briggs Committee] reconstituted so that a man of action would be the main executive."[7]

Conant did not immediately support Bush's plans for an accelerated nuclear program. "Wasn't this a development for the *next* war, not this one?" he asked at an NDRC meeting. On July 11, 1941, Bush received a message from Charles Lauritsen, an NDRC staffer then in London, that the British were embarking on a full-scale effort to develop a bomb. It was that message, coupled with a report by Ernest Lawrence at Berkeley that there might be another route to the bomb in addition to uranium—plutonium had been discovered at Berkeley—that convinced Conant to change his mind and back the bomb's development.

In March 1941, Bush convinced Roosevelt to establish a new agency that would not only direct research but involve itself in strategy and policy. This would be the Office of Scientific Research and Development (OSRD), to which the NDRC would report. Bush was named OSRD director, and Conant was put in charge of the NDRC, with Briggs's Uranium Committee, now renamed the S-1 Committee, under his direct control. Conant would be the civilian head of what would be given the cover name "the Manhattan Project" for secrecy reasons.

The British and American governments each wanted to control the bomb. The British were thinking ahead—they remembered what had happened after the last war, when the Americans had gone home, disarmed, and left a defeated Germany time to rebuild its war machine. The Americans, on the other hand, were unwilling to cede the atomic bomb even to their closest ally. Bush wanted to know everything the British had done on the bomb, and in late 1941 he got Roosevelt to request a gentlemen's agreement to share information. There was no written agreement, because each side hoped to get there first and to cut off the information flow when success seemed imminent. The historian Peter Parides writes that "the United States and Britain were playing a very dangerous game, one that was dictated by political motive and strategic considerations. It was a game Britain lost."[8]

The Americans extracted as much information as possible from the British. When Roosevelt gave the order to proceed with development of the bomb in March 1942, the Manhattan Project was born. The Americans had more money, engineering resources, and émigré scientists than did the British and soon took the lead. Bush, Conant, and Gen. Leslie Groves, the Project's military director, imposed a policy of "restricted interchange," refusing to give the British scientists any information that would not contribute to developing a weapon during the current war. Security considerations were certainly important in that decision, but both sides also had their eyes on the postwar strategic balance and on the profits to be made from nuclear energy. British scientists and administrators pressed Churchill to demand full information sharing, and Churchill duly pressed Roosevelt. More than a year later, in August 1943, the two leaders signed what would be known as the "Quebec Agreement": the two nations would pool their resources, and information would be freely exchanged among scientists working in the same field.[9] (This free exchange would eventually allow the Soviet spy Klaus Fuchs, a member of the British team, access to Los Alamos.)

By 1942 the underlying science was well understood, and the Manhattan Project was built as a massive, simultaneous engineering effort to overcome three different problems: first, designs for two bombs, one using uranium-235 and one using plutonium; second, the separation of fissionable uranium-235 from nonfissionable uranium-238; and third, the production and purification of plutonium. Few of the participants seem to have had moral qualms about what they were doing, although many did later. "I am unhappy to admit that I did not pay much attention to [the moral problems]," the physicist Hans Bethe wrote. "We had a job to do and a very hard one. The first thing we wanted to do was to get the job done."[10] The Manhattan Project has been the subject of a great number of books.* I will focus on three individuals who worked on the project's distinct challenges: Edward Teller on the design of the bomb, Harold Urey on uranium isotope separation, and Glenn Seaborg on plutonium production.

Teller was thirty-four years old when he moved to Los Alamos, where Robert Oppenheimer was in charge of the operation to design and test both a

---

* One of the best is Richard Rhodes, *The Making of the Atomic Bomb* (New York: Simon and Schuster, 1986).

uranium bomb and a plutonium bomb. Teller would spend two and a half years there.

Teller had been born in 1908 to a Jewish family in Budapest. He did not speak until the age of three, and his family thought he might be mentally retarded; his protective mother insisted on sitting poolside with a rope tied around his waist as he learned to swim. As an adolescent, he lived through Bela Kun's brief and violent 1919 Hungarian Communist regime, which viewed Teller's father, a lawyer, as a parasite. The anti-Semitic Miklos Horthy ousted Kun, and Teller left Hungary in 1926 to study in Germany. He received his Ph.D. working on the new quantum mechanics under Werner Heisenberg at Leipzig University and then spent two years at the University of Göttingen. In 1933, the Nazis expelled Jews from the German universities, and Teller left for Niels Bohr's laboratory in Copenhagen. He moved to the United States in 1935, became a naturalized citizen in 1941, and was invited to Robert Oppenheimer's summer session in Berkeley in 1942, where the initial planning for the bomb took place.

In 1939, Bethe had theorized that the energy of the sun was the result of the fusion of hydrogen atoms to form helium (work for which he would be awarded a Nobel Prize for 1967).[11] Fusion releases nuclear energy not by splitting a very heavy atom such as uranium into two lighter atoms, but rather by fusing two very light atoms such as hydrogen to form a heavier atom. Over dinner at the Columbia University faculty club in 1941, Teller discussed the idea of a fusion bomb with Enrico Fermi. It would take enormous heat to trigger the fusion reaction. Fermi thought that a uranium fission bomb might be hot enough to do the trick, and he suggested that deuterium, a heavier isotope of hydrogen, would work better than normal hydrogen as fuel for the fusion reaction.

Teller was fascinated. At first he calculated that a fission reaction would not be hot enough to set off hydrogen fusion, but a colleague convinced him that it would. By the time he arrived at Oppenheimer's summer planning session, the hydrogen fusion bomb—which the group nicknamed "the Super"—was all Teller wanted to talk about. There was one hitch, Teller suggested. While he was confident that an atomic bomb would generate enough heat to fuse deuterium in the Super, it might also fuse the nitrogen in the earth's atmosphere, thereby destroying the planet. Bethe redid Teller's calculations and found an error—his correction showed that there was no risk of atmospheric ignition. That naturally left everyone relieved. The Berkeley group's report to Washington concluded that the Super would be perhaps a thousand times more powerful than an atomic bomb. It was put on the Manhattan Project agenda, with Teller in charge.

For almost all the young scientists posted to the New Mexico desert, their time there would be one of the most intellectually stimulating of their lives, a period of intense camaraderie and shared effort. Not for Teller. Despite his brilliance, his only significant contribution to the bomb project came during an offhand conversation with another Hungarian, John von Neumann, over dinner. Oppenheimer's Los Alamos team had planned to bring both the uranium and plutonium bombs to critical mass through a "gun-type" assembly. One subcritical piece of nuclear material would be shot along a tube into another subcritical piece; together, they would exceed the critical mass, resulting in a chain reaction and explosion. The pure plutonium-238 produced in Berkeley's cyclotron would have worked in a device like that. But when the first reactor-produced plutonium arrived at Los Alamos from the pilot plant in Oak Ridge, Tennessee, it was "dirty"—contaminated with plutonium-239 and plutonium-240, which could not be removed by any chemical means. The dirty isotopes produced neutrons that would cause premature detonation of the plutonium-238 in the slow gun-type device, and a gun-type plutonium bomb would "fizzle," disintegrating before it could reveal its real power. So the Los Alamos scientists were considering an implosion trigger, in which chemical explosives would rapidly slam pieces of plutonium into a central critical mass. Teller's contribution was to realize that implosion would also compress the plutonium, which would reduce the required critical mass. Given the shortage of material, this would be a significant advantage.[12] Teller lost interest at that point and refused to work on the details of implosion, which were left to Klaus Fuchs, but the implosion trigger would prove successful in the first "Trinity" test of the atomic bomb on July 16, 1945.

The construction of the atomic bomb proved more difficult than anticipated, and the Super, which needed the bomb as its trigger, never received the attention that Teller thought it deserved. He was monomaniacal on the subject, and people avoided him. "While his ideas are always original and often brilliant," Rudolf Peierls said of him, "they are not always practical or timely. He pursues his ideas with great insistence, and this makes him act at times like a prima donna."[13] The historian William Broad writes that "the leaders of Los Alamos found him more of a hindrance than a help." Rather than focusing on the project assigned to him, he "preferred wide-ranging talks with the project's charismatic leader, J. Robert Oppenheimer, who often found himself pressed for time." Teller fell into open conflict with his old friend Bethe, who ran the Los Alamos physics section. He was removed from work on the atomic bomb and allowed to speculate on the Super. He had decided "that the atom bomb was a sure thing and unworthy of his attention."[14]

Harold Urey was born on an Indiana farm in 1893 and moved as a child to Montana, where his parents were homesteaders. After graduating from high school, he taught school for three years and then entered the University of Montana, where he received a degree in zoology with a minor in chemistry. He lived and studied in a tent during the school year and worked on a railroad gang during the summer. After graduating in 1917, he worked in industry for a few years before entering the Berkeley graduate program in chemistry in 1921. After receiving his Ph.D. in 1923, he went off to study with Niels Bohr in Copenhagen for a year.

In 1932, Urey separated a heavy isotope of hydrogen, deuterium, from ordinary hydrogen, for which he would receive the Nobel Prize in chemistry in 1934. The deuterium atom has both a neutron and proton in its nucleus, which is called the deuteron. Deuterium would have a special role in nuclear research: firing deuterons at uranium-238 led to observation of an isotope of plutonium; deuterium rather than ordinary hydrogen would be used as the fuel for the hydrogen bomb; and heavy water (water whose hydrogen was in the form of deuterium) could be used to control a nuclear reaction.

Urey was known for his generosity and willingness to share credit. His Nobel Prize was awarded in his name alone, but he gave half of his prize money to his collaborators. Mildred Cohn, a graduate student working for Urey at Columbia in the 1930's, remembers having two strikes against her as a Jewish woman; many of the job postings actually specified "Christian male." Urey worked hard to find her a position and lent her money to live on while she finished her research. He was also politically active, starting long before the war. As early as 1932, he had been staunchly anti-Nazi and anti-Fascist and had advocated world government. When European scientists fled Mussolini and Hitler, Urey and his wife welcomed them to America. Like Einstein, Urey feared that Germany would be the first to develop the atomic bomb, and he supported an American bomb program.

As World War II approached, Urey served on the Briggs Uranium Committee (which became the S-1 Committee, reporting to Conant). Under Urey's direction, the committee examined four approaches to separating uranium isotopes, all based on the fact that uranium-238 atoms are heavier than uranium-235 atoms: separation by centrifuge (heavier substances are spun preferentially to the outer wall), separation by thermal diffusion (lighter gases concentrate at the hotter end of a tube), separation by gaseous diffusion (heavier gases diffuse more slowly through a mesh than do lighter ones), and separation by electromagnetic means (ionized substances with lighter atoms are deflected further by a magnetic field than are heavier ones).

In May 1942, Urey advised using centrifuges (the preferred method for most nations producing enriched uranium today). Leslie Groves, the Manhattan Project's director, had no understanding of the technical issues but overruled Urey. Rather than choose one separation method and make it work, Groves jumped from one to another. Ten thousand workers began to build a thermal diffusion plant at Oak Ridge. Urey managed that effort, but he correctly believed it would have little relevance to the war effort. He also led the gaseous diffusion effort, which was more successful in producing uranium-235.[15]

"I was most unhappy during the war," Urey later wrote. "I had bosses in Washington who didn't like me, and I had people working for me who didn't like me." He felt he could not resign, but he confessed that "I was very close to a nervous breakdown during the war."[16] He told Mildred Cohn that he was so upset by the use of the bomb against Japan that he would never again work on military research.[17] He began speaking out after the war, writing an essay entitled "I'm a Frightened Man" for *Collier's* magazine, warning that nuclear weapons posed a great danger to the entire world.[18]

The atomic bombing of Japan moved Urey to the political left. He served as vice chairman of the Emergency Committee of Atomic Scientists, of which Einstein was chairman, opposing the use of atomic weapons and advocating peaceful use of atomic energy. In 1948, the chairman of the House Un-American Activities Committee, J. Parnell Thomas, attacked Edward Condon, who had played a leading role in the Manhattan Project and was then head of the National Bureau of Standards, saying he was "one of the weakest links in our atomic security." Urey and Einstein supported Condon, calling such accusations "a disservice to the interests of the United States."[19] When the Rosenbergs were sentenced to death for atomic espionage, Urey sent a telegram to Eisenhower, pleading for him to block their execution and later saying, "I doubt seriously that justice had been done."[20] Urey was called to testify before the Army-McCarthy hearings in 1953, where he was treated as a Communist fellow traveler. The University of Chicago, where he served on the chemistry faculty, ignored the accusations.

Glenn Seaborg was born in 1912, the son of Swedish immigrants who had settled in Ishpenning, Michigan. Seaborg's father was a mechanic, and the family lived in an all-Swedish neighborhood. He was so shy as a child that his mother arranged with his teachers for him to go to the bathroom without asking permission, because he was too embarrassed to raise his hand. Shyness was not a problem once he reached maturity. These are the opening paragraphs from his autobiographical website:

When the phone rang in the Radiation Laboratory one January afternoon I recognized the Boston accent from the newscasts. President-elect John F. Kennedy wanted to know: Would I join his administration as head of the Atomic Energy Commission?

I said that I needed to think it through.

Take your time, he replied, I'll call you tomorrow morning.[21]

Seaborg worked his way through school as a stevedore, received his Ph.D. in the chemistry program at Berkeley, joined the Berkeley faculty, and began working on the creation of new elements. In 1939, the periodic table ended with uranium, atomic number 92. In 1940, Edwin McMillan and Phillip Abelson from the Berkeley physics department irradiated uranium-238 with neutrons, producing a stable isotope of what McMillan suspected was element 94 (now named plutonium), but he did not have time to confirm this before leaving for MIT for war work. Seaborg wrote McMillan that he, Joe Kennedy (an instructor at Berkeley), and Art Wahl (Seaborg's student) would be happy to extend his work, to which McMillan agreed. Seaborg and his collaborators used deuterons rather than neutrons to bombard uranium-238 and succeeded in producing a different isotope of plutonium. Wahl managed to purify plutonium, based on a suggestion by Wendell Latimer, dean of the Berkeley College of Chemistry, and verify that the two isomers of plutonium were different.[22] Seaborg was quick to take the credit. He wrote McMillan, "These results came just in time to me in the [plutonium] project which I am doing for the Uranium Committee."[23] The Seaborg-Wahl-Kennedy crew, augmented by Emilio Segrè, produced enough plutonium for experiments that would demonstrate that it was fissionable—that it could support a nuclear chain reaction even more readily than uranium. A plutonium bomb was possible.

If a uranium bomb was to be constructed, the fissionable uranium-235 isotope would need to be separated from the inert uranium-238 isotope, which outnumbered it by a factor of 140 in naturally occurring uranium. That was the problem that Urey was managing. For a plutonium bomb, the problem was not concentration but creation—unlike uranium, plutonium did not occur in nature. But because plutonium was made by irradiating inert uranium-238 with neutrons, it might be produced as a by-product of uranium-235 separation. If the fissionable isotope of uranium-235 *could* be sufficiently concentrated in the midst of the surrounding inert uranium-238, a controlled chain reaction could produce neutrons that would transform the inert uranium-238 into plutonium. It would make sense to build both a uranium bomb and a plutonium bomb simultaneously, which is what the Manhattan Project did.

Seaborg went to work for a Manhattan Project team with the cover name "Metallurgical Laboratory" or "Met Lab." Located at the University of Chicago, its charter was producing and purifying plutonium for a bomb. Arthur Holly Compton, NDRC member Karl Compton's brother, was in charge of the Met Lab. On April 19, 1942, he visited Berkeley. The rumor at the chemistry department was that Compton had actually come to hire Seaborg's student Art Wahl but that Seaborg had not let Compton leave his office until he had convinced Compton to hire him as chief of the Plutonium Chemistry Section.[24] It was Seaborg's thirtieth birthday. Compton also invited a number of other Berkeley faculty members, graduates, and research fellows who had worked with Seaborg—in addition to Joe Kennedy and Art Wahl, he asked David Lipkin and Sam Weissman—to join the Manhattan Project. Fed up with the way Seaborg had monopolized scientific credit, however, they refused to work in Chicago with Seaborg and insisted on being posted to Los Alamos.[25]

Chemical separation of the isomers of uranium was not possible, as we have seen, but plutonium purification was a relatively simple chemical problem. It was complicated, however, by the radioactive mess in which plutonium was embedded after its production in a nuclear pile. When Seaborg started on the plutonium purification project, the only source of plutonium was bombardment of uranium in a cyclotron; the uranium nuclear pile that would produce plutonium in quantity did not yet exist. A mere two milligrams of plutonium were made in a cyclotron, but that turned out to be enough to plan the billionfold scale-up to industrial quantities. The Manhattan Project built a pilot plant at Oak Ridge and a production plant at Hanford, Washington.

Although Hanford produced plutonium successfully, it has been an environmental disaster. The bismuth phosphate method that was used for plutonium purification had a yield of only about 90 percent, and much of the remaining 10 percent and the waste fission products ended up in the Columbia River, the groundwater, and the air. While this may have been understandable under the pressure of development during World War II, it has caused long-term problems, and a high-yield plutonium purification process was introduced only in the 1960s. Seaborg was intimately involved in atomic energy, including serving as chairman of the Atomic Energy Commission, during the entire period that bismuth phosphate purification was in use.

The first American bomb, dropped on Hiroshima on August 6, 1945, was a uranium bomb; the second bomb, dropped on Nagasaki on August 9, used Seaborg's plutonium. Seaborg of course had no control over the decisions as to whether, where, and when the bombs would be used. Whatever the merits of the arguments about the use of the bombs, approximately seventy thousand people died either at once or from the immediate aftereffects of the Nagasaki bomb, with many more injured or to eventually suffer radiation poisoning. Most were civilians. One can imagine that Seaborg might have had any of several reactions to the news of the bomb—triumph, doubt, regret, or horror. Seaborg's journals are extremely detailed (to the point of recording what he had for lunch), and as published fill entire bookshelves. This however is his entry for August 9, 1945, his only mention of the Nagasaki bomb:

A plutonium bomb was dropped on Nagasaki shortly before 11:00 a.m. Japanese time, August 9 (yesterday our time). The announcement was the top headline in this morning's paper here.

I had a meeting with Provost Deutsch (President Sproul is out of town) [both of Berkeley] to tell him about my offer of a professorship at the University of Chicago (at $10,000 per year) with the additional inducement of other academic staff as well as graduate students in the Department of Chemistry to work with me. Deutsch was encouraging that the University of California's offer could be improved to reduce the discrepancy between it and that from the University of Chicago.[26]

THE DECISION

On April 12, 1945, President Roosevelt, vacationing at a favorite spa in Warm Springs, died of a cerebral hemorrhage. Harry Truman, sworn in as president that evening, seemed an unlikely successor. He was a failed Kansas

City haberdasher whose debts had been paid by the political machine of Kansas City's Boss Pendergast, whose patronage interests he had faithfully served—he was known as "the Senator from Pendergast." Under pressure from the Democratic Party's leaders, Roosevelt had selected Truman to replace the incumbent vice president, the left-leaning Henry Wallace, as his 1944 running mate. Truman had shown little experience or judgment in foreign affairs. When Germany invaded Russia in 1941, Senator Truman said, "If we see that Germany is winning we ought to help Russia and if Russia is winning we ought to help Germany, and that way let them kill as many as possible."[27]

Truman held his first cabinet meeting immediately after his swearing-in. After the meeting, Secretary of War Henry Stimson waited for the others to leave the room and then told the president that a project was under way to develop a new explosive of almost unbelievable destructive power. The next day, James Byrnes, whom Truman would soon appoint secretary of state, told the president "with great solemnity" that "we were perfecting an explosive great enough to destroy the whole world."[28]

Truman and his closest military and political advisors, with the exception of Stimson, seemed to have had no real understanding of the atomic bomb. Byrnes, a master Senate politician who had been Truman's mentor there, would see the bomb as a club to be used to bully the Russians; Hap Arnold, chief of the AAF, likely saw it in the same way as did Curtis LeMay, who said that he understood that the bomb would make a "big bang" but that it "didn't make much of an impression on me."[29] To them, it was just a bigger bomb. Stimson warned Truman that the United States could not keep its nuclear monopoly for long and urged the president to appoint a committee of leading citizens to advise him on its use and to consider international control. The president agreed, and named an Interim Committee that included Stimson, Byrnes, Bush, Conant, and Karl Compton. A scientific advisory panel, including Oppenheimer, Fermi, Lawrence, and Arthur Compton, was formed to provide technical expertise to the Interim Committee. The advisory committee excluded scientists who were hesitant to use the bomb, such as Szilard, James Franck, and Urey.

On May 31, the Interim Committee made its recommendation. Oppenheimer and Arthur Compton had advised the committee that the bomb would have the explosive equivalent of ten thousand tons of TNT and would kill about twenty thousand people if dropped over a city, with more injured by burns or radiation.[30] (Both estimates were low. The estimate of those killed was based on the assumption that Japanese civilians would take shelter from an air raid, while the actual bombing was by a single plane without advance warning.) The committee discussed alternatives to bombing a Japanese city—arranging a demonstration of the bomb for the Japanese, dropping it on a preannounced target in Japan, or dropping it on a neutral area, perhaps an uninhabited island. All these ideas were rejected. Dropping the bomb on an uninhabited area would not show its destructive power. And what if the bomb fizzled, or what if the Japanese brought American POWs to a preannounced site? The Interim Committee's minutes for May 31: "Secretary [Stimson] expressed the conclusion, on which there was general agreement, that we could not give the Japanese any warning; that we could not concentrate on a civilian area; but that we should seek to make a profound psychological impression on as many of the inhabitants as possible. At the suggestion of Dr. Conant the Secretary agreed that the most desirable target would be a vital war plant employing a large number of workers and closely surrounded by workers' houses."[31]

A number of Manhattan Project scientists, led by Szilard and James Franck, organized petitions that the bomb be demonstrated to the Japanese before use on civilians; other scientists circulated counterpetitions.[32] Truman never saw any of them. All recommendations, including the Interim Committee's, were funneled through Stimson, who decided what the president would or would not see. Stimson had his own biases. He headed the Army, and both Gens. Marshall and MacArthur, who was scheduled to lead the invasion of Japan in the same way that Eisenhower had led in Europe, strongly influenced him. They insisted that Japan could be forced to unconditional surrender only by a land invasion. Stimson hoped that the bomb might avert that invasion.

Belief in the necessity of invasion was not universal. The Navy and the AAF believed that a combination of blockade and bombing campaigns had already defeated Japan and that, given a few more months, it would surrender. But the advice that the Interim Committee and Stimson received was skewed. When the Interim Committee deliberated and made its recommendation to Stimson, he had Gens. Grove, Marshall, and Arnold present, but no Navy or AAF officers other than Arnold, who reported to Marshall and was unwilling to openly oppose him. The Interim Committee and Stimson, in their wishes to avoid American casualties in an invasion, never considered whether such an invasion would be necessary before recommending dropping the bomb on a Japanese city.[33]

In his advice to Truman, Stimson showed his disconnection from the conduct of the war in Japan. After the March 9–10 firebombing of Tokyo, he had asked Arnold whether there had been any deviation from the policy of precision bombing. When Arnold told him that there had been no change in strategy, that the civilian casualties were only incidental, Stimson accepted his answer. As late as May 16, Stimson told Truman that insofar as possible he was holding the AAF to precision bombing, and that similar rules would be applied to the atomic bomb. But he must have known what was happening, as his decisions and advice to the president show. Stimson removed Kyoto from the target list for both conventional and atomic bombing because of its historic and artistic treasures, saying he "did not want to have the reputation of the United States outdoing Hitler in atrocities," and he told Truman that he worried that Japan's cities would be so "thoroughly bombed out that the new weapon would not have a fair background to show its strength." Truman's response was to laugh and say he understood.[34] Stimson deceived himself about the firebombing campaign in Japan, and he deceived his new president. The historian Tami Biddle has written that over Hiroshima, "no moral threshold was crossed that had not been crossed much earlier in the year."[35]

On June 14, the Joint Chiefs met to plan the invasion, and they acted almost as if the atomic bomb did not exist. The Army was certain that an invasion would be necessary, and the Navy and AAF agreed to plan for a conditional invasion if blockade and bombing failed to end the war. On June 18, the Joint Chiefs met with Truman, who expressed his concern about the American casualties that would result from facing Japan's two-million-man homeland army. No one seemed able to offer a definitive alternative to an invasion. Gen. Ira Eaker represented Arnold, who did not attend. Like Arnold, Eaker was under orders to support Marshall, and he endorsed the decision to invade the southernmost Japanese island of Kyushu. As far as the Army was concerned, there was nothing to discuss. LeMay arrived for a meeting the next day, and Marshall slept through his presentation.[36]

At the Potsdam Conference in July, Truman received news of the successful Trinity test in New Mexico of the first atomic bomb, and he mentioned to Stalin almost in passing that America had "a new weapon of unusual destructive force." Stalin (who of course knew all about it from Klaus Fuchs and other spies) said that he hoped that the Americans "would make good use of it against the Japanese." America, Britain, and China agreed on the Potsdam Declaration, a July 26 ultimatum to Japan to surrender or face "prompt and utter destruction." It made no mention of the bomb, nor did it offer to preserve the emperor system. The declaration was delivered by radio broadcast rather than through neutral countries' diplomatic channels, which may have led the Japanese to view it as propaganda.[37]

Meanwhile, the Japanese were attempting to negotiate peace terms through the Soviet Union, which deliberately failed to forward messages to the United States. The Americans had cracked the Japanese diplomatic code, and the State Department and the Joint Chiefs were fully aware of the Japanese desire to negotiate an end to the war. The same intercepts showed that the Japanese were unrealistic in believing they could negotiate a peace that would allow them to avoid occupation, try their own war criminals, and demilitarize on their own. "It is true that the war was over before the atomic bomb was dropped," LeMay later said. "We knew that because we had broken their code. The Russians didn't say anything about it, and we couldn't say anything about it because that would tell them we had broken their codes."[38]

Japan was defeated, but that did not mean the war was over. Japan relied on its plan for *ketsugo*, a mobilization of the entire nation to resist to the death. By forcing unacceptable losses on the Allies, the Japanese cabinet

▓ James Conant and Vannevar Bush shake hands, supposedly during the Trinity test of the first atomic bomb at Alamogordo, New Mexico. In fact, this was a re-creation in a Boston garage by *The March of Time* a year later. *Courtesy HBO Archives.*

still hoped to negotiate a peace that would leave its political system intact. The United States had no clear plan to force surrender, so it pursued all paths, hoping that some combination of firebombing, blockade, the atomic bomb, and invasion would bring the war to an end.

Truman relied on his advisers and allies. The advice he received from the Interim Committee, the Joint Chiefs, Secretary of State Byrnes, Secretary of War Stimson, Churchill, and Stalin was unanimous: drop the bomb on Japan. Truman always acknowledged that the decision to use the bomb was his, but he signed no authorizing document other than a handwritten note on the back of a Stimson cable: "Reply to your [message]. Suggestions approved. Release when ready but not sooner than August 2. HST."[39] Gen. Groves said, "Truman did not so much say 'yes' as not say 'no.' It would indeed have taken a lot of nerve to say 'no' at that time."[40] Roosevelt had not managed the firebombing of Japan, and Truman would not manage the atomic bomb. The bomb was just a new, bigger explosive, and the details of its use would be a military decision. Stimson authorized Arnold to use it, and Arnold ordered Carl Spaatz, now in command of the AAF in the Pacific, to bomb any one of the four Japanese cities that had been intentionally left off the target list for incendiaries—Hiroshima, Kokura, Niigata, or Nagasaki—as soon as weather permitted after August 3.

On August 6, 1945, the B-29 *Enola Gay* dropped a uranium bomb on Hiroshima, resulting in at least ninety thousand deaths. The atomic bomb is, of course, the ultimate weapon for area bombing, but the AAF still pretended that it practiced precision bombing: the *Enola Gay*'s bombardier used his Norden bombsight to target the Aioi Bridge in the city center (and not the Hiroshima headquarters of the Japanese Fifth Army Division); he missed the bridge by eight hundred feet. With an atomic bomb, however, that was precise enough. Tokyo suspected something was wrong when Hiroshima's radio station went off the air and the telephone and telegraph lines went down. The Japanese army sent an airplane to Hiroshima and immediately censored all news of the bombing.

President Truman made a radio broadcast to the nation and followed with a second three days later: "The world will note that the first atomic bomb was dropped on Hiroshima, a military base. That was because we wished in this first attack to avoid, insofar as possible, the killing of civilians. . . . Having found the bomb we have used it. . . . We have used it to shorten the agony of war, in order to save the lives of thousands and thousands of young Americans."[41]

On August 9, the AAF dropped a plutonium bomb on its secondary target, Nagasaki, killing between sixty thousand and eighty thousand; the primary target, Kokura, was obscured by clouds.[42] The Americans wanted to send a message that there would be an unending rain of atomic bombs until Japan surrendered. The scheduling of the second bomb, only three days after the first, had nothing to do with giving the Japanese a space in which to consider surrender but was a tactical decision by the AAF. The second drop was originally scheduled for August 11, but the date was moved up because the weather on August 11 was predicted to be overcast. Weather, not diplomacy, set the date.[43]

■ Thomas Ferebee, the *Enola Gay*'s bombardier, with his Norden bombsight after the atomic bombing of Hiroshima. *Photo by Ted H. Lambert.*

On August 15, Japan surrendered, subject only to the reservation that the emperor could stay on the throne in a titular role.

The American public strongly approved of the bombings. In December 1945, four months after the bombings, *Fortune* magazine published the results of a public opinion survey:[44]

Alternatives	Responding
1. We should not have used any atomic bombs at all.	4.5%
2. We should have dropped one first on some unpopulated region, to show the Japanese its power, and dropped the second one on a city only if they hadn't surrendered after the first one.	13.8%
3. We should have used the two bombs on cities just as we did.	53.5%
4. We should have quickly used many more of them before Japan had a chance to surrender.	22.7%
5. Don't know	5.5%

Three-quarters of the respondents approved the way the bombs were used or regretted not using more. The great majority of those involved in producing the bomb were proud of their work.[†]

Two arguments have been made in support of the decision to use the atomic bombs: that the bombs saved American lives that would have been lost in an invasion, and that more Japanese lives would have been lost in continued firebombing and in an eventual invasion than were in fact lost at Hiroshima and Nagasaki. Both are probably correct in their way, although they assume that an invasion would have been required. The U.S. Strategic Bombing Survey, however, argued that "certainly prior to 31 December

---

[†] On August 12, only three days after Nagasaki and before the Japanese surrender, the United States released what has become known as the Smyth Report, a surprisingly detailed technical history of the Manhattan Project. (H.D. Smyth. *A General Account of the Development of Methods of Using Atomic Energy for Military Purposes under the Auspices of the U.S. Government, 1940–1945.* Washington, DC: Superintendent of Documents, 1945.) It has been called "How to Build an Atomic Bomb in Your Basement," and it has undoubtedly helped other nations in their bomb projects by detailing the approaches that worked and those that were abandoned. The chemists felt slighted (and some still do). Glenn Seaborg protested in a letter to H. D. Smyth, the Manhattan Project physicist who was the report's author: "A large number of chemists . . . have pointed out to me the extraordinary brief and undetailed treatment, compared to the treatment of physics problems, given to chemical problems and accomplishments in the Smyth Report. . . . I must say, as one who has been in a position to watch a good deal of the chemical development take place, that I also am struck by the imbalance between your treatment of the physical and chemical aspects of this great accomplishment." (Paul Pratter, "Uranium Hexafluoride: Development of the Atomic Bomb at Linde/Hooker," www.paulpratter.com/niagara/lindehooker.htm.)

1945, and in all probability prior to November 1, 1945 [the scheduled date for the invasion of Kyushu], Japan would have surrendered even if the atomic bombs had not been dropped and even if Russia had not entered the war."[45] But the British and the Americans were war-weary, and it would have been difficult to hold the Allied forces in place, waiting for a possible Japanese surrender, while the Russians fought in Manchuria.

Russia was in fact committed to entering the war, and did so on August 8, two days after the Hiroshima bombing. (Japanese ambassador Naotake Sato called on Foreign Minister Vyacheslav Molotov to ask his help in approaching the Allies to negotiate peace terms, and Molotov interrupted him to read the Soviet declaration of war on Japan.) The nuclear scholar Ward Wilson has made a plausible case that the Soviet entry, not the bomb, motivated the Japanese surrender. The Japanese cabinet began considering surrender only on the morning of August 9, a full three days after Hiroshima but a few hours after Russia's midnight entry into the war, which certainly dashed any Japanese hope that its *ketsugo* strategy of inflicting casualties would lead to a negotiated peace; Stalin, with twenty million Russians killed in the war, was not one to be deterred by casualties. The Soviets planned to invade the northern Japanese island of Hokkaido, and the Japanese undoubtedly preferred an American occupation to a joint American-Soviet occupation. Wilson argues that the bomb gave the emperor a way to save face: in his announcement of surrender, he could blame the enemy's use of "a new and cruel bomb" rather than the defeats of the Japanese navy and army in battle.[46]

The Japanese still had a home army of two million men, and the Japanese war party was still in charge. The bomb did not end the war; what it did was give the Japanese prime minister, Hideki Togo, the opportunity to go directly to the emperor, in contravention of the normal Japanese political practice, and let the emperor express his wish that the war should end.

The president and the Joint Chiefs later argued that they had used the bomb to force surrender. That, however, is hindsight, and they had no such confidence when the decision was made: Arnold said that the "abrupt surrender of Japan was more or less a surprise."[47] The bomb's use was motivated in part by internal divisions within the American leadership. Heywood

Hansell, the AAF general whom Arnold had replaced with LeMay, argued that Truman used the bomb not to convince the Japanese to surrender but to convince the U.S. Army that the invasion was unnecessary: "Nothing short of the atomic bombs would divert the single-minded determination of the US Army."[48] In the end, the reason was as Truman explained things in his radio address: "Having found the bomb, we have used it." Money had something to do with that. The United States had spent $2 billion developing the bomb, and it would have been difficult to explain to the American public why all that money had been spent on a weapon that sat on the shelf while American airmen and sailors continued to die.

Hap Arnold saw Japan's surrender as proof that Billy Mitchell had been right. "Fully recognizing the indispensable contribution of other arms," he wrote to Stimson, "I feel that air power's part may fairly be called decisive. The collapse of Japan has vindicated the whole strategic concept of the offensive phase of the Pacific war.—No invasion was necessary."[49] This of course ignored the facts that the AAF had, without acknowledgment, abandoned precision strategic bombing in favor of firebombing city centers; that it had dropped two atomic bombs, which were not even imagined within its strategy; and that the Soviet Union had entered the war. Nonetheless, two years later, in 1947, Arnold would get the independent air force that he and Billy Mitchell had always wanted.

9

The Weapon Not Used

During World War I's stalemate, chemical weapons made the trenches increasingly hellish. First chlorine, then phosgene, then mustard, "the king of poison gases"; first released from cylinders, then packed into artillery shells, then lobbed by mortars that dropped a forty-pound drum of gas into the enemy's trench. Worse yet was in the works—both sides planned to use long-range bombers to spray gas on enemy cities in 1919, had the war not ended with the November 1918 armistice.

As World War II approached, the combatants expected that gas would be used again, despite the Geneva Protocol that, with the exception of the United States and Japan, they had all signed. Every nation had chemical weapons stockpiled, had delivery systems, had defensive equipment, and had chemical warfare specialists. Every nation pledged no first use of gas, but if one nation had taken up chemical warfare, the others would have followed. World War II was the most deadly war in history, yet the world's enormous stockpiles of chemical weapons would, for the most part, sit unused.

Nuclear weapons have not been used since World War II, and it is worth comparing nuclear and chemical weapons. As would be the case with nuclear weapons in the Cold War, fear of retaliation had a great deal to do with forbearance to launch a chemical strike. Chemical retaliation was in fact more certain than nuclear retaliation: with nuclear weapons, one nation might convince itself that a first strike could eliminate an enemy's ability to retaliate, but there could be no such hope with chemical weapons. Each nation's leader knew that use of poison gas would be answered in kind.

Effective weapons have a way of forcing their use even if they do not fit their services' doctrines—America's AAF would embrace napalm and the atomic bomb in World War II, for example. But when the war began, gas did not have a reputation as an effective weapon—it had promised to break the stasis of trench warfare in the previous war, but it had failed. The RAF and the AAF both preferred high explosives and incendiaries to gas for strategic bombing. Even Hitler, who had no moral compunctions about any weapon, showed little interest in chemical warfare. He had been gassed as an enlisted soldier in World War I, and he never visited the German chemical weapons headquarters at Raubkammer; his idea of strategy was rapid movement by armor, infantry, and aircraft. When the Germans were advancing, from 1940 to 1942, they had no interest in gas because it would have slowed them down. From 1943 on, their cities were vulnerable to aerial gas attacks, especially after the Normandy invasion, when the Allies had air superiority. And near the end of the war in Europe, when Hitler might have been willing to use his secret nerve gases in scorched-earth revenge warfare, confusion and the interference of subordinates would have made gas attacks difficult to organize.

Roosevelt deserves much of the credit for the worldwide forbearance. Both he and his predecessor Herbert Hoover detested gas. When Congress passed a bill in 1937 promoting the Chemical Warfare Service to a Corps—with the same status as the infantry or artillery—FDR vetoed it, saying, "It has been and is the policy of this Government to do everything in its power to outlaw the use of chemicals in warfare. Such use is inhuman. . . . I hope the time will come when the Chemical Warfare Service can be entirely abolished."[1] He maintained that attitude throughout the war, threatening retaliation against any enemy's first use. And he kept Churchill, who several times considered using gas, on a short leash. America had not ratified the Geneva Protocol that barred first use of gas, but Roosevelt's policy made the country an effective signatory.

At critical points, most of the combatants considered initiating chemical warfare: the British against a feared German invasion after the fall of France in 1940; the Germans in their long retreat from Russia after Stalingrad in 1943; the Germans during the Normandy invasion in 1944; the British in retaliation against the German V-1 and V-2 attacks in 1944; the Germans against the Allies in the last days of the war in 1945; and the Americans in their planned invasion of the Japanese homeland in 1945 and 1946. Each time, gas was rejected or the decision was deferred. Only the Japanese used gas, against the Chinese, and they stopped after an American warning of retaliation.

At the start of the European war in September 1939, the American Chemical Warfare Service was even more unprepared than the rest of the Army. Congress had not funded the CWS's requests for retaliatory gas stocks, and the CWS's intelligence about the capabilities of the Axis powers was risible. The Army general staff expected gas to be used in the coming war, but it did not prepare. Some of the problem was institutional. The Army had not assimilated chemical warfare in the way that it had other weapons that had been introduced in World War I, the airplane and the tank—weapons that promised the possibility of a breakthrough on the battlefield. Many of the Army's generals had served as field officers in the previous war, where they had seen chemical weapons up close and had been repulsed. Gas casualties had swamped medical stations, and gas supplies had clogged transport. No one wanted to see that again, and the Army acted as if ignoring gas would prevent it. Moreover, money was scarce, with the Navy and the Army fighting over budgets. An Army dollar spent on chemical weapons was a dollar unavailable for troops, guns, and airplanes.[2]

Britain did not begin to prepare for chemical warfare until the Italians used gas in Ethiopia. The British pacifist movement was the strongest in Europe, and it included veterans who had been gassed in the first war. With a public that was strongly anti-gas, most of the government's chemical weapons funding was for civil defense—gas masks for every adult and child, and gas-proof shelters. At the war's start, Britain knew it would not be able to retaliate against a chemical attack on its Expeditionary Force in France, where the British expected 160 German bombers would deliver eighteen thousand gallons of mustard gas a day. Consequently, when Germany invaded Poland on September 1, 1939, the British ambassador to Switzerland delivered a message for the Germans: the British would not use gas if the Germans would not, to which the Germans agreed. Neither party, of course, trusted the other to comply. After war was declared, the British government immediately began to expand its stocks of chemical weapons.[3]

Germany's attitude was also unrealistic, but for different reasons. Of all the combatants, it was best prepared for chemical warfare. Germany's lack of confidence was rooted in the Versailles Treaty, which ended World War I and which had banned its possession of poison gas. While the Germans maintained a secret program of cooperative chemical weapons research and manufacture with the Soviet Union in the 1920s, they incorrectly believed that the British and the Americans had used that time to develop new weapons and stockpiles. Germany saw itself as a decade behind, when it was actually far ahead.[4] It possessed larger stockpiles of World War I gases, such as mustard and phosgene, and it had a civil defense system comparable to Britain's. It had also developed World War II's only new class of chemical weapons, nerve gases. In 1936, Gerhard Schrader, an organic chemist at the German chemical giant IG Farben, synthesized a new compound that he hoped would prove an effective insecticide. As he drove home that evening, he was almost unable to make out the road, he had a pounding headache, and he had trouble breathing. When he arrived home, he looked in the mirror and saw that his pupils had shrunk to pinpoints. Schrader was lucky—he spent two weeks in the hospital and eight more days in bed. He had inhaled a very small amount of his new compound, and it had nearly killed him. Tests on animals showed that it caused "nausea, vomiting, constriction of the pupils and the bronchial tubes of the lungs, copious drooling and sweating, abdominal cramps, diarrhea, muscular twitching, gasping for air, violent convulsions, slowing of respiration and heartbeat, and finally paralysis of the breathing muscles, culminating in death."[5] It was too dangerous for use as an insecticide (although it did kill bugs very effectively), but Schrader sent it to the War Office, whose scientists were impressed with its potential as a chemical weapon. They named it "tabun," from the German word for "taboo." Hermann Göring, the commander of Germany's Luftwaffe, ordered tests, which determined that one tabun-loaded bomblet could kill everyone within a hundred feet. In August 1939, the German army put tabun into production as one of its standard poison gases. That same year, Schrader discovered sarin, another nerve agent that is six times more powerful than tabun.[6]

Germany invaded France in May 1940, and France surrendered six weeks later. The Germans had no interest in using gas because it would have slowed their blitzkrieg, and the British did not consider gas because they feared for their soldiers, trapped on the beaches of Dunkirk until finally boat-lifted home. When France fell, the Americans increased the CWS budget for 1941 by a factor of thirty—a level still much too low to bring chemical stocks to anything close to their planned level. James Conant, as we have seen, had managed the development of the poison gas Lewisite— then supposed to be America's secret weapon—during World War I. As head of the chemistry section of the National Defense Research Committee, he was in charge of all civilian chemical research, including incendiaries, synthetic rubber, and poison gases. Conant visited the British chemical warfare headquarters at Porton Down in 1940, where he learned of an improved British synthesis of Lewisite and discussed a compound that had been developed there, British Anti-Lewisite (BAL), which neutralized Lewisite when applied to human skin. The Allies regarded BAL as a secret weapon: if they had it and the enemy did not, they could use Lewisite on the battlefield with impunity.[7]

The CWS had been producing Lewisite at an Edgewood Arsenal pilot plant since 1925. The CWS did have some concerns about the compound, finding it difficult to develop toxic concentrations in outdoor tests, and worrying that because Lewisite hydrolyzed (reacted with water), it might be less useful in the tropics or wet climates. But this did not derail the Lewisite train, perhaps because Lewisite was America's weapon, perhaps because of the new synthesis Conant had brought from England, perhaps because of BAL. The CWS had suspended an earlier study of Lewisite's hydrolysis because of budgetary reasons, and it did not investigate further. In 1940, as war approached, the CWS saw mustard and Lewisite as the gases with the greatest potential. Using the new synthesis that Conant had brought from England, the CWS constructed Lewisite plants at the Army's Pine Bluff, Huntsville, and Rocky Mountain Arsenals, which produced about twenty thousand tons in total. The Rocky Mountain plant, near Denver, had problems: repeated releases of Lewisite vapors, fumes so heavy that workers had to wear gas masks, a spill of thirty-five hundred gallons onto the factory floor, and a blast of crude Lewisite directly into the face of a worker.

If Lewisite and mustard were to be the CWS's staples of World War II, they needed to be studied and compared. The CWS tested the two compounds on about sixty thousand soldier "volunteers" during World War II. The worst of these tests were called "man-break" experiments. The subjects, dressed in battle uniforms, were sent into gas chambers that simulated the high temperatures and humidity of the tropics, and one of the gases was introduced at some particular concentration. The men stayed in the chambers for one to four hours, were left in their uniforms for another twenty-four hours, and were then tested for skin burns. If no burns appeared, the CWS repeated the test at higher concentrations until there was something to report—thus the name "man-break": keep testing until the men break. Some volunteers developed severe genital burns. After extensive testing, the CWS came to a conclusion: Lewisite did not work as well as mustard. It hydrolyzed easily, something Conant had known twenty-five years earlier. America's secret weapon of World War I, it turned out, did not work in the rain. In late 1943, the CWS discontinued production of Lewisite, but it took a conservative approach toward ending its possible use. It kept its current stocks of Lewisite as a backup to mustard, and both the United States and Britain continued Lewisite tests on humans.[8]

During the period between the fall of France and Pearl Harbor, Britain stood alone against the Axis and therefore was not constrained by allies. Had the Germans invaded, Britain almost certainly would have used gas against the invaders' beachheads, the Geneva Protocol notwithstanding. The British were unprepared for chemical warfare because, like the Americans, they had put chemical weapons at the back of the queue in the run-up to the war. Churchill exploded at a cabinet meeting in September 1940, demanding to know why the planned stocks of poison gases had not been produced. But even had the weapons existed, their use against a German invasion would have been disastrous for the British. The Germans certainly would have retaliated in kind, and they would not have attempted an invasion without air superiority. They had much larger stocks of gas, and Britain's cities were much closer to the Luftwaffe's continental bases than Germany's cities were to British bases.

Churchill pushed to build his chemical production and delivery systems. By the end of 1941, Britain was ready to use offensive chemical weapons on five hours' notice, with twenty thousand tons of gas in inventory and seven bomber squadrons trained in aerial spraying.[9] Both sides held back in 1940–41, however. The Germans, who were planning another blitzkrieg attack, this time on Russia, did not want gas introduced to the battlefield. Had Churchill decided to use gas, he would have had to overcome the opposition of both the British Army and the RAF, and he must have known that instigating chemical warfare would have made it difficult for the United States to enter the war as Britain's ally.

On May 11, 1942, Churchill proclaimed that the British would retaliate in kind if the Germans used chemical weapons against the Russians. A month later, Roosevelt announced that he would treat Japanese chemical attacks against the Chinese as if they had been made against Americans. (He did not clear this with Secretary of War Stimson, and the United States had no capability to enforce the threat.) For a few months, any local commander on either side could have triggered a cascade of chemical warfare, with each nation using gas in retaliatory support of its allies. The Americans and British tried to gain control of situation. In November 1942, they agreed that the decision to retaliate would be reserved to each nation's supreme command. But that still meant that the United States could be drawn into chemical warfare by a British decision, and vice versa. If any nation—the United States, Britain, Germany, or Japan—had pulled the trigger, all nations might have jumped in.

The Joint Chiefs asked the CWS what was needed for readiness and received an unrealistic response: 616,608 tons of Lewisite and mustard, the amount required for unrestricted offensive gas warfare in all theaters, with gas used as the primary weapon. That grandiose estimate was ignored, and both the Americans and British stocked chemical weapons only as needed for retaliation. Nonetheless, the retaliatory threat was real. The Germans had no doubt that, given Churchill's approach to high-explosive and incendiary bombing, he would spray and bomb their cities with poison gas.

Beginning in 1941, the Germans gassed millions of Jews and other civilians with carbon monoxide and hydrogen cyanide—by far the most deadly use of poison gas in history. But from the Nazi point of view that had nothing to do with the war, and they did not use gas on the battlefield while they advanced into Russia. In mid-1942 (just as their advance began to stall), they began to manufacture the nerve gas tabun, using concentration camp prisoners as workers. The prisoners suffered constantly from low-level tabun poisoning and were left to die untreated if they received a fatal dose. To test the effects of the gas, the Germans first used apes but found concentration camp inmates both cheaper and more available. They enlisted a Nobel laureate, Professor Richard Kuhn of the Kaiser Wilhelm Institute for Medicinal Chemistry in Heidelberg, to map the physiological mechanism by which tabun and sarin killed. He determined that the gases inhibited the enzyme cholinesterase, which left the nerve signals switched permanently "on" and led to asphyxiation. Kuhn developed a test-tube assay that allowed chemists to screen new cholinesterase inhibitors as nerve gas candidates.[10]

In 1941, the Germans overran the Ukraine. Their plan for 1942 was to split their army into two parts, one that would move south to capture the oil fields in the Caucasus, and another that would move east to capture the city of Stalingrad on the west bank of the Volga. The Germans advanced rapidly into the summer of 1942, but the Russians kept a tenuous hold on Stalingrad itself and established a strong defensive position on the Volga's east bank. On November 19, the Russians launched a pincer attack against units of Germany's Hungarian and Romanian allies to the north and the south of Stalingrad. The Soviet troops surrounded the German 6th Army, inflicting an estimated eight hundred thousand casualties on Axis troops (and suffering similar losses themselves). The Germans never managed to sustain an advance on the Eastern Front again.

Germany's rationale for gas use had changed. Before Stalingrad, gas on the battlefield would have slowed the German blitzkrieg, but after Stalingrad it would have slowed the Russian advance and the German retreat. Joseph Goebbels, Robert Ley, and Martin Bormann all urged Hitler to use chemical weapons, including the secret weapon tabun, against the Russians. At a May 15, 1943, meeting in the Wolf's Lair in eastern Prussia, Otto Ambros, IG Farben's expert on poison gas, gave Hitler an update on current stocks of gases. Germany had forty-five thousand tons in total, Ambros told Hitler, but its enemies likely had more, and they had larger production capacity. Hitler then asked about tabun—whether it was a German monopoly and whether the enemy had nerve gases as well. Ambros replied that he suspected the Allies might have nerve gases, and he based this on the disappearance of organophosphate compounds—compounds similar to tabun and sarin—from American scientific journals, which suggested that the Americans had classified such research. (He was wrong; the Allies were unaware of the existence of the German nerve gases and had no such weapons under development.) After hearing Ambros's reply, Hitler stood up abruptly and left the room. He ordered that tabun and sarin production be doubled. Still, fearing that some rogue officer would use them and spark Allied retaliation, he ordered that no chemical weapons be transported to the Russian front.[11]

Soon thereafter, American soldiers died from chemical weapons in a German air attack. The gas was not German tabun, however—it was mustard gas, manufactured at Edgewood Arsenal in Maryland.

After the Allies took Sicily in the summer of 1943, they crossed the Messina straits and landed at Salerno on the Italian mainland, just south of Naples. They captured Naples and Bari, the latter a port city of 250,000 located across the Italian boot from Naples, and began bringing in supplies to support an advance up the Italian peninsula for an attack on Rome. Gas was a worry for the Allied invaders. The invasion of southern Italy was the first successful breach of Axis-occupied continental Europe, and no one knew how fiercely the Germans would resist. Rumors circulated that the Germans had used gas against the Russians. Should the Germans use gas, the Allies planned to retaliate, so they shipped chemical weapons to Italy. (In fact, the Germans were destroying both their own chemical weapons stocks and Italian stocks, or removing them from Italy as rapidly as possible for the same reason that Hitler had ordered them pulled from the Russian front—they feared that local commanders would use them and trigger Allied chemical retaliation.)[12]

"Liberty" ships were a staple of the U.S. Merchant Marine in World War II; in all, 2,751 were launched. They were cheap and could be slapped together quickly from prefabricated sections (one was assembled, start to finish, in four and a half days in a publicity stunt). The Liberty ship *John Harvey* arrived in Bari's harbor on November 28, 1943, carrying a cargo of two thousand 100-pound mustard-gas bombs. The ship had loaded the bombs, along with a crew of seven CWS soldiers, in Baltimore. The cargo was secret—so secret that even the *John Harvey*'s master was not told what he carried, nor was the naval officer in charge of the Bari port. The harbor was crowded with cargo ships that had brought ammunition, bombs, and 100-octane aviation gasoline, and the *John Harvey* waited its turn to be unloaded.

Sailors and stevedores unloaded ships around the clock, and the harbor was brightly lit every night despite the risk of German air raids. A German ME-210 reconnaissance plane flew over Bari for three days, and Captain Jenks of the RAF, in charge of the harbor's defense, was worried. His supervisor, Air Marshal Sir Arthur Coningham, was not. In a press conference on the afternoon of December 2, he said, "I would regard it as a personal affront and insult if the Luftwaffe would attempt any significant action in this area."[13] This in spite of fact that the harbor was defended by a single anti-aircraft gun whose guidance system was inoperative, and that the RAF fighters stationed nearby were off supporting Allied bombing runs.

The German JU-88 bombers came in about 7:30 on the evening of Coningham's boast, below the radar at 200 miles per hour. The merchant ships, crammed side by side, were defenseless. Twenty-eight were sunk, and another twelve damaged. The *John Motley*, berthed alongside the *John Harvey*, was filled with ammunition, and exploded. The *John Harvey* went next. The mustard bombs were not fused and did not explode, but they cracked open. The toxic mustard spilled into the harbor, which was covered with oil from burning and damaged ships and from a severed pipeline on the quay. The oil provided an ideal solvent for the mustard, and it contaminated the sailors who jumped from their burning ships. A cloud of mustard-impregnated smoke from the burning oil rose over the city, choking all who breathed it.

Mustard does not do its work instantly. Within twenty-four hours of exposure, large blisters filled with yellow fluid form, and victims complain of intense itching and burning. Should the blisters cover more than 50 percent of the body, death usually results. Breathing mustard vapors destroys lung tissue, and contact with the eyes blinds. If the mustard from the explosion had been washed away quickly, the damage would have been reduced, but no one suspected gas because the CWS soldiers on board the *John Harvey*—the only ones who knew its cargo—had been killed. Sailors, many of them wounded and burned, were sent to the hospital in their mustard-soaked clothing; rescuers who had pulled them from the water were themselves covered in mustard; doctors and nurses handled the patients without time to wash. The U.S. destroyer *Bistera* entered the harbor after the attack and rescued oil-soaked sailors before heading for open sea. That night, the *Bistera*'s crew, blinded by the mustard, struggled to steer the ship to the harbor at Taranto.[14]

One nurse described what happened in the Bari hospital a few hours after dawn: the patients "were complaining of intense heat and stripping their clothes off . . . trying desperately to rip their dressings and bandages off . . . blisters as big as balloons." The medical staff suspected mustard poisoning but could get no information from the War Office in London. Stewart Alexander, a chemical weapons officer stationed in Algiers, arrived two days later. He had worked at Edgewood Arsenal and immediately identified the cause as mustard, but he had no idea of the source. A German gas attack was of course suspected. That rumor was put to rest when a fragment from an American bomb, smeared with mustard, was retrieved from the harbor. Alexander worked from a plan of the ships berthed in the harbor, marking the location of the sailors who had died or suffered the most severe mustard symptoms, and deduced that the *John Harvey* was the source.[15]

■ The German air raid on the Italian port of Bari, which released mustard gas that had been stored on the Liberty ship *John Harvey.* The oil-soaked sailor, pulled from the water, is unknowingly contaminated with mustard, as are his rescuers. Blisters will appear only hours later. *U.S. Army photograph.*

Both the British and the Americans attempted a cover-up. They were concerned that the Germans would believe that the Allies were planning to initiate gas warfare and would make a preemptive attack. There was no way to squelch the rumors. *Time* magazine reported that at a press conference, Secretary of War Stimson "was brusque, stiff, and cut the conference short . . . Stimson snapped, 'No! I will not comment on this thing!'"[16] U.S. documents on the attack were not declassified until 1959, and the British admitted nothing until 1986. Eisenhower, in his 1948 book, *Crusade in Europe*, described the attack on Bari: "One of the ships was loaded with a quantity of mustard gas. . . . Fortunately the wind was offshore and the escaping gas caused no casualties." Churchill denied in his memoirs that the Allies even had gas in Europe.[17]

By the end of December, 83 of the 628 who had been hospitalized had died. Bari's civilians who had appeared at the military hospital had been sent away untreated, and their dead may have exceeded a thousand.

When the Allied generals planned for the Normandy invasion, gas was very much on their minds. Mustard gas, which can persist for days, would have been the Germans' weapon of choice for making the beachheads untenable. Gen. Omar Bradley wrote in his memoir, "I reasoned that Hitler, in his determination to resist to the end, might risk gas in a gamble for survival.... [E]ven a light sprinkling of persistent gas on Omaha Beach would have cost us our foothold there."[18] The use of gas at Normandy might have had profound consequences. Had the Normandy landing been repelled, the war might have stretched on for some time, especially had the Germans later used gas to slow the Anglo-American and Russian advances. The first atomic bombs might have been used against Germany rather than Japan. But the Allies had achieved air superiority prior to the invasion, and the Germans had a good idea of what sort of retaliation they would face: the Allies had prepared two gas attacks on German cities, each by a formation of four hundred bombers.

The German V-1 "buzz-bomb" attacks on London began the week after the invasion, and the V-2 ballistic missile attacks two months after that. The British feared that the Germans would load gas in the missiles, and they distributed thirty million gas masks to their citizens. The Germans considered using chemical warheads in the rockets but believed that high-explosive warheads would do more damage.[19] Even without gas, the V-rockets terrified the British, and the British Chiefs of Staff considered gas attacks against the rocket launching sites. When his chiefs rejected the idea, Churchill was unhappy. He demanded a "cold-blooded calculation ... by sensible people and not by that particular set of psalm-singing uniformed defeatists." He got his cold-blooded calculation: the planning staff presented alternatives that included a combination of phosgene and high explosives on a thousand tactical targets or twenty German cities, and mustard attacks on fifteen hundred tactical targets or sixty cities. The upside, said the planning staff, was that the attacks would contribute to the collapse of German civilian morale; the downside was that the Germans would retaliate and that gas would likely slow the Allied advance and antagonize the French civilian population. Grumpily, Churchill gave up.[20]

By late 1944, Germany's defeat seemed inevitable. Bormann, Ley, and Goebbels again pushed for use of tabun against the Red Army. Hitler turned for advice to his armaments minister, Albert Speer, who told him that IG Farben's Ambros still thought it was likely that the Allies possessed nerve agents and that the German army recommended against gas use. Without asking permission, Speer then ordered that production of mustard and nerve gases be discontinued in favor of production of explosives.[21]

After the Allied firebombing of Dresden, the Nazi leadership again considered gas, but came to no decision. Hitler ordered that under no circumstances were chemical munitions, especially the secret nerve agents, to be captured by the advancing Allies. But the Wehrmacht feared destroying them, because the fumes might make the Allies believe that they were being attacked, so they attempted to move the weapons away from the front by rail and barge. In a smaller reprise of the German attack on Bari, an American bomber struck a railcar carrying tabun, killing four civilians. In his postwar testimony to Allied investigators, Speer claimed that Hitler ordered gas use near the end of the war but that he undermined the order's execution.[22] Perhaps. No document has been found with Hitler's order to use gas, and Speer's testimony came while he was successfully ingratiating himself with the Allies; Speer was the highest-ranking Nazi who neither was executed nor served a life term. In any case, it would have been much easier amid the collapse of the Reich for Hitler to order poison gas than it would for him to have gotten his order executed. The order would have had to filter through layers of resisting Wehrmacht staff to a willing field officer who was able to organize gas stocks and delivery equipment, transport the gear to one of the collapsing fronts, and then shell the advancing Allies.

Japan had not been subject to gas attacks in World War I and saw things differently than did the European and American combatants. Like the United States, Japan did not worry about civil defense—it believed that the Pacific Ocean was an effective barrier against air attacks on its homeland. The Japanese viewed gas as a tactical weapon like any other. They sent gas units to China, where they blithely used Lewisite and mustard without any apparent concern for their own prospects in an expanded war in which their enemies would have chemical weapons.[23]

Roosevelt threatened retaliation in 1942, but the Japanese saw it as an empty threat. They knew that the Americans were aware of Japanese chemical attacks in China and were not publicizing them. They concluded that Roosevelt was afraid that using gas against the Japanese would risk chemical retaliation by the Germans in Europe. Then in January 1944, the *New York Times* speculated that, given the brutal Japanese behavior in the Pacific War, the United States might in fact use gas. Japan immediately proclaimed a no-first-use policy. For some reason, Japan trusted Roosevelt's own no-first-use proclamation. The Japanese units that faced the Americans were given no chemical weapons; all the stocks were with the Kwantung army in China and in Manchuria, and the Japanese could not have made even a token retaliation had the Americans begun chemical warfare. Intercepted Japanese coded messages revealed that the Japanese knew that they were unprepared, and that they ordered their commanders to desist from using even smoke because the Americans might mistake it for gas and retaliate.[24]

In April 1945, Roosevelt died. Neither Japan nor the United States was a signatory to the 1925 Geneva Protocol, so there was no legal constraint against gas warfare by either party. Roosevelt's statements against use of chemical weapons had been his personal policies, and no one knew Truman's stance. And with Germany's surrender in May, the Americans no longer worried about gas warfare in the Pacific triggering retaliation in Europe.

The Americans had suffered horrific casualties in their advance across the Pacific, caused in part by the Japanese policy of fighting to the last man. Of twenty-one thousand Japanese defenders on Iwo Jima, 216 had surrendered. As the battle for Okinawa approached, the Japanese knew that they were outnumbered and would be defeated, but they spent months in the construction of dugouts that were impregnable to even direct shell hits, and they camouflaged the entrances so that they were nearly invisible. The Japanese did not try to prevent an American landing but waited in their caves, from which they inflicted as many casualties as possible. In the spring of 1945, American tests showed that nonpersistent gases such as phosgene were "the most promising of all weapons" against cave defenses, more so than napalm flamethrowers, whose flame streams could not turn corners once inside the cave. Gas was preferable: the cave's mouth could be targeted with chemical shells or bombs, or gas could be pumped into any opening. Once in, the gas would diffuse into side chambers, giving the Japanese defenders nowhere to hide.

The Americans scheduled the invasion of the Japanese home islands in two steps, as we have seen: the invasion of the southernmost island, Kyushu, for November 1, 1945, and the invasion of Honshu for March 1946. The Japanese home army comprised two to three million men, and the Americans expected that those troops would also dig in, just as the Okinawa defenders had.

Beginning in 1943, the U.S. Army's Special Projects Division, located at Fort Detrick, Maryland, studied anthrax, botulism, plague, and other biological weapons, and it tested a bomb to deliver botulism. The American policy was to use biological weapons, like chemical weapons, in retaliation only; the Japanese, however, had already used crude biological weapons in China. By early 1945, the American Special Projects Division had developed herbicides that could be sprayed over Japan to kill the rice crop, thereby starving the country into submission. Merck, a chemical manufacturer, sought a legal opinion on the herbicide's use, and the Army's judge advocate general ruled that a chemical that was not directly harmful to humans was not in violation of U.S. policy. (This was the same logic that would justify use of herbicides such as Agent Orange during the Vietnam War.) But the use of herbicides to starve Japan was rejected on two grounds: the necessary chemicals could not be manufactured and transported in time to spray the 1945 rice crop, and the United States could be responsible for feeding millions of starving civilians after a Japanese surrender.[25]

Because napalm bombing was working very well against Japanese cities, the Army Air Forces had little interest in switching to unproven bombing with poison gas. The Army ground forces, however, regarded gas as a useful weapon against dug-in defenses. In May and June 1945, George Marshall indicated that he favored using gas tactically "against those last pockets of resistance." In a meeting with Secretary of War Stimson, Marshall said that he saw gas as no more inhumane than phosphorus or flamethrowers, which were the standard methods for clearing cave defenses, and he forwarded a study supporting gas use to Adm. King. "If you agree with the proposed action," he wrote, "I believe we should discuss the subject informally with General Arnold and [chairman of the Joint Chiefs of Staff] Admiral Leahy." Marshall was not concerned with Japanese retaliation, possibly because he knew that the Japanese had no offensive capability outside of Manchuria and China. The United States planned to move its chemical stocks to China and Burma in preparation for the invasion.

Then Marshall reconsidered. In a June 21 note to Adm. Leahy, Marshall said that he thought moving chemical stocks would be a waste of transport and port facilities "unless we are contemplating [gas] use on other than a retaliatory basis." On July 3, the Joint Chiefs decided to delay the decision. President Truman had just departed for the Potsdam Conference, and there was no time to present a proposal for a new policy on chemical warfare to him and the other Allied leaders. By delaying, the Joint Chiefs effectively decided not to employ gas, at least not in the Kyushu invasion; there would not be sufficient time before the scheduled invasion date.[26] It is possible that the Joint Chiefs would have reconsidered that decision before the Honshu invasion planned for March, but that is speculative.

As World War II drew to its close, the Chemical Warfare Service seemed destined for a quick death. True, it had been responsible for the M-69 napalm bomb, which had incinerated Japanese cities, but its soldiers had spent the war operating smoke generators and flamethrowers, tasks that the infantry could have handled. Army budgets would shrink dramatically once the war ended, and many expected that the first thing to go would be the service that had been responsible for the weapons not used, the weapons that no one had wanted in the first place.

German nerve gas was the *deus ex machina* that saved the CWS. It happened quickly. The Americans, British, and Soviets all stumbled upon tabun munitions and German chemists in the war's final days: the Russians captured the German tabun plant at Dyhernfurth intact, and they captured a partially constructed sarin plant at Falkenhagen. The British interrogated Schrader, the chemist who had started it all; he gave them the chemical formulas for tabun, sarin, and other agents and told them that the Soviets had the tabun plant. Jürgen Von Klenck, the plant manager at Falkenhagen, fled to Bavaria after burying several thousand pages of technical documents, which he used as bargaining chips with the Americans.

The CWS sent Louis Fieser to Germany to interrogate Richard Kuhn, the Nobel laureate who had determined nerve gases' physiology and had also synthesized soman, a nerve agent even more deadly than sarin. Fieser had worked in Kuhn's lab before the war, and Kuhn received him warmly, denying that he had had anything to do with poison gases. Fieser does not mention the interview with Kuhn in his memoir, so he may have accepted Kuhn's story.[27]

Ambros, who had headed poison gas manufacture for the chemical conglomerate IG Farben, tried to pretend when captured that he was a paint chemist, but he was held for questioning by a joint American-British interrogation team. Paul Tarr, an American CWS intelligence officer, may have helped him evade arrest for two years. Ambros was eventually convicted of using forced labor at Auschwitz and sentenced to eight years. He served two years, was released, and was then hired by Dow Chemical as a consultant. The U.S., Britain, and the Soviet Union all grabbed chemists, bombs, chemicals, technical documents, and entire plants wherever they could and shipped them home. The American recruitment drive was called Project Paperclip after the paper clips attached to the resumes of the most desirable scientists, many of whom were sent with their families to Edgewood Arsenal and granted American citizenship.[28]

The chemical arms race was on. Given that the Soviets, who had an intact tabun plant, were in the lead, there was no talk of dismantling the CWS. While Roosevelt had vetoed the promotion of the CWS to higher status, in 1946 Truman signed a bill that did just that, making the CWS the Chemical Corps. He yanked ratification of the 1925 Geneva Protocol from the Senate docket. The Soviet atomic bomb test in 1949 further helped the Chemical Corps' cause—if the Russians had the bomb, the United States could not let them take the lead in chemical weapons. In 1949, Gen. Anthony C. McAuliffe (the hero of the Battle of the Bulge who had replied "Nuts" to the German demand for surrender at Bastogne) was appointed the Chemical Corps' chief, and in a 1950 speech to the American Chemical Society he revealed American plans for a new generation of chemical weapons that would attack the nervous system.[29]

When the Korean War began in 1950, the Chemical Corps' budget was tripled. The Army and the Air Force chiefs of staff recommended revoking the no-first-use policy so that gas might be employed to stop the "human wave" attacks of the Chinese People's Army. The Navy's admirals, who remembered Bari and would be responsible for transporting chemical weapons, saw potential disaster—in any accident on a ship, there would be nowhere to run—and delayed a policy change.

After Korea, the Chemical Corps' public relations department invited writers to educate the public on the Soviet threat. Cornelius Ryan, a journalist who would write the best-selling World War II accounts *The Longest Day* and *A Bridge Too Far*, wrote a cover story for *Collier's* that described the effect of a single Soviet Tu-4 bomber (the Soviet clone of the American B-29) spraying nerve gas on Washington, D.C. According to Ryan, nerve gas would be far more deadly than an atomic bomb. Ryan did not question *why* the Soviets would send a single plane in an unprovoked attack. He quoted Gen. Egbert F. Bullene, the Chemical Corps' chief, who saw the Soviet Union's ratification of the 1925 Geneva Protocol forbidding first use of chemical weapons as especially threatening. The treaty forbade the USSR's use of chemical weapons only against countries that had ratified the protocol, and the United States had not done so; that meant that there was no legal barrier to a Soviet attack. (Bullene's solution to this dilemma was not for the United States to ratify the treaty but for it to abandon its no-first-use policy).[30] In 1956, President Eisenhower did revoke the no-first-use policy, putting chemical weapons in the same class as nuclear weapons; first use was permissible, but only with presidential authorization.[31]

Environmental concerns were not at the top of the Chemical Corps' priority list. The Chemical Corps produced enormous amounts of sarin at its Rocky Mountain Arsenal near Denver and simply dumped the waste products into open ponds. Local farmers complained that their wells were polluted, and in 1962 the Chemical Corps drilled a twelve-thousand-foot well down to bedrock and pumped four million gallons of waste into it, after which Denver experienced its first earthquake in eighty years. The Chemical

Corps stopped pumping, and the earthquakes ceased; the Chemical Corps started again, and so did the quakes. Not until 1966, after it had dumped 163 million gallons of waste down the pipe and observed four thousand earth tremors, did the Chemical Corps stop pumping for good.[32]

By that time the Chemical Corps had come up with something better than sarin—a new nerve agent called VX, the most deadly chemical weapon in the American arsenal: a drop the size of a pinhead placed on the human skin would cause death. VX was not only more deadly than sarin, it was persistent—once an area was sprayed, it stayed poisoned for weeks. Food Machinery Corporation manufactured VX under Army contract at a plant on the Wabash River in Indiana. (In 1961, Food Machinery changed its name to FMC Corporation. Perhaps the FMC public relations department was behind the company's name change. It must have been difficult to fit "food" and "nerve gas" into the same corporate mission statement.) In 1962, the VX plant manager, speaking at a local Chamber of Commerce meeting, disclosed what the plant was manufacturing.[33]

For nerve gas to be used in battle, the Army needed a delivery system. It engineered the M-55 rocket, which weighed fifty-five pounds, carried five

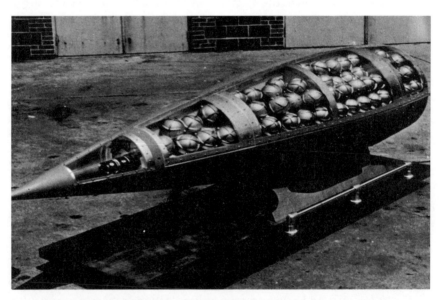

■ An "Honest John" rocket shown in cutaway with bomblets containing nerve gas, ca. 1960. *U.S. Army photo, courtesy Library of Congress.*

quarts of sarin or VX, and had a range of six miles. After the Army purchased 478,000 M-55s, it found that fifty thousand—roughly one in ten—of the sarin-filled rockets leaked. In 1968, the Chemical Corps decided to dispose of the leaking rockets by digging open-air trenches at Dugway, placing the M-55s nose down, covering them with loose material and gasoline, and burning them. It did not go well. Some of the rocket motors ignited, sending M-55s pinwheeling through the air, spewing nerve gas as they went. The rockets would need to be dumped at sea, and the Army already had a continuing program to load obsolete munitions on old Liberty ships, tow the ships out to sea, and scuttle them—Operation CHASE (Cut Holes and Sink 'Em). The leaking M-55s ended up two hundred miles off the coast of Atlantic City.[34]

In 1966, in field trials in Alaska, the Army accidentally left two hundred VX-filled artillery shells and three sarin-filled M-55 rockets on the frozen surface of Blueberry Lake. When spring came, the weapons all went to the bottom. Two years later, the Army drained the lake and retrieved them. Fifty-three caribou died near the lake three years later.[35]

In 1968, six thousand sheep were killed near Dugway Proving Ground in Utah in an accident involving field tests of VX. The Army denied everything at first, but later admitted that half a million pounds of nerve agents had been sprayed over the area over several years. It eventually agreed to pay compensation, though it continued to refuse to admit that the sheep had died from gas.[36]

When Soviet intelligence recruited an enlisted man at Edgewood Arsenal as a spy in 1969, the U.S. Defense Intelligence Agency set up a deceptive coup called Operation Shocker. The Soviet spy was a double agent, and he provided his Soviet controller with forty-five hundred pages of carefully crafted documents describing an imaginary new nerve agent, "GJ." The plan was to make the Soviets waste time and money. It worked in part; they took the bait but, spurred on by what they thought the United States had done, the Soviets developed an entire new class of nerve agents in the 1970s.[37]

In the late 1960s, chemical weapons were under fire on all sides. Press reports appeared that the Kennedy administration had earlier sent mustard

and nerve gas munitions to American-occupied Okinawa without inform-
ing the Japanese or the local government, and the Japanese requested that
the United States remove all chemical weapons. The United States admitted that Okinawa was not the only case—chemical weapons had been
secretly deployed in West Germany as well. The allies were up in arms.
Henry Kissinger, then national security adviser, advised newly inaugurated
President Nixon to cut his losses. Nixon announced a complete renunci-
ation of biological weapons, including destruction of all stockpiles, and a
return to a no-first-use policy on chemical weapons. He announced that the
United States would no longer manufacture "unitary" chemical weapons
(chemical weapons that were poisonous in themselves, such as mustard
and VX) but would move to safer "binary" weapons (weapons composed
of two nonpoisonous chemicals that reacted to form a poisonous chemical
only when mixed during a shell's flight or a bomb's drop).[38]

Americans were becoming environmentally conscious. The Army wanted to dump another load of chemical weapons at sea, including 12,000 tons
of sarin-filled bombs, 9,000 tons of mustard bombs, and 12,500 tons of
leaking M-55 rockets, most of which were stored at Rocky Mountain Arsenal. The munitions would travel by train through Indianapolis and Dayton
to Elizabeth, New Jersey (about ten miles from Manhattan), where they
would be loaded onto Liberty ships, towed out to sea, and sunk. Many objected, especially those along the planned train route, and the Army backed
off. Everything but the M-55s were incinerated on-site.[39]

In January 1973, the Army announced plans to downsize the Chemical Corps and eliminate its status as a separate branch.[40] It tried to merge
the Chemical Corps into the Ordnance Corps (the branch responsible
for developing and producing explosives) but found that "the missions
and culture of the two organizations were incompatible"—suggesting that
the Ordnance Corps had said that it wanted nothing to do with chemical
weapons.[41] But the Chemical Corps was saved again, this time by the 1973
Yom Kippur War between Egypt and Israel. Destroyed Egyptian tanks
were discovered to be equipped with sophisticated Soviet-supplied chemical warfare defenses. This suggested to the Chemical Corps' congressional
supporters that Soviet offensive capabilities were equally sophisticated,

and they refused to allow the corps to be downsized.[42] The Chemical Corps took as its mission the modernization of its stockpiles by moving to binary weapons. Its strategy for modernization was to neglect maintenance of the existing stockpile of unitary weapons, thereby creating a need for new weapons.[43]

In 1977, the Carter administration tried to negotiate an end to chemical weapons with the Soviet Union but failed. In 1982, the Reagan administration bought into the Chemical Corps's binary weapons program and increased its funding substantially. The Reagan administration's logic was as follows: our enemies have chemical weapons, so if they strike us, we must be able to retaliate in kind. The United States could have renounced chemical weapons unilaterally, kept the Chemical Corps focused on antidotes, anti-gas equipment, training, and defensive measures, and announced that it would treat any chemical attack as it would a nuclear attack—that it would retaliate with nuclear weapons, either tactical or strategic as appropriate. Instead, despite the evidence that chemical weapons had not provided any nation a strategic advantage through two world wars, the United States insisted that it must be able to respond in the same way that it was attacked.

In the late 1980s, world opinion began to swing against chemical weapons. Iran and Iraq were at war, and Iraq used mustard and sarin against Iranian troops as well as against its own Kurdish citizens; the United States tacitly favored Iraq and did not press the matter in the United Nations or other international forums. But corporations did not want to be identified with poison gases. In 1989, Mobay and Occidental Chemical refused to sell thionyl chloride, an intermediate in the manufacture of nerve gases, to Combustion Engineering, the CWS's prime manufacturing contractor. President George H. Bush and Soviet Premier Gorbachev began negotiating the Chemical Warfare Convention (CWC), a planned multinational agreement to go beyond the Geneva Protocol and mandate destruction of all chemical weapons beyond a "security stockpile" of five thousand tons.[44]

Then two things happened nearly simultaneously: the Soviet Union collapsed, thereby reducing the threat of chemical attack, and the United States led a coalition that invaded Iraq in the 1991 Gulf War. Czech and French coalition units both detected nerve gas on the battlefield, probably from destroyed Iraqi arms dumps. Their troops donned protective gear, but the U.S. commanders thought that the gas warnings were false alarms. On March 4, 1991, U.S. forces blew up the ammunition dump at Khamisiyah, where the Iraqi forces had stored nerve gas. Observers reported a substantial mushroom cloud. Of the 650,000 U.S. veterans of that war, nearly half have reported some symptoms of what has been called "Gulf War syndrome," including fatigue, loss of muscle control, headaches, dizziness and loss of balance, memory problems, muscle and joint pain, indigestion, skin problems, immune system problems, and birth defects in their children. The Pentagon denies any link between the destruction of the ammunition dump and the health problems. The issue remains controversial, and two scientific papers support the possibility of a causal link.[45]

The Gulf War refuted the notion that chemical weapons were a "poor man's atomic bomb" that would deter an attack by nations with larger conventional forces. Iraq had chemical weapons, had proven in its war with Iran that it was willing to use them, threatened the coalition forces with them, and then made no use of them even in the Scud missiles that it fired at Israel. After the Gulf War, the United States decided that retaining a five-thousand-ton security stockpile was unnecessary, and on May 13, 1991, President Bush announced that the United States would destroy its stockpiles of chemical weapons and would not employ them even in retaliation against an enemy's chemical attack; the effective date of that policy change would be the date that the CWC came into force, provided the Soviet Union was a signatory. The CWC came into force in 1997, after sixty-five countries ratified it. It outlawed use and production of weapons and mandated that all stockpiles be destroyed under international supervision. As of this writing—nearly a century after World War I—all countries have ratified the treaty with the exception of Angola, Burma, Egypt, Israel, North Korea, Somalia, South Sudan, and Syria. Approximately 75 percent of the world's (declared) stockpiles had been destroyed as of August 2012.[46] Eliminating chemical weapons is a work in progress.

The Cold War and the Hydrogen Bomb

E ven before the Manhattan Project began, Edward Teller found the idea of building the Super—a bomb that would use the heat of an atomic bomb to trigger the fusion of deuterium stored in an adjacent cylinder—irresistible. As we have seen in Chapter 8, Teller spent his time in the project thinking about little else. Oppenheimer, the project's technical leader, wanted to keep Teller as a generator of ideas, so he tolerated his obsession with the Super. He put him in charge of a small group and left him to do what he wanted.

After Japan surrendered, almost all the physicists at Los Alamos were eager to leave the isolation of the desert and return to academic life. Not Teller. When Oppenheimer told him that there was no longer a reason to work on the hydrogen bomb, he was deeply disappointed. He offered to stay on at Los Alamos if Oppenheimer would use his influence to support further work on the Super, but Oppenheimer refused; for him, the war had put an end to bomb projects. Teller decided to return to the University of Chicago. Before he left, however, he produced the *Super Handbook*, a summary of all his team's work, and he filed a patent disclosure for what would be called the "Booster," a device to increase the yield of a fission bomb by placing deuterium and tritium (a third isotope of hydrogen with two neutrons in its nucleus) at its center.[1]

James Conant, who had kept his position as president of Harvard while he served as civilian leader of the Manhattan Project, was not popular with many of the project's scientists, particularly with those who had signed a petition urging that the bomb be demonstrated to Japan before it was used on a city. They believed that Conant had kept the petition from Truman and had supported bombing civilians. It was Secretary of War Stimson who controlled access to Truman, but they were right about Conant's recommendation to bomb "a vital war plant employing a large number of workers and closely surrounded by workers' houses."[2] Oppenheimer had concurred in Conant's recommendation, but that was not generally known, and he did not receive the criticism that Conant did.

After the war's end, it was important to transfer the Manhattan Project's expertise to some permanent body. On October 5, 1945, the Truman administration proposed the May-Johnson bill, named after its congressional sponsors, Sen. Edwin Johnson and Rep. Andrew May. The bill had the support of both Conant and Vannevar Bush. It proposed an Atomic Energy Commission with part-time commissioners who would be appointed by the president but would be very difficult for him to remove. These seemed to be positions tailor-made for Conant and Bush, who would be able to keep their day jobs at Harvard and the Carnegie Foundation, respectively. Scientists objected to the bill's penalties for disclosing information and to the control of atomic energy by the military.[3] Leo Szilard and Harold Urey were especially critical, and Conant was oblivious to their complaints. He told National Academy of Sciences president Frank Jewett that before long, all the scientists would be behind the bill.

The bill failed, possibly because it lacked broad military support. The Manhattan Project had been run by the Army, and the May-Johnson bill came out of the War Department. The Navy had its own interests in nuclear weapons, as did the AAF leaders, who believed that they would soon win their independence and saw themselves as the logical custodians of atomic bombs. Both the Navy and AAF may have preferred civilian control to Army control. May-Johnson was replaced by a bill sponsored by Sen. Brien McMahon, an AAF ally. His bill, which passed, provided for a full-time Atomic Energy Commission (AEC) with no military involvement.[4] The AEC was to be given technical advice by a General Advisory Committee (GAC) headed by Oppenheimer and including among others Conant, Fermi, physicist Isidor Rabi, and Glenn Seaborg.

Teller, who was not invited to join the GAC, was still obsessed with fusion. He and six colleagues prepared a fifty-nine-page report, "A Prima Facie Proof of the Feasibility of the Super," which he presented at an April 1946 conference at Los Alamos. Klaus Fuchs, still three years away from detection as a Soviet spy, suggested a modification to Teller's Booster. He thought that moving the deuterium and tritium to a separate chamber might allow the radiation from the fission explosion to compress the fusion fuel enough to ignite it. He and John von Neumann filed for a patent on the idea. After the conference, Teller and his group circulated a report that concluded, "It is likely that the Super bomb can be constructed and will work . . . within two years." Most of those who had attended the conference found that claim incredible, because they had seen nothing to support it. In the autumn of 1946, Teller proposed a series of tests of prototype fusion devices to the new director at Los Alamos; all except the Booster were ignored. Teller suspected that Oppenheimer was sabotaging the Super.[5]

The AEC's chairman, David Lilienthal, relied on Oppenheimer and the GAC for advice, and they had given him no reason to be interested in the Super. At an October 5, 1949, AEC meeting, Lilienthal blocked Lewis Strauss, a conservative Republican AEC commissioner, from putting the Super on the agenda. Teller had Strauss's ear, and Strauss already despised Oppenheimer for both personal and political reasons. When Strauss discovered that Lilienthal had not informed President Truman of the possibility of the Super, he forced Lilienthal to call a special meeting of the GAC for October 29 to consider its development.

In the spring of 1946, Albert Einstein had organized the Emergency Committee of Atomic Scientists, an organization dedicated to international control of atomic weapons. Both Urey and Szilard, who had feuded with

Conant for years, were committee board members and were contributors to the *Bulletin of the Atomic Scientists*, dedicated to public education and discussion regarding nuclear issues. Conant, never one to share information, was at first dismissive of their efforts. In a speech at the Harvard Club, he said, "The time has not yet come for the civilians to participate in atomic knowledge to any great extent."[6] Conant, like Lilienthal, opposed development of the Super, and by 1949, with the Super on the table, he would have welcomed support even from left-leaning scientists who disliked him. He was not to get it from Urey.

Both sides prepared for the special GAC meeting. Teller was backed by a conservative Berkeley contingent: Ernest Lawrence, who led the Radiation Lab that had developed the calutrons that produced much of the Manhattan Project's uranium 235; Luis Alvarez, a physics professor who also worked at the Radiation Lab; and Wendell Latimer, the dean of the College of Chemistry at Berkeley, where Seaborg was a chemistry professor. The first three met with Teller at Los Alamos, where he showed them essentially the same information that had been available in 1946. They went from Los Alamos to Washington, where they met with senior figures at the Pentagon, with all the AEC commissioners, and with Sen. McMahon. Their message was a simple one—Russia may be ahead of us, and we cannot let them get the Super first. Lilienthal, who strongly opposed the Super, turned his head and looked out the window during their presentation to him.[7] Teller began recruiting scientists to work on the Super, and he initially convinced Hans Bethe. Two days later, Teller remembers, Bethe backed out—after talking with Oppenheimer, who showed Bethe a letter from Conant saying that the Super would be built "over my dead body."[8]

The only GAC member who did not attend the October meeting was Glenn Seaborg, and he sent Oppenheimer a letter with a wishy-washy endorsement for the Super: "Although I deplore the prospects of our country putting a tremendous effort into [the hydrogen bomb], I must confess that I have been unable to come to the conclusion that we should not."[9] Seaborg was a professor in the chemistry department that bomb proponent Latimer headed, and he was dependent on another bomb proponent, Lawrence, for use of the Berkeley cyclotrons. At the same time, he wanted to stay in Conant's and Oppenheimer's good graces. It is not surprising that he missed the meeting. Oppenheimer and Conant did not share Seaborg's letter with the other GAC members.

Because the GAC had no new evidence that the Super was technically feasible, it opposed a high-priority program. Even had new theoretical justifications been advanced, the GAC estimated that the Super would need five years. The bomb's limitless power would make it difficult to deliver, and it would have an explosive force hundreds of times that of fission bombs, with proportional radioactive contamination. Two additional documents expressed the moral concerns of the GAC members. The majority annex, signed by Conant, Oppenheimer, and four others, said that the bomb would represent "the policy of exterminating civilian populations."[10] The minority annex by Fermi and Rabi was even harsher, saying that development was wrong on fundamental ethical principles. Although Oppenheimer would be given both credit and blame for influencing the GAC's opposition to the bomb, it was Conant who took the lead; in conversations with Bethe a few days before the meeting, Oppenheimer had wavered, and he had written Conant on October 21 that it would be "folly to oppose [the Super's] exploration."

Conant swung the GAC against the Super. At the meeting's start, as many as five of the eight GAC members had favored an all-out development program, but the vote against the Super was in the end unanimous.[11] Conant said, "This whole discussion makes me feel I am seeing the same film, and a punk one, for the second time." Lilienthal said that Conant seemed weighed down by what he had done with the atomic bomb, and that he looked "almost translucent, so grey."[12] Two weeks later, the AEC endorsed the GAC's recommendation against development of the Super in a 3–2 split vote, with Lilienthal in the majority and Strauss opposed. When the Joint Chiefs of Staff met to discuss the GAC report, Sen. McMahon read it aloud to them, commenting as he went. Not surprisingly, the Joint Chiefs issued their own recommendation in favor of development.

Truman had appointed a three-man special committee to advise him on the Super—Lilienthal (opposed), Secretary of Defense Louis Johnson (in favor), and Secretary of State Dean Acheson (undecided). Johnson sent the Joint Chiefs' recommendation directly to Truman, bypassing Lilienthal and Acheson. Truman said he thought that the Joint Chiefs' ideas "made a lot of sense." When the three-man special committee met with Truman on January 31, he had already decided. "What the hell are we waiting for?" he asked. Lilienthal timed the meeting: seven minutes.[13]

In hindsight, none of the arguments against the Super would have made any real difference, even had Truman decided against it. The Soviet Union was hard at work on its own hydrogen bomb and would have succeeded eventually, which would have kicked off a crash American program that also would have succeeded. Some of those who might have been expected to oppose the Super were in favor: Harold Urey, Bernard Baruch, the financier and presidential adviser who had advocated international control of atomic weapons, and the Vatican all endorsed Truman's decision. Einstein did not endorse the decision, but he declined to oppose it, writing in a private letter, "As long as competitive armament prevails, it will not be possible to halt the process in one country."[14] Even Fermi, one of two GAC members most vociferously opposed to the Super on moral grounds, worked on the bomb once the president made his decision.

It is difficult to untangle the technical, ethical, personal, and political strands when assessing the different positions taken on the hydrogen bomb. Every GAC member was fed up with Teller, which may have predisposed their opposition to it; Urey disliked Conant and Oppenheimer, which may have entered into his support for it; and Conant and Oppenheimer have been accused of vanity in the inconsistency between their support of the atomic bomb project, which they had led, and their opposition to the hydrogen bomb project, which they would not.

Truman had had a tumultuous five years. He had taken office in April 1945. When Japan had surrendered in August 1945, the United States was alone at the top: Europe, Japan, and China were in ruins; the Soviet Union had lost twenty million dead and seemed exhausted; but America was undamaged and rich, and it alone had the atomic bomb, a weapon so powerful that it seemed to make all others obsolete. Then Stalin imposed Communist governments on almost all the territory that his troops occupied.

The fourth postwar year had been particularly dark. On August 29, 1949, the Soviet Union exploded its first atomic bomb, something that most in American intelligence thought would not happen for years. (Truman later told a senator that he could not believe "those asiatics" could build anything as complicated as the atomic bomb,[15] and after he left office in 1953 told the press, "I am [still] not convinced Russia has the [atomic] bomb.")[16] On October 1, 1949, Mao proclaimed the People's Republic of China, and the remnants of the Nationalist government and army retreated to Taiwan; this handed the Republican opposition a battle cry, "Who lost China?" And just days before Truman's meeting to decide on the hydrogen bomb, he learned that Klaus Fuchs had admitted that he had been a spy for the Soviet Union at Los Alamos during the Manhattan Project. Fuchs had worked on the most sensitive details of the implosion mechanism for the plutonium bomb and had been involved in the planning for the hydrogen bomb, including the Fuchs–von Neumann patent for radiation implosion. Fuchs's betrayal would soon be public, and Truman knew that many would see it as the explanation for the Russians' bomb. Things would soon get worse. On February 9, 1950, Sen. Joseph McCarthy would wave a paper that he claimed listed 205 Communists working in the State Department, marking the start of a wave of FBI investigations, congressional hearings, firings, and loyalty oaths. And on June 25, 1950, the North Korean Army would pour across the 38th parallel into South Korea, with the apparent support of both the Soviet Union and the People's Republic of China. The Communists seemed to be overtaking the United States on every front, and America's moment alone at the top was ending.

In the midst of this storm of bad news, Truman announced on January 31, 1950, that he had directed the AEC to "continue with its work on all form of atomic energy weapons, including the so-called hydrogen or super-bomb." Truman's announcement was nothing like Roosevelt's 1942 decision to build an atomic bomb. First, Truman's announcement was public, whereas Roosevelt's decision was secret; second, in 1950 no one knew if a fusion bomb was even possible, whereas in 1942 the physics of a fission bomb were well enough understood that success was nearly certain; third, fusion bombs (if they were physically possible, and if they could be carried in an airplane) would be so powerful that they might destroy the world, whereas atomic bombs had at least some military utility; fourth, the hydrogen bomb would require that the Hanford reactor produce tritium rather than plutonium for fission bombs and would pull Los Alamos and its scientists away from improving fission weapons, whereas the Manhattan Project did not divert resources from other war efforts; and finally, Truman's announcement was political, whereas Roosevelt's decision was military. Before his announcement, Truman did not ponder America's strategy for using a hydrogen bomb, the alternatives to its development, the possibility of international control of nuclear weapons, or the trade-offs between a hydrogen bomb and improved fission bombs. Given all his bad press, he just needed to look tough.

In 1950, America's military was in a sorry state. In an effort to reduce the nation's huge debt from World War II, Truman, with the support of his second secretary of defense, Louis Johnson, had cut the 1950 defense budget to a seventh of its 1945 level in inflation-adjusted dollars. Without a military draft, the quality of enlisted volunteers was poor. Dean Acheson, the secretary of state in Truman's second administration, pushed for a greatly increased defense budget, and Paul Nitze, an Acheson protégé, chaired a committee that authored NSC-68, a classified plan released in April 1950 that argued for tripling the defense budget. Before the Korean War, NSC-68 was going nowhere, but, as Acheson said, "Korea saved us."[17]

Gen. Hoyt Vandenberg had taken office as Air Force chief of staff in 1948. The Strategic Air Command (SAC), the bomber force whose mission was nuclear attack against any American enemy, was a mess. In a test, 101 out of SAC's 180 bombers could not even get off the ground. Vandenberg sent Curtis LeMay in to clean things up. LeMay came to SAC from a stint as commander of the new air force in Europe, where he had directed the Berlin airlift. On one of his first days on the job at SAC, LeMay walked in and told his operations commander, "Have 'em attack Wright. The whole damn command."[18] Without prior notice, he sent every SAC bomber to converge on Wright Field in Dayton for a simulated nuclear attack. It was not a success. Many of the planes were unable to get off the ground or were forced to turn back with mechanical problems, and not one plane scored a simulated hit on target. And pretending to bomb an Air Force base in Ohio was of course far easier than actually bombing the Soviet Union. Once LeMay had demonstrated SAC's problems, he set about rebuilding the command from the ground up.

SAC was not directly involved in Korea, but LeMay offered to repeat there what he had done in Japan: "I slipped a message 'under the carpet' in the Pentagon that we ought to turn SAC loose with incendiaries on some North Korean towns." But the rules were different in Korea, and LeMay's offer was not accepted. Korea was, as Vietnam would later be, a war with limited objectives and political restrictions on military action. "So we . . . eventually burned down every town in North Korea anyway, and some in South Korea too," LeMay later wrote. "We even burned down [the South Korean port city of] Pusan—an accident, but we burned it down anyway. Over a period of three years, we killed off—what—twenty percent of the population. . . . [T]his seemed to be acceptable, but to kill a few people at the start right away, no we can't stomach that."[19] He would say similar things in the 1960s about Vietnam.

SAC's mission was to direct an atomic attack, but SAC did not control the bombs—the civilian Atomic Energy Commission did. After the 1945 bombings of Hiroshima and Nagasaki, the United States produced plutonium and uranium bombs at a steady pace, but it kept its nuclear weapons at home, in what were known as "Q areas" in New Mexico, Texas, and Kentucky. Should LeMay receive an order to bomb Russia, he was to send his B-29s to the Q areas, where the commander should have received instructions to release the bombs. Because the B-29s did not have the range to reach Russia from the United States, they would first fly to bases in Newfoundland and England to refuel. Bomb assembly crews would arm the bombs there, and the B-29s would fly their missions. Although the Soviets had detonated their own atomic bomb a year earlier, the United States had not yet moved to a posture of rapid response: the whole procedure was designed to take six days. LeMay did not like the system, and by the time he left SAC in 1957, he had B-52 bombers on continuous runway alert, with KC-97 tankers ready to refuel them for an immediate attack on the Soviet Union. But in 1950, he worried about even being able to meet the six-day bombing schedule, and he managed to equip 250 bombers and staff them with crews trained to do so. Then Douglas MacArthur began poaching his planes and crews with plans to drop atomic bombs on Korea.

On August 5, 1950, six weeks after the North Korean army invaded the South, ten B-29s lined up for takeoff at Fairfield-Suisun Air Force Base, halfway between Sacramento and San Francisco. Each had an unarmed Mark IV atomic bomb, its plutonium core removed, in its belly. LeMay did not want to lose his bombers and his trained SAC crews to MacArthur. He had argued, had dragged his feet, and had insisted on flying to Washington to receive the order directly from Air Force chief of staff Hoyt Vandenberg. But the decision was final—ten atomic bombs were flying to Guam, within B-29 range of Korea. If the Chinese or Russian armies intervened in Korea, MacArthur, the theater commander, planned to turn the neck of the Korean peninsula into a zone so radioactive that neither enemy troops nor supplies could cross. But by delaying and arguing, LeMay had won the most important point: the bombs would stay under control of the Joint Chiefs of Staff, to which SAC reported. Before MacArthur could use the bombs, he would need the Joint Chiefs' permission. That meant that LeMay would have a chance to make his voice heard.

Gen. Robert Travis, the commander of the nuclear mission to Guam, rode as a passenger on one of the B-29s. Takeoff conditions were ideal, with the wind almost directly head-on at seventeen knots. The pilot ran a full power check and released the brakes for takeoff. Just as he lifted off, his number two engine failed, and he feathered its propeller. Then the landing gear failed to retract, and when he tried to make a 180-degree turn, he could not keep the left wing up. He slid the plane to the left to avoid a trailer court and crash-landed, left wing down, at 120 mph. The crew escaped with minor injuries, but twelve passengers, including Gen. Travis, were killed. Twenty minutes after the crash, the chemical high explosives in the atomic bomb detonated, scattering tamper uranium, killing seven more and injuring 173 others. Only nine atomic bombs arrived in Guam.

Truman's decision to press ahead with the hydrogen bomb did not make building it possible. It changed neither nuclear physics' principles nor physicists' understanding of them. Teller's "classic Super" consisted of a tank of liquid deuterium that would be ignited into fusion by the heat of a fission bomb. Fermi and physicists Stanislaw Ulam and Cornelius Everett did spreadsheet calculations—with paper and mechanical calculators, not with Microsoft Excel and computers—and their results were discouraging. A tank of liquid deuterium would ignite only if it contained a large amount of tritium, which could be produced only in limited amounts in the same nuclear reactors tied up in producing plutonium for atomic bombs. And if one end of the deuterium-tritium tank did ignite, the other end would burst before the fusion reaction reached it.

Meanwhile, Los Alamos planned a series of tests for 1951 that were code-named Greenhouse. Teller's Booster design, with a deuterium-tritium mixture embedded in the fission core, would be tested first. The next test on the schedule, code-named Greenhouse George, was similar to the Fuchs–von Neumann idea: the deuterium-tritium mixture would be enclosed in a separate chamber that would receive a radiation burst from the fission bomb. Physicist Robert Jastrow said, "Teller was trying to get support for the H-bomb project, and since he could not figure out how to build an H-bomb, he thought up the [George] project instead, as a demonstration for the people back in Washington."[20] In November 1950, the GAC met at Los Alamos to review the negative spreadsheet calculations on the Super and the planned Greenhouse tests. Teller took the floor. He managed to insult his colleagues, saying that he thought Los Alamos might not be strong enough to develop the Super if the tests gave positive results. He demanded that the entire laboratory be put at his disposal for a year after Greenhouse, although he had no new ideas for making fusion work.

Then came the breakthrough—although whose breakthrough remains a matter of dispute. In December 1950, Stanislaw Ulam was attempting to increase the yield of fission bombs by using implosion. Rather than use chemical explosives to compress a plutonium core, as the Fat Man bomb used on Nagasaki had done, Ulam was considering using one fission bomb to compress another. Sometime in January, he saw a way to apply the same idea to a fusion bomb. His wife found him staring out the living room window. "I found a way to make it work," he told her. "It is a totally different scheme, and it will change the course of history." Ulam informed Norris Bradbury, Los Alamos's director, and physicist Carson Mark the next day, before he spoke to Teller. Teller had considered compression many times, and he insisted it would make no difference: the fusion reaction would occur faster, he said, but the deuterium-tritium tank would also explode faster, exactly cancelling any advantage. In his conversations with Ulam and Mark, however, he realized he was wrong. The only compression that he had previously considered was from the shock wave and mass due to chemical explosives, but he now realized that compression by a fission primary would also exert radiation pressure, which chemical explosives would not. Pressure would be exerted on the deuterium-tritium mixture from the shock wave and the mass products of the fission explosion (atoms, protons, electrons, neutrons), and also from radiation products (mostly X-rays). The radiation, however, would get there first—it traveled at the speed of light. Ulam's compression scheme would work, Teller decided, but not exactly as Ulam explained it. Teller and Ulam wrote a March 9, 1951, report detailing their ideas, crediting themselves jointly for the work done.[21]

Teller would spend the rest of his life denying Ulam's role. He had spent ten years as a voice crying in the wilderness for his Super, and he was not about to cede any credit for the breakthrough idea. Between 1955 and 2001, he wrote five different accounts of the genesis of the idea of fusion by compression. For most people, memory blurs as time passes, but not for Teller. He recalled new details in each version of the episode, new conversations with participants who appeared in one story and then disappeared in another. But each of Teller's versions came to the same conclusion: he, not Ulam, deserved the credit.[22]

American prospects in the Korean War seesawed between catastrophe and total victory. The North Korean invasion of June 1950 pushed MacArthur's forces into the tiny Pusan Perimeter in the southeastern tip of the peninsula. With an amphibious landing at Inchon in September, MacArthur's troops pushed the North Korean army across the original boundary at the 38th parallel, captured the North Korean capital, Pyongyang, and seemed about to conquer all of Korea. In October, Communist Chinese troops crossed into Korea. LeMay's diary reported that by November 28, "the Korean battle" was "going very badly" and "the Chinese" had "made mincemeat out of our latest attack. Gen. MacArthur stated that conditions were out of control."[23]

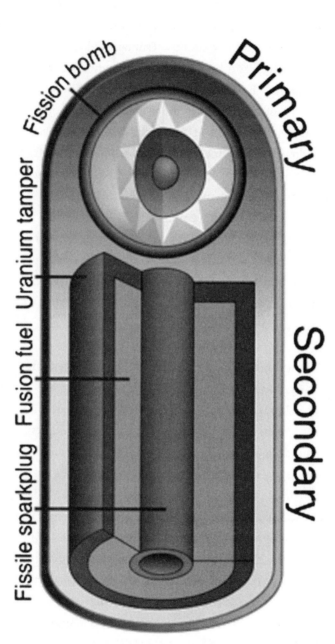

Fission bomb

Primary

Uranium tamper

Fusion fuel

Fissile sparkplug

Secondary

The Teller-Ulam device for the hydrogen bomb. A primary fission bomb ignites a secondary fission bomb that surrounds the fusion fuel.

At a November 30 press conference, Truman asserted that he would take whatever steps were necessary to stop the Communists. When a reporter asked if that included atomic bombs, Truman replied, "That includes every weapon we have," and he said that he had always considered the use of atomic weapons. The White House issued a clarification later that day: "Only the President can authorize the use of the atom bomb, and no such authorization has been given. If and when such authorization should be given, the military commander in the field would have charge."[24] MacArthur, of course, was that military commander. Banner headlines ran in every American newspaper saying that Truman might use the atomic bomb. Because the American forces were fighting under a United Nations mandate, Clement Atlee, the British prime minister, was able to raise his voice. He announced that he would go to Washington to see the president, and Truman backed off, saying that the United States had no intention of using the bomb. LeMay agreed. He wrote Air Force chief of staff Gen. Vandenberg that, after examining possible targets, he thought atomic bombs were inadvisable.

MacArthur was increasingly unhappy over Truman's attempts to negotiate a Korean ceasefire. In March, he sent an insubordinate letter directly to the Republican House minority leader, Joe Martin, saying that there was "no substitute for victory"; Martin read the letter into the *Congressional Record*. When two hundred Soviet bombers moved into Manchurian air bases, the Joint Chiefs proposed atomic retaliation in the event of a major attack and went to Truman for approval. Truman replied that Gen. MacArthur was unstable and that he could not give him control of atomic weapons. The Joint Chiefs got the point. They would support Truman's removal of MacArthur, and the new theater commander, Gen. Matthew Ridgway, would be given control of the nine atomic weapons that LeMay had sent to Guam a year earlier. Ridgway did not use them, and LeMay later got permission to ship them back from Guam to the United States. He never returned them to the AEC, and they became SAC property.[25]

Truman and Secretary of Defense Johnson had slashed the pre–Korean War defense budget under the assumption that possessing the atomic bomb would allow the United States to wage war on the cheap. Throughout the Korean War, both the military and the president had considered use of the bomb but had never found the right moment. Oppenheimer summed it up: "Are [atomic bombs] useful in ground combat? . . . What can we do with them?"[26] Truman had his own ideas, which the Joint Chiefs or even LeMay would have been unlikely to approve. In his diary, Truman imagined giving the Soviet Union a ten-day ultimatum: either withdraw all Chinese troops from Korea or America would use its atomic weapons to destroy every military base in Manchuria, including any ports and cities.[27]

In early 1950, despite Truman's decision to develop the hydrogen bomb, both Conant and Oppenheimer remained on the AEC's General Advisory Committee. In April, the National Academy of Sciences, America's most prestigious scientific organization, held an election for a new president, and the nominating committee proposed Conant, who said he would be happy to serve. Such a nomination usually resulted in rubber-stamp approval by the membership. When Conant's nomination came to the floor, it was met with what has been called the "revolt of the chemists." Wendell Latimer nominated Detlev Bronk, president of Johns Hopkins, and after emotional speeches supporting and opposing Conant, Bronk was elected 78–71. The opposition to Conant centered around two groups: right-wing scientists such as Latimer, who were disturbed by Conant's leadership role in the GAC's vote against the bomb, and scientists such as Urey, who resented his "authoritarian" behavior during World War II and the Manhattan Project.*

---

* Both groups had strong ties to the University of California in Berkeley. On the right, Willard Libby, now at Chicago, had received his Ph.D. in chemistry from Berkeley; Lawrence and Alvarez were physics professors and leaders at the Berkeley Radiation Laboratory; Teller had been on Berkeley's physics faculty; and Latimer, Joel Hildebrand, and Kenneth Pitzer were physical chemistry professors at Berkeley. On the left, Harold Urey, who criticized Conant as a bungler during the Manhattan Project and had opposed the idea of Conant heading the AEC, had received his Ph.D. at Berkeley. Oppenheimer, who supported Conant, had been a Berkeley physics professor prior to World War II. Seaborg, a politically ambitious Berkeley physical chemistry professor, characteristically avoided taking a stand on Conant's presidency but likely voted with Lawrence, his dean (Latimer), and his department chairman (Hildebrand).

The election was a public humiliation for Conant. According to one source, he never set foot in the National Academy building again.[28]

Oppenheimer called a meeting for June 16, 1951, to discuss plans for nuclear weapons tests. All the AEC commissioners, the top management of Los Alamos, and a majority of the GAC—but not Conant—attended. The results of both the Booster and George tests were discussed, and Teller was impatient to present his (and the unacknowledged Ulam's) plan for radiation compression. He was sure that Oppenheimer and the GAC would find some way to belittle the idea and avoid testing it. Bethe recalled that Teller could not contain himself as he listened to the proceedings, that he suddenly broke in and demanded to be heard immediately. Norris Bradbury, the director of Los Alamos, reminded him that his presentation was scheduled for later in the meeting, but Teller insisted and was allowed to speak.

When Teller sat down, Oppenheimer said that his proposal was "so sweet" that it had to be done. Bethe said later that Teller, as he did so often, had been pushing on a door marked "Pull."[29] The GAC's unanimous ethical objections to the bomb, made only eight months earlier, were not even discussed. Truman had already decided to build the bomb, the Korean War was under way, and the Russians would likely find the same compression solution. Nonetheless, Teller still suspected that secret forces, led by Oppenheimer, were trying to block him. He later remembered this meeting not as a triumph but as a cabal that tried to shut him up, a memory that was shared by no other attendee. The Greenhouse test series was finished, and the AEC scheduled a new series code-named Ivy. Teller saw his suspicions of persecution confirmed when he was denied the opportunity to manage the Ivy "Mike" test of his new idea for the hydrogen bomb. (Teller was repeatedly frustrated in his desires to manage, beginning with Oppenheimer's decision to put Bethe in charge of the theoretical division at Los Alamos. Even those who admired Teller believed that he would be a disaster as an administrator.)

Teller left Los Alamos in a huff and began lobbying for a second atomic weapons laboratory. As he saw things, Los Alamos was at best slow and bureaucratic, while at worst it was actively impeding progress on the hydrogen bomb. He found backing from AEC commissioner Strauss, Sen. Mc-Mahon, and the Air Force's chief scientist, David Griggs. The Air Force saw Los Alamos as Army-controlled, based on its World War II management by Army Gen. Leslie Groves, and it wanted a nuclear weapons lab that would focus on thermonuclear weapons suitable for strategic air attack rather than on small fission bombs for battlefield use. Teller got his laboratory, though not quite as he wanted it. Ernest Lawrence, head of Berkeley's Radiation Laboratory, organized support for a new AEC laboratory at Livermore, an hour's drive from Berkeley. Lawrence wanted Herbert York, not Teller, to be the new director, and he insisted that York would report to him. Teller swallowed his pride and accepted the arrangement.[30]

The Mike test of the Teller-Ulam hydrogen bomb took place just days before the 1952 presidential election. It was an unqualified success: it had been expected to yield 5 megatons, but it yielded 10.4 megatons—about five hundred times as powerful as the Hiroshima and Nagasaki bombs. The fireball was three miles wide. The AEC filmed the explosion, added music and a narrator, and played the result on commercial television.[31] According to Teller, Oppenheimer suggested that the Mike test bomb could be used to end the Korean War: build a similar device somewhere in Korea, trick enemy soldiers into congregating around it, and destroy them. Given Teller's creative memory (he told the story in two versions, one with Isidor Rabi present and one with him absent, and Rabi had no memory of the conversation), his account may say more about Teller than Oppenheimer.[32]

It would take the Soviet Union less than a year after Mike to detonate a primitive hydrogen bomb and two more years to test a bomb that used the Teller-Ulam compression scheme. Both countries began to build thermonuclear stockpiles. Over the next decade, both the United States and the Soviet Union (and Britain and France) tested hundreds of bombs in the atmosphere, spewing radioactive fallout.

In April 1954, eighteen months after the Mike test, *Time* magazine reported that Teller and Lawrence had been responsible for its success: "Teller became the director of the programme and in phenomenally short time found short cuts through Oppenheimer's technical objections."[33] The article gave full credit to Livermore, not Los Alamos, although the test's

■ The "Mike" device, the first American hydrogen bomb. It was not a weapon that could be dropped from an airplane. *U.S. Department of Energy photograph.*

director, Marshall Holloway, and most of the staff for Mike had come from Los Alamos. Because the test was classified, the article's errors were not corrected. The leaks behind the article may or may not have been Teller's fault, but the distorted press account angered many scientists.[34] And the Oppenheimer security hearings, which began just as the article was published, would further estrange Teller from many of his remaining friends.

Oppenheimer's critics—led by Sen. McMahon, AEC commissioner Strauss, and Air Force chief scientist Griggs, the same triumvirate that had lobbied for a second nuclear weapons lab—pushed Truman to remove Oppenheimer from the GAC. Oppenheimer was under FBI surveillance; he knew that his past political activities were under renewed investigation (his brother, wife, and lover were all at one time members of the American Communist Party, and he had admitted to having lied to the FBI about attempts by a Communist friend to involve him in espionage). Teller had been interviewed about Oppenheimer by the FBI in 1952. He had told the FBI that he blamed Oppenheimer for his difficulties in recruiting Bethe and others to work on the Super, and he offered his own psychological evaluation of Oppenheimer, describing him as erratic and depressive.[35]

In November 1953, William Borden sent an indictment of Oppenheimer to FBI director J. Edgar Hoover and to the Joint Committee on Atomic Energy, of which Borden had been general counsel. Borden's letter accused Oppenheimer of acting as a Soviet agent, beginning with his prewar years and continuing through the H-bomb development. The FBI amplified and documented Borden's accusations and reported to the White House, where President Eisenhower ordered Oppenheimer cut off from further access to classified information pending a security hearing. The White House, the AEC, and the FBI all hoped that Oppenheimer would resign from the GAC and from his position as a government consultant rather than force a hearing, but Oppenheimer wanted vindication. He was overconfident and did not prepare sufficiently for the hearing, where he contradicted himself repeatedly under committee counsel Roger Robb's sharp cross-examination.

The hearing was supposedly closed, but press leaks were a problem from the start. Many who had worked with Oppenheimer testified in his support, including Fermi, Rabi, Conant, Lilienthal, and Gen. Groves, whose testimony, however, was blunted when he admitted that although he was certain Oppenheimer had never been disloyal, he would not renew his security clearance under the current rules. Even the right-wing physicist John von Neumann, who favored immediate preventive nuclear war against the Soviet Union, testified in Oppenheimer's support. Others, led by the right-wing Berkeley contingent, testified against Oppenheimer (Lawrence managed to avoid testifying, saying he was ill). And then it was Teller's turn.

Teller had first learned about the Oppenheimer hearings from Curtis LeMay on a plane heading home from a thermonuclear test.[36] When Teller arrived in Washington to testify, he agreed to be briefed privately by Robb, and Teller later gave an account of that briefing. He said that he first told Robb that he did not think Oppenheimer was a security risk, but that after Robb showed him parts of Oppenheimer's (supposedly confidential) testimony, he told Robb that he could no longer say that. When Teller was called to testify the next day, Oppenheimer was present. Under Robb's questioning, Teller told Robb that he believed Oppenheimer to be loyal, but that Oppenheimer had behaved in ways that were hard to understand, and that he would "feel personally more secure if public matters would rest in other hands." He went on to say, "If it is a question of wisdom and judgment, as demonstrated by actions since 1945 [in other words, Oppenheimer's opposition to the H-bomb], then I would say he should not be granted clearance." As he left the room after two hours of testimony, he paused before Oppenheimer, held out his hand, and said, "I'm sorry." After a moment, Oppenheimer took his hand and replied, "After what you've just said, I don't know what you mean."[37]

Oppenheimer's security clearance was pulled in a 2–1 vote, which caused a press controversy and pressure for more information. Despite the AEC's assurance to all witnesses that their testimony would be confidential, the committee released the transcripts, and the reaction from his fellow physicists to Teller's testimony was immediate. Their distaste for him was not because of his political stance—others, like Lawrence and von Neumann, were at least as far to the right—but because of his publicity seeking, his refusal to share credit with Ulam, his exaggerated claims for his own contributions, and especially for his testimony against Oppenheimer. Teller said that his colleagues shunned him in the way that members of religious communities shun apostates. He arrived at Los Alamos for a meeting and was met by a *Life* magazine writer for a scheduled interview; it seemed to his colleagues that "Mr. H-bomb," as Teller had become known after the *Time* article about the Mike test, was feeding a reporter another grandiose story. After the interview, Teller went to the terrace for drinks with his colleagues. People turned away, and an old friend with whom he had shared a house refused to shake his hand. Teller returned to his room and wept.[38]

11

Missiles

Beginning on September 7, 1940, German bombers attacked London for fifty-seven consecutive nights; in total, the Blitz killed forty thousand British civilians. After May 1941, the RAF gained air superiority, Hitler turned the Luftwaffe toward Russia, and London's skies were mostly quiet for three years. In June, 1944, "doodlebugs"—as the British called them—began to appear over London. These were the first of the German "Vengeance weapons"—V-1 drone aircraft that carried a nineteen-hundred-pound warhead. The Germans launched eight thousand of them, mostly from fixed ramps in France and Holland. Guided by gyroscopic compasses and autopilots, they flew at two thousand to three thousand feet as they crossed the Channel toward London. People walking London's streets could hear the V-1's pulsejet engine's signature buzzing sound, which stopped suddenly when the bomb's odometer had ticked off the programmed distance to target. The bomb went into a steep dive then, but the sudden silence gave listeners a few seconds to find shelter. RAF fighters and antiaircraft gunners shot the V-1s down, or barrage balloons snared them, and only about half got through. Shortly after the

Normandy invasion, Allied troops captured the fixed V-1 launch sites, and the Germans replaced the V-1 with the V-2.

Where the V-1 was frightening, the V-2, the first modern ballistic missile, was terrifying. The first V-2 struck London on September 8, 1944; it landed in Slavelely Road in Chiswick, where it killed three people. The V-2 was unstoppable—it dropped at supersonic speed from as high as fifty-five miles, so its victims never heard or saw it coming. The first puzzled English newspaper accounts reported that the explosions might have been due to faulty gas mains. The V-2's mobile rail- and road-based launchers meant that its launch sites could not be bombed or captured. More than five hundred V-2s struck London, killing twenty-seven hundred civilians.

The V-2 actually preceded the V-1 in development. The German army (the Wehrmacht) had begun the V-2 project when, to the Wehrmacht's irritation, the Luftwaffe insinuated itself by offering additional funding. The simpler V-1 was initiated by the Luftwaffe alone after the V-2 was well under way. The U.S. Army and Air Force would later exhibit the same interservice squabbling over missiles, with no clear-cut division of responsibility.

The Treaty of Versailles, which ended World War I, restricted the dimensions of the German army's artillery guns. The treaty said nothing about rockets, however, and in 1930 Walther Dornberger, a German artillery officer, was put in charge of a rocket development program and began recruiting engineers. In 1932, he found Wernher von Braun at an amateur rocket club. Von Braun, a big, square-jawed twenty-year-old physics student with wavy blond hair, was fascinated with the idea of space flight—as a boy, he had strapped skyrockets to his wagon and sent it hurtling out of control. He was an enthusiastic recruit; he became a member of the Nazi Party in 1937 and joined an unarmed SS unit in 1940, both after (he later claimed) he had been told that he would not be able to continue his rocketry work if he refused.

Hitler spent as much money on the V-2 as America did on its Manhattan Project, but he got behind the program too late for it to have a significant effect on Germany's chances in the war. The timing mattered: Eisenhower said that it might have been disastrous had the Germans begun using the V-2 a few months earlier against the staging areas for the Normandy invasion.[1] The

Germans manufactured the first V-2s at Peenemünde, on the Baltic coast, and the British bombed the site in August 1943 after they identified a missile's silhouette in a reconnaissance photo. Using slave labor, the Germans constructed a safer underground factory in mountain tunnels near Nordhausen in eastern Germany. Many of the V-2 project's scientists and engineers had fond memories of the excitement and camaraderie of Peenemünde and Nordhausen, and photos of them at their test gauges look like photos of the Manhattan Project—if one ignores the Mittelbau-Dora concentration camp inmates in their striped uniforms, fifteen thousand of whom were compelled to work as scientists, technicians, assembly workers, and construction laborers.[2] They died at a rate of about 250 a week. Von Braun denied any complicity in their brutal treatment, but French prisoners later testified that he ordered beatings and watched as prisoners were hung by their wrists.[3]

On May 2, 1945, a week before the war's end, von Braun and most of his staff left Nordhausen and headed for southern Germany, where they arranged their surrender to the Americans; in an interview after the war, von Braun postdated his surrender to May 10, after V-E day, which absolved him of any charges that he betrayed the Reich before its collapse.[4] Like the Germans, von Braun's new American masters were more interested in rocketry for weapons than for space travel. Von Braun said that his aspirations were for the stars, but he accommodated both regimes.*

The Nordhausen V-2 site was within the area that the Allies had agreed would constitute the Soviet occupation zone, but an American artillery

---

* Tom Lehrer wrote the song "Wernher von Braun":

Gather round while I sing you of Wernher von Braun,
A man whose allegiance
Is ruled by expedience.
Call him a Nazi, he won't even frown.
"Ha, Nazi Schmazi," says Wernher von Braun.
Don't say that he's hypocritical,
Say rather that he's apolitical.
"Once the rockets are up, who cares vere dey come down?
Dat's not my department," says Wernher von Braun. . . .
    —Tom Lehrer, © 1965. He can be seen performing the
    song at www.youtube.com/watch?v=QEJ9HrZq7Ro.

colonel, Holger Toftoy, got there first and removed all the rocketry doc-
umentation—freight cars full of it—and parts for a hundred V-2 rockets.

The AAF was more interested in the winged V-1 than in the V-2. An AAF
officer, Clayton Bissell, wrote a 1944 paper comparing the effectiveness of
the Luftwaffe's conventional bombers in the Blitz with the later V-1 attacks
and concluded that, over comparable time periods, the V-1 was cheaper,
saved pilots' lives, and did more damage.[5] The AAF reverse-engineered a
captured V-1 and produced an identical flying bomb, which it named the
JB-2, in a matter of weeks. It ordered production of two thousand units, and
it proposed using thousands more in the invasion of Japan.[6]

The Army Ordnance Corps saw the V-2 as artillery, and the AAF saw the
V-1 as a pilotless airplane. Neither, however, was ready to cede ground to
the other. On October 2, 1944, the Army staff attempted to draw a line: the
AAF would be responsible for bombs or missiles dropped from airplanes
and for guided missiles that depended on aerodynamic forces (winged missiles, like the V-1), while the Army ground services would be responsible
for guided missiles that depended primarily on their own momentum (ballistic missiles, like the V-2).[7] That truce would turn out to be temporary.

In 1944, AAF chief of staff Hap Arnold recruited Theodore von Kármán,
a cofounder of the Jet Propulsion Laboratory, to head what would be called
the Scientific Advisory Board (SAB). In 1946 the SAB produced a thirteen-
volume strategic plan, *Toward New Horizons*.[8] Volumes VIII and IX covered guided missiles, which Arnold saw as the future of strategic air warfare.
"I see a manless Air Force. I see no excuse for men in fighter planes to shoot
down bombers," he told von Kármán. "When you lose a bomber, it is a
loss of seven thousand to forty thousand man-hours, but this crazy thing
[the V-2] they shoot over there takes only a thousand man-hours."[9] (It is
interesting that he made his analysis in terms of hardware costs rather than
the lives of the crew.) In a report released in late 1945, Arnold observed,
"We should be ready with a weapon of the general type of the German
V-2 rocket . . . ideally suited to deliver atomic explosives."[10] Arnold's health
was in decline by war's end—he had four heart attacks between 1943 and
1945—and he wanted to preserve his legacy of progressive thought for an
independent postwar Air Force. After the war, Arnold made the SAB, still

headed by von Kármán, a permanent part of the AAF structure, and he had it report directly to him as chief of staff.

Not everyone agreed that missiles were the future of military aviation. Vannevar Bush was dismissive. In his 1945 testimony before the Senate Committee on Atomic Energy, he said, "There has been a great deal said about a 3,000-mile high-angle rocket. In my opinion such a thing is impossible and will remain impossible for many years."[11] And many AAF officers, who had built the world's most powerful bombing force, saw no reason to place their bets on missiles. The B-29 had defeated Japan, the much larger B-36 was in production, the jet B-45 and B-47 bombers were in development, and the B-52 was on the horizon. The bomber wasn't broken, so why fix it?

Arnold appointed two of his protégés to key R&D positions. He named Curtis LeMay deputy chief of staff for research and development, where he was to coordinate all AAF R&D, and he named Col. Bernard Schriever, a bomber pilot who had flown forty missions in the Pacific, as the scientific liaison officer for the Air Materiel Command. LeMay's R&D group had little authority[12]—the real purchasing and planning power resided with the Air Materiel Command—and Schriever began to work closely with von Kármán and the SAB scientists. LeMay and Schriever were in overlapping, ill-defined positions, and they began what would be a long, contentious relationship.

In 1945, the AAF asked seventeen companies for proposals for pilotless aircraft, with plans to spend 34 percent of its 1947 R&D budget on missiles. Convair, the manufacturer of the new B-36 bomber, proposed the MX-774 ballistic missile, with a five-thousand-mile range. The MX-774 was not a modified V-2 but an independent engineering effort with swiveling engines, a thin skin, and an independent warhead—all concepts that the later Atlas intercontinental ballistic missile (ICBM) would use.

After Arnold left active service in February 1946, LeMay argued that von Kármán's SAB should report to him, in his role as R&D chief, rather than to his boss, Air Force chief of staff Carl Spaatz. Distracted by the approaching separation of the Air Force from the Army, Spaatz agreed. LeMay, as we have seen several times in this book, was a get-it-done-now commander with a short horizon. He wanted bombers that flew faster, farther, and higher, and he paid little attention to missiles or other long-range technology. By 1947, when LeMay left his R&D post to take command of the AAF in Europe, the SAB had disappeared from the AAF organization chart, and von Kármán's secretary had to fight to keep him from being evicted from his office.[13]

LeMay's lack of interest in missiles did not mean that he was willing to leave them to others. In a 1946 memo to Spaatz, he advised his boss on how to argue for AAF exclusivity: "The long-range future of the AAF lies in the field of guided missiles. In . . . many pilot requirements, we are reaching human limits. . . . The AAF *must* go to guided missiles." If it flew, LeMay thought, it belonged to the AAF, and he refused to share. When the Army ground forces and the Navy invited the AAF to join them in developing a test site for short- and medium-range missiles at White Sands, New Mexico, LeMay and the AAF declined. For a time, the AAF got exclusivity, at least from the Army's Field Artillery. In October 1946, the Army rescinded its 1944 memo that had given the Army ground services responsibility for R&D on ballistic missiles and handed it to the AAF; after the Air Force split off as a separate service, however, the Department of Defense announced in 1948 that the Army would regain R&D rights to its own "tactical" missiles, and the Air Force would have rights to "strategic" missiles. Neither "tactical" nor "strategic" was defined, and the struggle between the services would continue for years.[14]

Defense money flowed freely for a time—Convair's MX-774 missile was given a year's funding—but Truman clamped down hard on defense spending in 1947, and that policy would remain in place until the Korean War began in June 1950. When R&D funding shrank, the newly independent Air Force responded by protecting its bombers. In May 1947, it cancelled the MX-774 because it did not seem workable in the next eight to ten years. The Air Force had ignored the missile in any case. During its brief budgetary life, the Air Force had not sent Convair any design specifications. Working on its own, Convair had completed three test missiles by the time it received notice of cancellation. It launched them in 1948, and all three crashed and exploded. Convair continued a small ICBM research program with its own money.[15]

The Army was more interested in missiles than was the Air Force. It sent Von Braun, the other German scientists, and the captured V-2s to its new test range at White Sands, about forty miles from Fort Bliss, Texas, where the German scientists trained the Americans in V-2 launching techniques. During the war, the Germans had not had time to work on the V-2's many bugs, including wobbling when the fuel ran low and fracturing wiring harnesses, and the American and German engineers began identifying and fixing these.

Not all V-2 firings went smoothly. On the evening of May 29, 1947, Dr. Ernest Steinhoff, who had been the guidance expert at Peenemünde, attached two wires to the wrong lugs, and a V-2 headed south rather than north. It streaked across the El Paso sky, crossed the Rio Grande, and crashed into a cemetery in Juarez, Mexico. The other German scientists recalled that Steinhoff had made the same wiring mistake two years earlier, when he had launched a V-2 from Peenemünde that, instead of landing in the Baltic, struck neutral Sweden.[16]

The Germans left White Sands for Fort Bliss in 1947, and by 1949 they were in Huntsville, Alabama, where the Army established Redstone Arsenal as its missile command. Holger Toftoy, the officer who had recruited von Braun and others in Germany, was in charge at Redstone during the Korean War, and the team began development of the Redstone missile, a straightforward extension of the V-2 that was designed to carry an atomic warhead two hundred miles. They launched the first Redstone at Cape Canaveral on August 20, 1953. The Air Force was doing very little with its mandate for strategic missiles, while the Army had an experienced rocket team and a working tactical missile. And the Army had an expansive concept of "tactical."

In 1948, LeMay was named to head the Strategic Air Command, the bomber fleet whose mission was to launch a nuclear attack. SAC was a muddle when he took charge, but he built it into an effective striking arm. From its bases in England and southern Europe, SAC could hit almost any target in the Soviet Union. In 1951, as he was about to receive his fourth star, LeMay focused more than ever on new bombers. Schriever was still a colonel and in the same posting that Arnold had appointed him to five years earlier—scientific liaison officer to the materiel command. His job was to be open to new (and possibly silly) ideas, and he had, as noted, a difficult relationship with LeMay. Where LeMay was blunt and intimidating, Schriever was quiet and analytical. He had reported into LeMay's organization during World War II, but LeMay either did not know him or pretended not to. When Schriever approached LeMay with what Schriever himself later admitted was a particularly stupid idea—putting pontoons on bombers so that they could be dispersed around America's lakes and rivers—LeMay stared at him, took his cigar from his mouth, and said, "Did you say your name was Schriever?" Things did not improve in later meetings. Based on his World War II experience, LeMay wanted bombers that could fly at high altitude above the enemy's fighter and anti-aircraft defenses. Schriever argued that Soviet surface-to-air missiles would soon be able to reach any altitude (a prediction validated when Gary Powers's U-2 spy plane was shot down over the Soviet Union in 1960), and he made a presentation suggesting that flying bombers *under* the enemy's radar was a better strategy. LeMay and his staff stomped out of the room.[17]

LeMay and Schriever battled again, this time over LeMay's submarine envy. The Navy had developed a nuclear-powered submarine with essentially unlimited submersion time, and the USS *Nautilus*, the first nuclear submarine, sailed under the polar icecap in 1954. Range is to a bomber what submersion time is to a submarine—a bomber with unlimited range would allow SAC to strike anywhere in the world without refueling, and, flying for days on end, it would not be vulnerable to a Soviet sneak attack that could destroy it on the ground. LeMay dreamed of a nuclear-powered bomber, although it is far easier to float a nuclear reactor than to fly one. Schriever's job was to help specify the plane and recruit a team to build it. LeMay told Schriever that he did not want just any nuclear-powered bomber—he wanted a *supersonic* nuclear bomber. Schriever dutifully interviewed all the experts and told LeMay that it was impossible—a subsonic nuclear bomber could be built, but a supersonic nuclear bomber would require such high temperatures that the reactor would melt. That was not what LeMay wanted to hear—he wanted a "can-do" answer that Schriever was not giving him, and he was not one to let technological impossibility stand in his way. The Air Force loaded an operating nuclear reactor into a B-36 bomber and flew forty-seven flights over West Texas and New Mexico (including over the Fort Worth water supply) with a team of paratroopers in an accompanying bomber, ready to jump out and seal off the area in the event of a crash. The nuclear-powered bomber project continued in fits and starts until 1961, when Robert McNamara, Kennedy's new secretary of defense—who had been on LeMay's staff in the Pacific theater in World War II—finally killed it.[18]

In 1947, the AAF achieved what it had been fighting for since the days of Billy Mitchell—separation from the Army and status as a separate service, the U.S. Air Force. (The Army was likely glad to see the Air Force go; if things had continued as they had for the previous fifteen years, the ground forces would have wound up reporting to the air arm.) Congress passed a Unification Act that placed the Army, Navy, and Air Force under a single Defense Department. The Army and Navy lost their cabinet-level secretaries and their standing congressional committees, but the Navy at least kept its own airplanes and pilots, while the Army was told to depend on the Air Force for transport and battlefield troop support. Those were low-priority missions for the Air Force, which saw its strategic mission as paramount.

By 1952, Truman's last year in office, the nation was discouraged. The Korean War still dragged on, and Walter Winchell's radio broadcasts parroted Sen. Joe McCarthy's accusations of Communist spies in the government. Truman's approval ratings fell to 22 percent, and Eisenhower easily defeated the Democratic candidate, Adlai Stevenson, in the presidential election. But not even Eisenhower had any easy solutions to the looming Soviet menace, although he did negotiate an end to the war in Korea. Neither the United States nor its allies were prepared to spend enough money or draft enough soldiers to match the Warsaw Pact's conventional forces, and in 1953 Eisenhower proclaimed a "New Look" military policy that substituted inexpensive atomic weapons for expensive manpower. NATO's announced strategy in the event of Soviet invasion of Western Europe was "massive retaliation"—immediate strategic nuclear bombing of the Soviet Union's homeland and tactical nuclear bombing of the invading forces.

A nuclear battlefield, according to Army strategists, would be much deeper than a conventional battlefield and would require tactical nuclear strikes against formations and supply facilities hundreds of miles behind the front lines. The Defense Department had not yet set interservice guidelines for missiles, and New Look gave the Army justification for an expanded definition of "tactical."

The Army saw that the Air Force talked out of both sides of its mouth. Its external response to Army or Navy proposals for new missiles was to claim that it already had a better program under way. At the same time, it made ballistic missiles a low priority internally, preferring to spend R&D money on bombers and jet propulsion. Those missiles that it did fund were air-to-surface missiles and cruise missiles (subsonic guided missiles that were descendants of the V-1). The Air Force did not want ballistic missiles, but it certainly did not want the other services to have them. The Army was happy to use Wernher von Braun and his rocket team to stick its finger into what the Air Force saw as *its* missile pie.

Trevor Gardner, an assistant secretary of the Air Force for R&D, put the Air Force on the missile track in 1953. Gardner had worked briefly at Los Alamos, fabricating explosives, and had started his own aircraft parts supplier, where he had met Harold Talbott, Eisenhower's new secretary of the Air Force. Gardner was an intense man, a hard drinker and hard worker whose family had immigrated to the United States from Wales when he was a boy. He did not suffer fools gladly, and he was determined to get the Air Force moving on ballistic missiles.

Convair had continued to fund its MX-744 ICBM with its own money after the project's cancellation, and in 1951 it renamed the missile "Atlas" and managed to get a little support from the Air Force. The Air Force argument for refusing full funding for Atlas was circular: because the missile was supposed to carry a hydrogen bomb, the Air Force increased the missile's payload requirement so that it would be able to carry an early-1950s hydrogen bomb; because such a missile would be the size of the Empire State Building, there was no point in funding it. This argument ignored anticipated development of low-weight bombs, which John von Neumann and Edward Teller predicted would be available by 1960.[19] Gardner organized a Strategic Missiles Evaluation Committee to be chaired by von Neumann. In addition to academic scientists and industry leaders, Gardner added two ringers to the committee—Simon Ramo and Dean Wooldridge, engineers who had recently left Hughes Aircraft to set up their own company, Ramo-Wooldridge. Gardner wanted them to manage the Air Force's missile development process, but they had already turned Gardner's job offers down because they wanted their company to manufacture defense hardware. When Gardner, however, cut them off from hardware contracts on the grounds that their former employer, Hughes, was unhappy with them, they got the message and agreed to Gardner's plan. Gardner then summoned Schriever (now a brigadier general) to his office to meet Ramo and Wooldridge.

Von Neumann's committee predicted that, given an aggressive development program, the Atlas missile could be operational by the early 1960s. It also recommended that the traditional Air Force program for developing aircraft—using a contractor such as Boeing that would hire and control subcontractors as necessary—would not succeed. Gardner insisted that the missile be developed outside the bureaucratic Air Force channels. The Air Force fought him but eventually gave in; the alternative was to risk losing control of missiles altogether to some interservice Manhattan Project. Gardner established a centralized Air Force development office for guided missiles, put Schriever in charge, and made Ramo-Wooldridge the program manager.[20] Convair, the company that had kept the Atlas going for its years in the wilderness, did not get the prime contractor position it wanted and had to settle for building only the missile's airframe. As a backup in case Atlas did not work out, Gardner and Schriever would authorize the Titan ICBM project in 1955.

Thus in 1954, Curtis LeMay was in charge of the Air Force's strategic bombers, and Bernard Schriever was in charge of the Air Force's strategic ICBMs. From LeMay's point of view, bombers were America's strength and protection. They were reliable and reusable, could carry very large payloads, could be recalled and redirected during a mission, and had crews that could provide visual assessments of the damage done. Better bombers were in development, and still better bombers would follow. Missiles, on the other hand, were unreliable—perhaps a quarter of them crashed in tests, and they would be flying over the United States carrying nuclear warheads. Once launched, they could not be redirected or recalled, and no one would know whether the target had been destroyed.

Schriever would not have disagreed with LeMay's assessment of the short-term situation. Missiles were not ready in 1954. He was convinced, however, that they would be operational by the 1960s. They would be invulnerable to enemy fighter and antiaircraft defenses, would need no refueling or foreign bases, and would be inexpensive compared with bombers and their crews. Missiles would be the Air Force's future, unless LeMay and his allies grabbed all the R&D money for fancier bombers.

American bombers ringed the Soviet Union from bases in England, Europe, and Japan. For the Soviet Union, the situation was different: the Soviet Union had no bomber bases from which it could threaten the United States, and its military had no culture of strategic bombing. In 1954, American intelligence detected a new Soviet jet bomber, the Bison, which was similar in configuration to America's new B-52. On Soviet Aviation Day in 1955, the Russians proudly flew twenty-eight Bisons past the reviewing stand in three flights—nine Bisons, ten Bisons, and nine Bisons. LeMay argued in congressional hearings that he needed at least a thousand B-52s to close the bomber gap—if the Soviets were willing to show twenty-eight Bisons, they must have many more. According to the CIA, however, twenty-eight were all they had, and it was possible that the last flight of nine was the first flight returning for a second pass. By 1958, SAC had 1,769 bombers, including 380 B-52s; the Soviet Union had a bomber force a fraction that size, with eighty-five Bisons.[21] Moscow had decided that in order to threaten the United States, it needed ICBMs, not bombers. And as the CIA was well aware, the Soviet Union's ICBM was further along than Schriever's Atlas. On March 15, 1953, the Soviets successfully test-fired a missile eight hundred miles. America's only operational missile, the Redstone, had a two-hundred-mile range.

Eisenhower empanelled a committee to assess the military balance between the USSR and the United States. The committee's report, issued in February 1955, was full of foreboding that the Soviet Union would soon

surpass America in both hydrogen bombs and missiles, and it recommended that the United States develop an intermediate-range missile (IRBM)
for both land-and sea-launch. An IRBM would have a range of about fifteen
hundred miles—not enough to strike the Soviet Union from the United
States but close enough for European-based firings or for shipboard or
submarine launches. Such a missile, the committee suggested, could be developed more quickly than an ICBM, which had a projected date of 1962.
The Army, with its Huntsville team, believed that its Redstone tactical missile, a direct descendant of the V-2, could be extended in straightforward
fashion to have a range of fifteen hundred miles. The Army still had R&D
responsibility for tactical missiles, and while fifteen hundred miles might
seem a stretch for "tactical," no one in authority had defined an upper limit
on range. The Army proposed to build an IRBM that it called "Jupiter."

Gardner and Schriever, on the other hand, saw the IRBM as a distrac-
tion from the Atlas ICBM. Gardner tried to get the IRBM project killed
but failed. But if he was forced to propose an IRBM, he wanted it to be
a derivative of the Atlas so that the test results would at least speed Atlas
development. The Army pointed out that the Atlas had a very thin skin,
which was fine for an ICBM that would spend its time in outer space, but
not for an IRBM, as the skin would be ripped up in the upper atmosphere.
The Air Force was unwilling to leave any missile project to the Army and
proposed development of an entirely new IRBM, not based on Atlas, that
it called "Thor."

A strong secretary of defense would have stepped in and tamped down
the interservice rivalry. That did not happen. Charles Wilson, chairman of
General Motors, had joined the Eisenhower administration as defense secretary immediately after the 1953 inauguration. Wilson applied the sort of
thinking that had made him successful at GM. He saw those who reported
to him—the service secretaries, his assistant secretaries, and the Joint
Chiefs—as his corporate vice presidents. GM's corporate headquarters
was responsible for manufacturing and finance, while the divisions took
care of engineering and marketing; that strategy had made GM the world's
largest and most successful corporation, with "a car for every purse and purpose." At GM each automobile division—Chevrolet, Pontiac, Oldsmobile,

Buick, and Cadillac—introduced models on its own and did not worry about competing with models from other divisions. Wilson brought the GM philosophy to the Defense Department: "Leave the military stuff up to the military, and the production up to us," he said.[22]

Wilson saw himself as a manager, not as a policy maker. Choosing Jupiter or Thor was not his job, any more than choosing the Oldsmobile 98 or the Buick Roadmaster had been at GM. And as a good manager, he liked to see his team working in harmony. Making a decision to kill one of the missiles would have angered at least one of his chiefs of staff and service secretaries, so he allowed both services to proceed through the development phase. The time to choose would be when the winning missile was to be put into production. He announced that the IRBM was to have equal priority with the ICBM, but that it was not to slow development of the ICBM—ignoring the fact that the Atlas, Titan, Jupiter, and Thor projects would share the same small pool of qualified engineers and contractors.

Schriever appointed Col. Ed Hall as program director for the Air Force's Thor. Hall was a surprising choice, given the top-secret nature of the missile project and the national security obsessions of 1955—the FBI knew that his brother Ted, who had worked at Los Alamos during the Manhattan Project, had spied for the Soviet Union. Ted Hall was not prosecuted because the evidence against him would have been inadmissible in court, and because prosecution would have revealed other information that the FBI preferred to keep secret. The FBI apparently had no doubts about Col. Hall's patriotism, however, and Schriever respected the work he had done managing engine development for the Atlas missile.

Schriever and Hall were starting behind the von Braun team, but they found a way to catch up quickly. They hired "Dolph" Thiel, a German engineer who had worked for von Braun, and Thiel arrived with duplicates of the IRBM studies he had managed at Huntsville. The Air Force's Thor would be a copy of the Army's Jupiter. Both missiles would be almost exactly the same height, diameter, and weight, would carry the same payload, would be liquid fueled, would use the same engine (the engine that Hall had managed for the Atlas), and would mount the engine on gimbals for steering. The only important difference would be the heat shield. The Air

Force's Thor would use a copper shield, and the Army's Jupiter would use an "ablative" shield that would burn away during reentry. Had there been any justification for running two simultaneous development projects, it would have been that something might have been learned from two different approaches. Instead, the Air Force simply copied the Army's design. Wilson set up a flat-out race to see which team could be the first to either make its missile operational or kill the other team's missile through bureaucratic infighting. The United States was in a missile race with the Soviet Union, but the missile race that mattered most to the Army and Air Force was with each other.

The betting was that the Air Force would win the bureaucratic battle and that Jupiter would be cancelled. Eisenhower asked, "Why would the Army want a 1,500 mile missile for itself, because the first requisite of using that kind of weapon is that you have very good observation to find whether it is doing the job you thought it was . . . and that puts you right square in Air Force business."[23] Secretary Wilson listened, and he announced that whichever missile was put into production, the Air Force, not the Army, would be responsible for deployment. Furthermore, he at last defined the Army's responsibility for "tactical" missiles. Tactical missiles were to have a maximum range of two hundred miles—the range of the Redstone missile, which von Braun's team had first tested three years earlier. Wilson's directive did not kill the Jupiter program, but it meant that beginning June 30, 1957, the Air Force would be responsible for funding both Jupiter and Thor, although the Army's Huntsville team would remain responsible for Jupiter's technical management.

The Army did not back off. An Army colonel wrote an unauthorized response to Wilson's announcement, attacking Wilson's Air Force favoritism, Air Force industrial suppliers, and the entire southwestern United States, saying that "the Southeastern United States"—that is, Huntsville—was a more "strategically sound location." He released his memorandum to the press and was court-martialed, but he was a hero to von Braun and his team. The secretary of the Army tried to get von Braun's team a role in the space program, pointing out that an experimental Jupiter-C three-stage rocket had flown thirty-three hundred miles on September 6, 1956, and that it would have gone into orbit if the nose cone had not been weighted with sandbags.[24]

Wilson assumed that either Jupiter or Thor would show its technical superiority, thereby allowing him to cancel the other missile. It is hard to understand that assumption, given that the two missiles were nearly identical. In February, April, May, and June 1957 he repeated his assertions that only one missile would go into production. It seemed inevitable, based on Wilson's decision to give the Air Force deployment authority, that Jupiter would be cancelled.

But the tests gave the Army hope. Both missiles used the same Cape Canaveral test stand. Von Braun's Army team used the iterative development approach for Jupiter that it had used for the V-2 and for the Redstone missile: build, test, learn from the test, modify the missile, and then repeat that cycle until ready for production. Hall's Air Force team, with less experience but much more money, believed in concurrency: schedule tests without pause, and order production tooling even before the tests' completion. Concurrency, Schriever and Hall believed, would be the quickest path to operational status for Thor. And when it came time to choose, the Air Force would be able to argue that choosing Jupiter would mean wasting the sunk costs the Air Force had already expended on production setup for Thor.

The Air Force team showed its inexperience when it rushed to be the first to launch. Thor 101 exploded on the Cape Canaveral launch pad on January 24, 1957; a technician had dragged a hose that supplied liquid oxygen through the sand, contaminating a valve. Things did not improve on April 19, when a tracking technician incorrectly hooked up his display, so Thor 102 appeared to be heading for Orlando; a panicked range-safety officer detonated it just after launch. The liquid-oxygen tank of Thor 103 ruptured on May 20, severely damaging the launch pad, and an investigation showed that a technician had ignored a pressure gauge showing a danger reading.

The Army fared better. The first Jupiter launch, on March 1, broke up after seventy-two seconds, and the second, on April 12, lasted ninety-two seconds. But von Braun's team had attached sensors to every part of Jupiter and learned from the telemetry data: sloshing fuel was unbalancing

Wernher von Braun with a model of the Jupiter rocket. *Bundesarchiv, Bild 183-64549-0022 /CC-BY-SA.*

206 ■ AMERICAN ARSENAL

the missile. The third Jupiter, with its fuel problem fixed, sailed 1,625 miles downrange in the Caribbean.

Schriever blamed program director Ed Hall for Thor's failures. He was an easy man with whom to find fault—an argumentative, suspicious hard drinker who blamed Ramo-Wooldridge and other team members for Thor's problems and refused to delegate responsibility. And his public behavior could be unforgivable: during a Jupiter test, Hall was heard calling out "Blow! Blow! Blow!" as the Army rocket lifted from the pad. Schriever replaced him and then went back to his superiors to ask for more money for tests. On August 30, Thor 104 flew for ninety-six seconds; on September 20, Thor 105 flew 1,495 miles; and on October 11, Thor 106 flew 1,725 miles.

Both Schriever and his Army counterpart filed briefs with the Defense Department arguing that the other service's missile development project should be cancelled. Wilson was on the spot: he had two nearly identical missiles, both of which had proven their capabilities in test. He had proclaimed many times, however, that only one of them would be put into production.

Then the Soviet Union saved Jupiter, Thor, and Secretary Wilson. On October 4, 1957, it launched its Sputnik satellite. The 184-pound Russian satellite streaked across America's sky every ninety minutes, broadcasting beeping radio signals. Soviet premier Nikita Khrushchev said, "We have all the rockets we need: long-range rockets, intermediate-range rockets, and close-range rockets." A month later, the Russians launched the 1,120-pound Sputnik II, which carried a live dog. In case anyone had missed his earlier point, Khrushchev explained, "We have developed an intercontinental ballistic missile with a hydrogen warhead."[25] The American Navy tried to launch a satellite during a live television broadcast on December 6, but the rocket rose only four feet before exploding on the launch pad. Success finally came to the Americans on January 31, 1958, using a Juno rocket that was an adaptation of the Jupiter missile, but it was less than awe-inspiring; Khrushchev referred to the thirty-pound Explorer I as America's "grapefruit satellite." America's technological lead seemed to have vanished, and the Soviets ruled space. Unlike the Russian atomic bomb, the Soviets' achievement with Sputnik could not be minimized. They had not stolen the rocket from the United States—America had watched its own rocket explode on television. And the Russians had not gotten their rockets from the Germans—America was the country with Wernher von Braun, who appeared on Walt Disney's television show to talk about space travel.

The nation was panicked, and no politician was about to cancel any missile program. Soviet state planning had bested Wilson's capitalist-inspired competition. Despite his earlier disavowals, Secretary Wilson announced that both Jupiter and Thor would go into production. At that moment, more missiles looked like a very good thing, and as one assistant secretary of defense put it, cancelling the Air Force's Thor would have meant "a Congressional delegation from California would be down our necks. And elimination of the Army Jupiter program would have half the Alabama delegation plus a couple of representatives from the Detroit area fighting us." Besides, what if one of the missiles turned out not to work as advertised?

On December 15, 1957, *Pravda* reproduced the front page of the London *Daily Herald* after the American Vanguard rocket exploded on takeoff. The failure was called a "kaputnik" and a "stayputnik" in other newspapers. The Russian caption above the *Daily Herald*'s banner translates as "Publicity and Reality."

Sen. Lyndon Johnson, the Senate majority leader, congratulated Wilson on his decision.[26]

Once Thor and Jupiter were in production, the State and Defense Departments went looking for customers. They were not lining up. Sputnik had raised doubts in NATO about American technological superiority. Both Jupiter and Thor were vulnerable—they needed preparation before firing, and they required aboveground, fixed bases that would be primary targets for Soviet nuclear strikes in the event of war. Britain was eager to repair relations with the United States after the 1956 Suez fiasco and agreed to take four squadrons of fifteen Thors each.[†] But the Dutch and Germans all said a polite "no thank you," and President Charles de Gaulle cancelled a three-squadron agreement with a less-than-cordial *non* when he took office in France. The Scandinavians all said no, and Greece's government was deemed too unstable to risk placing missiles there. Italy, however, agreed to accept one squadron of Jupiters, and ever-reliable Turkey accepted two squadrons.[27]

Meanwhile, the United States successfully tested the Atlas ICBM in late 1958, and that meant that both Thor and Jupiter would soon be obsolete: the British Thors were deployed only from 1958 to 1963, and the Italian and Turkish Jupiters only from 1961 to 1963. Thor and Jupiter were the products of muddled thinking on several counts. First, the United States reacted impulsively to Soviet missile tests, deciding that it needed an IRBM without examining where such a missile would fit in its strategic plans. Second, although an IRBM would be useful only if it were stationed in Europe, the State and Defense Departments did not consult with NATO allies before beginning development. Third, Secretary of Defense Wilson allowed the Army and the Air Force to launch virtually identical R&D programs. And finally, under political pressure after Sputnik, the Eisenhower administration decided to build and deploy *both* missiles, missiles that were even then nearly obsolete and had no clear strategic mission. Missiles may have been America's future, but this was not a promising start.

[†] Britain, France, and Israel had seized Egypt's Suez Canal without notifying the United States, which forced them to withdraw.

12

War Games

On April 19, 1989, a twenty-eight-year-old white jogger was found in a pool of mud and blood in New York's Central Park. She had been raped and beaten—beaten so badly that she had no memory of the attack. The police grabbed five black teenagers, ages thirteen to sixteen, and interrogated them separately. The police had no physical evidence or witnesses against the boys, but four of the five confessed, implicating themselves and the others. Although all later recanted and pled not guilty, their confessions convinced the jury, and they received sentences of five to thirteen years.

Thirteen years later, their convictions were vacated. Matias Reyes, a prisoner then serving thirty-three years to life for murder and rape, confessed that he had been the sole Central Park rapist.

Why did four teenagers confess to a horrific crime that they did not commit? Researchers at the RAND Corporation, a Santa Monica think tank, would have understood. They had studied the problem forty years earlier, using John von Neumann's mathematical game theory. They had a name for the problem that the teenagers faced—the "prisoner's dilemma." RAND, however, was studying not the juvenile justice system but nuclear war.

Hap Arnold, commander of the Army Air Forces in World War II, looked to the long term. Most AAF commanders, operating under the stress of day-to-day combat, were at best able to fine-tune their operations, fiddling with bomber formations or revising target lists. Arnold left that to his subordinates and planned for an independent Air Force. But what then? The Army had its arsenals and proving grounds, and the Navy had its Naval Research Laboratory, but the new Air Force would start with very little. The war had temporarily drawn the nation's academic elite into the AAF—Robert McNamara, a Harvard business professor, for example. But Arnold knew that the scientists, engineers, and statisticians would return to academia and industry after the war. Arnold's health was bad, and he had only a little time to put the Air Force on an innovative path.

No one had a coherent plan for America's new atomic bomb. Some AAF leaders, including Curtis LeMay, saw it as a bigger bomb, to be used like any other. Some strategists and Manhattan Project scientists, however, thought that it changed everything. They predicted that America's monopoly on the bomb would be short-lived and that an arms race loomed, one that might threaten global destruction. Many on the right thought that atomic weapons were all that kept the Russians from marching straight to the English Channel. Many on the left wanted the bomb turned over to the United Nations, but efforts at international control failed because of American and Soviet intransigence. Thomas Edison and the Navy's admirals had miscommunicated during World War I, but this was more severe. Politicians, pundits, statesmen, scientists, and military officers all talked past each other.

Frank Collbohm, a former marine and a senior engineer at Douglas Aircraft, met Arnold in 1942 while working on radar. He suggested that Douglas build an organization of research scientists who would work under contract. On October 1, 1945, Arnold met with Collbohm and senior Douglas executives. He told them that he had $10 million in unspent dollars from his wartime research budget and that he would offer the money to Douglas to fund what would be called the RAND project—"RAND" standing for "Research and Development." Arnold appointed LeMay as his deputy chief of staff for research and development. On March 1, 1946, the day after Arnold left active command, the RAND contract was final, and LeMay was RAND's champion—at least for a while.[1]

John Williams, Collbohm's number two, had expansive ideas. In order to understand what the bomb meant and what to do with it, RAND would need not just mathematicians and physical scientists but economists, psychologists, and political scientists. Assembling a large interdisciplinary team would be expensive, and LeMay flinched when Williams told him his plans—LeMay wanted weapons *now*, and the $10 million that Arnold had given RAND would not go far. But LeMay listened to Williams and relented, perhaps hearing the recently retired Arnold's voice in his head. "Go ahead," he told Williams. "Spend what you have to spend. And do it *right*."[2]

As we have seen, LeMay left his R&D post in 1947 to take command of the Air Force in Europe, and he returned to America in 1948 to take charge of the Strategic Air Command. SAC's primary mission was an atomic attack on the Soviet Union if World War III erupted. Although it was formally part of the Air Force, SAC was almost a fourth service branch—it reported directly to the Joint Chiefs of Staff. LeMay developed his own intelligence data and target lists, which he refused to share with anyone outside SAC, including the Air Force staff. And while LeMay had been supportive of RAND in his R&D role, as SAC commander he saw RAND's staffers as smug intellectuals who wrote academic papers telling him how to do his job.

Bernard Brodie, a naval strategist who would join RAND in 1951, was among the first to consider how the bomb had changed war. The Navy and Army, Brodie wrote, would play only minor roles in a war in which both sides had atomic weapons, and air wars would be very different. In his 1946 book, *The Absolute Weapon*, he used the British defense against the German V-1 rocket as an example.[3] On the RAF's best day, it had shot down 97 of 101 V-1s targeted at London. It was an amazing achievement, Brodie noted. On the other hand, had those V-1s carried atomic bombs, London would have been destroyed. Defense against the atomic bomb needed to be perfect, and perfection was impossible. He drew conclusions: the shortage of fissile material meant that atomic bombs would be limited in number, so nations would target their enemies' most important assets, their cities; America must remain constantly on war alert, as there would be no time to build fighting strength as the Allies had done in World Wars I and II; and a surprise atomic attack by either side would result in a retaliatory attack against the aggressor's cities. He concluded that atomic weapons could not be used in any rational way. Their only purpose was to *deter* war, and a nation's military would have as its only purpose averting war. His conclusions were not universally embraced, especially by SAC and the Air Force.[4]

At the time that Brodie wrote, his prediction that the United States and the Soviet Union would face off with atomic bombs was not yet fact. America still had a monopoly on the bomb, and some argued that a preventive war against the Soviet Union was the rational choice: get the Russians before they get the bomb. The recent experience of Pearl Harbor inspired American fears of a sneak attack. In September 1945, a month after World War II's end, the Joint Chiefs endorsed a call for action should an enemy prepare for war: "I don't like the word 'defense,'" Arnold said. "We should shoot to insure the safety of America. . . . This country should capitalize on the atomic bomb, if necessary, to assure world peace." Army Gen. Leslie Groves, who had run the Manhattan Project, proposed attacking the Soviet atomic research facilities in order to maintain the American monopoly.[5] (Israel executed this sort of preventive attack against Iraq in 1981 and against Syria in 2007.) In 1950, even after the first Soviet atomic bomb detonation, Secretary of the Navy Francis Matthews made an Orwellian call for the United States to fill its "inescapable role" through an atomic attack on the Soviet Union, thereby becoming "the first aggressor for peace."[6] Gen. Robert Gow, the U.S. military attaché in Moscow, had his diary stolen from his Frankfurt hotel room, and the East German press published extracts: "War! As soon as possible! Now! . . . Communism must be destroyed!"[7] Churchill suggested to Eisenhower that he attack the Soviet Union before the Russians could build a stockpile of atomic weapons.[8] Former Air Force secretary and future senator and presidential hopeful Stuart Symington also argued for preventive war, and the *New York Times* reported that Secretary of Defense Louis Johnson did as well. Sen. Lloyd

Bentsen, who would be the Democrats' 1984 vice presidential candidate, proposed using atomic bombs against Communist bases in Manchuria.[9] Even the English pacifist Bertrand Russell advocated preventive atomic war against the Soviet Union, although he later denied doing so.[10]

Cooler heads prevailed. Neither Truman not Eisenhower considered an unprovoked attack on the Soviet Union. Even if such an attack succeeded, what next? Occupy Russia? Eisenhower wrote to James Forrestal, Truman's first secretary of defense, "Conquering the Russians is one thing, [but] finding out what to do with them afterward is an entirely different problem."[11] Although neither Truman nor Eisenhower advocated *preventive* atomic war, they did not renounce *preemptive* war—a first strike against the Soviet Union if it was seen to be preparing to strike the United States. Eisenhower did say, however, that he thought such a strike was politically and constitutionally infeasible, as it would require a secret session of Congress. And neither president renounced use of atomic weapons in a conventional war. Indeed, both threatened their use in Korea, and Eisenhower told the Joint Chiefs in 1956 that atomic weapons would be used in any "general war," which meant any war in which the United States was engaged directly against the Soviet Union, and that he would unleash SAC as soon as he saw that the Russians were on the move.[12] This was a policy of "massive retaliation," first announced publicly by Secretary of State John Foster Dulles in 1954. American responses to a Soviet invasion of Western Europe would not be local and proportionate but general and massive—an attack with atomic bombs on Russian strategic targets and cities. This was America's "nuclear guarantee" to its NATO allies, and, like any guarantee, its value could only be tested if its holders tried to redeem it. If Soviet troops seized Berlin, would America really risk New York and Washington?

The Korean War broke out in 1950, four years after Brodie dismissed the Army's ground troops as useless. Conventional war clearly still had a place in the atomic age, but new *de facto* rules were in force: the two nuclear powers could not engage each other directly, because that would lead to general nuclear war under America's doctrine of massive retaliation. Furthermore, a nuclear power could not use nuclear weapons against a non-nuclear power, as Truman found when the American public and America's allies condemned his threats to use atomic bombs in Korea. So nuclear weapons, which America had made the centerpiece of its military strategy, seemed to be useless in any war that America might fight. But strategists at RAND and elsewhere refused to abandon the idea that somehow, some way, it must be possible to wage nuclear war rationally.

Game theory was one of RAND's tools. Invented by John von Neumann, game theory allows mathematical analysis of competitive games that involve two or more players who have incomplete information about the other's assets and intentions—games such as poker or nuclear war. The best move for each player, according to game theory, is the move that will lead to the best (or least bad) outcome, assuming that the opponent also makes his best move. An example is the prisoner's dilemma, faced by the five teenagers accused in the rape and beating of the Central Park jogger. The analysis is easier if we reduce the problem from five accused to two: two prisoners are arrested, but the prosecuting attorney has no evidence for a conviction on serious charges. If neither confesses, the prosecutor can convict both of a minor charge, and they will each serve a year. The prosecutor approaches both prisoners with an offer: confess and go free, while your partner will receive twenty years. But there is a catch—if both prisoners confess, both will serve five years—less than the full twenty because they have shown repentance and acknowledged their guilt. Although the optimal *joint* strategy is for both to stay silent, the optimal *individual* strategy depends on many factors: how much each prisoner trusts the other, how much he values his reputation as a "stand-up guy," and how much he dreads prison. (When there are five defendants, as in the Central Park case, the temptation to confess increases, because the prosecutor can tell each prisoner that if any one of the other four confesses first, he will receive a long sentence.)

The prisoner's dilemma applies to nuclear war. If both powers in a nuclear standoff refuse to launch a first strike, the world and the arms race continue (analogous to both parties staying silent); if one party launches a surprise attack, the other will be destroyed and his retaliatory capability will be degraded, so damage to the attacker will be reduced (analogous to one party confessing); and if both parties launch before either is struck, damage to both will be severe, but not as severe for either as suffering an attack without the ability to counterlaunch (analogous to both parties confessing).

RAND applied itself to this problem. The optimal strategy, RAND said, depends on how much damage each attacker could do in a first strike, how much damage each attacker could do in retaliation, and how each party felt about the potential damage. Game theory is mathematical, so it worked only if numbers could be assigned to each outcome, and it was RAND's job to come up with the numbers. It asked the Air Force how much damage it could do—how many bombers would get through enemy defenses. In order to justify a larger attacking force, the Air Force predicted that most of its bombers would be shot down. The Soviet Union, of course, was not disclosing its force levels, so RAND relied on intelligence estimates of Soviet strength from the CIA and the Air Force. Throughout the Cold War, Air Force estimates of Soviet forces were greatly inflated, because that justified more and better American bombers (and later more and better missiles). The Air Force was RAND's customer, so RAND used Air Force numbers in its calculations.

But the damage numbers were just the start. RAND needed to evaluate how both parties would *value* the damage. How bad, for example, was killing three million American civilians? Would killing six million be twice as bad, less than twice as bad, or more than twice as bad? How would the Soviets answer similar questions? Addressing all this required knowledge of each nation's "utility function," a mathematical formulation of damage and death. If America felt that six million of its citizens dead would be less than twice as bad as three million dead, for example, its utility function's rate of increase was declining as the death toll rose. RAND's planners felt capable of assessing American utility functions (which required answering questions such as "How many American lives would we sacrifice to protect our NATO allies from Soviet occupation?"). Setting values for the Communists' utility functions was harder. After all, the Russians had lost twenty million dead in World War II and had kept going, and the Chinese Communists had sent their troops in human waves against American soldiers in Korea. They seemed to be more callous. The Air Force issued contracts to RAND to assess Soviet thinking, and RAND produced *The Operational Code of the Politburo*.[13] Once RAND had fed the Air Force's unreliable and politically motivated estimates into its own wholly invented utility functions, it had the numbers that it needed to simulate nuclear war.

Not all of RAND's work was worthless. Albert Wohlstetter's 1953 analysis of the Air Force's strategy for its overseas bomber bases, for example, was insightful. The United States had ringed the Soviet Union with SAC bases. LeMay, SAC's commander, wanted his bombers as close as possible to their targets. Wohlstetter pointed out that if the bombers were close to the Russians, the Russians were also close to the bombers, which were, for the most part, sitting undefended on runways. As we have seen, an attack on the Soviet Union in 1953 would have taken about a week to organize—the bombs would have been flown from the United States to the overseas bases. The Russians would observe the mobilization and would strike first, Wohlstetter argued, destroying the bases and bombers. Wohlstetter recommended that the bombers be kept in blast-hardened hangars in the United States and that the overseas bases be used only for refueling the bombers on the way to execute their missions.

LeMay disagreed. He did not want to spend money protecting his bomber force. If the bombers were vulnerable, his answer was to buy more bombers, to buy longer-range bombers (the intercontinental B-52 was in the works), and, most important, to get the first blow in without waiting to be attacked. And LeMay had other motivations: Wohlstetter's study had been commissioned by the Air Force staff, while LeMay and SAC reported directly to the Joint Chiefs. If LeMay accepted the RAND study, he would be letting the Air Force staff run his show. When Wohlstetter flew to SAC's headquarters in Omaha to present his case, LeMay skipped the briefing entirely, and his deputy, Tommy Power, who had led the firebombing of Tokyo, walked out at the end of the presentation. LeMay compromised on the bombing strategy but not on hardened hangars. B-47 and B-36 bombers would take off loaded with bombs from U.S. bases, would be refueled by tankers in the air, would strike their targets, and would return to the overseas bases for post-strike recovery. When Wohlstetter argued that the tankers would cost so much that there would not be enough money for bombers, LeMay's response was simple: SAC needed more money.

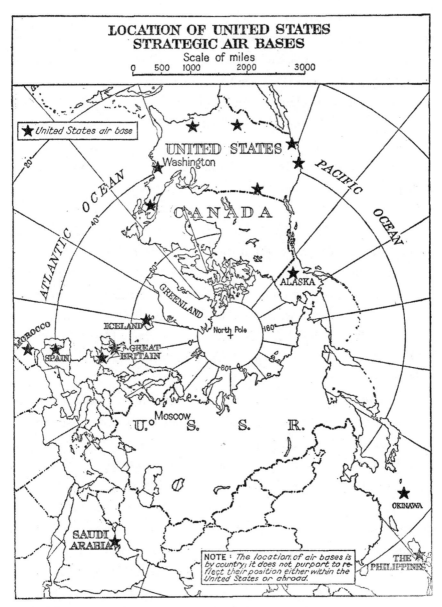

LOCATION OF UNITED STATES STRATEGIC AIR BASES
Scale of miles
0   500   1000   2000   3000

United States air base

UNITED STATES
Washington

CANADA

PACIFIC OCEAN

ATLANTIC OCEAN

ALASKA

GREENLAND

ICELAND

North Pole

GREAT BRITAIN

SPAIN

MOROCCO

U. Moscow S.   S.   R.

OKINAWA

SAUDI ARABIA

NOTE : The location of air bases is by country; it does not purport to reflect their position either within the United States or abroad.

THE PHILIPPINES

SAC bases ringing the Soviet Union. *Henry Kissinger,* Nuclear Weapons and Foreign Policy (*New York: Harper and Brothers, 1957*), 108.

Wohlstetter's logic was sound, but the quantitative inputs for his study were inflated Air Force and SAC estimates of Soviet forces, which made the risk of a "nuclear Pearl Harbor" seem much more plausible than it was. And the Wohlstetter study never considered Soviet motivation. Why would the Russians attack overseas SAC bases knowing that their cities would be destroyed in attacks from U.S. bases? That approach would be characteristic of RAND's analyses—looking not at what the Russians would want to do but at what they could do, all based on inflated intelligence estimates.[14]

The savants at RAND and elsewhere continued to argue about proper use of nuclear weapons. In 1951, Bernard Brodie joined RAND, where he changed his tune. Limited nuclear war *was* possible, he now said, and it could be fought through tacit signals between careful, rational opponents— for example, "I haven't nuked your cities yet, so don't nuke mine and we can confine nuclear war to the battlefield."[15] William Kaufmann, a Princeton political scientist who joined RAND in 1956, thought that the United States could respond to a Soviet invasion of Western Europe with attacks on military targets that would escalate to attacks on cities only if the Russians refused to withdraw.[16] Henry Kissinger, a young Harvard professor, made his name with a 1957 book that saw limited nuclear war as a strategic option.[17]

But limited war was not part of SAC's worldview. LeMay planned to use every bomb he had in a "Sunday punch" that would destroy the Soviet Union's ability and will to fight. In 1957, a blue-ribbon commission, known as the Gaither Committee after its chairman, Horace Rowan Gaither, a founder of RAND, evaluated a proposal for a huge civil defense program of fallout and blast shelters. When Gaither fell ill, Robert Sprague, founder of Sprague Electric, served as acting chairman, and he and other committee members flew to Omaha to meet with LeMay. Sprague asked to see a surprise alert of the entire SAC force. Not a single plane managed to take off in the six-hour time allotted to react to a surprise Soviet attack. Sprague and his fellow panel members were appalled, but LeMay was unconcerned. He told Sprague that the Soviets would never be able to mount a general surprise attack. The rumors—always denied—that American spy planes flew over the Soviet Union every day were true, LeMay said, and "if I see that the Russians are amassing their planes for an attack, I'm going to knock the shit out of them before they get off the ground."

"But General LeMay, that's not national policy," Sprague replied.

"I don't care. It's my policy. That's what I'm going to do."[18]

Two months later, Sprague discovered how little the Eisenhower administration knew about SAC's plans. At a lunch with LeMay and Air Force secretary James Douglas, Sprague told Douglas that if the Soviets launched a surprise attack, SAC would get almost no fueled, crewed, atomic-loaded planes off the ground for retaliation. When Douglas protested that he had been told that at least 167 planes would survive and turned incredulously to LeMay for confirmation, LeMay said, "Mr. Sprague is correct." And if the secretary of the Air Force had no clue, Sprague thought, it was unlikely that the president knew any more. Military tradition called for taking the offensive and striking hard, and that was what LeMay—and, for that matter, the rest of the Air Force, the Army, and the Navy—had been trained to do. In World War II, playing defense had led to the French defeat, the bombing of Pearl Harbor, loss of the Philippines, and half of European Russia overrun. LeMay was uninterested in the Gaither Committee's civil defense plans and in protecting SAC against surprise attack. What he wanted was more and better bombers. In World War III, he planned to strike first.

Sprague presented the Gaither Commission's conclusions on civil defense to Eisenhower and warned that SAC was vulnerable to a "bolt from the blue" surprise attack. Like LeMay, Eisenhower was not worried. He was a student of military history and believed that wars did not arise from nowhere, that if the Russians attacked, it would be during an international crisis, and that there would be time to put SAC on alert. Besides, the top-secret U-2 spy planes' flights over the Soviet Union would give warning of any impending attack, just as LeMay had told Sprague. Eisenhower did order SAC to be put on increased alert, but neither he nor Secretary of State John Foster Dulles was interested in a massive civil defense buildup that would strip funding from the military budget and frighten the voters.[19] Eisenhower did not believe the nation could survive a nuclear war, and he never saw much merit in civil defense. As he thanked the Gaither Commission members, he told them he now realized he had asked the wrong question. "You can't have this kind of war," he said. "There just aren't enough bulldozers to scrape the bodies off the streets."[20]

As mentioned in chapter 11, the Air Force claimed that the Russians were building new Bear and Bison bombers that threatened the continental United States, and that America was behind in a "bomber gap." The Soviet bombers existed, though not in numbers close to Air Force or SAC estimates, which were based on extrapolation. If a U-2 spy plane photographed a building believed to be devoted to bomber production, SAC would assume two production shifts a day, use the size of the building to calculate how many bombers could be manufactured each month, and then use those numbers to determine how many bombers the Soviets had then and would have later. They ignored the fact that the Soviets had no bases close enough to support attacks on the United States with a return flight, so in any mass attack the Soviet Union would lose its bomber force as its planes crashed or ditched. (When one airplane designer suggested to Soviet premier Khrushchev that the bombers could land in Mexico after attacking, Khrushchev exploded, "What do you think Mexico is—our mother-in-law? You think we can simply go calling any time we want?")[21]

With the Soviet announcement of a test of an ICBM and the launch of Sputnik in 1957, the bomber gap morphed into a missile gap. The United States planned to have sixty-five ICBMs by 1961, when the Air Force and the CIA estimated that the Soviets would have five hundred ICBMs aimed at the United States; SAC had its own estimate of one thousand. These estimates were based on smudges and unidentified objects in U-2 overflight photos—farmers' silos, monasteries, and war memorials were all identified as disguised Russian missiles. But after initially supporting the Air Force estimates, the CIA began backtracking. Its staffers were monitoring Russian ICBM tests, and they were seeing very few. In 1960, the Air Force announced very high estimates of Soviet missiles; the CIA's were lower, those of the Army and Navy (who were trying to keep the Air Force from grabbing an even bigger piece of the budget pie) lower still. Even the lowest of these turned out to be too high. With its 1960 Discover satellite, the United States was able to survey the entire Soviet Union and count ICBMs.

It found not one thousand, not five hundred, but four. In his 1960 presidential campaign, John Kennedy blamed the Eisenhower administration for a "missile gap." Because the data from the U-2 flights were classified, neither Eisenhower nor Republican presidential candidate Richard Nixon could respond effectively.[22] The election was close, and the missile gap may have made Kennedy president.

In 1958, Wohlstetter, still at RAND, published a paper that was especially unpopular with SAC and the Air Force. In "The Delicate Balance of Terror," he said that there seemed to be a great deal of confusion about "deterrence," a word much bandied about in discussions of strategy.[23] The Soviet Union, Wohlstetter said, was not deterred from launching a nuclear attack because the United States had powerful *first-strike* capability, as the Air Force argued when it demanded more bombers and missiles. In fact, increasing America's first-strike capability might make the Russians believe that an attack was imminent and tempt them to launch their own first strike. Rather, Wohlstetter said, deterrence arose from an assured United States *second-strike* capability that would survive any Soviet first strike. Hardening missile silos and bomber hangars was one way to do that, but land-based missiles would still be vulnerable to a direct hit. The best second-strike force would be submarine-launched Polaris missiles, which were then in development. The submarines' locations would be unknown, and the Russians would not be able to bomb them. In 1960 it was not possible for a submarine or a ship at sea to locate itself precisely, so Polaris missiles were not as accurate as land-based missiles. This inaccuracy was actually a deterrent, according to Wohlstetter, because the Soviets would know that Polaris missiles could not be used in a first strike against their missiles or airfields, but could be used only in a second strike against their cities.

Although Wohlstetter did not say so explicitly, the implication was clear: if all the United States wanted was deterrence of a Soviet first strike, the Air Force's land-based missiles would be unnecessary once Polaris came online. Furthermore, Wohlstetter wrote, the Air Force was deploying Thor and Jupiter IRBMs in England, Italy, and Turkey, and those were worse than useless as a deterrent. Their liquid-fueled rockets would take hours to launch, and they were so close to the Soviet Union that a Soviet first strike would easily destroy them on the ground. Considered from the Soviet point of view, their only possible use was in an American first strike, and that could motivate the Soviets to launch a surprise strike against them during an international crisis. His argument was similar to the one he had made five years earlier against SAC's bomber bases: all missiles were not created equal—IRBMs were not the same as ICBMs—and missiles too close to their targets were the very opposite of a deterrent.

Many nuclear war strategists were bookish introverts who shunned publicity, but Herman Kahn, a RAND analyst and protégé of Wohlstetter, became the public face of rationalized Armageddon. Kahn had left CalTech with only a master's degree in nuclear physics, although he did assist Hans Bethe and Edward Teller at Livermore in designing the hydrogen bomb. Kahn was a complex man, both manic and nearly narcoleptic, morbidly obese, and sometimes unintelligible in his rapid and disjointed speech.* He was a consultant to the Gaither Commission on civil defense, and he gave three-day seminars urging the nation to prepare for the coming war, a war that most preferred to ignore.

Kahn's message was simple: nuclear war, either intentional or accidental, was inevitable. By 1973, he said, there would be fifty thousand nuclear weapons, each with a button. "You're worried about somebody making the wrong connection. You know, he turns the dial just for kicks. He presses the button because he likes to look at red lights. . . . People just literally can't resist passing without pressing buttons. I'm one of them myself."[24] His analogy for the occasional nuclear explosion was a lion roaming the streets of New York—there would be deaths, and people would be terrified, but even five or ten lions would kill fewer people than died in pedestrian traffic accidents. There were limits, Kahn admitted: a hundred lions might make the city uninhabitable, just as a hundred accidental nuclear explosions might be too many for the world to handle.[25]

---

* Kahn can be seen at www.youtube.com/watch?v=1-QwGBDbd3M in a 1976 video of a television panel discussion on the advisability of plutonium breeder reactors. He was not a doctrinaire right-winger. He appears with Margaret Mead, with whom he mostly agrees.

Like his RAND colleagues Kaufmann and Brodie, Kahn believed in the possibility of fighting limited nuclear war with proportionate, analytical responses. He divided deterrence into three types and advocated strategies for nuclear war with forty-four levels of escalation. America's announced policy of massively retaliating against any Soviet conventional attack in Europe was unrealistic, he said. "Even if we think we are sincere . . . when the time comes to act it will just not be worth it." He told an Air Force general that SAC's plan for a massive one-time strike was nothing more than a "war orgasm" (later abbreviated to "wargasm"). Civil defense was important, he said, not just because it might reduce the death count in a war from a hundred million to fifty million—a good thing in itself—but because it would make the Russians know that we meant business, and it would give us "the ability to convert [from conventional war to nuclear war] *at our discretion*" (italics in the original).[26] He encouraged construction of private and public fallout shelters. (When Kahn installed a fallout shelter in his own yard, he could not fit through the entrance.) The majority of nuclear war survivors and their descendants, he said, would live normal and happy lives. Although some food would be radioactive, that problem could be solved by rationing: class A food, the least contaminated, would be reserved for children and pregnant women; classes B and C, more contaminated, would be rationed by price according to degree of radioactivity; class D, still more contaminated, would be fed to people over forty because their cancers were unlikely to develop before they died of other causes; class E, the most contaminated, would be fed to animals.

In 1960 Kahn published *On Thermonuclear War*, a rambling treatise that borrowed from ideas originated by Wohlstetter and others at RAND. It included scenarios for World Wars III through VIII. When Kahn asked Wohlstetter for his opinion on the book's manuscript, Wohlstetter advised him to burn it. But the book became a best seller, and Kahn appeared regularly on television and radio. Listening to Kahn talk about nuclear war was hypnotizing—here was someone willing to speak about the unspeakable.[27]

Reviews of Kahn's book were mixed. He was compared to Adolf Eichmann, who was then on trial in Israel, for his bland assessment of horror.

■ Herman Kahn in 1965. *Library of Congress Prints and Photographs Division.*

James Newman said in *Scientific American*, "No one could write like this; no one could think like this."[28] But some pacifists and leftists, including Bertrand Russell and Norman Thomas, welcomed the book, arguing that it exposed the thinking that went on in the Pentagon.[29]

In 1964, Stanley Kubrick made the film *Dr. Strangelove*. Kubrick had begun with the idea of a serious film about nuclear war, but after a few hours talking with Kahn, he decided that it worked better as black comedy.[30] Some of the film's language and ideas were taken directly from Kahn's book— Kahn had, for example, invented the idea of the "doomsday machine," the device that in the film destroys the world, although he did not endorse its use as a deterrent, and the "mineshaft gap" arose from his suggestion that factories could be moved to abandoned mines. When the film appeared, Kahn complained that Kubrick had cribbed so much from his book that he deserved royalties. Kubrick replied, "That's not how it works, Herman!"[31]

Kahn was one of several who were thought to be models for Kubrick's character Dr. Strangelove, a former Nazi who appears in a wheelchair and speaks with a German accent. Others named as models include Edward Teller, John von Neumann, Wernher von Braun, and Henry Kissinger (then coming to prominence as a consultant to the National Security Council). Those four had German or Hungarian accents, von Neumann spent the last years of his life in a wheelchair, and von Braun had been a Nazi and an SS officer. Peter Sellers, the actor who played Strangelove, said that he modeled his character's wavy hair and accent after Kissinger. Teller once told an interviewer, "My name is not Strangelove. I'm not interested in Strangelove. What else can I say? Look. Say it three times more, and I throw you out of this office."[32]

The United States and the Soviet Union were like two gunslingers facing each other in the street, but with an important difference: if a gunslinger draws first and aims well, he will live and his enemy will die. In the nuclear gunfight, the bullets would travel slowly enough—thirty minutes or so—that the enemy could shoot too, and then both gunmen would die. Bertrand Russell compared the standoff to the teenage game of chicken, in which two drivers head straight for each other on the highway's centerline. The first to swerve is called chicken and loses face. Kahn noted that a winning strategy in chicken was to appear irrational, to fling empty whiskey bottles from the car, to wear dark glasses, and, once the car reaches high speed, to throw a steering wheel out the window.[33] For that strategy to succeed, it is important that the player only *appear* crazy—if both players are actually irrational, both will die. Kahn suggested that the desire to appear irrational might be the reasoning behind the appointment of LeMay as SAC commander, because no one could doubt that he was willing to execute America's nuclear war plans. But, said Kahn, LeMay needed an assistant whose job, upon outbreak of war, was to shoot LeMay.[34]

When President Kennedy was inaugurated in January 1961, he appointed Robert McNamara, the president of Ford Motor, as secretary of defense. Charles Wilson, one of McNamara's predecessors under Eisenhower and the former chairman of General Motors, had believed in leaving "the military stuff up to the military." Under Wilson, the total defense budget allocated by Congress had been distributed among the services, and each service spent its share pretty much as it wished. As we have seen, that had led to the wasteful development of nearly identical missiles, Jupiter and Thor, by the Army and Air Force. McNamara's approach was different. He believed in top-down management using "systems analysis"—a quantitative examination of each mission, its technical requirements, its feasibility, its schedule, and its costs. Systems analysis had worked for McNamara at Ford, and he planned to impose it at Defense, despite the demands from congressional committees and the individual services for control over allocations of funds. The Air Force felt especially threatened by McNamara—after LeMay retired from active service, he wrote *America in Danger*, an anti-McNamara diatribe—but the Army and Navy came to despise McNamara too.[35] Sunk costs were irrelevant to McNamara. Immediately after taking office, he tried to kill LeMay's pet project, the supersonic B-70 bomber, despite its seven years of development. He eventually succeeded, although it took him two years to put the final nail in its coffin. And if two services planned similar weapons, McNamara ordered them to use a common development platform, as he did with the F-111 fighter shared between the Air Force and Navy (which the Navy never deployed).

Two weeks after McNamara took office, he received a briefing on the nation's plan for nuclear war—the Single Integrated Operational Plan (SIOP-62), scheduled to go into effect April 1, 1961.[36] The Air Force had formulated the idea of the SIOP in 1960, when the Navy's Polaris missiles were about to come online. If Polaris could not be stopped, the Air Force wanted the Navy's submarine fleet placed under SAC's command; when that idea did not wash, SAC insisted that it have control of the Polaris target list in order to eliminate duplication between Air Force and Navy targets. Once SAC got control of the targets, it assigned Soviet missile bases and airfields to the relatively inaccurate Polaris, which was supposed to be a second-strike weapon against cities, and then assigned its own missiles to hit the same targets because Polaris could not be trusted to hit them. Using its inflated projections of Soviet missile counts and its estimates that Soviet defenses would destroy a large fraction of its bombers, the Air Force planned multiple attacks on each target. One city the size of Hiroshima was scheduled to be bombed four times with a total explosive force more than five hundred times that of the first atomic bomb. The SIOP presented to McNamara stipulated that in the event of any armed conflict with the Soviet Union, the United States would send 2,164 megatons of hydrogen bombs against 654 targets within the Soviet Union.

And that was not the worst of it—that was the plan for an immediate response to a Soviet attack using only the SAC planes that were on alert. Plan 1-A of SIOP-62 (the title "1-A" suggests that it was the preferred option; it was certainly LeMay's) was an all-out preemptive first strike on the Soviet Union if it seemed about to launch an attack on America. Then the entire nuclear force, 3,200 nuclear weapons, would be sent against 1,060 targets in the USSR, Eastern Europe, and Communist China. Nothing would be held back, and bombs directed against missile silos and hardened hangars would be set to explode at ground level for maximum destructive force, where they would also generate maximum fallout.

John Rubel, an assistant secretary of defense, recalls sitting through the horrifying SIOP presentation to McNamara. It was February 3, 1961, at SAC's command center near Omaha, where SAC would manage nuclear war should the SIOP be executed. The command center was set up that day as for a school Christmas pageant—rows of folding chairs facing a stage where the briefers would flip through charts on easels. The walls were covered with maps of the Soviet Union, China, and Eastern Europe (this was before the days of electronic displays). SAC commander Gen. Tommy Power sat in the front row next to Secretary of Defense McNamara, with Rubel and other high-ranking officials near the front. Behind them were generals in decreasing order of rank, with one-star generals at the rear of the room. The briefers, one with a pointer and one to flip the pages, went through a few charts and matter-of-factly described the first wave of the nuclear attack.

Stanley Kubrick could not have done it better. The briefers stepped back, and two airmen appeared with tall stepladders, one from each wing. They walked to symmetrical points, erected their ladders, climbed at the same pace, and simultaneously pulled at red ribbons. A clear plastic sheet whooshed down in front of a map, with red dots marking each nuclear strike. The airmen descended, picked up their ladders, and simultaneously moved into the wings, only to reappear with each new wave—carrier-based bombers, SAC bombers already aloft, SAC bombers on alert, SAC bombers on standby, Polaris missiles from submarines, Atlas land-based missiles, Thor and Jupiter IRBMs in Europe. . . . Power stopped the briefers at one point, turned to the audience, and told a prepared joke: "I just hope none of you have any relatives in Albania, because they have a radar station there that is right on our flight path, and we take it out." McNamara, appalled, did not laugh. One briefer predicted a hundred million Soviet dead and three hundred million Chinese dead, and that was just from fallout. It did not include the dead from blast or fire, the dead in Eastern or Western Europe, the dead elsewhere from fallout, or the dead in the United States from Soviet retaliation. Someone broke in: "May I ask a question?"

Power turned and said, "Yeah, what is it?"

"What if this isn't China's war? What if this is just the Soviets? Can you change the plan?"

"Well, yeah, we can," Power said begrudgingly. "But I hope nobody thinks of it, because that would really screw up the plan."[37]

A week later, McNamara sat through another presentation, this time by William Kaufmann, whom McNamara had hired along with twenty-three other RAND analysts as his assistants in the Defense Department. Kaufman argued for a doctrine of "counterforce," targeting Soviet military sites rather than cities, and for a rationally conducted, limited nuclear war, with each side sending tacit signals and threats to each other by the targets that it bombed. McNamara, always susceptible to a reasoned argument, saw this as an alternative to the horrific SIOP plans, and he threw the Defense Department's "Whiz Kids" at formulating a detailed counterforce strategy.

Under Eisenhower and Wilson, the RAND geeks had worked for the Air Force. Under Kennedy and McNamara, the Air Force was working for the geeks. After LeMay sat through a briefing by Harold Brown (a future secretary of defense in the Carter administration), he protested, "Why, that son of a bitch was in *junior high school* while I was bombing Japan!"[38]

Daniel Ellsberg, on loan from RAND to the Office of Naval Research, got permission to look at all Navy war plans—high-level plans as presented to the Joint Chiefs as well as the low-level operational plans for ship commanders. He examined the plans for the Navy's Pacific Command, whose basic mission was to bomb cities in China should the United States go to war with that country. Even if the Pacific Command was ordered to attack the Soviet Union, Ellsberg discovered, the command's plan book was so rigid that it could not avoid bombing China as well. Ellsberg extended his examination to the Air Force and Pentagon, where he found the same thing at every level. Whatever the president ordered, by the time things filtered through the chain of command, only a single, inflexible, and all-out war plan would reach the submarine, bomber, and missile crews. Whatever RAND's analysts thought, limited nuclear war was impossible—the president would not be able to do anything other than order an all-out attack. Ellsberg wrote McNamara a detailed memo with recommendations for a revised SIOP, one that envisioned escalating stages of nuclear war. McNamara made that U.S. policy in May 1961, to be included in next year's SIOP-63. When the Air Force refused to spend the money to implement his new plan, McNamara cut off funding for Minuteman missiles until it complied.[39]

In June 1961, before the new plan could be put in place, the Soviet Union tested the recently inaugurated Kennedy's mettle by threatening to cut off West Berlin. Young, educated East Germans used Berlin as an exit gate from Communism, and Khrushchev was determined to stop the flow. East German troops delayed NATO forces traveling along the autobahns to Berlin but eventually let them pass, and American and Russian tanks, gun turrets swiveling, faced each other at Berlin's Checkpoint Charlie. "Berlin is the testicles of the West," Khrushchev is reported to have said. "When I want the West to scream, I squeeze on Berlin." If Soviet troops had blockaded Berlin, the first step in the Joint Chiefs' plan book was to send a few brigades down the autobahn as a test. If Soviet troops engaged, starting what was by definition "general war," the next step was SIOP-62.[40]

Fearing the catastrophe if the all-out SIOP was implemented over Berlin, a group at the National Security Council proposed a first strike against Soviet military targets—no Soviet cities to be attacked. They estimated such a war would result in two to three million American deaths and European deaths in the low tens of millions. Both McNamara and Kennedy considered this, but the hawkish Paul Nitze was fiercely opposed—what if things did not go according to plan? What if the Russians did not behave "rationally" by accepting our no-cities nuclear signal and were left with enough bombs and capability to hit Washington and New York? The

Soviets eventually wound down the military standoff in Berlin and fixed their emigration problem by building the Berlin Wall, but the episode left McNamara and the Defense Department shaken. The year 1961 was probably the high-water mark in American nuclear superiority over the USSR, and if there had ever been a time to execute a counterforce first strike, that was it. But for all their tough-guy posturing and planning, the nation's civilian leaders backed away.[41]

An American first strike was not on the table when the Soviets sent missiles to Cuba in 1962, although Kennedy did consider both conventional bombing of the Cuban missile bases and an invasion of Cuba. The Soviets had armed their nuclear missiles, and they might have launched them rather than watch them be destroyed by bombs. An invasion might also have escalated into nuclear war, because the Russian commander in Cuba had tactical nuclear weapons and authorization to use them. Khrushchev eventually agreed to remove the missiles in return for a public American promise not to invade Cuba and a secret agreement to remove the Jupiter IRBMs from Turkey.

McNamara took his new counterforce plan public in 1962 with speeches at the NATO conference in Athens and at a commencement at the University of Michigan. The reaction was not positive. America's European allies saw the no-cities strategy as an attempt to keep the United States and the Soviet Union safe while confining an escalating nuclear war to Europe. As far as America's NATO allies were concerned, counterforce was an abrogation of America's nuclear guarantee. Besides, the United States did not fully control nuclear weapons. The British and French both had nuclear forces that targeted Soviet cities, and the United States would not be able to execute its "no-cities" strategy if its allies bombed Moscow and Leningrad. McNamara backed off, saying the United States had no plans for confining nuclear war to Europe, although he kept the secret target list focused on military installations. In any case, counterforce did not solve McNamara's big problem—the Air Force's continuing demands for more bombers and missiles. The Air Force kept finding more Soviet missile bases and airfields, all of which had to be targeted several times over, just to make sure. Two weeks after Kennedy's assassination, McNamara announced a new doctrine—"assured destruction." Once the Soviet Union was destroyed, there was no point in destroying it again. Alain Enthoven, a former RAND analyst, calculated that four hundred 1-megaton bombs would kill almost as many Russians and do almost as much industrial damage as could be done with larger strikes. The Defense Department assigned four hundred megatons to each of the three "legs" of the military triad—bombers, land-based missiles, and submarine-launched missiles—so that *each leg* would individually be able to destroy the USSR.

The Soviets rapidly deployed ICBMs in the 1960s and approached parity with the United States. "Assured destruction" became "mutual assured destruction" (MAD). In any nuclear war, according to MAD, both sides would be destroyed, so no rational leader would launch a nuclear first strike. MAD was a modernized version of the ancient practice of hostage taking, in which one power held prominent citizens of its enemy as hostages, threatening to execute them if the enemy made war. MAD could in theory be a stable strategy, but that required rules: each side must target the other's cities rather than the other's strike force (eliminating the temptation for a preemptive first strike), and neither side could deploy anti-missile defenses (so each side could be seen to be vulnerable to the other's retaliatory strike). To work, MAD would require verifiable arms control. While there were some moves in this direction (foremost among them the 1972 anti-ballistic-missile treaty), MAD never became a strategic doctrine for either the United States or the Soviet Union, and both sides continued to seek advantage.

McNamara cut the authorization for Minuteman missiles to one thousand, but he gave the Air Force a consolation prize: he approved the development of an advanced Minuteman missile with multiple independent re-entry vehicles (MIRV) capability. Each MIRVed missile would be able to carry several warheads, each of which would be independently targetable. When he approved MIRV development, McNamara ignored critics who pointed out three drawbacks. First, once both sides had developed MIRV capability, the temptation for a first strike would only increase: before MIRV, one first-strike missile could at best destroy one unlaunched enemy missile, but a MIRVed first-strike missile that carried three warheads could destroy three missiles sitting in their silos. Second, the Soviets had larger throw-weight missiles and would be able to pack more warheads into each missile. And finally, MIRV would make arms control more difficult, because while surveillance satellites could count the number of missile silos, they could not count the number of warheads on the missiles.[42] The United States deployed the Minuteman III in 1970 with three warheads, and the Soviet Union, as predicted, followed in 1974 with the SS-18 with eight warheads.

The Trident missile, which replaced the submarine-launched Polaris, also compromised the MAD balance. Polaris was the perfect second-strike weapon—too inaccurate to destroy military targets but accurate enough for cities. Trident was MIRVed and was accurate enough to be an effective first-strike weapon. Eventually, 30 percent of America's nuclear warheads would be placed on Trident.

RAND analyst Martin Shubik devised a game called the "dollar bill auction" that models the Cold War arms race. A dollar bill is up for sale, and either you or your opponent can bid any amount for it, starting with as little as one cent. Shubik's auction has a special rule, however: even if yours is not the high bid, you still must pay the winning bid, but you will get nothing in return. So the bids start low and escalate—one cent, ten cents, fifteen cents. . . . Even when one player bids a full dollar, the bidding continues. The low bidder bids $1.01, because dropping out would mean immediate loss of a dollar with no compensation. There is no logical end to the game: the "winning" bidder will pay far more than the dollar is worth, and the losing bidder will pay the same and get nothing.[43] The United States and the Soviet Union spent forty-five years bidding for that dollar.

Four Lessons from Vietnam

A week after he took office in 1961, President Kennedy approved an American counterinsurgency program to supply arms and advisors to the Diem regime in South Vietnam. His defense secretary, Robert McNamara, placed his faith in analytical thinking, a faith he shared with other Kennedy advisers who continued to manage the war through the Johnson administration. The United States' defeat in Vietnam is a complex story that has been studied and debated in thousands of books and articles; this chapter will focus on four particular cases and the thinking behind them. In each case, American leaders tried to solve problems analytically, but they did so with tunnel vision. Had they questioned their assumptions, results might have been better.

THE REDEYE MISSILE

In 1969, I was drafted into the U.S. Army and was sent to Aberdeen Proving Ground, along with a number of other soldiers who were scientists or engineers, to work on weapons tests. Aberdeen was then evaluating the performance of the Redeye bazooka-style anti-aircraft missile. The Redeye was a first-generation MANPAD (man-portable air defense) system, designed for use by an individual infantryman against low-flying jets and helicopters. The Redeye saw its first deployment in 1967 after eight years of development; the Army replaced it in 1981 with the Stinger, which has been featured in films, television dramas, and video games.*

Unlike the Stinger, the Redeye did not work all that well. As described in an Army historical report, "it could not go fast enough, it could not maneuver soon enough, and it could not discriminate well enough." The Redeye's sensor "saw" infrared radiation (heat) rather than visible light. It was designed to lock onto a low-flying jet's or helicopter's exhaust, follow it, and detonate. But the sensor was not up to the job; it could only identify a very bright (hot) target silhouetted against a dark (cold) background. That meant that the Redeye could see a jet only if it had a clear view of its exhaust (in other words, if it was looking at the rear of a jet that might have just dumped its munitions on the soldier who was firing the missile) and that it had trouble seeing the much dimmer helicopter exhausts at all.[1]

While I was at Aberdeen, a soldier-engineer (whose name I do not recall) who was working on the Redeye project test team told a story. I am not vouching for the story's accuracy—it was all more than forty years ago. With that caveat, the story: The Redeye team's civilian project leader was told to prepare a presentation for a general from the Pentagon. When the general and his staff arrived, the team members assembled in a briefing room, and the Redeye project leader began flipping through his charts and slides. After a few minutes, the general broke in, "Can this missile hit a truck?"

That was a question from left field, and it stopped the presenter cold. Every soldier-engineer in the room had the same thought: hit a truck? The Redeye could barely see the superheated exhaust of a 1,500-horsepower helicopter outlined against a cold sky. The idea that it could hit a 100-horsepower truck, sitting on the warm earth, with maybe a foot of not-very-hot

* For example, the 2007 film *Charlie Wilson's War*, starring Tom Hanks and Julia Roberts.

exhaust pipe showing, was absurd.[†] But no one said anything, because saying that to a general might result in a transfer to an infantry company in the Mekong Delta.

The team leader took a long time to phrase his answer. "Sir, the infrared radiation from a truck's exhaust is just not intense enough for the missile's sensor to pick up." Good answer, everyone thought. That should end it.

"What if we put thermite on the truck?" the general asked. Thermite, a mixture of a metal and a metal oxide, burns white-hot and was often used to simulate a jet's exhaust in drones that were dragged across the sky as targets in missile tests.

Another long pause from the team leader. "Yes, sir, the sensor would see the thermite."

"Let's try it," the general said. So the team went out to the test range, hoisted a truck up onto a stand with a crane, placed a pot of thermite on the truck, stood back a few hundred yards, lit the thermite, launched the missile, and blew up the truck.

One test wasn't enough. The general wanted a statistical analysis, so the experiment was repeated again and again. And not with old run-out trucks from the motor pool but with brand-new two-and-a-half-ton trucks. Worked every time. The next step would have been to convince the North Vietnamese to drive around with thermite on their tailpipes, but that was not part of the story as I heard it.

I remembered the story when I came across a previously classified Army document that describes a "Helicopter Redeye Air-Launched Missile

---

[†] The radiation emitted per unit area by a hot body is proportional to the fourth power of its temperature as measured in Kelvin. The hottest exposed part of a truck is the exhaust pipe as it extends from under the body. The exhaust temperature of an average pre-1974 U.S. car (before catalytic converters were required) is about 600K, and this is probably a good guess for a 1967 Soviet Zil-131 truck, which was widely used by the North Vietnamese. The U.S. HU-34 helicopter, which was the reference for the Redeye performance specification, has an exhaust temperature of 1,173K. Thus the radiation per unit area of a truck exhaust would be less than 10 percent of that of a helicopter exhaust, and almost all of a truck's exhaust is concealed beneath the body or hood. In addition, the lower temperature of the truck exhaust would shift its radiation spectrum toward the far infrared, so the Redeye's mid-infrared sensor would be even less sensitive for that target.

(RAM)" program, a plan to mount the Redeye inside a helicopter for use against enemy trucks: "Early in 1970, additional acquisition and firing tests . . . were conducted to evaluate the anti-truck capability of the helicopter-borne system." The tests were done at Aberdeen "to determine the terminal aim points." The report concluded that although "the feasibility of the helicopter RAM system was established," it was "not recommended for use."[2] If Aberdeen established "the feasibility of terminal aim points," it could have done so only by using thermite or some other artificial hot target. Using the Redeye against trucks was hopeless, as any of the project engineers could have demonstrated using only a slide rule.

However misguided the attempt, it is easy to see why the Pentagon wanted to turn the Redeye into an anti-truck weapon. The Redeye was a weapon for which the Army had no immediate use—its forces in South Vietnam had absolute air superiority, so there were no enemy jets or helicopters to shoot at. The Army's problem in Vietnam was not airplanes but trucks that carried supplies down the Ho Chi Minh Trail through Laos. After the 1968 Tet Offensive, the North Vietnamese Army (NVA) moved into South Vietnam in force, and it needed a steady flow of supplies. If a Redeye missile could see through the jungle canopy that covered the roads, snake through the vegetation, fly up a truck's exhaust pipe, and then explode, it might win what had become an unwinnable war.

Even the Stinger, which has a far better sensor than the Redeye, cannot see a truck. But it has proved effective against jets and helicopters, as was demonstrated by the missiles that the CIA provided to the mujahidin fighting the Russians in Afghanistan (although the role of the Stinger in the Russian defeat has been overstated).[3] In 1968, the Soviet Union came up with a competitor to the Redeye, known as the Strela or the SA-7; a newer version, the SA-14, with capabilities similar to the Stinger's, was deployed in 1974. As of 2011, China, North Korea, Egypt, Israel, and other countries have manufactured MANPADs (often copying existing systems, which is much easier than developing one from scratch). Between 500,000 and 750,000 MANPADs are estimated to exist, 90 percent of them in state inventories. Guerrilla and terrorist organizations are estimated to possess the missing 10 percent, and the United States has destroyed more than 32,000 MANPADs since 2003. At least fifteen successful MANPAD attacks on civilian aircraft have been reported.[4] When the Reagan administration sent Stingers to the Afghani mujahidin through Pakistan, Pakistan first skimmed off some Stingers as a "missile tax" and then sent the rest on to the rebels, who fired some, sold some, gave some to allies such as Iran, and kept some for future use. Under President George H. Bush, the CIA began a buyback program, offering $30,000 for a Stinger, no questions asked. The CIA's offering price eventually went up to $200,000, and this probably did collect almost all the Stingers—those who sold at that price could take the money and buy cheaper Soviet-manufactured MANPADs on the black market.[5]

The risk in supplying MANPADs to guerrilla forces should have been no surprise to either the CIA or the military—RAND had warned of the dangers in a 1975 report.[6] Both the United States and the USSR developed MANPADs without much thought—they must have seemed like bazookas that could be pointed at airplanes rather than at tanks, and what country would argue against giving its soldiers that? But a little thought would have shown the falseness of that analogy. Why would the United States, the Soviet Union, or any country that relies on air superiority and on civilian jet travel want to develop a weapon that allows a lone gunman to shoot down airplanes? Both the United States and the USSR could have sponsored UN resolutions to ban MANPADs in the early 1960s. I know of no record of the matter even being discussed.

CHEMICALS: AGENT ORANGE AND TEAR GAS

At South Vietnamese president Diem's request, the U.S. Army's Chemical Corps supplied the South Vietnamese Army two types of chemicals: riot control agents (RCAs) such as tear gas, and herbicides, of which the best-known is Agent Orange, which has resulted in cancers, birth defects, and stillbirths.[7] But the herbicides' health problems were at first unknown, and it was RCAs that fueled an immediate controversy.

President Kennedy and Secretary of Defense Robert McNamara worried that using RCAs in combat would subject the United States to charges of chemical warfare given that the 1925 Geneva Protocol banned the use in war of "asphyxiating, poisonous, or *other* gases" (my italics). They knew that the legalistic argument that neither the United States nor South Vietnam was a signatory to the protocol would mean little to world opinion. Claims that the gases were nonlethal would not wash either, because the South Vietnamese used the gases to flush Viet Cong guerrillas from their bunkers or tunnels so that they could shoot them. The South Vietnamese were especially indiscriminate in their use of RCAs; they once sprayed six thousand civilians to clear what they intended to be a free-fire zone. Peter Arnett, then working for the Associated Press, reported in 1965 that U.S. and Vietnamese forces were "experimenting with non-lethal gas warfare," and most readers saw only "gas warfare" rather than "non-lethal." The North Vietnamese claimed that the South Vietnamese used nerve gases as well, and President Johnson had to answer reporters' questions. Newspapers across the country ran the story on the front page and published editorials opposing gas use. McNamara told journalists off the record that he would rather "lose the war" than authorize more tear gas. "If by itself it would save the situation, I wouldn't [use gas]. . . . My God, I don't want to go through that again."

McNamara's concern was not for morality or even legality but for the public relations damage. He temporarily suspended the theater commander's authority to use RCAs, but both the American and South Vietnamese armies used them throughout the war.[8] Eventually American outrage dissipated: gas in Vietnam did not photograph as well as napalm and helicopters, and the American public became blasé after watching one group of American anti-war protesters after another tear-gassed on television. Not until April 8, 1975, did President Ford sign an executive order banning the use of RCAs in offensive operations and requiring presidential authorization for defensive uses and rescue missions.

Kennedy and McNamara also feared the world's response to herbicide spraying, which began the year before the publication of Rachel Carson's *Silent Spring*, a best seller that decried the environmental effects of indiscriminate pesticide use. Diem wanted to use herbicides to deny the Viet Cong cover for roadside ambushes and attacks on bases, to defoliate the cover over Viet Cong supply routes, to destroy the mango swamps in which Viet Cong took refuge, and to starve the Viet Cong by killing crops in areas they controlled. The military situation was deteriorating badly in late 1961—the Viet Cong temporarily seized Phuoc Thanh, a provincial capital only fifty-five miles from Saigon, and publicly beheaded Diem's province chief. A joint American–South Vietnamese group presented a plan to defoliate half of South Vietnam, a plan that would have consumed chemicals faster than the American chemical industry could produce them. Kennedy rejected that proposal, but on November 30, 1961, he approved a less ambitious plan that included defoliation of supply routes and combat areas, although it held back on authorizing crop destruction. The United States at first planned to fly the spraying missions using planes painted with South Vietnamese markings, but it gave this up after realizing that the deception would not be credible.[9]

Agent Orange was the most-used herbicide in Vietnam. It and the other military herbicides were nothing special—they were merely formulations of herbicides that were commonly used in the United States. The chemical that caused the problems is dioxin, an unintended contaminant of 2,4,5-T, a broadleaf-plant defoliant that constituted half of Agent Orange.[†] While 2,4,5-T is itself relatively harmless—eating a teaspoonful of pure 2,4,5-T would not be fatal—dioxin was known as early as 1957 to be one of the most poisonous man-made compounds, and the manufacturing process for 2,4,5-T inevitably produces trace amounts of dioxin.[10]

Crop dusters routinely applied 2,4,5-T in the United States, but the most famous applicators were the aircrews of Operation Ranch Hand in Vietnam. The U.S. Air Force used modified C-123 airplanes—big, slow, ugly transports—for Ranch Hand, with up to six planes flying side by side. Each plane delivered a thousand gallons of herbicide in an 8.7-mile swath that took about four and a half minutes. An enlisted man in the rear managed the tanks and the spray nozzles, and two active pilots worked in unison. The left-seat pilot flew the plane, kept left-right spacing with other

---

[†] Dioxin's full chemical name is 2,3,7,8-tetrachlorodibenzo-p-dioxin, and 2,4,5-T's is 2,4,5-trichlorophenoxyacetic acid.

■ Operation Ranch Hand pilots spraying Agent Orange in Vietnam. *U.S. Air Force photograph.*

planes, and turned the sprayer on and off, while the right-seat pilot controlled power and altitude, monitored the instruments, and maintained fore-and-aft spacing with other planes. Each pilot had to be ready to take over if the other was hit by ground fire, which was common. The C-123s were not armored, and the Ranch Hand units were among the most decorated of the war—many received Purple Hearts for combat wounds. Flying slowly, at low altitude, straight and level, they were easy targets for any soldier with an AK-47.

So that Operation Ranch Hand could be called a joint U.S.-Vietnamese operation, each plane's crew included a South Vietnamese "commander," who was only a passenger—any random enlisted man would fit the bill. The planes took off just after dawn, when the winds were quiet, and they flew out of the sun to make enemy ground fire more difficult.[11] The crews began wearing black berets (which led to disagreements with Army Special Forces soldiers, who wore authorized green berets) and purple scarves in honor of the first herbicide they had sprayed, Agent Purple.

Air Vice Marshal Nguyen Cao Ky of the South Vietnamese Air Force, known for his black flying suit and pearl-handled pistols, awarded the Ranch Hand crews his violet scarf after flying a sortie with them. When Gen. William Westmoreland banned unauthorized uniform items, Ky called the American ambassador and forced a dispensation for Ranch Hand crews.[12]

Ranch Hand began on a small scale, clearing vegetation along roads and canals. In October 1962, after dithering for almost a year, Kennedy approved a crop destruction program, although he tried to keep it under tight control. All attempts to limit defoliation and crop destruction ultimately failed. From 1962 to 1964, Ranch Hand sprayed 250,000 gallons; in 1965, 400,000 gallons; in 1966, 1.6 million gallons; and projected needs for 1967 were 5.6 million gallons and for 1968 11.9 million gallons. To put this in perspective, the Army planned to spray Vietnam at more than a hundred times the density of agricultural herbicidal spraying as done in the United States.[§] That calculation alone should have set off alarms that Ranch Hand was out of control. In 1967, Secretary of Agriculture Orville Freeman protested when the entire U.S. production of 2,4,5-T was allocated to the military, leaving nothing for American farmers.[13]

The attempt to spray "Viet Cong crops" was especially counterproductive. A 1967 RAND report noted that food was plentiful in Vietnam and that the Viet Cong fighters accounted for only 1.5 percent of the population and consumed no more than 3 percent of the food, so starving the Viet Cong was unlikely to work. Furthermore, the Viet Cong were not themselves farmers, so "Viet Cong crops" were crops grown by peasants from whom the Viet Cong demanded a tax in kind; when the peasants' crop was reduced by spraying, the Viet Cong still took what they needed, leaving the peasants with less. RAND interrogators interviewed Vietnamese farmers and discovered, not surprisingly, that the farmers blamed the South Vietnamese government and the United States for starving them to

[§] All of Vietnam has an area one-thirtieth that of the United States; total agricultural herbicide use in the United States in 1965 was 2.4 million gallons.

get at the Viet Cong. The farmers reported that after spraying runs they suffered runny noses, nausea, cramps, and diarrhea, and that some infants had died. The RAND report's authors suggested that it might help if the military undertook an education campaign to explain to the farmers why their crops were being destroyed.[14]

In 1966, the American Association for the Advancement of Science passed a resolution demanding an investigation of herbicides' effects, arguing that they might have long-term consequences. The Department of Defense funded a supposedly independent evaluation and report, which found no cause for alarm but advised further study.[15] In the fall of 1969, a National Institutes of Health study came to light that showed birth defects in mice who had been subjected to even small amounts of 2,4,5-T. The study was from 1966, and it had not reached the Food and Drug Administration (FDA) until 1968. Then the FDA sat on it for a year before passing it to the Agriculture and Defense Departments. Ralph Nader's consumer watchdog group said that a White House staffer had told it that the report was suppressed because it would have helped the antiwar movement; an FDA spokesman blamed pressure from chemical companies, especially Dow. In response, Dow claimed that it had a new manufacturing process that would produce a "clean" herbicide with greatly reduced dioxin, called Orange II. But it was too late for that. Herbicide use in Vietnam was banned in 1970. Drums of Agent Orange and other herbicides were removed from South Vietnam to remote Johnson Island in the Pacific in 1972 and incinerated at sea in 1977.[16]

Dioxin proved disastrous to the health of both the Vietnamese and the Americans, and the area around former U.S. bases remains contaminated. For years, the Department of Veterans Affairs took a hard line on compensation, denying veterans' claims unless the condition appeared during service or within a year after discharge. That position finally changed in 2010, when the VA announced that Agent Orange should be presumed to be the cause for a number of diseases. Almost all of the 230,000 veterans' claims have been processed at a total cost of $3.6 billion.[17] A federal court dismissed a 2004 class-action lawsuit against U.S. chemical companies by Vietnamese civilians and veterans.[18]

THE M16 RIFLE

We left with 72 men in our platoon and came back with 19. Believe it or not, you know what killed most of us? Our own rifles. Before we left Okinawa, we were all issued the new rifles, the M-16. Practically every one of our dead was found with his rifle torn down next to him where he had been trying to fix it.

— Letter from a Marine Corps rifleman in Vietnam[19]

In 1967, at the height of the Vietnam War, the U.S. Army changed its standard-issue rifle from the M14 to the M16. Within weeks, reports came in from soldiers in combat: their rifles had jammed, and they were helpless. The decision to change to the M16 was top-down. McNamara ordered it after years of squabbling between the M16's opponents (including Army chief of staff Gen. Earl Wheeler, Sen. Ted Kennedy, the Army's Ordnance Department, the National Rifle Association, and America's NATO allies) and its supporters (including the Army's Infantry Board; the commander of American ground forces in Vietnam, Gen. William Westmoreland; and Curtis LeMay).

McNamara made his decision for the M16 in 1962, just as U.S. Special Forces troops entered Vietnam. The Viet Cong were armed with the Soviet AK-47, which performed much better in automatic mode than did the M14. The M16, McNamara believed, matched the modern Army's needs better than did the M14. It was shorter and lighter than the M14, so it was easier to carry; it fired a lighter bullet, so soldiers could carry more ammunition; it was at least as lethal; it was just as accurate out to two hundred yards; and it was much more accurate than the M14 when fired in automatic mode—important in jungle warfare, where the enemy is often seen only at close range. Compared to a missile or a fighter plane, a rifle is not a high-technology weapon, and the decision must have seemed straightforward to McNamara's analytical mind. He ended the discussion and ordered all the armed services to adopt the M16. Five years after he ordered the change, it blew up in his face. The problems were not technological but sociological—he had looked only at the rifle, not at the people and organizations that would be responsible for introducing and supporting it.

Rifles were first issued as standard infantry weapons in the Civil War, and the Army had a long tradition of valuing marksmanship—the best rifle was, by its definition, the most accurate rifle. The Army Ordnance Department's armory in Springfield, Massachusetts, had produced weapons for the infantry since the Revolutionary War. Starting in 1892, Ordnance had standardized on a .30-caliber round in all its rifles—the Krag-Jorgenson, used in the Spanish-American War; the M1903 Springfield, used in World War I; the Garand M1, used in World War II and Korea; and the M14, the successor to the M1. The heavy .30-caliber round was aerodynamically stable, and a skilled marksman could fire it accurately out to twelve hundred yards.

The Ordnance Department was responsible for producing the Army's rifles. It was the infantry, however, that would use them, and it had its own group of experts—the Infantry Board. The board thought accuracy was overrated and that aimed fire had little to do with success on the battlefield. What was important instead was volume of fire—firing in bursts rather than single aimed shots. While the M14 could be fired in automatic mode, its spray of heavy .30-caliber bullets made it uncontrollable. What was needed, the Infantry Board said, was a weapon that fired a lighter, higher-velocity round. The board and its predecessor had fought and lost two battles for a lighter round—first in 1928 and then in 1950, when the United States had forced the .30-caliber round on its allies as the NATO standard over British objections. The .30-caliber round was an article of faith for the Ordnance Department, and it developed the M14 rifle as the Army's standard weapon to fire it.

The Infantry Board did not give up. Its commander, Col. Henry Neilson, visited Eugene Stoner, a rifle designer at ArmaLite, a small-arms manufacturer, and discussed a lightweight rifle that would fire a high-velocity .22-caliber bullet. ArmaLite named its prototype rifle the AR-15, and Neilson ordered ten of them. They arrived at Fort Benning, Georgia, just as the Army announced that the M14 would be the new standard. Neilson was impressed with the AR-15's performance, and he shipped the prototypes to the Ordnance Department and to the Arctic Test Board for further tests. Neither was happy. The Ordnance Department said that the rifle's narrow barrel retained water, and the Arctic Test Board reported that the small bullet was unstable in the dense air at temperatures of -65°F. The Infantry Board did not see either of these as a problem. The barrel water was easy to clear by tipping the rifle with the chamber open, and it was unlikely that any soldier would (or could) fire his rifle at -65°F.

Army chief of staff Maxwell Taylor overruled the Infantry Board. The M14 would remain the standard, and the Army would dedicate its research efforts to a futuristic weapon that would fire bursts of darts rather than bullets. But ArmaLite, the AR-15's manufacturer, was a private company, and its sales agents did not give up. They approached Asian military buyers, who were enthusiastic about the lighter AR-15 for their smaller soldiers. Because the AR-15 was not standard U.S. equipment, however, it was ineligible for purchase by allies using American military-assistance funds, so ArmaLite needed an American military buyer.

Curtis LeMay, the Air Force chief of staff, was in the market for a rifle to replace the Air Force's World War II–era inventory of weapons. The ArmaLite agents invited him to a Fourth of July picnic in 1960, where he shot watermelons with an AR-15. He put in a request to buy eighty thousand of them, using money that had been appropriated for a different project. The request went nowhere—McNamara refused to allow him to shift the funds, and congressional supporters of the M14 refused the Air Force permission to purchase any AR-15s at all.

In June 1961, an article in the *New York Herald Tribune* called the M14 a "major blunder . . . the result of an official Army ordnance policy . . . to get rid of short-range, light impact spray-fire weapons."[20] Bad publicity got McNamara's and Kennedy's attention, and McNamara began to look at the AR-15 again. He agreed to purchase a thousand for testing in Vietnam, where both Vietnamese troops and American advisers were enthusiastic about the new rifle. Charles Hitch, one of McNamara's hires from RAND, issued what came to be called the "Hitch Report," which concluded that the AR-15 was superior to the M14 in every way.

Cyrus Vance, the secretary of the Army, asked the Army staff for their opinions, which vehemently opposed reconsidering the M14 decision. Choosing its rifle was the most fundamental Army decision, and it was not the business of civilians in the Department of Defense to stick their noses in. The Army staff insisted that it needed one rifle that it could use anywhere, and it cited an article in *American Rifleman*—the publication of the National Rifle Association—that was critical of the AR-15, saying that its bullet was unstable in cold air and recommending an increase in the spin that was imparted by the barrel's rifling. McNamara pressed Army chief of staff Earl Wheeler to decide in favor of the AR-15. Wheeler was caught in the middle—he couldn't accede to McNamara's demands without losing credibility with his own staff. Congress, meanwhile, was largely pro-M14, because military contractors were already producing the weapon or its parts in various congressional districts. Wheeler kicked the problem to a committee. He decided that he needed more tests—of a weapon that the Army had tested repeatedly for five years.

The Army cooked the new tests to make the AR-15 look bad. Secretary Vance threw the results out and forced Wheeler to agree to purchase a hundred thousand AR-15s for paratroopers and Special Forces units and to reduce M14 purchases accordingly. But the M14 remained the Army's standard weapon, and Ordnance had not yet approved the AR-15 for production, so Wheeler could not issue a purchase order.

McNamara did not trust the Army to push the AR-15 through its production system. He created a parallel structure, the Technical Coordinating Committee (TCC), comprising representatives from the Army, Air Force, and Marines, along with civilians from the Defense Department. Had the Army taken the AR-15 as it had existed in 1962 into production, instituted acceptance criteria that treated both the rifle and its ammunition systematically, and developed training and maintenance procedures, the jamming problems that surfaced in Vietnam in 1967 would have been avoided. Instead, the committee tinkered with the design. It changed the spin ratio in the rifle barrel as the *American Rifleman* had recommended, it added a manual bolt-assist anti-jamming device to ram a cartridge into the chamber (against the advice of the Air Force and Eugene Stoner, the rifle's designer), and it changed the trigger-pull pressure.

The Army still stalled. By fall of 1963, it had let no contracts for production, and it sent McNamara another memo saying that the AR-15 was unsatisfactory. McNamara responded by shutting down M14 production, which provoked screams from Sen. Ted Kennedy and the congressional delegation from Massachusetts, where the Springfield Armory and several of the M14's suppliers were located. The Army relented. In November 1963, the AR-15, as modified by the TCC, was put into production with a grudging "one-time" Army order for eighty-five thousand experimental units. It was now an official Army weapon, and it received a new name—the M16. The M14, however, remained the standard rifle.

American ground troops began arriving in Vietnam in 1965, and the heat was on. Westmoreland, the theater commander, said that his soldiers and the South Vietnamese troops needed M16s. In February 1967, the Army announced that the M16 was the standard Army weapon for Vietnam, and began replacing all M14s.

The jamming complaints began almost immediately. Congressional and Army investigations would show that even when the rifle was properly maintained, it had a jamming problem. In an effort to alleviate a problem with occasional accidental firing when a single round was introduced manually (not the usual combat situation), the Army had, without sufficient test, changed the ammunition to use a slower-burning powder. That resulted in a faster "cycle rate" between rounds fired, which made the rifle six times more likely to jam. In late 1967, the Army modified the M16 by slowing its cycle rate and by chrome-plating its chamber to resist corrosion. In 1969, analysts found that the slower-burning powder left a sticky calcium carbonate residue that contributed to jamming. That was fixed in a new powder specification.

Those were the technical problems, but nontechnical, systematic problems contributed to jamming. Despite the powder change, the rifle's manufacturer still tested using the old powder, as was specified in its contract—there was no connection between the rifle as tested before shipment and as used in combat. Poor training and management of the exchange of M14s for M16s in Vietnam may have been the biggest problem. Troops who had arrived with M16s after training with the weapon in the United States were almost uniformly happy with it, and most jamming reports came from units that had their M14s swapped out in the field. Many of them reported that they had received no training in cleaning and maintenance of the M16, and that cleaning kits were not always distributed. Inspectors reported that they found M16s so filthy that they could not see daylight through the barrel. Governor George Romney of Michigan (Mitt Romney's father) sent the troops in Vietnam a Christmas present of Dri-Slide, a commercial lubricant manufactured in his state. Dri-Slide might have worked better or worse than the Army lubricant, but it had not been tested, and it complicated the analysis of the jamming problem. Not until 1969 was the M16 performing reliably.

There was plenty of blame to go around. The Army staff had waffled for ten years after receiving the first AR-15 prototype. The Army then ordered a risky, rushed change of its most basic infantry weapon—the rifle—in the midst of a war, with no clean lines separating development, procurement, and deployment. Secretary McNamara mistrusted the existing Army structures and set up the TCC as a parallel organization. But, with no resources of its own, the TCC was forced to rely on the Army's technical and logistics functions. And the Army Ordnance Department, relieved of its responsibilities by the creation of the TCC, took an "I told you so" attitude to the M16's problems.[21]

BOMBING

The United States bombed North Vietnam for more than three years under President Johnson with a graduated, on-and-off campaign, called "Rolling Thunder," lasting from March 1965 to October 1968. After Nixon took office in 1969, he ordered shorter but more intensive campaigns—"Linebacker I," lasting from May to October 1972, and "Linebacker II," for twelve days in December 1972. The hawkish view—LeMay's, for example—was that the Rolling Thunder campaign was aimless, politically limited, and ineffective; and that the intensive Linebacker attacks would have won the war if they had been continued.

A 1986 article in *Air Force* magazine reported that the Air Force pushed for large-scale bombing of "strategic targets" in the North as early as 1964, but that "military amateurs . . . in Washington . . . believed that close support of ground forces was the way to victory."²² If "strategic targets" are those vital to the enemy's ability to wage war, however, no strategic targets existed in North Vietnam in 1964. Before 1968, the Communist armed forces in South Vietnam consisted almost wholly of Viet Cong guerrillas, who supplied themselves locally. McNamara testified in 1967 that the Viet Cong required at most a hundred tons of supplies a day from the North, and that trying to stop that small flow by bombing was impossible. And the supplies that the Viet Cong did import from the North—armaments, ammunition, and medical supplies—were manufactured in the Soviet Union and China, which even the Air Force did not advocate bombing. The Air Force wanted to target North Vietnam's Haiphong Port and the rail lines from Hanoi to China, but American bombing accuracy was only slightly better than in World War II. Johnson and his advisors feared striking Soviet or Chinese ships in the harbor, or dropping stray bombs into Chinese territory. They remembered Korea, where reaching the Yalu River had drawn China into the war. Now, only a few years after the Cuban missile crisis, the United States was unwilling to risk a direct confrontation with either the USSR or China, both of which were nuclear powers.²³

Much of the Air Force's criticism of Rolling Thunder was valid. Rolling Thunder was not really strategic bombing, but rather what Robert Pape has called "coercive bombing"—bombing aimed at causing an enemy enough pain that he will accommodate the bomber's demands.²⁴ Two of the Johnson administration's bombing goals were political and had nothing to do with North Vietnam: to signal America's firmness to its allies worldwide, and to boost the morale of the South Vietnamese government, which was near collapse. The third goal, to impose such costs on North Vietnam that it would cease supporting the Communist insurgency in the South, showed how profoundly American leaders misunderstood the situation.²⁵ "We didn't know them well enough to empathize," McNamara said much later. "We saw Vietnam as an element of the Cold War, not as what they saw it—a civil war."²⁶

Johnson's advisors believed that North Vietnam was a Soviet-Chinese client state in the same way that South Vietnam was a U.S. client state, and that the United States could negotiate a settlement with North Vietnam's great-power masters. This disregarded twenty-five years of history—North Vietnam had been fighting the French and then the Americans since the end of World War II. The 1954 Geneva Conference on Vietnam had established North and South Vietnam as temporary states pending unification after elections. The United States refused to allow elections because, as President Eisenhower said, "80 per cent of the population would have voted for the Communist Ho Chi Minh."[27] Johnson and his advisors tried to use Rolling Thunder to force North Vietnam to abandon its central war aim—the unification of Vietnam.[28]

Different bombing strategies were on the table as Rolling Thunder was planned: Maxwell Taylor, President Johnson's military advisor, proposed starting off small and "tightening the noose," escalating the intensity and the targets until North Vietnam capitulated; the Army's Earl Wheeler argued for a campaign focused on combat support of ground troops in the South and at the same time interdicting supplies from the North; finally, Curtis LeMay wanted to hit the North hard, striking all the targets on the Air Force's list immediately. In the end, the United States pursued all three strategies, one after the other: escalation in the spring and summer of 1965, interdiction from summer 1965 to the end of 1967, and general bombing of all targets through the fall of 1967, after which there was no way to escalate because all targets had been destroyed.[29] Johnson stopped the bombing in October 1968 in an effort to initiate peace talks with North Vietnam and to help the Democratic presidential candidate Hubert Humphrey.

The United States estimates that Rolling Thunder killed fifty-two thousand Vietnamese, cost the United States almost $10 for every $1 of damage done, and delivered more explosive tonnage than in either the Korean War or in the Pacific theater of World War II.[30] It achieved virtually nothing. The civilians in the White House and Defense Department micromanaged the campaign—President Johnson reportedly bragged that "they can't bomb an outhouse without my approval." But the outcome would have been little different had the Air Force been unleashed to destroy all the allowable targets in 1964. Bombing power stations in North Vietnam could not stop the Viet Cong in South Vietnam, and nothing short of nuclear weapons would have made the North Vietnamese abandon their goal of a unified Vietnam.

■ Secretary of Defense McNamara and the Joint Chiefs of Staff with President Johnson at his Texas ranch, 1964. McNamara is second from left in the white shirt, behind Johnson leaning forward; LeMay is facing the camera with his cigar. *LBJ Presidential Library.*

In January 1968, during Tet, the Vietnamese New Year, the Viet Cong and North Vietnamese Army (NVA) launched attacks on more than a hundred towns. By military standards, their attacks were a failure—the Viet Cong suffered irreplaceable losses, and almost all the initial Communist gains were reversed. The Tet Offensive marked a turning point in the war, however, because the attackers' temporary victories—among them occupying the grounds of the American embassy in Saigon and capturing the city of Hué—appeared on television, and the American public began to see the Vietnam War as unwinnable.

Nixon defeated Hubert Humphrey in the 1968 presidential election. Nixon and his foreign policy advisor, Henry Kissinger, pursued a policy of "Vietnamization"—providing air support, increased equipment, and training to the South Vietnamese military while gradually withdrawing American ground troops. American war aims had changed. Although the Nixon administration did not publicly renounce the Johnson administration's goals for an independent, non-Communist South Vietnam, its private goals were to remove American troops while providing enough assistance to South Vietnam so that it would not immediately collapse. Kissinger has denied that he ever said that he sought a "decent interval" before the fall of Saigon. Whether or not he uttered those exact words, Nixon's White House tapes are revealing. In August 1972, Nixon was worried that a defeat in Vietnam would affect the 1972 election results negatively. "So we've got to find some formula that hold the thing together a year or two," Kissinger can be heard telling Nixon, "after which, Mr. President, Vietnam will be a backwater . . . by January '74 no one will give a damn."[31]

The Paris peace talks, begun in 1968 under Johnson, went nowhere. Starting in 1968, North Vietnam began to move its Army south to shore up the Viet Cong, which had been shattered during Tet. On March 30, 1972, the NVA launched its largest offensive of the war. Nixon had reduced U.S. troop levels from more than half a million when he took office to sixty-nine thousand, so the South Vietnamese Army bore the brunt of the ground fighting.[32]

The NVA advanced rapidly at first, capturing the provincial capital Quảng Tri City. Nixon responded with bombing, and he refused to repeat what he saw as Johnson's mistake—he would not call off the attacks until North Vietnam agreed to peace terms. The Nixon-Kissinger foreign policy had made aggressive bombing less risky. Nixon moved toward a policy of recognition of Communist China and détente with the Soviet Union. In 1969, China and the USSR were engaged in a seven-month border war with each other. While both Communist powers continued to supply and support North Vietnam, each feared isolation and wanted an improved relationship with the United States. Fear of a larger war, which had restrained Johnson, would not restrain Nixon and Kissinger. They expanded the bombing list to include targets near the Chinese border, in the North Vietnamese capital, Hanoi, and in the port of Haiphong. New laser-guided "smart" bombs allowed American bombers to strike targets that had been inaccessible in Johnson's Rolling Thunder campaign four years earlier. The NVA commander, Gen. Giap, had sent all but one of his divisions into South Vietnam. Unlike the Viet Cong guerrillas in the 1960s, his conventional forces required a steady flow of supplies and reinforcements, which the American bombers were able to attenuate. Linebacker did more damage in six months than Rolling Thunder did in four years, and the South Vietnamese Army advanced and retook Quàng Tri. In October 1972, North Vietnam and the United States agreed on a basis for negotiations: the North Vietnamese would not demand the replacement of the Thieu regime, and the Americans would agree to a cease-fire in place, allowing the NVA to remain in South Vietnam. On October 26, Kissinger announced that "peace is at hand." The United States halted the bombing.

Peace was not at hand. The problem was South Vietnamese president Thieu, whose resolve had been stiffened by his army's successes during the Linebacker campaign. He feared that the Americans were preparing to abandon him, and he refused to agree to a continuing North Vietnamese presence in the South. On December 19, the United States kicked off Linebacker II. In twelve days, the American planes dropped 13 percent of the tonnage dropped in six months of Linebacker I. Although Linebacker II's bombs were dropped on North Vietnam, its message was directed at South Vietnam. Linebacker II was meant to demonstrate to the Thieu regime that it could count on America, that America remained ready to use its airpower to guarantee South Vietnam's survival. Thieu, however, continued to balk, and Nixon gave him an ultimatum, warning that he would initial the peace agreement alone if necessary, saying, "In that case I shall have to explain publicly that your Government obstructs peace. The result will be an inevitable and immediate termination of U.S. economic and military assistance."[33] Thieu signed, and the United States supported his regime—for two years. Watergate brought Nixon down, and in March 1975 the NVA began its final advance. The South Vietnamese Army and the Thieu regime collapsed within days.[34]

The lesson that some airpower believers take is the following: Rolling Thunder failed because it was politically limited and halfhearted; Linebacker succeeded because it hit every target hard and quickly. But the difference had little to do with the level of force. Rolling Thunder failed because the Viet Cong guerrillas needed little in the way of supplies from the North before 1968, and because the United States unrealistically demanded that North Vietnam abandon its central goal of a unified nation. Linebacker, on the other hand, succeeded because the NVA's conventional troops needed supplies and reinforcements from the North, and because American and North Vietnamese goals in 1972 were not fundamentally opposed: both wanted the United States out of Vietnam, and North Vietnam could accept Nixon's and Kissinger's demand for a "decent interval" before its final victory.

Star Wars

In 1979, presidential candidate Ronald Reagan visited the North American Aerospace Defense Center's hardened bunker, buried deep in Cheyenne Mountain, Colorado. NORAD's mission is to warn of an air attack on America or Canada, and its chiefs wanted to show Reagan a simulated Soviet nuclear attack. The big-screen maps displayed satellite pickup of enemy missiles as they emerged from their silos in northern Russia. The missiles' rocket motors cut out after a few minutes, and they began their outer-space journey across the North Pole. Reagan watched, fascinated, and asked, "What happens now?" The NORAD commanders explained that they could follow the missiles' flight precisely, first by satellite and then, as they neared Canada, by radar. The missiles crossed Canada, and Reagan asked again, "What happens now?" The NORAD commanders had nothing new to say: "We continue to track the missiles."

The answer Reagan was expecting was "Now we shoot them down." Although he was little more than a year from becoming the nation's commander in chief, he was unaware that America had no defense against Soviet missiles, and that nuclear war was deterred only by fear of mutual destruction. That seemed wrong to him. The nation that had built the atomic bomb and put a man on the moon should be able to defend itself.[1]

Immediately after Reagan's 1981 inauguration, a core group of his kitchen cabinet, calling itself "High Frontier," began considering missile defense. High Frontier was led by Karl Bendetsen, who had been an undersecretary of the Army under Truman and later chairman of Champion International, a forest products company. Bendetsen was a leading member of the Committee on the Present Danger, a revival of an anti-Communist organization that James Conant and others had founded in 1950. Only two High Frontier members were scientists—Edward Teller and his protégé George Keyworth, Reagan's science adviser.[2] Keyworth later admitted that he was in that office because Teller had proposed him and President Reagan admired Teller.[3] The Reagan administration redefined Keyworth's job—in other administrations, the science adviser had been a neutral assessor of science proposals, but Reagan's team expected Keyworth to be a cheerleader for the administration. He would have a difficult job of it. The High Frontier team was full of powerful figures with wacky ideas, and Keyworth would need to manage them while also placating Teller, who repeatedly pressed Keyworth to arrange direct meetings between him and the president.

Reagan's secretary of state, George Shultz, admired Reagan's vision and his ability to articulate his ideas in ways that resonated with the American public. But, Shultz wrote, he "could fall prey to a serious weakness: a tendency to rely on his staff and friends to the point of accepting uncritically—even wishfully—advice that was sometimes amateurish and even irresponsible."[4] What Reagan heard from the High Frontier group, from his White House staff, and from his cabinet (with the notable exception of Shultz) would show little concern for the costs, technological feasibility, or strategic impact of anti-missile defense. And Teller's advice to Reagan would be worse than amateurish—it was at first manipulative and later deceitful.

Teller, by this time a retired director of Livermore National Laboratory, was excited about the X-ray laser. A laser emits a pencil beam of energy composed of a small number of frequencies. Laser presentation pointers, for example, emit visible light—red, green, blue, or violet—at a frequency (color) determined by the laser's material. Visible lasers first appeared in the 1960s. By the early 1970s, lasers operated in the far-ultraviolet part of the spectrum, where the invisible beam can be very destructive: ultraviolet lasers are used commercially to machine metal. Moving beyond the ultraviolet to higher-energy X-ray lasers proved difficult, however. X-ray lasers require a much shorter, more energetic pulse, and because mirrors do not work in the X-ray region, which precludes amplifying the laser's beam with multiple reflections. Not until November 14, 1980—a few days after Reagan's election—did scientists at Livermore National Laboratory simultaneously demonstrate two different X-ray lasers in an underground test code-named "Dauphin." Commercial applications for their lasers were likely to be limited, however; they had used a nuclear bomb as their lasers' energy source. The lasers flashed, the X-ray sensors detected a burst of radiation, and then everything disappeared in the nuclear blast.[5]

Commercial applications were not what interested Teller, who saw the X-ray laser as a death ray that could destroy Soviet missiles. Livermore called the potential weapon "Excalibur," after the sword that King Arthur pulled from a stone. Excalibur would take the undirected force of a hydrogen bomb and pack it into beams of X-rays, each a million times as intense as the bomb itself. Hitting a missile with another missile is like shooting a bullet to knock down another bullet—the shooter must lead the target so that the two missiles arrive at the same point at the same instant. Laser beams, however, operate at the speed of light. No worries about leading the missile: just aim the laser like a flashlight, fire, and watch the missile disappear.

By 1980, the nose cone of a Soviet ICBM was packed with as many as ten nuclear warheads and a number of decoy warheads. An ICBM begins its flight in "boost phase," with its engines firing for three or four minutes. For a missile, boost phase is a period of maximum visibility and vulnerability—satellites can see its hot exhaust, and all its warheads are still in its nose cone, where they can be destroyed with a single strike. After boost phase, attacking a missile is harder—the nose cone opens, and each warhead must then be identified and targeted separately among the decoys. A laser beam, Teller thought, would be fast enough to destroy an ICBM in the few minutes of boost phase. He planned to place Excalibur in high orbit. As enemy missiles left the atmosphere, the Excalibur controller would pick up the bright plumes of the missiles' rocket engines. Excalibur's hydrogen bomb would then detonate, its X-ray lasers would flash for a few milliseconds, and the Soviet missiles, warheads still inside, would disappear.

We have seen Teller at Los Alamos during the development of the first-generation nuclear weapon, the atomic bomb, and as the champion of the second-generation nuclear weapon, the hydrogen bomb. At age seventy-two, he saw himself as the architect of the third-generation nuclear weapon, the directed X-ray beam. But unlike the atomic and hydrogen bombs, Teller claimed, his last device would not destroy cities but defend them—he would entitle his 1987 book *Better a Shield than a Sword*.[6]

Soon after Reagan's inauguration, Teller and Lowell Wood, a midlevel Livermore scientist who had Teller's backing, went to Washington to brief congressional leaders on the X-ray laser and to lobby for funding. Immediately after their trip, an article appeared in *Aviation Week and Space Technology* (a trade publication commonly called "Aviation Leak"): "X-ray lasers based on the successful Dauphin test are so small that a single payload bay on the space shuttle could carry to orbit a number sufficient to stop a Soviet nuclear weapons attack."[7] The article described the X-ray laser as if it were an existing weapon rather than a one-off test rig that had been destroyed in a nuclear blast beneath the Nevada desert. Teller (or someone he had briefed) was almost certainly the source for this misinformation, and Teller would repeatedly make similar exaggerated claims. Officials in the Reagan administration, with limited understanding of nuclear technology, ate it up. Who could doubt the father of the hydrogen bomb?

Teller dominated the discussions within the High Frontier group. At the first formal meeting on September 14, 1981, the group talked about defending America's new MX missile by using space-based weapons. Teller saw that as only a starting point. High Frontier's goal, he said, should be to protect America's cities—"assured survival" rather than "assured destruction." That idea—defending America's cities with a shield based on the X-ray laser or any other technology—had no foundation. When challenged, Teller would say that it was impossible to lie about the future, meaning that any claim that did not violate the law of physics was permissible.[8] But the Soviet Union had more than ten thousand warheads mounted on twenty-four hundred missiles. For "assured survival," the anti-missile shield would need to be perfect. And even if the shield stopped every ballistic missile, it would do nothing to stop bombers or cruise missiles. Teller's goal was impossible on its face, but it was one he shared with President Reagan.

The High Frontier team comprised three factions. The first was led by retired Army Gen. Daniel Graham, who wanted to resurrect a 1950s proposal named "BAMBI" that the Kennedy administration had cancelled as unworkable. BAMBI envisioned hundreds of space-based stations, each containing several rockets that would track rising missiles using infrared sensors, speed after them, and unfurl sixty-foot rotating "spider webs" to snare them. Sen. Malcolm Wallop, a conservative Republican from Idaho, led the second High Frontier faction. He proposed launching twenty-four "battle stations" equipped with chemical lasers that would be powered by fuels similar to those used in rockets; Wallop claimed his entire system could be in place before the end of the 1980s. And the final faction was led by Teller, who pushed Excalibur.

Teller had personal scientific credibility, and he had the resources of Livermore and the support of Keyworth, Reagan's science adviser. Keyworth told Congress that Sen. Wallop's chemical lasers were too low in energy—1,444 battle stations would be required, he said, not the twenty-four Wallop claimed. And Teller outmaneuvered Gen. Graham at every turn. When Graham argued that X-ray lasers orbiting in space would be vulnerable to enemy attack, Teller and Wood responded at the next meeting with a new basing plan: the lasers would not orbit but would "pop up" when needed. When American satellites detected Russian missiles, Teller said, rockets would launch the Excalibur modules into space, where they would deploy, lock onto their targets, explode their hydrogen bombs, fire their laser beams, and thereby stop the Soviet attack cold—all in the three or four minutes before the enemy missiles finished their boost phase. Graham left the White House group in a huff and published an incoherent account of his ideas with a forward by science fiction writer Jerry Pournelle.[9]

After besting his High Frontier opponents, Teller persuaded Bendetsen that Excalibur was the solution. Bendetsen wrote Reagan's adviser Edwin

Meese an urgent letter, saying that that Livermore could deliver a fully wea-
ponized device in five years and that increased funding of the X-ray laser
was so important that it could not wait for his full report. Bendetsen gave
the president a two-page summary of his final report on January 8, 1982,
repeating what Teller and Wood had told him. Reagan wrote to thank Bendetsen and assured him that "we will be moving ahead rapidly."[10]

A new White House panel, chaired by physicist Edward Frieman, was
asked for an in-depth study. Frieman, who knew Teller's reputation, refused to put him on the panel. Teller repeatedly asked Keyworth to arrange
a private meeting with the president, repeating his promises that Excalibur
would be a weapon in five years. Keyworth, who was skeptical of Teller's
claims and aware of Reagan's impressionability, was trying to distance
himself from his mentor and stalled Teller's requests to meet with Reagan.
When Teller appeared on William Buckley's television program, *Firing Line*,
he complained that he had not met with the president since his inauguration, which was untrue. But his claim applied enough political pressure to
get him his presidential audience. As he shook Reagan's hand, Teller said,
"Mr. President, third generation, third generation," a greeting that confused
the president. *Aviation Week and Space Technology* claimed—with no cited
source—that Teller had asked for a $300 million increase in funding for
the next several years. Keyworth thought the meeting was a disaster. After
Teller asked Reagan for funding, Meese and national security adviser William Clark cut the meeting short. Always persistent, Teller sent the president a thank-you letter that summarized his claims, and he followed that
with a draft for a suggested presidential speech.[11]

Livermore scientists briefed the Frieman panel on Excalibur and refused
to back Teller's prediction that a weapon could be produced in anything
close to five years—their estimate was that, given a billion dollars in increased funding, scientific feasibility might be determined in six years. And
that would be only the first of seven phases in weapons development. If all
went well, and if the money tap were opened full bore, a weapon might appear in fifteen years. When Teller heard the details of the Livermore presentation, he was furious. He demanded—and got—a second presentation by
Livermore scientists to the panel, which was even less encouraging about

the X-ray laser than the first had been. It suggested that Excalibur would only be effective against missiles launched from sites close to the United States because of power and altitude limitations.

By the time the panel's report arrived at the White House, however, its conclusions no longer mattered. The president had made up his mind that defending America from nuclear attack would be his signal achievement.[12]

Teller and others had been busy lobbying while the panel had deliberated. Adm. James Watkins, the chief of naval operations, met with Teller on January 20, 1983, and Teller converted him to the Excalibur cause. National security adviser Robert McFarlane and presidential adviser John Poindexter encouraged Watkins to get the Joint Chiefs of Staff on board. Watkins briefed the Joint Chiefs before their meeting with the president on February 11, and they agreed to present a unified, positive front on missile defense—including the representative of the Air Force, the service that had historically preferred spending on offensive weapons. McFarlane and Watkins stage-managed the presidential show, with McFarlane breaking in on Watkins's presentation with, "Wait a minute. Are you saying that . . . we

▪ A Livermore Laboratory rendering of an Excalibur hydrogen bomb exploding and triggering three X-ray laser beams aimed at warheads. The device in the foreground is apparently labeled "CCCP." *Lawrence Livermore National Laboratory.*

might be able to develop an effective defense against ballistic missiles?" and Watkins responding, "Yes, that's exactly what I'm saying. . . . Would it not be better if we could . . . protect, rather than avenge our people?" Reagan later said that his meeting with the Joint Chiefs was a turning point in his commitment to missile defense.[13]

McFarlane claimed to be the one who convinced Reagan that the time was right to make a public announcement despite the technological risks and the cost. Success with the president required that McFarlane adapt to Reagan's way of thinking. Reagan was convinced, McFarlane later wrote, "that we were . . . heading toward Armageddon, the final battle between good and evil. 'I'm telling you, it's coming,' he would say. 'Go read your Scripture.'"[14]

President Reagan did not inform Secretary of State Shultz about his meeting with the Joint Chiefs until the following day. Shultz was taken aback. From what he knew, missile defense was difficult and perhaps impossible. After all, the United States had dismantled its limited Safeguard anti-missile site in North Dakota in 1974 because it had been determined to be ineffective. America's entire nuclear strategy was based on deterrence, not defense, and deterrence had worked for almost thirty-five years. And now, without consultation with America's allies, the president had a new strategy based on untested, undeveloped technology.

Reagan spoke to the nation on television on March 23, with Teller in the audience grinning and applauding. Reagan had not informed Shultz of his intended speech until two days earlier, when Shultz protested that the Joint Chiefs were not capable of judging the technical issues and that America's allies would see missile defense as a retreat to "Fortress America." Reagan called Keyworth in. According to Shultz, Keyworth gave only vague answers to his questions about the science. Shultz did manage to get important changes made to Reagan's speech—neither the X-ray laser nor other technologies were mentioned; nothing was said about deployment; the timeline was changed from a few years to the end of the century; the existing deterrent strategy would be maintained in the meantime; and America would continue to abide by the Anti-Ballistic Missile treaty with the Soviet Union. But Reagan refused to allow Shultz to give America's allies any advance notice of the speech.

Those allies, along with scientists, nuclear strategists, and the Soviets, all reacted negatively to Reagan's anti-missile shield, which was now named the Strategic Defense Initiative (SDI) and quickly dubbed "Star Wars" in the press. Britain's Margaret Thatcher saw SDI as an American retreat from its promised nuclear umbrella; most scientists thought SDI was a pipe dream; many nuclear strategists thought SDI would make nuclear war *more* likely, because it would give the Soviets an incentive to launch a first strike before America's shield made their missiles useless; and Soviet premier Yuri Andropov saw SDI as America's attempt to block Soviet retaliation after an American first strike.[15] But the American public responded positively.[16] The president wanted to eliminate nuclear war, after all.

A week later, Teller wrote a *New York Times* op-ed piece titled "Reagan's Courage" in which he made veiled references to the X-ray laser.[17] But the laser had a political problem—it was triggered by a nuclear bomb, and Reagan's stated ambition was to make nuclear weapons obsolete. Secretary of Defense Caspar "Cap" Weinberger seemed especially clueless, repeatedly asking an aide, "It's not a bomb, is it?" before he briefed Congress.[18] Teller appeared before the House Armed Services Committee in April 1983 and said the laser's nuclear explosions would be "relatively small." He took the opportunity to call the plans of Wallop and Graham, his High Frontier rivals, "outlandish," and he called for a massive increase in funding for the X-ray laser. On May 23, Reagan awarded Teller the National Medal of Science, America's highest scientific honor.

Despite Teller's political successes, the X-ray laser was faring poorly in technical and strategic evaluations. The underground "Cabra" test of the laser, two days after Reagan's SDI speech, showed no X-ray signals. Now that the SDI program was public, the president asked a former head of NASA, James Fletcher, to chair yet another panel, this one to assess different SDI approaches and recommend funding levels. The Fletcher panel asked an obvious question: how would the Soviets counter an X-ray laser? The answer was that it would not be very difficult to do so: the X-rays' energy would be dissipated in the earth's atmosphere, and the Soviets could program their missiles to end their burst phase and disperse their MIRVed warheads while still within the atmosphere, or they could depress their missiles' arcs so that they never left the atmosphere at all. Soviet fast-burn boosters could also speed the boost phase and end it before the X-ray lasers could "pop up." But the Fletcher panel still recommended allocating $1 billion to the X-ray laser out of a total of $26 billion in SDI funding. Even if the laser was useless as an anti-missile weapon, it could still be used to knock out Soviet satellites. That was an urgent problem—if the Soviets had their own X-ray lasers mounted on satellites, they could knock out all of America's space-based SDI weapons before they could be used. Rather than being the key to SDI, the X-ray laser might make SDI impossible. That part of the Fletcher report was classified and unavailable to the public. But the report's unclassified summary seemed disconnected from the rest of the report, and it endorsed the X-ray laser enthusiastically. The report's summary was not written by anyone on the panel, Fletcher said, but by "someone at the White House." The summary spurred articles that touted the potential of the X-ray laser in *Aviation Week and Space Technology*, *Scientific American*, and the *New York Times*.

The "Romano" test of the X-ray laser, an underground nuclear explosion that repeated the failed Cabra test, did detect X-rays and showed that longer-tubed lasers gave exponentially more brilliant bursts, just as theory would predict. Lowell Wood claimed that Romano showed that X-ray lasers would make anti-missile defense cheaper than offense—one hydrogen bomb could fire ten or a hundred lasers, each of which would destroy a missile that contained ten MIRVed warheads, so the Soviets could not win by just deploying more missiles. Teller reported the Romano results in an excited letter to Keyworth, claiming "quantitative" agreement with experiment—an exaggeration—and ignoring the criticisms in the Fletcher report. Teller wrote on Livermore letterhead, and he repeatedly used phrases such as "we have developed," implying that he spoke for the laboratory, though he did not copy his letter to any Livermore officials. Roy Woodruff, the Livermore associate director responsible for the laser program, eventually learned of Teller's letter. He confronted Teller, who conceded that he might have exaggerated but refused to write a correcting letter, saying it would ruin his reputation. Roger Batzel, the laboratory director, did not permit Woodruff to correct Teller's letter, saying everyone knew that Teller often overstated results.

Other scientists gave the Romano data a critical look. George Maenchen, a Livermore scientist, suspected that the Romano brilliance measurements were false results from the beryllium reflectors used to bounce the radiation to the sensors. Los Alamos scientists conducted their own "Correro" test and showed that Maenchen was right, and they concluded that Excalibur's X-ray beams might not have the intensity to do the job. Edward Walbridge, a scientist at Argonne National Laboratory, pointed out in *Nature* magazine that the laser beams would diffuse as they traveled, and that at 1,240 miles, the beams would be two hundred feet in diameter—too broad to do much damage. Excalibur was too dim and too unfocused to be the anti-missile death ray that Teller wanted it to be.

Teller and Wood responded with a Livermore plan for "Excalibur Plus," a focused X-ray laser a thousand times more powerful than Excalibur, and then with "Super Excalibur," a thousand times more powerful than Excalibur Plus. Super Excalibur's beam would have a trillion times the energy density of a hydrogen bomb, and it would be able to destroy Soviet missiles even when they were within the atmosphere. Teller ignored or glossed over concerns about the vulnerability of space-based weapons and about treaties banning weapons in space, and he abandoned the pop-up plan. Instead, Super Excalibur would ride in a stationary geosynchronous orbit, twenty-two thousand miles above the Soviet Union. Immediately after Reagan's 1984 reelection, Teller wrote key government officials to claim that a single Super Excalibur battle station, "the size of an executive desk," would be incredibly light and cheap. It might generate as many as a hundred thousand independently aimable beams, each of which could destroy a missile. Again, he wrote on Livermore stationery. This time, however, he copied Livermore's director, Batzel, but not Woodruff. Super Excalibur existed only on paper, but Batzel again refused to allow Woodruff to write a correcting letter.

Livermore's "Cottage" test on March 23, 1985, showed brightness increases in the laser—a *Scientific American* article announced an increase by a factor of a million—and Teller and Wood rushed to Washington to brief Gen. James Abrahamson, whom Reagan had appointed SDI director, and William Casey, the CIA director. Reagan personally promised Teller an additional $100 million in funding.

But then Super Excalibur began to crumble. Scientists at Livermore's rival laboratory, Los Alamos, took a close look at the Cottage results and applied Maenchen's analysis. The beryllium reflectors, they said, were contaminated with oxygen and were emitting a false glow when struck by X-rays. The December 28 "Goldstone" test used hydrogen gas rather than beryllium reflectors, and it proved to be the swan song for the X-ray laser, which showed only about 10 percent of the predicted brightness. That made focusing even more important, but the April 1987 "Delamar" test showed that the laser's beam had not narrowed. Super Excalibur was a bust, although Teller kept selling it, saying that only the government's secrecy laws kept him from telling the world how well it worked.

Woodruff, fed up by Teller's and Wood's undermining and by lack of support from his boss, had resigned as the laboratory's associate director. Teller blamed him for Excalibur's failure. Woodruff had not, Teller said, been "a constructive member of the team." Worse, from Teller's point of view, Woodruff had exposed Teller's exaggerations and damaged Livermore's reputation by his resignation. On a *60 Minutes* segment, Teller became so upset that he ripped off his headset and stormed off the set when he was questioned about Woodruff.[19]

Robert Gates, who would later serve as CIA director and secretary of defense, was then deputy director of the CIA. "Amid the countless skeptics that such a defensive umbrella could ever be built," he later wrote, "there were two small groups of people who believed it probably could. The first was Ronald Reagan and a small group of his advisers. The second was the Soviet leadership."[20] After a long period of nuclear inferiority, the Soviets had in the 1970s caught up to a position of superiority in land-based missiles, although not in submarine-based missiles or stealth bomber technology. The USSR's economy was struggling, and a new arms race was something the Soviet Union could not afford. SDI threatened the USSR's hard-won nuclear parity, and it seemed impossible to the Soviets that the United States would spend so much money on something that could not work. Yuri Andropov and Konstantin Chernenko, Soviet leaders during the early days of SDI, were followed by Mikhail

Gorbachev in 1985. Reagan and Gorbachev were scheduled to meet for the first time in Reykjavik in October 1986, and SDI was at the top of the Soviet agenda.

Teller and others wrote Reagan a letter pleading with the president not to use SDI as a bargaining chip in arms reduction talks, which was Secretary of State Shultz's plan. They need not have worried. Even when Gorbachev offered complete, mutual elimination of nuclear weapons if the United States would keep SDI work "to the laboratories," Reagan refused to budge. SDI was not on the table. Reagan and Gorbachev met a year later, in Washington, and Teller said that when the president introduced him to Gorbachev in a reception receiving line, Gorbachev refused to shake his hand. When the president said, "This is the famous Dr. Teller," Gorbachev supposedly replied, "There are many Dr. Tellers." There is no independent confirmation for this story, and given Teller's history with the truth and a photo of him and Gorbachev at the reception engaged in what seems to be friendly conversation, Teller may have invented the snub.

Andrei Sakharov, Teller's counterpart as the father of the Soviet hydrogen bomb, apparently convinced Gorbachev to decouple arms control negotiations from SDI. He called SDI a "Maginot line"—even if SDI were deployed, it would be easy to evade. Sakharov addressed an American gathering in honor of Teller in 1988, where he warned that SDI devices in space would be objects of attack during an international crisis, and that their presence alone could itself lead to nuclear war. While he did not say so explicitly, Sakharov worried that even an unworkable SDI might tempt both sides to launch a first strike—what was important was who *believed* it would work. If the Soviets believed in America's SDI, they would be tempted to strike first, before its deployment made their missiles useless; if the Americans believed in their own SDI, they would be tempted to strike first and use SDI to mop up whatever the Soviets could launch in a retaliatory attack. If SDI was an American bluff, it was a very risky bluff that put the world at risk.[21] And while some have claimed that the threat of SDI bankrupted the Soviet Union, the USSR never wasted close to what the United States did on an anti-missile effort.[22]

Excalibur collapsed, but Teller and Wood did not leave the stage. While their exaggerations may have made their names mud among scientists, they were still stars at the White House, and they immediately began promoting another Livermore project, "Brilliant Pebbles," without missing a beat. Thousands of small rockets—the Pebbles, each weighing about five pounds—would orbit Earth in swarms, waiting to fire their engines and smash into enemy missiles when called upon to do so. Unlike Excalibur, no nuclear weapon would be involved—in fact, no explosives at all. The Pebbles would be like bullets, destroying missiles through the kinetic force of the collision. Teller and Wood briefed SDI director Abrahamson on Brilliant Pebbles in October 1987, and then briefed President Reagan and his top aides in March 1988. They brought a Pebble model with them that they draped in black velvet when news photographers were allowed into the briefing room. According to Teller, the program would be cheap—$10 billion to both build and deploy a hundred thousand Pebbles. Then the engineers took a look. By 1989, the Pebbles had grown to a hundred pounds, their number had dropped to forty-six hundred, and the system cost had ballooned to $55 billion. Critics noted that Pebbles would operate in outer space, and the Soviets could easily send their missiles through the high atmosphere, or could release their MIRVed warheads and decoys while still in the atmosphere—the same objections they had made against Excalibur. Teller did what he had done against those earlier objections: he ignored them. Brilliant Pebbles was in many ways similar to Gen. Graham's revival of BAMBI, which Teller had called "outlandish" and had criticized as vulnerable to attack. The president loved it, and Brilliant Pebbles became the new centerpiece of SDI.

Just before Reagan left office, he awarded Teller the Presidential Citizens Medal. When Teller was asked which president had the best grasp of science, he quickly answered, "No competition—Ronald Reagan," whose strength, Teller said, was his ability to listen. "The people who would not listen were Ford, Kennedy, Eisenhower, and above all, Jimmy Carter."[23]

In 1989, Reagan passed SDI on to his heirs, who, one after another, have had to deal with the legacy. Reagan had promised protection from nuclear threat and spent a fortune on a system that was still in the R&D stage. Even

■ Edward Teller receiving the Presidential Citizens Medal in 1989. *Lawrence Livermore National Laboratory.*

though SDI was impossible and enormously expensive, no president could just say "Never mind" and walk away. Immediately after his 1988 inauguration, George H. Bush announced that he would "vigorously pursue" SDI, but he retreated when he had the opportunity: When he gave his State of the Union speech in January 1991, the nation's attention was focused on the Gulf War, the Soviet Union was collapsing, and he was at the peak of his personal popularity. He announced that SDI would be changed to "Global Protection Against Limited Strikes" (GPALS), which would use Brilliant Pebbles technology to protect America's missiles but not its cities. The number of Pebbles, which had started at 100,000 and then been reduced to 4,600, was cut to between 750 and 1,000.

Bush had other priorities, in part because of the Gulf War. Patriot, an anti-missile system designed to protect against short-range tactical missiles, saw its first service in 1991 against primitive Iraqi Scud missiles. Initially, the Army claimed an 80 percent success rate in Iraq, and Bush, when he visited the Raytheon plant that manufactured the Patriot, upped that to 97 percent when he declared, "Patriot is 41 for 42: 42 Scuds engaged, 41 intercepted." Later analysis showed the success rate to have been much lower, perhaps 10 percent.[24] The Patriot was developed outside of the SDI program, and some argued that the money spent on SDI's impossible dream would have been more productively spent on theater missile defenses (TMDs) such as Patriot.[25]

Immediately after his election, Bill Clinton announced that he rejected the idea of a space-based system but that he would fund TMDs such as the Patriot—missiles that would protect troops from shorter-range missiles and that would not violate the ABM treaty. On May 13, 1993, he renamed the SDI office, calling it the Ballistic Missile Defense Office (BMDO) and slashing its funding. That marked the end of Brilliant Pebbles, which like Excalibur was never deployed. The Republicans objected and made reinstating SDI a cornerstone of their 1994 "Contract with America." Perhaps due to political pressure, Clinton's 1998 defense budget requested $6.6 billion for the years 2000–2005 to support deployment of national missile defense against "rogue nations" such as North Korea.[26]

When George W. Bush won the presidency in 2000, he again made missile defense a priority. Donald Rumsfeld, Bush's secretary of defense, was a believer, as were Paul Wolfowitz and Richard Perle; Rumsfeld had headed the 1998 congressional Commission to Assess the Ballistic Missile Threat to the United States. Not surprisingly, his panel had identified a grave and underestimated threat. In June 2001, Bush submitted an $8.3 billion request for missile defenses.

The attack on America came three months later, not by missiles but by hijacked airplanes, and not by a rogue state, but by the stateless Al Qaeda. Gen. Eugene Habiger, the retired commander of the Strategic Air Command, called the effort to defend against nuclear missiles misdirected. "There's a great leap of faith," he said, "between being able to build a missile and being able to put a warhead on that missile that can survive the temperature extremes, the G-loading, the fusing requirements, [and] the vibration." He said that if he were advising Saddam Hussein or the leader of North Korea on how best to attack the United States, a missile would be the last thing he would recommend, because the Strategic Air Command would know exactly where it came from. He worried about other delivery systems than missiles: "There are tens of thousands of Conex containers—those metal containers that come into the United States on cargo ships every day, tens of thousands—all you have to do is build a nuclear device, and when that Conex container gets into lower Manhattan, you set it off. I'm not concerned about an incoming ICBM. I'm more concerned about . . . a nuclear device that you put in a trunk, a travel trunk. That's what caused me to lay awake at night, not any incoming missile."[27]

Nonetheless, the Bush administration continued to push missile defense after the 9/11 attacks. Clinton's BMDO was renamed the Missile Defense Agency (MDA), and the United States announced in December 2001 that it would unilaterally withdraw from the ABM treaty. The Bush administration partially deployed its anti-missile system, called Ground-Based Midcourse Defense (GMD), with thirty interceptor bases in California and Alaska. Reagan had promised that SDI would protect America's cities from thousands of Soviet missiles; even if GMD worked perfectly (and it has only been about 50 percent effective against drones in tests), it could stop no more than thirty.

After Barack Obama took office in 2009, his administration announced a shift toward a system placed in Europe to defend against shorter-range Iranian missiles, a plan closer to Clinton's approach. But in March 2013, the administration announced plans to add fourteen missiles to the Alaska site to defend against North Korean threats.[28] A 2012 report by the National Research Council recommended adding another base in Maine or upstate New York to GMD. The report said nothing about whether improving port security, as Gen. Habiger suggested, might be a better way to use the $10 billion spent on missile defense each year. As always, the report brought out critics on all sides.[29] Missile defense in America has less to do with technology or strategy than with politics. Each administration starts anew.

15

Smart Bombs and Drones

In the last years of the twentieth century, two weapons changed the way that America fights air wars: smart bombs (bombs that "see" a target using a television camera or a radiation sensor, or that head for a programmed location) and UAVs (unmanned aerial vehicles). Smart bombs came into their own in the first Gulf War. Reconnaissance UAVs proved their worth in Bosnia and Kosovo in the late 1990s, and offensive UAVs began firing missiles in Iraq, Afghanistan, Pakistan, and elsewhere a few years later.

The American public got its first look at smart bombs on January 17, 1991. Iraq had invaded Kuwait five months earlier, and President George H. Bush had put together a UN-backed coalition to force its withdrawal. Iraq had the world's fourth-largest army, at 955,000 men, and it faced a coalition force only two-thirds that size. America's last experience of a real war had been the long disaster of Vietnam—nineteen years from start to finish, 58,000 American dead, and 153,000 wounded—and even experienced military officers feared that the Gulf War might be a reprise of Vietnam.

Gen. Edward Meyer, a former Army chief of staff, predicted that America would suffer ten thousand to thirty thousand casualties in driving Iraq out of Kuwait.[1] Saddam Hussein was counting on exactly that and reportedly told U.S. ambassador April Glaspie, "Americans cannot stand 10,000 dead."[2]

Americans watched the war in their living rooms. Tomahawk cruise missiles flew by journalists' Baghdad hotel windows and blew up government buildings. One after another, American fighter planes "plinked" Iraqi tanks with Maverick missiles, and CNN replayed the video clips: the pilot locked the missile's sensor onto the tank's image, pushed a button, and the missile did the rest. By the time the coalition's ground attack began in mid-February, the Iraqi army had already been seriously degraded. One Iraqi general said, "During the Iran war, my tank was my friend because I could sleep in it and know I was safe. . . . During this war my tank became my enemy. . . . [N]one of my troops would get near a tank at night because they just kept blowing up."[3] Although only 8 percent of the bombs dropped were smart bombs, they did 75 percent of the damage.[4]

Gen. Meyer and Saddam Hussein vastly overestimated U.S. casualties— only 346 Americans died in the Gulf War, and less than half of those in combat. On a statistical basis, American soldiers in the war zone were safer than had they stayed at home in civilian life.[5] Iraqi casualties, both military and civilian, were much higher, but even they were low by the standards of Vietnam—four thousand Iraqi civilians and thirty-five thousand soldiers dead, while about one million Vietnamese civilians and two million soldiers had died. Smart bombs made that reduction possible. One Iraqi battalion commander reported that only one of his soldiers was killed in the air war, but that all his vehicles were hit.[6] The Gulf War coalition destroyed Iraq's military capabilities, but it left Baghdad standing—unlike Tokyo, Hiroshima, Nagasaki, Dresden, Hamburg, or Berlin in World War II. The Air Force was finally able to deliver what it had promised in the 1930s: striking military targets while avoiding homes, schools, and hospitals. Where the Norden bombsight had failed, smart bombs succeeded.

The Gulf War taught America that future wars should be nearly bloodless, at least for its own soldiers. (On average from September 11, 2001, through 2012, about 540 Americans died each year in Iraq and Afghanistan. More died on average *every two days* in World War II, and that from an America with less than half the 2012 population.) And world opinion would no longer tolerate the widespread civilian casualties of Korea or Vietnam. On February 13, two fighter-bombers used laser-guided smart bombs to attack Baghdad's Amiriyah shelter, which had been mistaken for a military command center. A bomb went down the shelter's airshaft and killed 408 civilians, provoking outrage in the Arab world and protests in Europe and America.

Engineers have been tinkering with UAVs since the early days of aviation. In World War I, the Naval Consulting Board, chaired by Thomas Edison, funded a gyroscopic autopilot for an anti-ship "aerial torpedo" to be developed by Elmer Sperry and Peter Hewitt. The torpedo was designed to fly a preset magnetic course at a fixed altitude, wait until an engine revolution counter determined that it had achieved the desired range, and then dive onto an enemy ship that was had been calculated to be below. In flight tests, an autopilot-controlled seaplane flew a thirty-mile course and automatically dropped a bag of sand that missed the target by two miles, which was not bad for 1917. The Navy placed an order for six aerial torpedoes— stripped-down airplanes without seats or pilot controls that could carry a payload of a thousand pounds of explosive. The torpedo's initial flight tests were unsuccessful, and the war ended before it saw service. Sperry also contributed an autopilot to the Army for a UAV, the "Kettering Bug," named after its designer, Charles Kettering. The Bug could carry two hundred

■ The World War I UAVs—the Curtiss-Sperry aerial torpedo and the Kettering Bug.

pounds of explosives seventy-five miles. After a successful flight test, the Army ordered a hundred planes. Like the Navy's aerial torpedo, the Bug did not see combat.

Neither the Navy's aerial torpedo nor the Army's Bug had any external guidance, and both services saw the need for radio control if UAVs were to hit a specific target such as a ship or an artillery emplacement. The Navy lost interest in radio-controlled planes in the mid-1920s, while the Air Corps persisted into the 1930s, when it abandoned investment in UAVs in favor of the Norden bombsight and the B-17 heavy bomber.[7]

Germany's World War II V-1 "buzz bomb," like America's World War I aerial torpedo, was an unguided UAV flying on autopilot. Its mission was to hit any populated area in southern England, which did not require intelligence. The most successful smart bomb of World War II was the Japanese Kamikaze plane. Its guidance system was a human pilot, but it proved what a guided bomb could do. Kamikaze attacks sank 34 U.S. ships, damaged 384 others, and killed 4,900 sailors. Fourteen percent of the Kamikazes survived intense anti-aircraft fire and fighter defenses to strike a ship, and they sank 8.5 percent of those they struck.[8]

"Operation Aphrodite" was a plan to turn worn-out B-17 and B-24 heavy bombers into smart bombs: strip out all guns, armor, seats, and other unnecessary gear; stuff the bomber with thirty thousand pounds of high explosive; put a television camera in the nose; and fly it by radio from a mother ship, which would direct the plane to its target. Twenty were launched, and all failed—shot down, crashed because of control problems, or exploded prematurely. Lieutenant Joseph P. Kennedy, John Kennedy's older brother, died in an Aphrodite explosion on August 12, 1944. The Allied generals abandoned Aphrodite as unworkable in late January 1945.

Throughout its history, the Air Force has shown more interest in new aircraft than in new munitions. The Korean air war was mostly fought with World War II weaponry, with the exception of new jet fighters.[9] After Korea, the Eisenhower administration's New Look military strategy emphasized nuclear weapons. The Air Force entered the Vietnam era with an array of nuclear missiles, a fleet of B-52 strategic bombers designed to carry four nuclear bombs each, fighter-bombers designed for high-speed, low-level nuclear attack, conventional "iron" bombs that were little advanced from those it had possessed in 1945, and only two smart bombs, both developed by the Navy.

Aware that it needed better weapons, the Air Force enlisted Texas Instruments and the Army's Redstone Arsenal to develop what would become the Paveway laser-guided smart bomb: one plane would shine a pulsed, invisible, infrared laser beam on a target, and another plane, flying at approximately twelve thousand feet, would drop a bomb anywhere in a one-thousand-foot-diameter imaginary "basket" around the target, which was reflecting infrared radiation from the first plane's laser beam. The bomb would look for radiation at the right infrared frequency that had a beat that synchronized with the laser's pulsing. When it found that combination, it would lock on, head for the target, and destroy it. Texas Instruments had not yet designed a defense system, so it faced credibility problems in a competition against a rival system proposed by a more experienced North American Aviation subsidiary. The responsible Air Force officer bypassed the normal contracting process and convened a "generals board" that included recently retired Air Force chief of staff Curtis LeMay. The Air Force approved Paveway and sent units to Vietnam for combat testing in 1968—just as President Johnson announced a halt to bombing of North Vietnam.

From 1965 to 1968, as we have seen, the United States had rained bombs on North Vietnam in Operation Rolling Thunder. The Thanh Hoa Bridge across the Song Me River, for example, was the target of eight hundred American sorties that dumped ten thousand pounds of explosives. The bombs had scarred the bridge, but the anti-aircraft guns and surface-to-air (SAM) missiles that surrounded it shot down 104 American pilots, and the bridge remained standing. The Long Bien Bridge across the Red River in Hanoi was another apparently impregnable target—three hundred anti-aircraft guns and eighty-five SAM sites kept twenty-six supply trains crossing the bridge every day from China and the port of Haiphong. In 1972, when Nixon renewed bombing of North Vietnam with the Linebacker campaign, smart bombs took out both bridges in a matter of days.[10]

Political success did not follow military success. As a bombing exercise, Linebacker was enormously successful, but the United States lost the war. Linebacker did convince the Air Force to continue to invest in improved short-range smart bombs such as Paveway. These were launched from warplanes in combat, and they fit solidly into the Air Force's precision bombing doctrine. Long-range cruise missiles, developed in the 1970s and introduced in the early 1980s, were another story. These jet-propelled, subsonic unmanned airplanes are descendants of the German V-1 buzz bomb. They fly at low altitude to evade enemy radar, are self-guided to fly a programmed route, have a range of about fifteen hundred miles, and can carry either a nuclear or conventional warhead of up to two thousand pounds. They are smart bombs, but they make the pilot less important. They do not need a sophisticated bomber—subsonic B-52s, submarines, or surface ships could launch them from a distance. In 1977, President Jimmy Carter cancelled the Air Force's prized supersonic B-1A bomber when cruise missiles became available. A French general said in an interview, "The B-1 is a formidable weapon, but not terribly useful. For the price of one bomber, you can have 200 cruise missiles." Air Force officers groused that the United States might as well subcontract the next war to Pan Am.[11] But at a cost of more than $1 million each, cruise missiles are not weapons for routine use. Their advantage is that they can be launched from afar, but they cost significantly more than short-range smart bombs, carry a smaller payload, and are somewhat less accurate, so the Air Force's pilots and warplanes kept a role in aerial combat.

Immediately after the Gulf War, the Air Force and Navy began development of the Joint Direct Attack Munition (JDAM) guidance kit, which could be bolted onto conventional bombs. JDAM bombs are ideal for fixed targets such as airfields, oil refineries, or power plants. GPS navigation systems are susceptible to jamming, so JDAM couples GPS guidance with an inertial guidance system that determines the bomb's position by measuring its acceleration, similar to the guidance systems used in ICBMs. JDAM is inexpensive (about $20,000 per kit) and, unlike laser- or television-guided smart bombs, does not require target visibility—feed it the coordinates of the target, and cloud cover and dust are no impediment.[12]

Smart bombs became standard munitions. In the 1995 NATO bombing campaign in Bosnia, 98 percent of the bombs dropped were smart. In the 1999 bombing in the Kosovo operation, precision bombing finally won a war without the need for a land invasion: Serbian premier Slobodan Milosevic gave up when he lost popular support after NATO hit Belgrade government buildings, the telephone system, and the Yugoslav power grid.[13] "Precision" did not mean that the operation was bloodless or free from blunders, however. NATO hit an Albanian refugee column that it mistook for a Serbian convoy, and a JDAM bomb destroyed the Chinese embassy in Belgrade when someone entered the wrong GPS coordinates.

In the 1970s, the Pentagon assigned the Army the job of developing a battlefield reconnaissance drone code-named "Aquila." The drone's specifications kept growing: night vision, laser designation for smart bomb attacks, a secure data link, armor. Only a few expensive prototypes were built, and the program was canceled in 1987. But when Israelis drones proved their worth in scouting Syrian radar sites in the Bekaa Valley in 1982, the Navy took note and acquired the Pioneer drone from an Israeli defense firm. The Pioneer was a simple reconnaissance drone, much like the original specification for the Aquila. The Navy used it successfully as a spotter for its battleships' sixteen-inch guns in 1991 in the Gulf War.[14]

The Air Force was less interested in UAVs than was the Navy, and it invested in them later than it did in smart bombs. It was the CIA, congressional Republicans, an Israeli engineer, and a small San Diego defense firm—not the Air Force—that would make the UAV an important American weapon.

Abraham Karem, an Israeli designer of drone aircraft, moved to the United States in the 1970s but was unable to find a job with a defense firm. So he started his own company, Leading Systems, and worked above his garage. He received seed money from the Pentagon to develop an unmanned drone aircraft. His UAV exceeded its contract's specifications, flying 650 hours without a crash, but the contract for further development went to another Israeli defense firm, and Leading Systems went broke.

Two brothers, Neal and Linden Blue, owned a cocoa and banana plantation in Nicaragua in the 1970s. They became friendly with the Nicaraguan dictator Anastasio Somoza, who was opposed in a guerilla war by the Sandinista Liberation Front, and the Blues saw UAVs as a way to attack the Sandinistas' gasoline storage tanks. They bought a small defense contractor, General Atomics, from Chevron in 1986. General

Atomics purchased Leading Systems' assets in bankruptcy and kept Karem working on an improved version of his drone, the GNAT-750, which made its first flight in 1989. The CIA and the Turkish government bought multiple GNAT-750s.

The Blues were looking to the long term: they believed that once the Air Force saw that it was in danger of losing control of a growing segment of military aviation, it would bend to the inevitable, just as it had in the 1950s when it took up missiles despite seeing them as a threat to its prized bomber fleet.[15] And rather than just wait for the Air Force to come to its senses, the Blues pushed. General Atomics spent more on political contributions as a percentage of sales than did any other defense contractor. Its specialty was offering junkets to key congressional staffers (a practice that is now illegal). Its congressional supporters included conservative Southern Californian Republican representatives Jerry Lewis and Randy "Duke" Cunningham. In 2005, Cunningham pled guilty to federal charges relating to bribery (not by General Atomics), and Lewis's reputation was sullied by charges of favoritism toward General Atomics and other contractors.[16] Lewis was not indicted, but

■ Neal Blue, CEO of General Atomics, with a Predator. *Photo by Gregg Segal.*

when the Republicans regained control of Congress in 2010, his party did not offer him his old post as chairman of the House Appropriations Committee.

General Atomics developed the Predator as the GNAT-750's successor, and it first saw service in Bosnia in 1995. Predators were at that time reconnaissance-only airplanes, roughly the size of a small Cessna. They were underpowered (Rotax, the company that manufactured the engine, was best known for snowmobiles), were not equipped with radar to see through clouds, had no de-icing equipment, and were difficult to land. Lewis had forced the Predator on the Air Force in 1994 with an earmark. "If it had not been for an earmark, the Predator would not have been in Bosnia," Lewis told Fox News in 2006. "And that mission served our country very, very well. A classic illustration of earmarks at their best."[17] General Atomics' political strategy worked—Congress forced the Air Force to invest in drones. In 2000, Republican senator John Warner laid out his goal for the Pentagon: one-third of its purchased aircraft should be unmanned by 2010. The Congressional Unmanned Systems Caucus remains a potent political force as of this writing, with sixty representatives who are members.[18]

There was some resistance. Most Air Force generals come from the ranks of fighter pilots, and as Hap Arnold pointed out in 1944, drone aircraft threaten to make fighter pilots obsolete. When the Air Force did reluctantly take up UAVs, it hired a civilian contractor to control them. Only when it found that its contractor was hiring retired Navy pilots did it assign its own pilots to unmanned aircraft, and even then it paid them less than "real" pilots and gave them no career advancement credit for flight hours.[19] By September 2001, nineteen of the sixty-eight Predators that had been delivered to the Air Force had been lost, many due to operator error.[20] The Air Force viewed them as toys. General Atomics fixed the Predator's performance problems—bigger turboprop engine, de-icing equipment, higher ceiling, greater payload. But it still had customer problems with the Air Force.

Gen. John Jumper was named Air Force chief of staff the week before the 9/11 attack on the World Trade Center. He had commanded U.S. and Allied air forces in the Bosnia and Kosovo campaigns. Unlike many in the Air Force, Jumper saw the potential of UAVs, though their limitations frustrated him. A Predator operator could spot an enemy tank, for example, but that was it. The operator would then have to send the location of the tank to a bombing coordinator, who would send two planes—a designator plane to "paint" the tank with a laser beam, and a second plane to destroy it with a smart bomb. During that delay, the tank might have fired on American troops or left the area entirely. Jumper's solution was to add a "laser ball" to his Predators so that an operator could designate a target, keep the laser beam on it even if it moved, and then call in a plane for a laser-bomb strike. But for "fleeting, perishable targets that don't require a big warhead and that we can just go ahead and take care of," Jumper saw even that as an unnecessary delay. He armed the Predator with its own laser-guided missiles—a pair of hundred-pound Hellfire anti-armor missiles. That solution married a UAV to a smart bomb; Predators could fly for hours, their operators sitting in cubicles in trailers near Las Vegas, taking breaks so that their attention did not flag, going home to their families as they handed the planes—still in flight—over to the next shift. When a target appeared, an operator could designate it with his laser ball and destroy it with his Hellfire.*[21]

The post-9/11 war in Afghanistan showed what an armed Predator could do—kill Al Qaeda leaders. Smart bombs can hit a target, but a Predator armed with a smart bomb can often identify what is *inside* the target. It can hover above a building for hours, watching people entering and leaving, and it can follow an automobile down a highway. Commanders could make fine distinctions about acceptable "collateral damage" to civilians—should a car carrying an Al Qaeda leader and an unknown companion be destroyed? What about a leader and his wife? What about a leader and his three children? In the past, bombs had been made bigger to compensate for their inaccuracy, but smart bombs reversed that trend. Their precision meant

---

* The Air Force leaders who followed Jumper may not have shared his enthusiasm for UAVs. Shortly after Jumper retired as chief of staff in 2005, the Air Force canceled its X-45 unmanned fighter development program. Some observers thought that the Air Force worried that the X-45 was a threat to its F-35 and F-22 fighters' development, which were late and over budget. David Hambling, "Who Killed the Killer Drone—and Why?" Defense Tech, May 8, 2006, http://defensetech.org/2006/05/08/who-killed-the-killer-drone-and-why; P. W. Singer, *Wired for War* (New York: Penguin Press, 2009), 253–254.

that bombs could be made *smaller*, just big enough to destroy a targeted house but leave the neighbor's house standing.

As of this writing, the drone's operator, not a computer, decides when an American weapon will be fired. The operator examines the video feed and determines whether an attack is authorized under his orders. (Although visual confirmation is no guarantee, as leaked 2007 footage of a mistaken and deadly helicopter attack on civilians in Iraq shows.)[22] But computers will become more involved, and the idea that humans can effectively oversee computers is illusory: in 1988, the guided-missile cruiser USS *Vincennes* shot down Iran Air Flight 66, killing all 290 on board. The airliner was ascending, was flying its scheduled route, and had its civilian transponder operating, but the *Vincennes's* Aegis computer system mistook the Airbus A300 for an Iranian F-14 fighter-bomber. Pressed for time, and believing the *Vincennes* was under attack, the crew accepted the computer's "advice" and fired two missiles at the plane, destroying it.[23]

As image-recognition and artificial intelligence software improve, computers will demonstrate an improved ability to distinguish tanks from taxis and terrorists' vans from school buses. Operators will learn to trust the computers, and when the computer says to fire, operators will obey. As UAVs proliferate, American drones will face enemy drones on the battlefield, and delays to call a human operator will be seen as intolerable. Computers will be given authority to fire, just as computers have been given the authority to risk billions of dollars in flash trading against other computers despite the occasional disastrous loss.

Allowing computers to make life-and-death decisions may be inevitable, but it is frightening. In his 1953 short story "Second Variety," science fiction author Philip K. Dick imagined a war in which autonomous American killer robots could distinguish and kill enemy soldiers. Then the military took the next step—giving the computerized factories that produced the killer robots autonomy to design improved models. Dick's story does not end well for the human race.[24]

UAVs and smart bombs are not yet an incarnation of Dick's nightmare scenario, and they have transformed America's arsenal. Older weapons were unusable: chemical weapons were simultaneously horrifying and militarily ineffective, and nuclear bombs are disproportionate—like arming bank guards with dynamite.[25] Combinations of smart bombs with UAVs, however, have shown themselves to be both usable and adaptable.

When to use them is another question. After Vietnam, the United States embraced what came to be known as the "Weinberger-Powell doctrine," named after Reagan's secretary of defense, Caspar Weinberger, and Joint Chiefs of Staff chairman Colin Powell. According to the doctrine, before the United States would initiate military action, national security must be threatened; all political, economic, and military means must be exhausted; a clear objective and a plausible exit strategy must exist; and the action must have broad public and international support. The 1991 Gulf War fit the Weinberger-Powell doctrine, but later interventions in Somalia, Bosnia, and Kosovo arguably did not. In the run-up to Bosnia, Secretary of State Madeleine Albright asked Powell, "What's the point of having this superb military that you're always talking about if we can't use it?"[26]

After 9/11, with the availability of smart bombs and UAVs, the Weinberger-Powell doctrine is effectively obsolete. Military force is often the first choice for the United States, supplanting diplomacy or other efforts. America is supposedly not at war in Yemen or Pakistan or Somalia, but Air Force drones strike there regularly. Because there is no risk to the pilots, there is little public scrutiny. And the CIA operates its own drones, with no public scrutiny at all. Legal and ethical questions remain unanswered: Should a Predator attack on a known terrorist in his car be considered an act of war or an assassination? What about terrorists who are American citizens? Who decides on legitimate targets?

At present, the United States has a technological lead in both smart bombs and UAVs. Historically, however, no nation has been able to maintain a weapons monopoly indefinitely—the American monopoly of the atomic bomb lasted only four years, and its monopoly of the hydrogen bomb less than that. Once other nations begin to use drones routinely, America may have to rethink its position on cross-border anti-terrorist attacks. What, for example, would the United States say about Russian UAV attacks on Chechen rebels in the mountains of neighboring Georgia, or a drone attack that the Chinese considered launching against a drug lord in Burma?[27]

China has offered its drones for sale at an air show, and other countries have doubtless produced them as well.[28] Export controls are unlikely to be effective in controlling proliferation. The United States sells UAVs and smart bombs to its allies, and the weapons are lost on the battlefield. Reverse-engineering the hardware of captured weapons would be relatively simple, although re-creating the firmware, which is certainly encrypted, would be more difficult. (The Iranians, however, claim they decrypted the video of a crashed American drone.)[29] But America's enemies have competent programmers and hackers, and digital espionage requires nothing more than access to the right computer.

Iran and North Korea waste their time trying to make seventy-year-old nuclear weapons and fifty-year old ICBMs. They are repeating Saddam Hussein's mistake—developing weapons that oppose the United States symmetrically. Tanks and airplanes failed Hussein, but Iraqi insurgents have used suicide bombers and IEDs, decidedly asymmetric weapons, far more effectively against coalition forces in both Iraq and Afghanistan. A better R&D strategy for America's enemies would be to develop robotic IEDs that combine off-the-shelf technologies—an explosive-stuffed model airplane guided by GPS, for example, or an IED built using a radio-controlled car with a video camera in its nose. The next arms race has only just begun.

Epilogue

This book has left many of its protagonists dangling midcareer. Some later developments:

Thomas Edison remained active after World War I, although his productivity naturally declined with age. He spent time in Florida with his friend Henry Ford, a man even more cantankerous and eccentric than Edison. When Edison died of diabetes in 1931, Ford encouraged Edison's son Charles to preserve his last breath in a test tube, which the Henry Ford Museum displayed for years.

Josephus Daniels left government service at the end of the Wilson administration in 1921 and resumed editing the *Raleigh News and Observer*. He remained a force in North Carolina's Democratic politics and supported his former subordinate, Franklin Roosevelt, for president in 1932. Roosevelt appointed Daniels as ambassador to Mexico, apparently forgetting that Daniels had been secretary of the Navy in 1914, when the Navy had occupied the Mexican port of Veracruz. The occupation killed (among many others) six teenage cadets at the military academy, whom Mexico commemorates in a national holiday every February 13. Daniels nonetheless served as ambassador until 1941, when he returned to North Carolina to edit his newspaper and to write a multivolume autobiography. When Roosevelt died in 1945, Daniels rode on his funeral train from Raleigh to his burial in Hyde Park. Daniels's autobiography, his biography of Wilson, his cabinet diaries of the Wilson administration, and his books on the Navy are important eyewitness accounts of fifty years of North Carolina and national politics.

Toward the end of his life, Daniels said that he regretted the viciousness of the 1898 white supremacy insurrection in Wilmington, although he continued to insist on its necessity. He died in 1948.

Billy Mitchell resigned from the Air Corps after his 1926 court-martial. While he continued to promote his airpower theories, he had lost his platform. He died in 1936, but he remained a hero to the Army Air Force, which in 1941 named the B-25 medium bomber the "Mitchell." Gary Cooper played Mitchell in the (historically inaccurate) 1955 film *The Court-Martial of Billy Mitchell.*

Carl Norden returned to Switzerland, where he died in 1965.

Curtis LeMay retired from the Air Force in 1965, after serving four years as Air Force chief of staff. He despised President Johnson and Secretary of Defense McNamara, both of whom he saw as deceptive and unwilling to face up to what was required to win the Vietnam War. In 1968, he agreed to be the vice presidential running mate of George Wallace, who was running a third-party campaign on a "law and order" platform that was a thinly disguised appeal to racism. LeMay was not a racist—he had pushed for integration of the Air Force before Truman's 1948 decision to integrate the military—but he hoped to win enough votes for Wallace to defeat the Democratic candidate, Hubert Humphrey, who he thought would continue Johnson's policies in Vietnam. Wallace's Air Force friends Carl Spaatz and Ira Eaker begged him not to run. His daughter Janie said of him, "He was the worst person possible to go into politics."

She was right. When Wallace introduced LeMay as his running mate at a press conference, LeMay did not explain why Wallace would be the best choice for America or why he had decided to join the ticket. Instead, he launched into his philosophy of war—that all weapons, including nuclear weapons, should be available for use in Vietnam. When Wallace tried to interrupt, LeMay cut him off. In another press interview, LeMay expressed his support for legalized abortion, a position guaranteed to upset Wallace's conservative base.

The Wallace-LeMay ticket received 13 percent of the vote, substantially less than had been expected. LeMay's reputation was indelibly stained. He was tarred as a segregationist, and he withdrew from public life. He died in 1990.[1]

Tommy Power, who led the 1945 bombing raid on Tokyo and chaired the 1961 SIOP briefing that appalled Secretary McNamara, served as commander of the Strategic Air Command from 1957 to 1964. When William Kaufmann of RAND proposed targeting Soviet military installations rather than cities, he remembers Power saying, "Restraint? Why are you so concerned with saving their lives? The whole idea is to kill the bastards. At the end of the war if there are two Americans and one Russian left alive, we win!"[2] Power died in 1970.

James Conant feigned indifference to his 1950 defeat in the election for the presidency of the National Academy of Sciences, saying that everything had come out for the best and that his opponent, Detlev Bronk, would make a fine president.[3] But the rejection must have hurt, and it may have influenced his 1953 decision to resign the presidency of Harvard and to accept the post of American high commissioner of occupied Germany. When the United States recognized the West German government in 1955, Conant became its first American ambassador. He served until 1957, when he returned to the United States to write on education and on the philosophy and history of science, and to work on his autobiography. He died in 1978.

Harold Urey moved to the University of Chicago after World War II and developed a new field, cosmochemistry, which attempted to explain the chemical composition of the planets and stars. He speculated that earth's early atmosphere might have been composed of water, ammonia, methane, and hydrogen, and in a groundbreaking experiment, he and his student Stanley Miller combined these substances and subjected them to electrical sparks to simulate lightning. They found that amino acids, fundamental building blocks of life, appeared as reaction products in the flask.

Late in his career, Urey moved to the University of California, San Diego, where he continued full-time research after retirement, publishing 105 papers. When asked why he was still working so hard, he replied, "Well, I'm no longer tenured." He died in 1981.

Glenn Seaborg got everything he demanded from the University of California after the war—full professorship, salary, staff, facilities, and budget. He later served as associate director of Berkeley's Lawrence Radiation Laboratory, as chancellor of the university at Berkeley, as chairman of the Atomic Energy Commission, and as president of the American Chemical Society. He won the Nobel Prize for Chemistry in 1951, and was the only then-living scientist to have an element named for him—seaborgium, element number 106. He worked with every president from Truman to Nixon, and he gave his autobiography the title *A Chemist in the White House.* He died in 1999.

Robert McNamara became increasingly discouraged about American prospects in Vietnam. After President Johnson refused to accept his recommendations to freeze American troop levels and to stop bombing, McNamara resigned as secretary of defense in early 1968. He kept his objections to himself, and Johnson nominated him to be president of the World Bank, where he served until 1981. He did not admit his opposition to the war until long after Johnson's 1972 death. McNamara died in 2009.

Daniel Ellsberg, the RAND analyst who uncovered the rigidity of America's nuclear targeting in 1961, is best known for his role in leaking what became known as the Pentagon Papers to the *New York Times*, which published a series of excerpts in 1971. They showed that Truman, Eisenhower, Kennedy, and (especially) Johnson had systematically deceived the American public about American actions in Southeast Asia.

Ellsberg has remained politically active, writing and speaking on military policy, disarmament, the need for government transparency, and civil rights. He lives in Berkeley, California.

Herman Kahn left RAND in 1961 to found the Hudson Institute, a policy research and consulting firm. He continued to appear on television panels and to write, responding to his critics in his books *Thinking about the Unthinkable* and *On Escalation*. He died at age sixty-one in 1983.

Lowell Wood, Teller's associate and the scientist behind SDI's failed Excalibur and Brilliant Pebbles weapon systems, is still at Livermore as of this writing. In 2011, he proposed a solution to the world's global warming problem: burn sulfur and spray the emitted particles into the stratosphere, where they would reflect the sun's energy and cool the planet. Anti-nuclear activists had long warned of "nuclear winter," an ice age caused by dust blocking the sun after a nuclear war, and Wood's idea is a controlled version of that—more particles would mean lower temperatures, according to Wood, and implementation would be inexpensive—$100 million per year, less than the cost of a wind farm. Many recalled similar cost claims for his SDI weapons. Wood has no experience as a climate scientist, and many researchers were outraged at his blasé suggestion of massive, untested interference with Earth's atmosphere.[4]

Robert Oppenheimer moved to the Virgin Islands after losing his security clearance. He continued to write and lecture on the need for free exchange of scientific ideas and on the failure of nuclear weapons as a centerpiece of foreign policy. He remained a polarizing figure. When he gave a series of lectures at Harvard in 1957, influential alumni protested, but 1,200 people packed the lecture hall. Kennedy awarded Oppenheimer the Enrico Fermi award in 1963, indicating that he was now politically acceptable. (Kennedy had given Teller the same award the previous year, possibly in an attempt to tamp down the outrage at Oppenheimer's award, an attempt that did not succeed.) Oppenheimer died of throat cancer at age sixty-two in 1967.

Edward Teller was summoned to the White House two months before his death in 2003, when President George W. Bush awarded him the Presidential Medal of Freedom, the nation's highest civilian honor. This was in addition to a medal from Kennedy and two from Reagan. He is almost certainly America's most presidentially decorated scientist.

Roy Woodruff resigned as director of Livermore's nuclear weapons programs in 1986 when the lab's director, Roger Batzel, refused to allow him to correct Teller's exaggerated claims for the Excalibur X-ray laser. Batzel did not take the resignation well. He isolated Woodruff in a small, windowless office that Livermore scientists called "Gorky West" after the Russian city of Gorky, to which the Soviet Union had sent Andrei Sakharov in internal exile for speaking out against the treatment of dissidents. Woodruff left Livermore for Los Alamos in 1990.

George Keyworth, Teller's protégé, who was Ronald Reagan's national science adviser, has served on a number of nonprofit and corporate boards. He was asked to resign from Hewlett-Packard's board in 2006 over allegations that he had leaked negative information about its CEO, Carly Fiorina, to CNET. He remains a fellow at the Hudson Institute, founded by Herman Kahn, and a director of General Atomics, the manufacturer of the Predator drone aircraft.

SOURCES AND ACKNOWLEDGMENTS

Like any broad survey, this book relies on the work of others. When referencing documents that I have not personally seen, I have not cited the archives where the documents may be found but have referred the reader to the sources from which I took the quotes or information. These are usually more accessible and embed the material in a larger context than I have done. Rather than listing all sources in a bibliography, I give a full citation in the first mention in each chapter of any reference. For the reader interested in going more deeply into the subject matter of this book, I found the following books, Web resources, and films especially useful:

Abella, Alex. *Soldiers of Reason: The RAND Corporation and the Rise of the American Empire*. Boston: Mariner Books, 2008.

Armacost, Michael H. *The Politics of Weapons Innovation: The Thor-Jupiter Controversy*. New York: Columbia University Press, 1969.

Batchelder, Robert C. *The Irreversible Decision, 1939–1950*. Boston: Houghton Mifflin, 1961.

Beard, Edmund. *Developing the ICBM: A Study in Bureaucratic Politics*. New York: Columbia University Press, 1976.

Biddle, Tami Davis. *Rhetoric and Reality in Air Warfare: The Evolution of British and American Ideas About Strategic Bombing, 1941–1945*. Princeton, NJ: Princeton University Press, 2002.

Biddle, Wayne. *Dark Side of the Moon: Wernher Von Braun, the Third Reich, and the Space Race*. New York: W. W. Norton, 2009.

Broad, William J. *Teller's War: The Top-Secret Story Behind the Star Wars Deception*. New York: Simon and Schuster, 1992.

Brown, Frederic. *Chemical Warfare: A Study in Restraints*. New Brunswick, NJ: Transaction, 2006.

Burr, William. "The Creation of SIOP-62: More Evidence on the Origins of Overkill." National Security Archive, www.gwu.edu/~nsarchiv/NSAEBB/NSAEBB130/index.htm.

Clark, Ronald W. *The Greatest Power on Earth: The International Race for Nuclear Supremacy*. New York: Harper and Row, 1980.

Clodfelter, Mark. *Beneficial Bombing: The Progressive Foundations of American Air Power, 1917–1945*. Lincoln: University of Nebraska Press, 2010.

Clodfelter, Mark. *The Limits of Airpower: The American Bombing of North Vietnam*. New York: Free Press, 1989.

Couffer, Jack. *Bat Bomb: World War II's Other Secret Weapon*. Austin: University of Texas Press, 1992.

Cronon, E. David. "Thomas A. Edison, Unorthodox Submarine Hunter." Madison Literary Club, www.worldwar1.com/sfedsub.htm.

Ghamari-Tabrizi, Sharon. *The Worlds of Herman Kahn: The Intuitive Science of Thermonuclear War*. Cambridge, MA: Harvard University Press, 2005.

Gillespie, Paul G. *Weapons of Choice: The Development of Precision Guided Munitions*. Tuscaloosa: University of Alabama Press, 2006.

Goodchild, Peter. *Edward Teller: The Real Dr. Strangelove*. Cambridge, MA: Harvard University Press, 2004.

Guillain, Robert. *I Saw Tokyo Burning*. Garden City, NY: Doubleday, 1981.

Hallion, Richard P. "Precision Guided Munitions and the New Era of Warfare." Air Power Studies Centre, Fairbain, Australia, APSC Paper no. 53, 1995, www.fas.org/man/dod-101/sys/smart/docs/paper53.htm.

Hargittai, Istvan. *Judging Edward Teller: A Closer Look at One of the Most Influential Scientists of the Twentieth Century*. Amherst, NY: Prometheus Books, 2010.

Heller, Charles. "Chemical Warfare in World War I: The American Experience, 1917–1918." Combat Studies Institute, U.S. Army Command and General Staff College, http://usacac.army.mil/cac2/cgsc/carl/resources/csi/Heller/HELLER.asp.

Hershberg, James. *James B. Conant: Harvard to Hiroshima and the Making of the Nuclear Age*. New York: Alfred A. Knopf, 1993.

Jeffrey, Thomas B. *From Phonographs to U-Boats: Edison and His "Insomnia Squad" in Peace and War, 1911–1919*. A Guide to Thomas A. Edison Papers, part V: 1911–1919. Bethesda, MD: LexisNexis, 2008.

Kaplan, Fred. *The Wizards of Armageddon*. New York: Simon and Schuster, 1983.

Kozak, Walter. *The Life and Wars of General Curtis LeMay*. Washington, DC: Regnery, 2009.

McFarland, Stephen L. *America's Pursuit of Precision Bombing, 1910–1945*. Smithsonian History of Aviation Series. Washington, DC: Smithsonian Institution Press, 1995.

McNaughter, Thomas L. *The M16 Controversies: Military Organizations and Weapons Acquisitions*. New York: Praeger Scientific, 1984.

Morris, Errol. "The Fog of War: Eleven Lessons from the Life of Robert S. McNamara." DVD. Sony, 2004.

Parides, Peter K. "To Run with the Swift—Vannevar Bush, James Conant and the Race to the Bomb: How American Science Was Drafted into Wartime Service," in *The Atomic Bomb and American Society: New Perspectives*, ed. Rosemary B. Mariner and G. Kurt Piehle. Knoxville: University of Tennessee Press, 2009.

Poundstone, Willliam. *Prisoner's Dilemma*. New York: Doubleday, 1992.

Renaker, John. *Dr. Strangelove and the Hideous Epoch: Deterrence in the Nuclear Age*. Claremont, CA: Regina Books, 2000.

Rhodes, Richard. *Dark Sun: The Making of the Hydrogen Bomb*. New York: Simon and Schuster, 1995.

Sheehan, Neil. *A Fiery Peace in a Cold War: Bernard Schriever and the Ultimate Weapon*. New York: Vintage Books, 2009.

Sherry, Michael S. *The Rise of American Air Power: The Creation of Armageddon.* New Haven, CT: Yale University Press, 1987.

Singer, P. W. *Wired for War.* New York: Penguin, 2009.

Skates, John Ray. *The Invasion of Japan: Alternative to the Bomb.* Columbia: University of South Carolina Press, 1994.

Tucker, Jonathan B. *War of Nerves: Chemical Warfare from World War I to Al-Qaeda.* New York: Anchor Books, 2006.

Vilensky, Joel A. *Dew of Death: The Story of Lewisite, America's World War I Weapon of Mass Destruction.* Indianapolis: University of Indiana Press, 2005.

I have extracted some writing from my earlier book *Cathedrals of Science: The Personalities and Rivalries that Made Modern Chemistry* (Oxford University Press, 2008), in particular the American experience of chemical weapons in World War I (Chapter 2 of this book) and the role of Glenn Seaborg and Harold Urey in the Manhattan Project (Chapter 8 and the Epilogue of this book). For those who have read *Cathedrals of Science,* my apologies for the repetition.

Above all, I would like to thank my wife, Ellen Pulleyblank Coffey. The staff at Oxford University Press has been especially helpful, including my editor, Timothy Bent; his assistant, Keely Latcham; production editor Joellyn Ausanka; and copy editor Sue Warga. Many have helped by reviewing drafts of this book, including Daniel Coffey, Joseph Coffey, Rebecca Coffey, Nan Gefen, Joseph Joyce, Maureen Joyce, Richard Leskosky, David Mattson, Jonathan Omer-Man, Connie Rubiano, Michael Whitt, and Peter Yedidia.

NOTES

Introduction

1. Patrick Coffey, *Cathedrals of Science: The Personalities and Rivalries That Made Modern Chemistry* (New York: Oxford University Press, 2008).
2. Daniel Ford, *The Button: The Pentagon's Command and Control System—Does It Work?* (New York: Simon and Schuster, 1985), 28.
3. John H. Rubel, *Doomsday Delayed: USAF Strategic Weapons and SIOP-62, 1959–1962; Two Cautionary Tales* (Latham, MD: Hamilton Books, 2008), 12.
4. Ike Jeanes, *Forecast and Solution: Grappling with the Nuclear: A Trilogy for Everyone* (Blacksburg, VA: Pocahontas Press, 1996), 306.

Chapter 1

1. John Milton Cooper, *Woodrow Wilson* (New York: Vintage, 2009), 352.
2. "Edison Won't Invent Man-Killing Devices," *New York Times*, October 26, 1914.
3. "Edison's New Naval Device," *New York Times*, November 1, 1914.
4. Matthew Josephson, *Edison: A Biography* (New York: McGraw-Hill, 1959), 454.
5. "U.S. Navy Submarines," Department of the Navy, Navy Historical Center, August 22, 2006, www.history.navy.mil/photos/shusn-no/ss-no.htm.
6. Thomas B. Jeffrey, *From Phonographs to U-Boats: Edison and His "Insomnia Squad" in Peace and War, 1911–1919*, A Guide to Thomas A. Edison Papers, part V: 1911–1919 (Bethesda, MD: LexisNexis, 2008), 81.
7. Joseph L. Morrison, *Josephus Daniels, the Small-D Democrat* (Chapel Hill: University of North Carolina Press, 1966), 48–49.
8. Josephus Daniels, *Editor in Politics* (Chapel Hill: University of North Carolina Press, 1941), 284.
9. Miller Reese Hutchison to Josephus Daniels, September 12, 1935, Thomas A. Edison Papers, X042G2, Rutgers University.
10. Miller Reese Hutchison to Howard A. Banks (an aide to Daniels), January 14, 1915, Thomas A. Edison Papers, X042G2.
11. "F-Boats All Unsafe, Naval Board Finds," *New York Times*, September 1, 1915.
12. "Deadly Gas in Submarines," *New York Times*, March 27, 1915.
13. "Edison Lessens Submarine Peril," *New York Times*, April 18, 1915.
14. "Edison Will Head Navy Test Board," *New York Times*, July 13, 1915.
15. "Edison's Plan for Preparedness," *New York Times*, May 30, 1915.

16. Miller Reese Hutchison to Josephus Daniels, September 12, 1935, Thomas A. Edison Papers, X042G2.
17. Miller Reese Hutchison to Josephus Daniels, November 6, 1915, Thomas A. Edison Papers, X042G2.
18. Naval Consulting Board minutes, December 23, 1915, Thomas A. Edison Papers, X018G.
19. Thomas A. Edison to Thomas Robins, February 4, 1919, Thomas A. Edison Papers, MF48; 281:17.
20. "Navy Heads Warned of E-2 Months Ago," *New York Times*, January 20, 1916.
21. "E-2 Court of Inquiry Is Named by Daniels," *New York Times*, January 18, 1916.
22. "A Foreign Navy Uses Edison Battery, Too," *New York Times*, January 17, 1916.
23. "Edison Man Warned by E-2 Inquiry Board," *New York Times*, January 21, 1916.
24. "Knew of E-2 Danger but Warned No One," *New York Times*, January 23, 1916.
25. Josephus Daniels to Thomas A. Edison, December 20, 1916, Thomas A. Edison Papers, X042G1.
26. Thomas A. Edison to Josephus Daniels, December 22, 1916, Thomas A. Edison Papers, X042G1.
27. Miller Reese Hutchison to Josephus Daniels, December 17, 1916, Thomas A. Edison Papers, X042G2.
28. Josephson, *Edison*, 450.
29. "Daniels Gets E-2 Findings," *New York Times*, February 15, 1916.
30. Jeffrey, *From Phonographs to U-Boats*, 90.
31. *Philadelphia Record*, December 31, 1916, Thomas A. Edison Papers, X042G2.
32. Miller Reese Hutchison to Josephus Daniels, February 19, 1936, Thomas A. Edison Papers, X042G2.
33. E. David Cronon, "Thomas A. Edison, Unorthodox Submarine Hunter," Madison Literary Club, www.worldwar1.com/sfedsub.htm.
34. Lloyd N. Scott, *Naval Consulting Board of the United States* (Washington, DC: Government Printing Office, 1920), 160–192.
35. David K. van Keuren, "Science, Progressivism, and Military Preparedness: The Case of the Naval Research Laboratory, 1915–1923," *Technology and Culture* 33 (1992): 710–36.

Chapter 2

1. Lance Sergeant Elmer Cotton, 1915, quoted in "Chlorine Gas," Spartacus, www.spartacus.schoolnet.co.uk/FWWchlorine.htm.
2. Fritz Haber, *Fünf Vorträge* (Berlin: Verlag von Julius Springer, 1924), 36, quoted in Daniel Charles, *Master Mind: The Rise and Fall of Fritz Haber, the Nobel Laureate Who Launched the Age of Chemical Warfare* (New York: Ecco, 2005), 173.
3. Maj. Charles Heller, "Chemical Warfare in World War I: The American Experience, 1917–1918," Combat Studies Institute, U.S. Army Command and General Staff College, http://usacac.army.mil/cac2/cgsc/carl/download/csipubs/LP10_ChemicalWarfareInWWI-TheAmericanExperience_1917.pdf
4. Charles, *Master Mind*, 173–74.
5. Heller, "Chemical Warfare in World War I."

6. Ibid.
7. Ibid.
8. A. Hunter Dupree, *Science in the Federal Government: A History of Policies and Activities to 1940* (Cambridge, MA: Harvard University Press, 1957), 320. Quoted in Gilbert F. Whittemore, "World War, Poison Gas Research, and the Ideals of American Chemists," *Social Studies of Science* 5 (1975): 149.
9. Elmer Sherwood, *Diary of a Rainbow Veteran* (Terre Haute, IN: Moore-Langen, 1929), 154–55.
10. Hervey Allen, *Toward the Flame: A Memoir of World War I* (Lincoln: University of Nebraska Press, 2003), 36, 57.
11. Marvin Gordon, Barry R. Sude, Ruth Ann Overbeck, and Charles Hendricks, "A Brief History of the American University Experimental Station and U.S. Navy Bomb Disposal School, American University," Office of History, U.S. Army Corps of Engineers, Washington, DC, 1994, http://64.78.11.86/uxofiles/enclosures/SpringValley_History.pdf
12. "N. B. Scott, 'Gassed,'" *Washington Post*, August 4, 1918.
13. "Had Deadliest Gas Ready for Germans; 'Lewisite' Might Have Killed Millions," *New York Times*, May 25, 1919.
14. Joel A. Vilensky, *Dew of Death: The Story of Lewisite, America's World War I Weapon of Mass Destruction* (Indianapolis: University of Indiana Press, 2005), 20.
15. Daniel Patrick Jones, "The Role of Chemists in Research on War Gases in the United States During World War I," Ph.D. dissertation, University of Wisconsin, 1969, 150.
16. Julius A. Nieuwland, letter to Amos A. Fries, November 14, 1922, University of Notre Dame Archives, quoted in Vilensky, *Dew of Death*, 26.
17. James Hershberg, *James B. Conant: Harvard to Hiroshima and the Making of the Nuclear Age* (New York: Alfred A. Knopf, 1993), 4.
18. John Leonard, "Good Man, Dull Book," *New York Times*, March 4, 1970.
19. James B. Conant, *My Several Lives: Memoirs of a Social Inventor* (New York: Harper and Row, 1970), 43–45.
20. Hershberg, *James B. Conant*, 38–39.
21. Ibid., 45.
22. Jones, "The Role of Chemists in Research on War Gases," 139.
23. Vilensky, *Dew of Death*, 31.
24. Leo P. Brophy, Wyndham D. Miles, and Rexmond C. Cochrane, *The Chemical Warfare Service: From Laboratory to Field* (Washington, DC: Office of the Chief of Military History, Department of the Army, 1959), 16–17.
25. Jones, "The Role of Chemists in Research on War Gases," 139.
26. Charles H. Herty, *Reserves of the Chemical Warfare Service* (Washington, DC: National Research Council, 1921), 2.
27. Vilensky, *Dew of Death*, 42–45.
28. Hershberg, *James B. Conant*, 47.
29. Vilensky, *Dew of Death*, 45, 39.
30. Ibid., 43.
31. Ibid., 52.

32. Winford Lewis, "How the American Chemists Silenced Germany," *Chemical Bulletin* 6 (January 1919): 4–6, quoted in Vilensky, *Dew of Death*, 50.
33. Conant, *My Several Lives*, 49–50.
34. Herman Skolnik and Kenneth Reese, *A Century of Chemistry: The Role of Chemists and the American Chemical Society* (Washington, DC: American Chemical Society, 1976), 456.
35. Ludwig Fritz Haber, *The Poisonous Cloud: Chemical Warfare in the First World War* (Oxford: Clarendon Press, 1986), 291.
36. Colin Nicholson, *Longman Companion to the First World War* (Harlow, UK: Longman, 2001, 248).
37. Hearings on Senate 2691, 2693, and 2715, 66th Congress, 94, quoted in Herty, *Reserves of the Chemical Warfare Service*, 4.
38. "Council Meeting," *Journal of Industrial and Engineering Chemistry* 1919, 395, quoted in Whittemore, "World War, Poison Gas Research, and the Ideals of American Chemists," 157.
39. Amos A. Fries, "Chemical Warfare," *Journal of Industrial and Engineering Chemistry* 1920, 429, quoted in Whittemore, "World War, Poison Gas Research, and the Ideals of American Chemists," 157.
40. "Sibert's Transfer Stirs Army Men," *New York Times*, March 1, 1920.
41. Daniel P. Jones, "American Chemists and the Geneva Protocol," *Isis* 71, no. 3 (1980): 428.
42. Ibid., 430.
43. Winford Lee Lewis, "Duties of a Reserve Officer in Time of Peace," *Chemical Warfare* 11, no. 10 (1925), 4.
44. Jones, "American Chemists and the Geneva Protocol," 432.
45. "General Fries Assails Anti-War Drives," *New York Times*, July 5, 1925.
46. Jones, "American Chemists and the Geneva Protocol," 433.
47. Ibid., 439.
48. Pany R. Sinish and Joel A. Vilensky, "WMDs in Our Backyards," *Earth Island Journal*, Winter 2005.
49. Theo Emery, "A House in Washington May Solve a 1918 Mystery," *New York Times*, November 29, 2012.
50. Theo Emery, "Zeroing in on Mystery of an Old Site Called Hades," *New York Times*, March 17, 2012.

Chapter 3

1. Mark Clodfelter, *Beneficial Bombing: The Progressive Foundations of American Air Power, 1917–1945* (Lincoln: University of Nebraska Press, 2010).
2. Paul H. Jeffers, *Billy Mitchell: The Life, Times, and Battles of America's Prophet of the Air* (St. Paul: Zenith Press, 2006), 109–11.
3. William Mitchell, *Memoirs of World War I: From Start to Finish of Our Greatest War* (New York: Random House, 1960), 59.
4. Clodfelter, *Beneficial Bombing*, 15; Douglas Waller. *A Question of Loyalty: Gen. Billy Mitchell and the Court-Martial That Gripped the Nation* (New York: HarperCollins, 2004), 119.

5. Mark Clodfelter, "Molding Airpower Convictions: Development and Legacy of William Mitchell's Strategic Thought," in *The Paths of Heaven: The Evolution of Airpower Theory*, ed. Phillip S. Meilinger (Maxwell Air Force Base, AL: Air University Press, 1997), 89.

6. Waller, *A Question of Loyalty*, 120–21.

7. Giulio Douhet, *The Command of the Air*, ed. Richard H. Kohn and Joseph P. Harahan (Washington, DC: Office of Air Force History, 1983), 44.

8. Maj. William Mitchell, memorandum to chief of staff, AEF, June 13, 1917, quoted in I. B. Holley, *Ideas and Weapons* (New Haven, CT: Yale University Press, 1953), 47.

9. David R. Mets, *Master of Airpower: General Carl A. Spaatz* (New York: Random House, 1997), 34.

10. Phillip S. Meilinger, "Trenchard, Slossor, and Royal Air Force Doctrine Before World War II," in *The Paths of Heaven: The Evolution of Airpower Theory*, ed. Phillip S. Meilinger (Maxwell Air Force Base, AL: Air University Press, 1997), 42.

11. Mitchell, *Memoirs of World War I: From Start to Finish of Our Greatest War*, 146, quoted in Clodfelter, *Beneficial Bombing*, 27.

12. Maj. Raynal C. Bolling to chief signal officer of the Army, subject: Report of Aeronautical Commission, August 15, 1917, quoted in Robert Frank Futrell, *Ideas, Concepts, Doctrine: Basic Thinking in the United States Air Force 1907–1960* (Maxwell Air Force Base, AL: Air University Press, 1989), 1:20.

13. Holley, *Ideas and Weapons*, 141–45.

14. H. H. Arnold, *Global Mission* (New York: Harper and Brothers, 1949) 67–68, quoted in Clodfelter, *Beneficial Bombing*, 31.

15. Douhet, *Command of the Air*, 6–7.

16. "Had Deadliest Gas Ready for Germans; 'Lewisite' Might Have Killed Millions," *New York Times*, May 25, 1919.

17. Phillip S. Meilinger, "Giulio Douhet and the Origins of Airpower Theory," in *The Paths of Heaven: The Evolution of Airpower Theory*, ed. Phillip S. Meilinger (Maxwell Air Force Base, AL: Air University Press, 1997), 10–15.

18. Meilinger, "Trenchard, Slossor, and Royal Air Force Doctrine Before World War II," 49.

19. Quoted in Andrew Boyle, *Trenchard, Man of Vision* (London: Collins, 1962), 472.

20. Waller, *A Question of Loyalty*, 145.

21. Ibid., 23.

22. Eugene M. Emme, "The American Dimension," in *Air Power and Warfare: Proceedings of the Eighth Military History Symposium, USAF Academy*, ed. Alfred E. Hurley and Robert C. Ehrhardt (Washington, DC: U.S. Government Printing Office, 1979), 67, quoted in Clodfelter, *Beneficial Bombing*, 47.

23. Waller, *A Question of Loyalty*, 23.

24. Arnold, *Global Mission*, 158–59.

25. Futrell, *Ideas, Concepts, Doctrine*, 1:39.

26. Clodfelter, *Beneficial Bombing*, 52–53.

27. Ibid., 53–65.

28. Haywood S. Hansell Jr., "Notes for a Lecture on the Development of the U.S. Concept of Bombardment Operations" (1951), quoted in David MacIsaac, *Strategic Bombing in World War Two: The Story of the United States Strategic Bombing Survey* (New York: Garland, 1976), 9–10.
29. Clodfelter, *Beneficial Bombing*, 73–74.
30. Thomas H. Greer, *Development of Air Doctrine in the Army Air Forces, 1917–1941* (Washington, DC: Office of Air Force History, 1985), 94–99, quoted in Clodfelter, *Beneficial Bombing*, 74.
31. Clodfelter, *Beneficial Bombing*, 78.
32. DeWitt S. Copp, "Frank M. Andrews: Marshall's Airman," Air Force History and Museums Program, www.afhso.af.mil/shared/media/document/AFD-100924-041.pdf.
33. Clodfelter, *Beneficial Bombing*, 87.
34. Ibid., 98.

Chapter 4
1. Stephen L. McFarland, *America's Pursuit of Precision Bombing, 1910–1945* (Washington, DC: Smithsonian Institution Press, 1995), 94.
2. Ibid., 27, 84.
3. Ibid., 72.
4. Ibid., 50–54.
5. Ibid., 97.
6. Ibid., 114–17.
7. Stewart Halsey Ross. *Strategic Bombing by the United States in World War II: The Myths and the Facts* (Jefferson, NC: McFarland, 2003), 131.
8. McFarland, *America's Pursuit of Precision Bombing*, 128.
9. Ibid., 135.
10. Ibid., 143.
11. Ibid.
12. Loyd Searle, "The Bombsight War: Norden vs. Sperry," *IEEE Spectrum*, September 1989, 64.
13. Ibid.
14. McFarland, *America's Pursuit of Precision Bombing*, 145.

Chapter 5
1. Walter Kozak, *The Life and Wars of General Curtis LeMay* (Washington, DC: Regnery, 2009), 1–17.
2. Curtis E. LeMay and MacKinlay Kantor, *Mission with LeMay: My Story* (New York: Doubleday, 1965), 208.
3. Errol Morris, "The Fog of War: Transcript," www.errolmorris.com/film/fow_transcript.html.
4. "Appeal of President Franklin D. Roosevelt on Aerial Bombardment of Civilian Populations, September 1, 1939," http://tdl.org/txlor-dspace/bitstream/handle/2249.3/396/Appeal_of_President_Franklin_D.pdf?sequence=167.
5. Winston Churchill, memo to minister of aircraft production, July 8, 1940, quoted in Winston Churchill, *The Second World War, Volume 2: Their Finest Hour* (Boston: Houghton-Mifflin, 1949), appendix A, 643.

6. "Hitlers Bombenterror: Die Angriffe der Deutschen auf Europas Städte," *Der Spiegel* Special 1/2003, www.spiegel.de/spiegelspecial/a-290080-3.html.
7. Stephen L. McFarland, *America's Pursuit of Precision Bombing, 1910–1945* (Washington, DC: Smithsonian Institution Press, 1995), 166.
8. Ibid., 166.
9. Phillip S. Meilinger, "The Prescient Planners of AWPD-1," *Air Force Magazine* 94, no. 7 (2011).
10. James Agee, "Films," *The Nation*, July 17, 1943, 82.
11. Leonard Maltin, "Introduction to *Victory Through Air Power*," *Walt Disney Treasures: On the Front Lines* (Disney, 2004), DVD.
12. Quoted in Mark Clodfelter, *Beneficial Bombing: The Progressive Foundations of American Air Power, 1917–1945* (Lincoln: University of Nebraska Press, 2010), 109.
13. B-24 Best Web, www.b24bestweb.com/a-tisketa-tasket1.htm.
14. LeMay and Kantor, *Mission with LeMay*, 278.
15. Ibid., 571.
16. Randall Jarrell. *Little Friend, Little Friend* (New York: Dial Press, 1945), 58.
17. LeMay and Kantor, *Mission with LeMay*, 298.
18. Gregory Fremont Barnes, *American Bomber Crewmen, 1941–1945* (Colchester: Osprey, 2008), 56.
19. *WWII, the Ultimate Collection*, disc 6, side B (Brentwood Home Video, 2004).
20. LeMay and Kantor, *Mission with LeMay*, 231–32.
21. Ibid., 234.
22. Clodfelter, *Beneficial Bombing*, 122.
23. Ibid., 126.
24. Ibid., 128–132.
25. Ibid., 134.
26. McFarland, *America's Pursuit of Precision Bombing*, 182.
27. Clodfelter, *Beneficial Bombing*, 153.
28. Ibid., 162–63.
29. Ibid., 168–69.
30. Ibid., 175.
31. Ibid., 149.
32. Ibid., 150–51.
33. Ibid., 179–80.
34. Gian P. Gentile, *How Effective Is Strategic Bombing? Lessons Learned from World War II to Kosovo* (New York: New York University Press, 2001), 25–32.
35. John Kenneth Galbraith, *A Life in Our Times: Memoirs* (Boston: Houghton Mifflin, 1981), 196, quoted in Gentile, *How Effective Is Strategic Bombing?*, 46.
36. Gentile, *How Effective Is Strategic Bombing?* 58–61.

Chapter 6
1. John D. Roberts, "The Beginnings of Physical Organic Chemistry in the United States," *Bulletin of the History of Chemistry* 19 (1996): 51.
2. James B. Conant, *My Several Lives: Memoirs of a Social Inventor* (New York: Harper and Row, 1970), 236–37; James Hershberg, *James B. Conant: Harvard to Hiroshima and the Making of the Nuclear Age* (New York: Alfred A. Knopf, 1993), 128.

3. Louis F. Fieser, *The Scientific Method* (New York: Reinhold, 1964), 9.
4. Ibid.
5. Ibid., 202.
6. Jack Couffer, *Bat Bomb: World War II's Other Secret Weapon* (Austin: University of Texas Press, 1992), 47.
7. Fieser, *The Scientific Method*, 11-13.
8. Ibid., 14.
9. Ibid., 16.
10. Ibid., 23.
11. Ibid., 23-24.
12. Ibid., 25.
13. Ibid., 25-33.
14. Ibid., 34-42.
15. Ibid., 45.
16. Photo in ibid., 48.
17. Ibid., 49-52.
18. Leo P. Brophy and George J. B. Fisher, *The Chemical Warfare Service: Organizing for War* (Washington, DC: Office of the Chief of Military History, Department of the Army, 1959), 43-46.
19. Quoted in Gian P. Gentile, *How Effective Is Strategic Bombing? Lessons Learned from World War II to Kosovo* (New York: New York University Press, 2001), 17.
20. H. S. Hansell, *Strategic Air War Against Japan* (Maxwell Air Force Base, AL: Air War College, Airpower Research Institute, 1980), 4.
21. Leo P. Brophy, Wyndham D. Miles, and Rexmond C. Cochrane, *The Chemical Warfare Service: From Laboratory to Field* (Washington, DC: Office of the Chief of Military History, Department of the Army, 1959), 185.
22. Ibid.
23. Lynn Eden, *Whole World on Fire: Organizations, Knowledge, and Nuclear Weapons Devastation* (Ithaca, NY: Cornell University Press, 2004), 88.
24. Ibid.
25. "Design and Construction of Typical German and Japanese Test Structures at Dugway Proving Grounds, Utah," Standard Oil Company, 1943, 13, http://www.scribd.com/doc/35617392/Standard-Oil-Design-and-Construction-of-Typical-German-and-Japanese-Test-Structures., quoted in Tom Vanderbilt, *Survival City: Adventures Among the Ruins of Atomic America* (Chicago: University of Chicago Press, 2010) 72.
26. "Dugway Proving Grounds," Japan Air Raids.org, www.japanairraids.org/?page_id=31; "Fire Warfare: Incendiaries and Flame Throwers," Office of Scientific Research and Development and National Defense Research Committee, Summary Technical Report of Division 11, Volume 3, www.japanairraids.org/?page_id=1095; "Design and Construction of Typical German and Japanese Test Structures at Dugway Proving Grounds, Utah."
27. Army Air Force films of the tests at Eglin can be seen in *Incendiary Attack for Japanese Cities, Air War: Pacific, Volume 1* (IMD Films, 2008). The structures at Eglin were much less sophisticated than those at Dugway.

28. Kenneth P. Werrell, *Blankets of Fire* (Washington, DC: Smithsonian Institution Press, 1996), 49.

29. Couffer, *Bat Bomb*, 6.

30. Ibid., 7.

31. Ibid., 5, 102.

32. Ibid.

33. Ibid., 1–14.

34. Ibid., 15–19.

35. Fieser, *The Scientific Method*, 121.

36. Couffer, *Bat Bomb*, 45–47.

37. Fieser, *The Scientific Method*, 127.

38. Couffer, *Bat Bomb*, 118.

39. Ibid., 119–20.

40. Fieser, *The Scientific Method*, 129.

41. Couffer, *Bat Bomb*, 120–23, 144–47.

42. Ibid., 208–9.

43. Ibid., 211.

44. Ibid., 226.

45. Fieser, *The Scientific Method*, 133–34.

46. Nick Ut, "Kim Phuc" (Associated Press, 1972), http://culturevisuelle.org/blog/6837.

47. "Maybe: Harry S Truman LL.D. (Hon.)," *Harvard Crimson*, June 2, 1965.

48. "The Man Who Invented Napalm," *Time*, January 5, 1968.

49. Marshall Gates, "Louis Frederick Fieser, April 7, 1899–July 25, 1977," *Biographical Memoirs*, vol. 65 (Washington, DC: National Academies Press, 1994), 158.

Chapter 7

1. Robert Guillain, *I Saw Tokyo Burning* (Garden City, NY: Doubleday, 1981), 182.

2. Ibid., 183–86.

3. Quoted in Michael S. Sherry, *The Rise of American Air Power: The Creation of Armageddon* (New Haven, CT: Yale University Press, 1987), 276.

4. Both Spaatz and Kuter quoted in Mark Clodfelter, *Beneficial Bombing: The Progressive Foundations of American Air Power, 1917–1945* (Lincoln: University of Nebraska Press, 2010), 169–70.

5. Sherry, *The Rise of American Air Power*, 102, 159–60.

6. Errol Morris, "*The Fog of War*: Transcript," www.errolmorris.com/film/fow_transcript.html.

7. Sherry, *The Rise of American Air Power*, 167–68.

8. Curtis E. LeMay and MacKinlay Kantor, *Mission with LeMay: My Story* (New York: Doubleday, 1965), 332.

9. Tami Davis Biddle, *Rhetoric and Reality in Air Warfare: The Evolution of British and American Ideas About Strategic Bombing, 1941–1945* (Princeton, NJ: Princeton University Press, 2002), 265.

10. Sherry, *The Rise of American Air Power*, 179–81.

11. Ibid., 238.

12. Douglas J. MacEachin, "The Final Months of the War with Japan," Center for the Study of Intelligence, Central Intelligence Agency, CSI 98-10001, December 1998; John Ray Skates, *The Invasion of Japan: Alternative to the Bomb* (Columbia: University of South Carolina Press, 1994).

13. Richard H. Kohn and Joseph P. Harahan, eds., *Strategic Air Warfare: An Interview with Generals Curtis E. LeMay, Leon W. Johnson, David A. Burchinal, and Jack C. Catton* (Washington, DC: Office of Air Force History, 1988), 54–55.

14. Clodfelter, *Beneficial Bombing*, 205–6.

15. Quoted in ibid., 208.

16. Haywood S. Hansell Jr., *Strategic Air War Against Germany and Japan* (Washington, DC: Office of Air Force History, 1986), 218.

17. Clodfelter, *Beneficial Bombing*, 210–11.

18. Sherry, *The Rise of American Air Power*, 257–58.

19. Ibid., 178.

20. Ibid., 300.

21. Ibid., 180.

22. Clodfelter, *Beneficial Bombing*, 217–20.

23. LeMay and Kantor, *Mission with LeMay*, 352–53.

24. Ibid., 353.

25. Ibid., 355.

26. Ibid., 353–54.

27. Sherry, *The Rise of American Air Power*, 289.

28. St. Clair McKelway, "A Reporter with the B-29s," *New Yorker*, June 7, 16, 23, and 30, 1945, June 23 issue, 35.

29. Sherry, *The Rise of American Air Power*, 290.

30. Clodfelter, *Beneficial Bombing*, 221–22.

31. Quoted in ibid., 223.

32. Sherry, *The Rise of American Air Power*, 31.

33. Ibid., 109.

34. Ibid., 116.

35. Biddle, *Rhetoric and Reality in Air Warfare*, 264.

36. Sherry, *The Rise of American Air Power*, 228.

37. Ibid., 229–30.

38. Ibid., 219–21.

39. Stephen L. McFarland, *America's Pursuit of Precision Bombing, 1910–1945* (Washington, DC: Smithsonian Institution Press, 1995), 205.

40. Clodfelter, *Beneficial Bombing*, 227–28.

41. Sherry, *The Rise of American Air Power*, 299.

42. Harry S. Truman, *Memoirs* (Garden City, NY: Doubleday, 1955), 1:416, cited in Sherry, *The Rise of American Air Power*, 316.

43. LeMay and Kantor, *Mission with LeMay*, 384.

44. Sherry, *The Rise of American Air Power*, 285–87.

45. Ibid., 311.

46. Biddle, *Rhetoric and Reality in Air Warfare*, 269.

47. "Appeal of President Franklin D. Roosevelt on Aerial Bombardment of Civilian Populations, September 1, 1939," http://tdl.org/txlor-dspace/bitstream/handle/2249.3/396/Appeal_of_President_Franklin_D.pdf?sequence=167.

Chapter 8

1. Ronald W. Clark, *The Greatest Power on Earth: The International Race for Nuclear Supremacy* (New York: Harper and Row, 1980), 36–38.
2. Ibid., 50.
3. Ibid., 49–50.
4. Ibid., 71–72.
5. Peter K. Parides, "To Run with the Swift—Vannevar Bush, James Conant and the Race to the Bomb: How American Science Was Drafted into Wartime Service," in *The Atomic Bomb and American Society: New Perspectives*, ed. Rosemary B. Mariner and G. Kurt Piehler (Knoxville: University of Tennessee Press, 2009), 27.
6. Karl Compton to Vannevar Bush, March 17, 1941, quoted in Parides, "To Run with the Swift," 29.
7. Minutes of the Meeting of the Advisory Committee of the National Academy on Uranium Disintegration, May 5, 1941, quoted in Parides, "To Run with the Swift," 30.
8. Parides, "To Run with the Swift," 35.
9. Clark, *The Greatest Power on Earth*, 132–53.
10. Quoted in Robert C. Batchelder, *The Irreversible Decision, 1939–1950* (Boston: Houghton Mifflin, 1961), 43–44.
11. Hans Bethe, "Energy Production in Stars," *Physical Review* 55 (1939): 434.
12. Edward Teller, *Memoirs: A Twentieth-Century Journey in Science and Politics* (Cambridge, MA: Perseus, 2001), 175–77.
13. Rudolf Peierls, *Bird of Passage: Recollections of a Physicist* (Princeton, NJ: Princeton University Press, 1985), 199–200.
14. William J. Broad, *Teller's War: The Top-Secret Story Behind the Star Wars Deception* (New York: Simon and Schuster, 1992), 33.
15. James Arnold, Jacob Bigeleisen, and Clyde Hutchinson, "Harold Clayton Urey: April 24, 1893–January 5, 1981," in *National Academy of Sciences Biographical Memoirs* (Washington, DC: National Academy of Sciences, 1995), 382.
16. Harold Urey, oral history interview by John Heilbron, March 24, 1964, Niels Bohr Library, American Institute of Physics, College Park, MD.
17. Mildred Cohn, "Harold Urey: A Personal Remembrance. Part II." *Chemical Heritage* 24, no. 1 (2006): 12.
18. Harold Urey, "I'm a Frightened Man," *Collier's*, January 5, 1946.
19. Jessica Wang, "Science, Security, and the Cold War: The Case of E. U. Condon," *Isis* 83 (1992): 249.
20. Arnold, Bigeleisen, and Hutchinson, "Harold Clayton Urey," 390.
21. Glenn Seaborg, "Meet Glenn Seaborg," Lawrence Berkeley Laboratory, www.lbl.gov/Publications/Seaborg/bio.htm.

22. J. L. Heilbron and Robert W. Seidel, *Lawrence and His Laboratory* (Berkeley: University of California Press, 1989), 461.
23. Seaborg to McMillan, March 8, 1941, quoted in Heilbron and Seidel, *Lawrence and His Laboratory*, 463.
24. Author's interview with Jacob Bigeleisen, who was a Berkeley graduate student in 1942, 2006.
25. Author's interview with Samuel Weissman, 2005.
26. Glenn Seaborg, Ronald Kathren, and Jerry Gough, *The Plutonium Story: The Journals of Professor Glenn T. Seaborg 1939–1946* (Columbus, OH: Battelle Press, 1994), 745.
27. "Our Policy Stated," *New York Times*, June 24, 1941.
28. Harry S. Truman, *Year of Decisions* (Garden City, NY: Doubleday, 1955), 11.
29. Michael S. Sherry, *The Rise of American Air Power: The Creation of Armageddon* (New Haven, CT: Yale University Press, 1987), 270.
30. Arthur Holly Compton, *Atomic Quest: A Personal Narrative* (New York: Oxford University Press, 1956), 216, 237.
31. "Notes of Meeting of the Interim Committee, May 31, 1945," Miscellaneous Historical Documents Collection, Harry S. Truman Library and Museum.
32. Batchelder, *The Irreversible Decision*, 59–60.
33. Ibid., 119.
34. Sherry, *The Rise of American Air Power*, 293–96.
35. Tami Davis Biddle, *Rhetoric and Reality in Air Warfare: The Evolution of British and American Ideas About Strategic Bombing, 1941–1945* (Princeton, NJ: Princeton University Press, 2002), 270.
36. Sherry, *The Rise of American Air Power*, 306–8.
37. Ibid., 330–41.
38. Richard H. Kohn and Joseph P. Harahan, eds., *Strategic Air Warfare: An Interview with Generals Curtis E. LeMay, Leon W. Johnson, David A. Burchinal, and Jack C. Catton* (Washington, DC: Office of Air Force History, 1988), 69.
39. "Henry Stimson to Harry S. Truman, with Handwritten Truman Reply on Reverse, July 30, 1945," Harry S. Truman Administration, Elsey Papers, Harry S. Truman Library and Museum.
40. Robert Jungk, *Brighter than a Thousand Suns* (New York: Harcourt, 1958), 208.
41. "Radio Report to the American People on the Potsdam Conference," August 9, 1945, Harry S. Truman Library and Museum.
42. "Frequently Asked Questions," question 1, Radiation Effects Research Foundation, www.rerf.or.jp/general/qa_e/qa1.html.
43. Batchelder, *The Irreversible Decision*, 151–53.
44. "The Fortune Survey," *Fortune*, December 1945, 305.
45. Batchelder, *The Irreversible Decision*, 120.
46. Ward Wilson, *Five Myths About Nuclear Weapons* (Boston: Houghton Mifflin, 2013), 21–53.
47. H. H. Arnold, *Global Mission* (New York: Harper and Brothers, 1949), 598.
48. Haywood S. Hansell Jr., *Strategic Air War Against Japan* (Air War College, Airpower Research Institute, 1980), 92.
49. Quoted in ibid., ii.

Chapter 9

1. Frederic Brown, *Chemical Warfare: A Study in Restraints* (New Brunswick, NJ: Transaction, 2006), 124–25.
2. Ibid., 149–87.
3. Jeffrey W. Legro, *Cooperation Under Fire: Anglo-German Restraint During World War II* (Ithaca, NY: Cornell University Press, 1995), 160–62.
4. Ibid., 178, 184–87.
5. Jonathan B. Tucker, *War of Nerves: Chemical Warfare from World War I to Al-Qaeda* (New York: Anchor Books, 2006), 28–29.
6. Ibid., 36–40.
7. Joel A. Vilensky, *Dew of Death: The Story of Lewisite, America's World War I Weapon of Mass Destruction* (Indianapolis: University of Indiana Press, 2005), 78–85.
8. Ibid., 84–101.
9. Legro, *Cooperation Under Fire*, 173.
10. Tucker, *War of Nerves*, 46–54.
11. Ibid., 56–61.
12. Gerald Reminick, *Nightmare in Bari: The World War II Liberty Ship Poison Gas Disaster and Cover-Up* (Palo Alto, CA: Glencannon Press, 2001), 27–29.
13. Ibid., 10.
14. Constance M. Pechura and David P. Rall, *Veterans at Risk: The Health Effects of Mustard Gas and Lewisite* (Washington, DC: National Academies Press, 1993), 43–44.
15. Reminick, *Nightmare in Bari*, 109–32.
16. "Bari Facts," *Time*, December 27, 1943, 19.
17. Dwight D. Eisenhower, *Crusade in Europe* (Garden City, NY: Doubleday, 1948), 204; Reminick, *Nightmare in Bari*, 165–76.
18. Omar N. Bradley, *A Soldier's Story* (New York: Henry Holt, 1951), 279.
19. Tucker, *War of Nerves*, 64–66.
20. Legro, *Cooperation Under Fire*, 164–66.
21. Tucker, *War of Nerves*, 68.
22. Legro, *Cooperation Under Fire*, 192–93.
23. Brown, *Chemical Warfare: A Study in Restraints*, 246–47.
24. John Ray Skates, *The Invasion of Japan: Alternative to the Bomb* (Columbia: University of South Carolina Press, 1994), 97.
25. Ibid., 84–95.
26. Brown, *Chemical Warfare: A Study in Restraints*, 271–81.
27. Tucker, *War of Nerves*, 83–92; Louis F. Fieser, *The Scientific Method* (New York: Reinhold, 1964).
28. Tucker, *War of Nerves*, 92–116.
29. Ibid., 124–25.
30. Cornelius Ryan, "G-Gas—a New Weapon of Chilling Terror," *Collier's*, November 27, 1953, 88–95.
31. Tucker, *War of Nerves*, 155.
32. Ibid., 156–57.
33. Ibid., 172.
34. Ibid., 197–99.

35. Ibid., 201.
36. Ibid., 203–12.
37. Ibid., 188–89.
38. Ibid., 215–17.
39. Ibid., 217–20.
40. "Army Chemical Corps to Be Phased Out," *Chemical and Engineering News*, January 22, 1973, 3.
41. *War of Nerves*, 224.
42. Ibid., 228–29.
43. Ibid., 241.
44. Ibid., 289–95.
45. James Dao, "Paper Links Nerve Agents in '91 Gulf War and Ailments," *New York Times*, December 13, 2012; J. J. Tuite and R.W. Haley, "Meteorological and Intelligence Evidence of Long-Distance Transit of Chemical Weapons Fallout from Bombing Early in the 1991 Persian Gulf War," *Neuroepidemiology* 40 (2013): 160–77; R. W. Haley and J. J. Tuite, "Epidemiologic Evidence of Health Effects from Long-Distance Transit of Chemical Weapons Fallout from Bombing Early in the 1991 Persian Gulf War," *Neuroepidemiology* 40 (2013): 178–89.
46. "Demilitarisation," Organisation for the Prohibition of Chemical Weapons, www .opcw.org/our-work/demilitarisation.

Chapter 10

1. Peter Goodchild, *Edward Teller: The Real Dr. Strangelove* (Cambridge, MA: Harvard University Press, 2004), 110–12, 118.
2. "Notes of Meeting of the Interim Committee, May 31, 1945," Truman Presidential Library.
3. Daniel J. Kevles, *The Physicists: The History of a Scientific Community in Modern America* (Cambridge, MA: Harvard University Press, 1995), 349–51.
4. James Hershberg, *James B. Conant: Harvard to Hiroshima and the Making of the Nuclear Age* (New York: Alfred A. Knopf, 1993), 258–63.
5. Goodchild, *Edward Teller: The Real Dr. Strangelove*, 119–29.
6. Hershberg, *James B. Conant*, 303.
7. Goodchild, *Edward Teller: The Real Dr. Strangelove*, 145.
8. Hershberg, *James B. Conant*, 472.
9. Glenn Seaborg, *A Chemist in the White House: From the Manhattan Project to the Cold War* (Washington, DC: American Chemical Society, 1998), 40–44, quoted in Istvan Hargittai, *Judging Edward Teller: A Closer Look at One of the Most Influential Scientists of the Twentieth Century* (Amherst, NY: Prometheus Books, 2010), 194.
10. Hershberg, *James B. Conant*, 476.
11. Ibid., 473–78; Hargittai, *Judging Edward Teller*, 194–97.
12. David E. Lilienthal, *The Journals of David Lilienthal: The Atomic Energy Years, 1945–1950* (New York: Harper and Row, 1964), 581, quoted in Goodchild, *Edward Teller: The Real Dr. Strangelove*, 151.
13. Goodchild, *Edward Teller: The Real Dr. Strangelove*, 153–55.
14. Walter Isaacson, *Einstein: His Life and Universe* (New York: Simon and Schuster, 2007), 501, quoted in Hargittai, *Judging Edward Teller*, 207.

15. Richard Rhodes, *Dark Sun: The Making of the Hydrogen Bomb* (New York: Simon and Schuster, 1995), 373.

16. "Truman Scored for Doubting Russians Have Atomic Bomb," *New York Times*, January 27, 1953.

17. Hershberg, *James B. Conant*, 498.

18. Curtis E. LeMay and MacKinlay Kantor, *Mission with LeMay: My Story* (New York: Doubleday, 1965), 432.

19. Richard H. Kohn and Joseph P. Harahan, eds., *Strategic Air Warfare: An Interview with Generals Curtis E. LeMay, Leon W. Johnson, David A. Burchinal, and Jack C. Catton* (Washington, DC: Office of Air Force History, 1988), 88.

20. Rhodes, *Dark Sun: The Making of the Hydrogen Bomb*, 456.

21. Ibid., 463–468.

22. Hargittai, *Judging Edward Teller*, 225–37; Rhodes, *Dark Sun: The Making of the Hydrogen Bomb*, 468–71; Goodchild, *Edward Teller: The Real Dr. Strangelove*, 174–86.

23. Rhodes, *Dark Sun: The Making of the Hydrogen Bomb*, 448.

24. "The President's News Conference, November 30, 1950," Truman Presidential Library.

25. Rhodes, *Dark Sun: The Making of the Hydrogen Bomb*, 449–51.

26. Ibid., 452.

27. Ibid., 452–54.

28. Hershberg, *James B. Conant*, 484–90.

29. Goodchild, *Edward Teller: The Real Dr. Strangelove*, 189.

30. Ibid., 187–202.

31. "Operation Ivy," Joint Task Force 132, USAF, http://archive.org/details/operation_ivy.

32. Hargittai, *Judging Edward Teller*, 264.

33. "The Making of the H-Bomb," *Time*, April 12, 1954, 21–24.

34. Goodchild, *Edward Teller: The Real Dr. Strangelove*, 212–13.

35. Ibid., 196–97.

36. Ibid., 231.

37. Ibid., 244.

38. Ibid., 232–50.

Chapter 11

1. Dwight David Eisenhower, *Crusade in Europe* (New York: Doubleday, 1948), 260.

2. See photograph of French physicist Charles Sadron in Michael B. Petersen, *Missiles for the Fatherland: Peenemünde, National Socialism, and the V-2 Missile* (Cambridge: Cambridge University Press, 2009), 196.

3. Wayne Biddle, *Dark Side of the Moon: Wernher Von Braun, the Third Reich, and the Space Race* (New York: W. W. Norton, 2009), 123–26.

4. Ibid., 190 n. 4.

5. Roy Irons, *Hitler's Terror Weapons: The Price of Vengeance* (London: HarperCollins, 2002), 199–203.

6. John Ray Skates, *The Invasion of Japan: Alternative to the Bomb* (Columbia: University of South Carolina Press, 1994), 91–92.

7. Edmund Beard, *Developing the ICBM: A Study in Bureaucratic Politics* (New York: Columbia University Press, 1976), 21–22.
8. See http://catalog.hathitrust.org/Record/003133242.
9. Michael S. Sherry, *The Rise of American Air Power: The Creation of Armageddon* (New Haven, CT: Yale University Press, 1987), 187.
10. H. H. Arnold, *Third Report of the Commanding General of the Army Air Forces to the Secretary of War: November 12, 1945* (Washington, DC: Army Air Forces, 1945), 68.
11. Beard, *Developing the ICBM*, 69–71.
12. Ibid., 112.
13. Neil Sheehan, *A Fiery Peace in a Cold War: Bernard Schriever and the Ultimate Weapon* (New York: Vintage Books, 2009), 124–25.
14. Beard, *Developing the ICBM*, 37–44.
15. Ibid., 49–67.
16. G. Harry Stine, *ICBM: The Making of the Weapon That Changed the World* (New York: Orion Books, 1991), 84–85, 113–14.
17. Sheehan, *A Fiery Peace*, 143, 160–62.
18. Ibid., 155–59.
19. Ibid., 177–78.
20. Beard, *Developing the ICBM*, 153–94.
21. Sheehan, *A Fiery Peace*, 150–51.
22. Michael H. Armacost, *The Politics of Weapons Innovation: The Thor-Jupiter Controversy* (New York: Columbia University Press, 1969), 74.
23. Ibid., 114.
24. Ibid., 123–28.
25. Stephen I. Schwartz, *Atomic Audit: The Costs and Consequences of U.S. Nuclear Weapons Since 1940* (Washington, DC: Brookings Institution Press, 1998), 129 n. 159.
26. Armacost, *The Politics of Weapons Innovation*, 172–79.
27. Ibid., 180–218.

Chapter 12

1. Fred Kaplan, *The Wizards of Armageddon* (New York: Simon and Schuster, 1983), 55–59.
2. Sharon Ghamari-Tabrizi, *The Worlds of Herman Kahn: The Intuitive Science of Thermonuclear War* (Cambridge, MA: Harvard University Press, 2005), 52–53.
3. Bernard Brodie, *The Absolute Weapon: Atomic Power and World Order* (New York: Harcourt, Brace, 1946, 29–30.)
4. Kaplan, *The Wizards of Armageddon*, 24–32.
5. Karl P. Mueller, Jasen J. Castillo, Forrest E. Morgan, Negeen Pegahi, and Brian Rosen, *Striking First: Preemptive and Preventive Attack in U.S. National Security Policy* (Santa Monica, CA: RAND Corporation, 2006), 124–25.
6. Ghamari-Tabrizi, *The Worlds of Herman Kahn*, 107.
7. Ibid., 108.
8. Mueller et al., *Striking First: Preemptive and Preventive Attack in U.S. National Security Policy*, 127.

9. Willliam Poundstone, *Prisoner's Dilemma* (New York: Doubleday, 1992), 141.

10. Ibid., 70–71, 78–80, 195–96.

11. Mueller et al., *Striking First: Preemptive and Preventive Attack in U.S. National Security Policy*, 148.

12. Ibid., 139–40.

13. Nathan Leites, *The Operational Code of the Politburo* (Santa Monica, CA: RAND, 2007; original publication 1951).

14. Kaplan, *The Wizards of Armageddon*, 97–110.

15. Bernard Brodie, *Strategy in the Missile Age* (Princeton, NJ: Princeton University Press, 1959).

16. John Renaker, *Dr. Strangelove and the Hideous Epoch: Deterrence in the Nuclear Age* (Claremont, CA: Regina Books, 2000), 204–10.

17. Henry Kissinger, *Nuclear Weapons and Foreign Policy* (New York: Harper and Brothers, 1957).

18. Kaplan, *The Wizards of Armageddon*, 132–34.

19. Ibid., 148–52.

20. Ghamari-Tabrizi, *The Worlds of Herman Kahn*, 192.

21. William Taubman, *Khrushchev: The Man and His Era* (New York: Norton, 2004), 243.

22. Kaplan, *The Wizards of Armageddon*, 155–73.

23. Albert Wohlstetter, "The Delicate Balance of Terror," *Foreign Affairs* 37 (1958): 211–34.

24. Ghamari-Tabrizi, *The Worlds of Herman Kahn*, 13–14.

25. Herman Kahn, *On Thermonuclear War* (New York: Free Press, 1960), 375–76.

26. Ibid., 647–48.

27. Kaplan, *The Wizards of Armageddon*, 220–31.

28. James R. Newman, "Books: Two Discussions of Thermonuclear War," *Scientific American*, March 1961, 197.

29. Ghamari-Tabrizi, *The Worlds of Herman Kahn*, 17–23.

30. Ibid., 275.

31. Alex Abella, *Soldiers of Reason: The RAND Corporation and the Rise of the American Empire* (Boston: Mariner Books, 2008), 96.

32. Gary Stix, "Infamy and Honor at the Atomic Café: Edward Teller Has No Regrets About His Contentious Career," *Scientific American*, October 1999, 44.

33. Poundstone, *Prisoner's Dilemma*, 212.

34. Ghamari-Tabrizi, *The Worlds of Herman Kahn*, 218.

35. Curtis E. LeMay and Dale O. Smith, *America Is in Danger* (New York: Funk and Wagnalls, 1968).

36. William Burr, "The Creation of SIOP-62: More Evidence on the Origins of Over-kill," National Security Archive, www.gwu.edu/~nsarchiv/NSAEBB/NSAEBB130/index.htm.

37. John H. Rubel, *Doomsday Delayed: USAF Strategic Weapons and SIOP-62, 1959–1962; Two Cautionary Tales* (Latham, MD: Hamilton Books, 2008), 23–27.

38. Ghamari-Tabrizi, *The Worlds of Herman Kahn*, 47.

39. Kaplan, *The Wizards of Armageddon*, 263–85.

40. Abella, *Soldiers of Reason*, 162–65.
41. Kaplan, *The Wizards of Armageddon*, 291–304.
42. Ronald L. Tammen, *MIRV and the Arms Race: An Interpretation of Defense Strategy* (New York: Praeger, 1973).
43. Poundstone, *Prisoner's Dilemma*, 260–70.

Chapter 13
1. Mary T. Cagle, *History of the Redeye Weapon System* (Huntsville, AL: U.S. Army Missile Command, 1974), 84-85.
2. Ibid., 159–60.
3. Alan J. Kuperman, "The Stinger Missile and U.S. Interventionism in Afghanistan," in *The New American Interventionism: Essays from Political Science Quarterly*, ed. James Carley Demetrios (New York: Columbia University Press, 1999).
4. "Man-Portable Air Defence Systems (Manpads)," Small Arms Survey, www .smallarmssurvey.org/fileadmin/docs/H-Research_Notes/SAS-Research-Note-1.pdf.
5. Kuperman, "The Stinger Missile and U.S. Interventionism in Afghanistan."
6. Brian Michael Jenkins, *High Technology Terrorism and Surrogate War: The Impact of New Technoloogy on Low-Level Violence* (Santa Monica, CA: RAND Corporation, 1975), 13.
7. Fred A. Wilcox, *Waiting for an Army to Die: The Tragedy of Agent Orange* (Santa Ana, CA: Seven Locks Press, 1989).
8. D. Hank Ellison, *Chemical Warfare During the Vietnam War: Riot Control Agents in Combat* (New York: Routledge, 2011), 1–28; William M. Hammond, *Public Affairs: The Military and the Media, 1962–1968* (Washington, DC: Center of Military History, United States Army, 1988), 157.
9. William A. Buckingham, *Operation Ranch Hand: The Air Force and Herbicides in Southeast Asia 1961–1971* (Washington, DC: Office of Air Force History, 1982), 9–22, 28.
10. Michael Gough, *Dioxin, Agent Orange: The Facts* (New York: Plenum Press, 1986), 27–34.
11. Paul Frederick Cecil, *Herbicidal Warfare: The Ranch Hand Project in Vietnam* (New York: Praeger, 1986), 48–52; Gough, *Dioxin, Agent Orange: The Facts*, 49.
12. Cecil, *Herbicidal Warfare*, 31; Wilbur J. Scott. *The Politics of Readjustment: Vietnam Veterans Since the War* (New York: Aldine de Gruyter, 1993), 80–81.
13. Buckingham, *Operation Ranch Hand*, 133.
14. Russell Betts and Frank Denton, *An Evaluation of Chemical Crop Destruction in Vietnam* (Santa Monica, CA: RAND Corporation, 1967).
15. Buckingham, *Operation Ranch Hand*, 138–40.
16. Cecil, *Herbicidal Warfare*, 160–65.
17. Alex Horton, "VA Nearly Done with Agent Orange Claims," *VAntage Point* blog, U.S. Department of Veteran Affairs, June 19, 2012, www.blogs.va.gov/VAntage/7229/va-nearly-done-with-agent-orange-claims.
18. *Vietnam Association for Victims of Agent Orange/Dioxin v. Dow Chemical Co.*, United States Court of Appeals for the Second Circuit, decided February 22, 2008, www .warlegacies.org/Agent%20Orange/Appealdecision.pdf.

19. William Beecher, "Weapons Dispute: M-16: Dandy or Dud?" *New York Times*, June 11, 1967.

20. A. J. Glass, "The M14: Best Army Rifle—or 'a Major Ordnance Blunder'?" *New York Herald Tribune*, June 26, 1961.

21. Thomas L. McNaughter, *The M16 Controversies: Military Organizations and Weapons Acquisitions* (New York: Praeger Scientific, 1984).

22. John L. Frisbee, "Practice of Professionalism," *Air Force*, August 1986, 113; Mark Clodfelter, *The Limits of Airpower: The American Bombing of North Vietnam* (New York: Free Press, 1989), 206–8.

23. Guenter Lewy, *America in Vietnam* (New York: Oxford University Press, 1978), 383–85.

24. Robert A. Pape, *Bombing to Win: Air Power and Coercion in War* (Ithaca, NY: Cornell University Press, 1996).

25. Lewy, *America in Vietnam*, 374.

26. Errol Morris, "*The Fog of War*: Transcript," www.errolmorris.com/film/fow_transcript .html.

27. Dwight David Eisenhower, *Mandate for Change* (Garden City, NY: Doubleday, 1963), 449.

28. Clodfelter, *The Limits of Airpower*, 40–52.

29. Pape, *Bombing to Win*, 177–89.

30. Lewy, *America in Vietnam*, 381, 404; Carl Berger, ed., *The United States Air Force in Southeast Asia* (Washington, DC: Office of Air Force History, 1977), 366.

31. "Nixon, Kissinger, and the 'Decent Interval,'" Miller Center, http://whitehousetapes .net/clips/1972_0803_vietnam/index.htm.

32. Clodfelter, *The Limits of Airpower*, 149.

33. Henry Kissinger, *White House Years* (New York: Little, Brown, 1979), 1469.

34. Clodfelter, *The Limits of Airpower*, 148–202.

Chapter 14

1. Adam Curtis, "Pandora's Box 2: The Brink of Eternity," http://www.youtube.com/ watch?v=d_REHDxhfKg, at 35:20. Based on a story told by Herbert York, former assistant secretary of defense for research and engineering and director of Lawrence Livermore Laboratory.

2. William J. Broad, *Teller's War: The Top-Secret Story Behind the Star Wars Deception* (New York: Simon and Schuster, 1992), 106; George P. Shultz, *Turmoil and Triumph: My Years as Secretary of State* (New York: Charles Scribner and Sons, 1993), 263.

3. William J. Broad, *Teller's War*, 104.

4. Shultz, *Turmoil and Triumph*, 263.

5. Jeff Hecht, "The History of the X-Ray Laser," *Optics and Photoionics*, May 2008.

6. Edward Teller, *Better a Shield than a Sword: Perspectives on Defense and Technology* (New York: Free Press, 1987).

7. Broad, *Teller's War*, 91–93.

8. Istvan Hargittai, *Judging Edward Teller: A Closer Look at One of the Most Influential Scientists of the Twentieth Century* (Amherst, NY: Prometheus Books, 2010), 97.

9. Daniel Graham, *High Frontier: A Strategy for National Survival* (New York: Tom Doherty Associates, 1983).
10. Broad, *Teller's War*, 107–16.
11. Ibid., 116–20; Peter Goodchild, *Edward Teller: The Real Dr. Strangelove* (Cambridge, MA: Harvard University Press, 2004), 342–44.
12. Broad, *Teller's War*, 127–31.
13. Ibid., 122–26.
14. Robert C. McFarlane and Zofia Smardz, *Special Trust* (New York: Cadell and Davies, 1994), 228.
15. Shultz, *Turmoil and Triumph*, 246–61.
16. Sanford A. Lakoff and Herbert Frank York, *A Shield in Space? Technology, Politics, and the Strategic Defense Initiative: How the Reagan Administration Set out to Make Nuclear Weapons "Impotent and Obsolete" and Succumbed to the Fallacy of the Last Move* (Berkeley: University of California Press, 1989), 361–62n66.
17. Edward Teller, "Reagan's Courage," *New York Times*, March 30, 1983.
18. Broad, *Teller's War*, 140.
19. Ibid., 143–215.
20. Robert M. Gates, *From the Shadows: The Ultimate Insider's Story of Five Presidents and How They Won the Cold War* (New York: Simon and Schuster, 2007), 263.
21. Hargittai, *Judging Edward Teller*, 413–16, 418–23.
22. For a contemporary discussion of Soviet responses, see Benjamin S. Lambeth and Kevin N. Lewis, *The Strategic Defense Initiative in Soviet Planning and Policy* (RAND, 1988).
23. Broad, *Teller's War*, 245–65.
24. Eric Schmitt, "Israel Plays Down Effectiveness of Patriot Missile," *New York Times*, October 31, 1991.
25. William J. Broad, "The Patriot's Success: Because of 'Star Wars' or in Spite of It?" *New York Times*, February 10, 1991.
26. Craig Cerniello, "Cohen Announces NMD Restructuring, Funding Boost," *Arms Control Today*, January/February 1999.
27. Sherry Jones, "Missile Wars," PBS *Frontline* (2002), www.pbs.org/wgbh/pages/frontline/shows/missile/interviews/habiger.html.
28. Thom Shanker, David E. Sanger, and Martin Fackler, "U.S. Is Bolstering Missile Defense to Deter North Korea," *New York Times*, March 15, 2013.
29. William J. Broad, "U.S. Missile Defense Strategy Is Flawed, Expert Panel Finds," *New York Times*, September 11, 2012.

Chapter 15

1. Richard P. Hallion, "Precision Guided Munitions and the New Era of Warfare," Air Power Studies Centre, Fairbain, Australia, APSC Paper no. 53, 1995, www.fas.org/man/dod-101/sys/smart/docs/paper53.htm.
2. Paul G. Gillespie, *Weapons of Choice: The Development of Precision Guided Munitions* (Tuscaloosa: University of Alabama Press, 2006), 156.
3. Hallion, "Precision Guided Munitions."

4. Gillespie, *Weapons of Choice*, 137–38.
5. James V. Writer, Robert F. DeFraites, and John F. Brundage, "Comparative Mortality Among U.S. Military Personnel in the Persian Gulf Region and Worldwide During Operations Desert Shield and Desert Storm," *Journal of the American Medical Association* 275, no. 2 (1996): 118–21.
6. Hallion, "Precision Guided Munitions."
7. Gillespie, *Weapons of Choice*, 14–25.
8. Hallion, "Precision Guided Munitions."
9. Gillespie, *Weapons of Choice*, 45–65.
10. David A. Koplow, *Death by Moderation: The U.S. Military's Quest for Useable Weapons* (Cambridge: Cambridge University Press, 2009), 1–3.
11. "Carter's Big Decision: Down Goes the B-1, Here Comes the Cruise," *Time*, July 11, 1977.
12. Peter Grier, "The JDAM Revolution," *Air Force Magazine*, September 2006.
13. Benjamin S. Lambeth, *NATO's Air War in Kosovo: A Strategic and Operational Assessment* (Santa Monica: RAND Corporation, 2001), 17–65.
14. P. W. Singer, *Wired for War* (New York: Penguin Press, 2009), 56–57.
15. Jen DiMascio, "New Drones Net Rosy Skies for Makers," Politico.com, November 23, 2009, http://www.politico.com/news/stories/1109/29828.html.; Barney Gimbel, "The Predator," CNN Money, October 28, 2008, http://money.cnn.com/2008/10/28/magazines/fortune/predator_gimbel.fortune/index.htm.
16. W. J. Hennigan, "Drones Create a Buzz in Southern California Aerospace Industry," *Los Angeles Times*, September 21, 2010.
17. Jen DiMascio, "New Drones Net Rosy Skies for Makers"
18. Home page of the caucus: http://unmannedsystemscaucus.mckeon.house.gov.
19. Singer, *Wired for War*, 59, 253.
20. Bill Yenne, *Attack of the Drones: A History of Unmanned Aerial Combat* (St. Paul, MN: Zenith Press, 2004), 64.
21. Ibid., 85–86.
22. Dan Froomkin, "WikiLeaks Video Exposes 2007 'Collateral Murder' in Iraq," *Huffington Post*, originally posted June 5, 2010, updated May 25, 2011, www.huffingtonpost.com/2010/04/05/wikileaks-exposes-video-o_n_525569.html.
23. Singer, *Wired for War*, 124–26.
24. Philip K. Dick, *Second Variety and Other Classic Stories* (New York: Carol, 2002).
25. Ward Wilson, "The Myth of Nuclear Necessity," *New York Times*, January 13, 2013.
26. Thomas Blood, *Madam Secretary: A Biography of Madeleine Albright* (New York: Macmillan, 1999), 182.
27. Jane Perlez, "Chinese Plan to Kill Drug Lord with Drone Highlights Military Advances," *New York Times*, February 20, 2013.
28. Mark McDonald, "Growth in China's Drone Program Called 'Alarming,'" *IHT Rendezvous* blog, *New York Times*, November 27, 2012.
29. Robert Mackey and Rick Gladstone, "Iran Shows Video It Says Was Made by U.S. Drone," *New York Times*, February 7, 2013

Epilogue

1. Walter Kozak, *The Life and Wars of General Curtis LeMay* (Washington, DC: Regnery, 2009), 365–88.
2. "William Kaufmann, 90; MIT Political Scientist Reshaped Kennedy's Defense Strategy," *Boston Globe*, December 26, 2008.
3. James Hershberg, *James B. Conant: Harvard to Hiroshima and the Making of the Nuclear Age* (New York: Alfred A. Knopf, 1993), 490.
4. Jeff Goodell, "Can Geo-Engineering Save the World?" *Rolling Stone*, October 4, 2011.

INDEX

Aberdeen Proving Ground, 233–34, 236
ABM treaty, 231, 270–71
Abrahamson, James, 265
Acheson, Dean, 173–74, 176
ACS (American Chemical Society), 37, 39–41, 93, 162, 288
ACTS (Air Corps Tactical School), 54–56, 68, 96, 113
Adams, Roger, 33, 90, 99–100
Adamsite, 33
AEC (Atomic Energy Commission), 131, 134, 170–71, 173, 175, 182–86, 187, 288
aerial torpedo, 274–75
Afghanistan, 12, 236, 272–73, 281, 284
Agee, James, 11, 76
Agent Orange, 160, 237, 239–40, 242
Agent Purple, 240
Aioi Bridge, Hiroshima, 140
Air Corps Tactical School. *See* ACTS
Air Force (USAF)
  Cold War strategy, 210–29
  missiles, 192–208
  nuclear weapons, 185
Air Materiel Command, 193
Aircraft Production, Bureau of, 48
airpower doctrine
  air superiority, 47, 83–84, 151,157, 189, 236–37
  origins, 49–51
AK-47 rifle, 240, 243
Al Qaeda, 270, 281
Alamogordo, 139
Albright, Madeleine, 283
Alexander, Stewart, 75, 155

Allen, William, 108
Alvarez, Luis, 172, 183
Ambros, Otto, 153, 162
American Chemical Society. *See* ACS
American Expeditionary Force, World War I, 29–30, 45, 47, 148
American Rifleman magazine, 246
American University, 30–31, 34, 36–37, 41–42, 90
Amiriyah shelter, 274
Andrews, Frank, 57–59
Andropov, Yuri, 263, 266
Anti-Ballistic Missile (ABM) treaty, 262
Aphrodite, Operation, 275
applesauce incendiary gel, 95, 100
Aquila UAV, 278
AR-15 rifle, 244–48
Arctic Test Board, 244–45
Argonne National Laboratory, 265
ArmaLite, 244–45
Army Air Corps, 79, 52–61, 64–71, 96, 113, 275, 286
Army Air Forces (AAF). 8–9, 44–45, 55, 60–72, 75, 77–144
  atomic bomb, 140–44
  chemical weapons, 146, 160
  European theater, 73–90
  Pacific theater, 105–20
  Postwar, 171, 192–94, 197, 210
Army Air Service, 45–46, 48–49, 51–54
Army Aviation Section, 45–46
Army-McCarthy hearings, 131
Army Ordnance Corps, 95, 243–44, 248
Army Signal Corps, 46

Arnold, Henry "Hap"
   inter-war years, 49, 59–60
   post–World War II, 192–93, 195,
      210–12
   World War I, 45
   World War II, 76, 80–85, 87, 106,
      109–16, 118–20, 137–38, 140,
      143–44, 161, 192
assured destruction, 231, 258
Atlas ICBM, 193, 198–99, 201–2, 208, 227
atomic bomb, 8, 10, 93, 122
   decision to use, 134–44
   Einstein letter, 123
   plutonium bomb, 10, 125–29, 132–34,
      140, 176–79
   Soviet bomb, 174–75
   uranium bomb, 129–32
Atomic Energy Commission. See AEC
Auschwitz, 162
autopilots, 70–71, 189, 274–75
AWPD/1, 75–76, 113

B-1A bomber, 277
B-17 "Flying Fortress" bomber, 9, 57–59,
      61, 66–67, 69, 74, 76–80, 82–83, 85,
      98, 275
B-18 bomber, 57
B-24 bomber "Liberator," 61, 76–77, 275
B-25 "Mitchell" bomber, 78, 101, 286
B-29 bomber, 61, 106, 108–11, 113,
      115–18, 163, 177–78, 193
B-36 bomber, 193, 197, 216
B-45 bomber, 193
B-47 bomber, 193
B-52 bomber, 177, 193, 200, 216, 275
B-70 bomber, 226
B-san (B-29 bomber), 106
BAL (British Anti-Lewisite), 149
Ball, George, 87–88
Ballistic Missile Defense Office
      (BMDO), 270
BAMBI, 259
Bari, 153–56, 163
Bartlett, Paul D., 93
Baruch, Bernard, 174
bat bomb, 99–103

battery, Edison alkaline, 14–15, 17–18,
      20–23, 25
battery, lead-acid, 14, 18, 23, 25
Batzel, Roger, 264, 290
Bekaa Valley, 278
Belgrade, 278
Bendetsen, Karl, 256, 259–60
Benning, Fort, 244
Bentsen, Lloy, 212–13
Berkeley, University of California, 125,
      127–28, 132–34, 172, 183, 185,
      187, 288–89
Berkeley Radiation Laboratory, 183, 185
Berlin airlift, 176
Berlin crisis, 229–30
Bethe, Hans, 10, 126–29, 172–73, 184,
      186, 222
Big Week, 84
bin Laden, Osama, 12
biological weapons, 50, 160, 166
Bison bombers, 200, 220
Bissell, Clayton, 192
Bistera, USS, 155
Bliss, Fort, 195
Blitz, London, 55, 74, 189, 192
Bloeker, Jack von, 100
Blue, Linden, 278
Blue, Neal, 279
Blueberry Lake, 165
BMDO (Ballistic Missile Defense
      Office), 270
Boeing, 57–58, 76, 199
Boeing 299 prototype of the B-17, 57
Bohr, Niels, 122, 127, 129
Bolling, Raynal, 48
bombardier's Code of Honor, 69
bomber gap, 10, 200, 220
bombing
   atomic bombing, 138–46
   coercive bombing, 249
   incendiary bombing, 49, 74, 82,
      107–19, 152
   precision bombing doctrine, 8–9,
      55–56, 67, 85, 88, 96, 99
   precision bombing, lack of success, 74,
      81, 113–15

bombing (*continued*)
  transition to area bombing, 7, 75–76, 80, 81–83, 86, 88, 108, 114, 116–17, 119, 140
bombsight shortage, 72
bombsights, 61–72
  calculations required, 62–64
  dive-bombing, 68
  Norden, 5, 8–9, 65–72, 74, 80, 82, 88, 108–9, 113, 140, 273, 275
  Radar, 82
  Sperry, 65, 68–72
  Wimperis, 65
Bonus March on Washington, 33
Booster, 170–71, 184
Borden, William, 187
Bormann, Martin, 153, 157
Bosnia, 272, 280, 283
Bradbury, Norris, 179, 184
Bradley, Omar, 157
Braun, Wernher von, 11, 190–91, 195, 198, 202–5, 207, 225
Briggs, Lyman, 123–24
Briggs Uranium Commission, 123–25
Brilliant Pebbles, 9, 268–70, 289
Britain, Battle of, 59, 75
British Anti-Lewisite (BAL), 149
Broad, William, 129
Brodie, Bernard, 9, 211–13, 218, 223
Bronk, Detlev, 183, 287
Brown, Harold, 228
Bruchmüller, Georg, 28
Bryan, William Jennings, 4
Buckley, William, 260
Buenos Aires, 59
Bullene, Egbert, 163
Bulletin of the Atomic Scientists, 172
burst phase of an ICBM, 263
Bush, George H. W., 167–68, 237, 269, 272
Bush, George W., 6, 270–71, 290
Bush, Vannevar, 6, 91, 93, 118, 123–26, 135, 139, 170, 193, 269–70, 272
Byrnes, James, 9, 135, 139

C-1 adaptor, 70
C-123 transport, Operation Ranch Hand, 240

Cape Canaveral, 195, 204
Caproni bomber, 49
Cardaniac, 71
Carlsbad Army Air Base, 92, 101, 103
Carlsbad Caverns, 100
Carnegie Foundation, 123, 170
Carson, Rachel, 238
Carter, Jimmy, 7, 167, 228, 268, 277
Casablanca conference, 80, 112
Casey, William, 265
CBO (Combined Bombing Offensive), 80
chain reaction, nuclear, 122, 128, 132
Charlie Wilson's War, 234
CHASE (Cut Holes and Sink 'Em), 165
Chemical Corps, 162–7, 237
Chemical Warfare Association, 40
Chemical Warfare Convention (CWC), 167–68
Chemical Warfare Service. *See* CWS
chemical weapons, 3–5
  attempts to limit, 38–41, 165–68
  inter-war years, 49, 51, 93, 95
  post–World War II, 162–68
  World War I, 26–42
  World War II, 145–61
Chennault, Claire, 109
Chernenko, Konstantin, 266
Chiang Kai-shek, 109–10
Chinese embassy in Belgrade, 278
chlorine, 15, 18, 20, 26–28, 30, 35, 38
cholinesterase inhibitor, 152
Churchill, Winston, 50, 74, 76, 80–81, 111, 118, 126, 139, 146, 151–52, 156–57, 212
CIA, 100, 200, 215, 220, 236–37, 265–66, 278–79, 283
civil defense, 218–19
Clarion, Operation, 86
Clark, William, 260
Clausewitz, Carl von, 6
Clinton, William, 6, 270–71
COA (Committee of Operations Analysts), 80–81, 86–87, 113, 118
coastal defense mission, Air Corps, 56–57
Coffin, Howard, 48
Cohn, Mildred, 130

Cold War nuclear strategies
assured destruction, 231, 258
counterforce, 228, 230
limited nuclear war, 218, 223, 228–29
massive retaliation, 197, 213
mutual assured destruction (MAD), 231
overseas bases, 216–72
preemptive war, 213, 227, 231
preventive war, 187, 212–13
Collbohm, Frank, 210
Collier's magazine, 131
Cologne, 108
combat box bomber formation, 79
combat support mission, Air Corps and
AAF, 56–57, 250
Combined Bombing Offensive (CBO), 80
Combustion Engineering, 167
Committee of Operations Analysts. *See*
COA
Compton, Arthur, 133, 135–63
Compton, Karl, 124, 133, 135
Conant, James, 5–6
Cold War, 170–74, 187
early life, 33–34
Harvard presidency, 87, 90
later life, 287
National Academy election, 183–84
World War I, 32, 34–37, 40–41
World War II, 87, 90–93, 124, 125–26,
130, 135–36, 149–50
Condon, Edward, 131
Conex containers, 271
Coningham, Arthur, 154
Consolidated Aircraft, 76–77
Convair, 193–94, 198–99
Cooke, Charles, 20–22
Coolidge, Calvin, 6, 40, 53
Cooper, Gary, 286
cosmochemistry, 287
Couffer, Jack, 92, 100–103
counterforce strategy, 228, 230
Cowan, Howard, 86
Craig, Malin, 57, 59
crop destruction program, Vietnam,
239, 241
cruise missiles, 277
Cuban missile crisis, 5, 230, 249

Cunningham, Randy "Duke," 279
Cut Holes and Sink 'Em (CHASE), 165
CWC (Chemical Warfare Convention),
167–68
CWS (Chemical Warfare Service), 35,
37–41, 54, 91–96, 99–101, 103,
146–47, 149–51, 161–62, 167

D-Day, 83–84
Daniels, Josephus, 4, 13, 16–20, 22–25,
51–52, 285–86
Dayton, 166, 176
de Gaulle, Charles, 208
"Death of the Ball-Turret Gunner," 77
Defense Department, 194, 197–98, 202,
206, 208, 228, 230–31, 242, 246
"dehousing" euphemism, 99
deterrence, 221–24, 262
Detrick, Fort, 160
deuterium, 127, 129, 132, 169–71,
179–80
Diem, Nguyen van, 233, 237–38
dioxin, 239, 242
Disney, Walt, 10–11, 75–76, 207
dive bombers, 56, 68, 70, 72
divinylacetylene, 92–93
d'Olier, Franklin, 87
dollar bill auction, 232
Donovan, William, 99
Doolittle, Jimmy, 85
doomsday machine, 224
Dornberger, Walther, 190
Douglas, James, 219
Douglas Aircraft, 210, 219
Douhet, Giulio, 46, 49–51, 53, 55
Dow Chemical, 242
Drague, Herbert, 69
Dresden, 85–86, 158
Dri-Slide, 248
drones. *See* UAVs
Drum, Hugh, 57–58
Dugway Proving Grounds, 96, 98, 103,
118, 165
Dulles, John Foster, 213, 219
Dunkirk, 149
DuPont Chemical, 92–95, 100
Dyhernfurth, 161

E-2 submarine, 18, 20–23, 25
Eaker, Ira, 80–84, 86, 138
Edgewood Arsenal, 35, 93, 153
Edison, Charles, 14
Edison, Thomas, 5, 11–25, 210, 274, 285
Edison Storage Battery Company, 21
Edwards Air Force Base, 101
Eglin Field, 98
Eighth Air Force, 76–80, 85, 88–89, 108–9
Einstein, Albert, 121, 123–24, 130–31,
    171, 174
Eisenhower, Dwight, 6–7
  chemical weapons, 163
  Cold War nuclear strategy, 197–98,
    200–201, 203, 208, 212–13, 219,
    221, 225, 228
  Oppenheimer security hearings, 187
  Vietnam, 250
  World War II, 80, 83–85, 111, 131,
    136, 156,190
Ellsberg, Daniel, 228–29, 289
Embick, Stanley, 58
Enola Gay, 140–41
Enthoven, Alain, 231
Everett, Cornelius, 178
Excalibur X-Ray laser, 9, 257–61, 265–66,
    268, 270, 289–90

F-4 submarine, 18, 22
F-22 fighter, 281
F-35 fighter, 281
F-111 fighter, 226
Fairchild, Muir, 96
Fairfield-Suisun Air Force Base, 178
Falkenhagen, 161–62
FBI, 65, 69, 175, 186–87, 202
FDA (Food and Drug Administration), 242
Ferebee, Thomas, 141
Fermi, Enrico, 127, 135, 171, 173–74,
    178, 187
Field Artillery, 194
Fieser, Louis, 91–95, 100, 102–4, 162
Fifth Air Force, 120
fission, 126–26, 132–33
flak, 77, 79–80, 85
Fletcher, James, 263–64

Flying Tigers, 109
FMC Corporation, 164
Food and Drug Administration (FDA), 242
Food Machinery Corporation, 164
Ford, 15, 226, 268, 285
Ford, Gerald, 6, 41, 238
Ford, Henry, 5, 285
Ford Motor, 225
Forrestal, James, 213
Foulois, Benjamin, 45, 65
Fourteenth Air Force, 109
Franck, James, 135–36
Freeman, Orville, 241
Freeman, Roger H., 89
Frieman, Edward, 260
Fries, Amos, 39–41
Frisch, Otto, 124
Frisch-Peierls memorandum, 124
Fuchs, Klaus, 126, 128, 138, 171, 175
Fuchs-von Neumann patent, 179
fusion, 127, 169, 171, 178–80

GAC (General Advisory Committee),
    171–74, 179, 183–84, 186–87
Gaither, Horace, 218
Gaither Commission, 218–19, 222
Galbraith, John Kenneth, 87
game theory, 209, 214–15
Gardner, Trevor, 198–99, 201
gaseous diffusion, 130
gasoline use in incendiaries, 93–94
Gates, Marshall, 104
Gates, Robert, 266
General Advisory Committee. See GAC
General Atomics, 278–80, 290
General Motors, 201–2
Geneva Conference on Vietnam, 250
Geneva Protocol on chemical warfare,
    40–41, 145, 147, 150, 159, 162–63,
    167, 238
German-Japanese Village, 96–99, 103, 118
GHQ reserve, 46
Giap, Vo Nguyen, 252
Glaspie, April, 273
GMD (Ground-based Mid-course
    Defense), 271

GNAT-750, 279–80
Goebbels, Joseph, 153, 157
Gorbachev, Mikhail, 267
Gorin, Frank, 40
Göring, Hermann, 149
Gotha bomber, 48
Gow, Robert, 212
GPALS, 269
GPS guidance for smart bombs, 277–78, 284
Graham, Daniel, 259, 263, 268
Grierson, C. M., 86
Guillain, Robert, 106–7
Gulf War, 167–68, 269, 272–73, 277–78

Haber, Fritz, 27–28, 38
Habiger, Eugene, 270–71
Hahn, Otto, 122
Haiphong, 249
Hall, Ed, 202, 204, 206
Hall, Ted, 202
Hamburg bombing, 81–82, 87, 96, 108, 118, 273
Handley-Page bomber, 48–49
Hanford reactor, 133–34, 176
Hankow bombing, 114, 119
Hansell, Haywood, 56, 106, 113–15, 144
Harding, Warren, 39
Harris, Arthur "Bomber," 75–76
Harvard University, 5, 9, 32–4, 87, 90–91, 93–96, 100, 104, 170, 287, 289
Heisenberg, Werner, 127
Heller, Joseph, 78
Hellfire missile, 281
herbicides, 160, 237, 239, 242
Hershberg, E. B., 92–94
High Frontier, 256, 258–59, 263
Hildebrand, Joel 183
Hiroshima, 5, 8–9, 109, 119, 134, 137, 140–43, 177, 226, 273
Hitch, Charles, 245
Hitler, Adolf, 4, 74, 87, 121, 123, 130, 137, 146, 153–54, 157–58, 189–90
Ho Chi Minh Trail, 236
Honest John rocket, 164
Hoover, Herbert, 146

Hoover, J. Edgar, 69, 187
Hudson Institute, 289–90
Hughes Aircraft, 199
Humphrey, Hubert, 250–51
Huntsville Arsenal, 203
Hussein, Saddam, 10, 270, 273, 284
Hutchison, Miller Reese, 15–23, 25
hydrogen bomb
    decision to develop, 171–76, 178
    George test, 6, 179, 184
    Greenhouse tests, 179, 184
    Ivy tests, 184
    Mike test, 184–86, 188
    Soviet bomb, 185
    Teller-Ulam implosion process, 179–81, 184

ICBM, 193, 199–202, 220, 222, 231, 257, 277, 284
IED (improvised explosive device), 284
IG Farben, 148, 153, 158
incendiary bombs, 49–50, 74, 91, 93–100, 103, 107, 113–14, 116–19, 140, 146, 149, 152, 177
incendiary gels, 92, 94–5, 99–100
Inchon, 180
Infantry Board, 244–45
Interim Committee, 135–37, 139
invasion of Japan, 5, 112, 119–20, 136–39, 142–44, 147, 160–61, 192
Iran, 167–68, 237, 282, 284
Iraq, 10, 50, 167–68, 212, 269, 272–73, 282, 284
IRBM, 201–2, 208, 222
Iwo Jima, 111, 119, 159

Japanese gas use, 147, 151, 158
Japanese surrender, 111–12, 119, 142–43, 160
Jarrell, Randall, 77
Jastrow, Robert, 179
JB-2 copy of V-1 rocket, 192
JDAM (Joint Direct Attack Munition), 277–78
Jet Propulsion Laboratory, 192
jetstream, 113, 115

Jewett, Frank, 170
John Harvey, USS, 154–56
John Motley, USS, 154
Johnson, Edwin, 170
Johnson, Louis, 173, 182, 212
Johnson, Lyndon, 6, 208, 238, 248–52, 276, 288
Jumper, John, 280–81
Juno rocket, 206
Jupiter IRBM, 201–8, 221, 225, 227, 230, 243

Kahn, Herman, 10, 222–25, 289–90
Kamikaze planes, 119, 275
Karem, Abraham, 278–79
Kármán, Theodore von, 192–94
Kaufmann, William, 10, 218, 223, 228, 287
KC-97 tanker, 177
Kennedy, Jackie, 7
Kennedy, Joe (physical chemist), 132–33
Kennedy, John F., 6–7, 233, 288–90
    chemical weapons, 165, 238–39, 241
    Cold War nuclear strategy, 228–30, 259, 268
    missile gap, 221
Kennedy, Joseph (brother of John), 275
ketsugo strategy, 143
Kettering, Charles, 274
Kettering bug, 275
Keyworth, George, 256, 259–60, 262, 264, 290
Khamisiyah, 168
Khrushchev, Nikita, 206, 220, 229–30
King, Ernest, 112, 161
Kissinger, Henry, 10, 225, 252–54
Klenck, Jürgen von, 162
Kobe, 115, 117
Kokura, 140
Korea, 7, 163, 175–78, 180, 182–85, 194–95, 197, 213–14, 249–50, 274–75
Kosovo, 272, 277, 283
Krag-Jorgenson rifle, 244
Kubrick, Stanley, 224, 227
Kuhn, Richard, 152, 162
Kun, Bela 127

Kuter, Laurence, 68, 108
Kuwait, 272–73
Kwantung army in China, 159
Ky, Nguyen Cao, 241
Kyoto, 137

La Cheppe, 44
La Follette, Robert, 4
Laos, 236
Latimer, Wendell, 132, 172, 183
Lauritsen, Charles, 125
Lawrence, Ernest, 125, 135, 172, 183, 185, 187–88
Lawrence Livermore National Laboratory, 261, 269
lead bombardier, 72, 80, 82
Leading Systems, 278–79
Leahy, William, 161
Lehrer, Tom, 191
LeMay, Curtis, 6–7, 9–10
    Director of AAF R&D, 193–96
    early life, 73
    Europe and the Eighth Air Force, 74, 76–80
    later life, 276, 286–87
    Rex sighting, 59
    SAC Command, 176–78, 180, 182–73, 187, 197, 199–200, 210–11, 216, 218–19, 225
    Twentieth Bomber Command in China, 109–10
    Twenty-First Bomber Command on Guam, 113–17, 119–20, 135, 138, 144
    Vice-Chief and Chief of AF Staff, 225–28, 243, 245, 248, 250–51
Lewis, Randy 279
Lewis, Winford Lee 32, 37, 40
Lewisite, 31–32, 35–37, 40–42, 49, 93, 149–51, 158
Ley, Robert, 153, 157
Libby, Willard, 183
Liberty ships, 154, 165–66
Lilienthal, David, 171–74, 187
limited nuclear war, 218, 223, 228–29
Linebacker bombing of North Vietnam, 248, 253, 276

Lipkin, David, 133
Little, Arthur D. Company, 94
Livermore National Laboratory, 185, 222, 256–61, 264–65, 268, 289–90
London Daily Herald, Sputnik, 207
Long Bien Bridge, 276
Los Alamos, 36, 126, 128–29, 133, 169, 171–72, 175–76, 179, 184–86, 188, 198, 202, 258, 265–66, 290
Luftwaffe, 70, 74, 84, 149, 151, 154, 189–90, 192
Lusitania, 18

M-1 rifle ,72, 244
M-14 rifle, 247
M-16 rifle, 5, 243
M-47 bomb, 93–94
M-55 rocket, 164–66
M-69 bomb, 94–96, 98–99, 103, 107, 109, 113–14, 161
M1903 rifle 244
MacArthur, Douglas, 7, 111–12, 136, 178, 180, 182
MAD (mutual assured destruction), 231–32
Maenchen, George, 265
Manchuria, 109, 143, 159, 161, 182–83
Manhattan Project, 6, 9–10, 33, 72, 104, 125–26, 128, 130–33, 136, 142, 169–70, 172, 175–76, 183, 190–91, 202, 210, 212
Mao tse-Tung, 114, 175
March, Peyton, 38
Marianas, 105, 111, 113, 115
Mark, Carson, 179
Marshall, George, 59–60, 80, 95, 109, 111–12, 118, 136–37, 160–61
Martin, Glen L. Company, 57
Martin, Joe, 182
massive retaliation, 197, 213
Matthews, Francis, 212
Maverick missiles, 273
Maxim brothers, 14
May-Johnson bill, 170–71
McAuliffe, Anthony, 162
McCarthy, Joseph, 197

McFarland, Stephen, 118
McFarlane, Robert, 261–62
McKelway, St. Clair, 117
McMahon, Brien, 171–73, 185–86
McMillan, Edwin, 132
McNamara, Robert, 6–7
    later life, 286–88
    Secretary of Defense, 210, 226–31, 237–38, 243, 245–49, 251
    World War II, 120
McRaven, William, 12
MDA (Missile Defense Agency), 271
Meese, Edwin, 260
Meitner, Lise, 122
Méliès, Georges, 14
Memphis Belle, 77–78
Mendelsohn, Eric, 96
Menoher, Charles, 49, 52
Merck, 160
Metallurgical Laboratory (Met Lab), 133
Metz, 47
Meyer, Edward, 273
Midway, Battle of, 106
Milller, Stanley, 288
Milosevic, Slobodan, 278
Mines, Bureau of, 29–30, 32, 38
Minh, Ho Chi, 250
Minuteman missiles, 229, 231–32
MIRV, 231–32, 263–64, 268
Missile Defense Agency (MDA), 271
missile gap, 10, 220–21
Mitchell, Billy, 7, 43–49, 51–54, 58–59, 75, 111, 117, 144, 197, 286
Mittelbau-Dora concentration camp, 191
Mobay Chemical, 167
Molotov, Vyacheslav, 143
morale bombing, 55, 75, 86, 249
Morris, Errol, 120
Mountbatten, Lord, 111
Muroc Army Air Base 101
Mustang fighter, 83
mustard gas, 27–28, 30–32, 34–35, 373–78, 42, 93, 145, 148, 150–51, 153–58, 165–67
mutual assured destruction (MAD), 231–32

MX-774 missile, 193–94, 198
MX missile, 258

Nader, Ralph, 242
Nagasaki, 5, 8–10, 109, 119, 134, 140,
    142, 177, 179, 273
Nagoya, 113–17
Nakajima aircraft factory, 113
napalm, 4, 8–9, 90–91, 94–95, 100,
    102–4, 107, 114, 117–18, 146,
    159–60, 238
NASA, 263
National Academy of Sciences, 104, 124,
    170, 183–84, 287
National Bureau of Standards, 123, 131
National Defense Research Committee.
    See NDRC
National Institutes of Health, 242
National Medal of Science, 263
National Research Council, 271
National Rifle Association, 243, 246
National Security Council, 225, 229
Nautilus, USS, 196
Naval Consulting Board, 11
Naval Research Laboratory, 20, 22, 25,
    123, 210
NDRC (National Defense Research
    Committee), 87, 91, 93–96, 98, 103,
    124–25, 149
Neilson, Henry, 244
Neumann, John von 128, 171, 187–88,
    198–99, 209, 214, 225
neutrons, 122, 129, 132, 170, 180
"New Horizons," 192
New Look military policy, 197–98, 275
Newman, James, 224
Nieuwland, Julius, 32
Niigata, 140
Nimitz, Chester, 23, 111
Nitze, Paul, 87, 176, 229
Nixon, Richard, 6, 166, 221, 248, 251–54,
    276, 288
NORAD (North American Aerospace
    Defense Command), 255
Norden, Carl, 65, 67, 69–72, 286
Norden bombsight, 5, 8–9, 65–72, 74, 80,
    82, 88, 108–9, 113, 140, 273, 275

Nordhausen, 191
Normandy invasion, 84, 146–47, 157,
    190
Norris, James, 40
Norstad, Lauris, 113–17, 119
North American Aerospace Defense
    Center, 255
North American Aviation, 276
North Korea, 168, 175, 177–78, 180, 236,
    270–71
North Vietnam, 235, 238, 249–50,
    252–54, 276
North Vietnamese Army. See NVA
NSC-68, 176
Nunn, Sam, 9
NVA (North Vietnamese Army), 236,
    251–54

Oak Ridge,128, 130, 133
Obama, Barack, 6, 9, 12, 271
Occidental Chemical, 167
Office of Scientific Research and
    Development, 98, 125
Office of Strategic Services, 99
Okinawa, 119, 159–60, 166, 243
Omaha, SAC headquarters, 218, 227
Omaha Beach, 157
"On Thermonuclear War." 223
"Operational Code of the Politburo," 215
Oppenheimer, J. Rober,t 10, 36, 126–29,
    135–36, 169–74, 183–88, 289
Ordnance Corps, 166, 244
Osaka, 117
OSRD (Office of Scientific Research and
    Development), 98, 125
Ostfriesland battleship, 52
overseas bases, 216–17

P-47 "Thunderbolt" fighter, 83
P-51 "Mustang" fighter, 83
Panetta, Leon, 12
Pape, Robert, 249
Paperclip, Operation 11, 162
Parides, Peter, 125
Paris peace talks, Vietnam War, 252
Patrick, Mason, 45–46, 52–53
Patriot missile, 269–70

Patton, George, 33
Paveway smart bomb, 276–27
Peacekeeper/Peacemaker missile, 11
Pearl Harbor, 4, 60, 70–71, 76, 106, 109, 111, 118, 150, 212, 219
Peenemünde,191, 195
Peierls, Rudolf, 124, 129
Pentagon Papers, 288
Perle, Richard, 270
Perry, William, 9
Pershing, John, 29, 35, 45–49, 51–52
Phosgene, 27–28, 30, 35, 145, 148, 157, 159
Phúc, Phan Thị Kim, 104
Pine Bluff Arsenal, 150
Pioneer UAV, 278
Pitzer, Kenneth, 183
Ploesti, 82
Poindexter, John, 261
Polaris missile, 221, 226–67, 232
Porter, William, 95
Porton Down, 149
Potsdam Conference, 138, 161
Potsdam Declaration, 138
Powell, Colin, 283
Power, Thomas, 7, 216, 227, 287
Powers, Gary, 196
Pravda, 207
preemptive war, 213, 227, 231
Predator UAV, 11, 279–81, 283, 290
Presidential Citizens Medal, 268–69
Presidential Medal of Freedom, 290
preventive war, 187, 212–13
"Prima Facie Proof of the Feasibility of the Super," 171
prisoner's dilemma, 210, 214
Progressivism, 4–5, 43
Pusan, 177, 180
Pyongyang, 180

Q areas, 177
Quàng Tri, 252–53
Quebec Agreement, 126
Quebec conference, 76

Rabi, Isidor, 171, 173, 185, 187
Radiation Laboratory, Berkeley, 131, 172

RAF (Royal Air Force), 49–50, 74, 80–82, 84–87, 108, 118, 146, 151, 154, 189, 211
Ramo, Simon, 199
Ramo-Wooldridge, 199, 206
Ranch Hand, Operation, 239–41
RAND, 9, 209–11, 214–16, 218, 221–23, 228–29, 231–32, 237, 241–42, 245, 287–89
Raubkammer, 146
Raymond, Antonin, 97
Raytheon, 269
RCAs (riot control agents), 237–38
Reagan, Ronald 5–6, 9, 11
  chemical weapons, 167
  SDI (Strategic Defense Initiative), 255–60, 262–63, 265, 267–68, 271
  Stinger missile, 237
Redeye MANPAD, 233–36
Redstone Arsenal, 276
Redstone missile, 195, 200–201, 203–4
Regensburg raid, 82
Rex, Italian liner, 59
Reyes, Matias, 209
Reykjavik, 267
Rhodes, Richard, 126
Ridgway, Matthew, 182
riot control agents, 237–38
Robb, Roger, 187
Rocky Mountain Arsenal, 150
Rolling Thunder, 248–50, 252–53
Romney, George, 248
Roosevelt, Eleanor, 99
Roosevelt, Franklin, 4, 7
  atomic bomb, 121–26
  chemical weapons ,146, 151, 158–59, 162
  preparation for World War II, 59, 69, 71, 74
  World War I, 16–17
  World War II, 76, 80–82, 87, 99–100, 109–11, 114, 118, 134–35, 139, 175
Roosevelt, Theodore, 4
Rosenbergs, 131
Rostow, Walt, 87
Rotterdam, bombing of, 119

Rouen, 76
Royal Air Force. *See* RAF
Rubel, John, 7
Rumsfeld, Donald, 270
Russell, Bertrand, 213, 224
Ryan, Cornelius, 163

S-1 Committee. 125, 130, 132
SA-7 MANPAD, 236
SA-14 MANPAD, 236
SAB (Scientific Advisory Board), 192–94
SAC (Strategic Air Command), 6–8,
    176–78, 182, 195–96, 200, 211–13,
    216–23, 225–27, 270, 287
Sachs, Alexander, 123
Saint-Mihiel, 47
Saint-Nazaire, 79
Sakharov, Andrei, 267, 290
SAM missile, 276
Sandinista Liberation Front, 278
sarin, 149, 152–53, 161–65, 167
Sato, Naotake, 143
Sault Ste. Marie, 68
SBAE, 70
Schoeffel, Malcolm, 65
Schrader, Gerhard, 148–49
Schriever, Bernard, 193, 195–96,
    199–202, 204, 206
Schweinfurt raid, 82–83
Scientific Advisory Board (SAB), 192–94
Scott, Nathan, 31
Scud missile, 168, 269–70
SDI (Strategic Defense Initiative), 5,
    263–64, 266–71, 289
Seaborg, Glenn, 10, 126, 131
    early life, 131–32
    Cold War, 171–73, 183
    later life. 288
    Manhattan Project, 132–34, 142
SEALs attack on bin Laden, 12
"Second Variety," 282
Segal, Gregg, 279
Segrè, Emilio, 132
Sellers, Peter, 225
Serbian war, 278

Seversky, Alexander de, 65, 75–76
Seversky Aircraft, 75
Shenandoah dirigible, 53
Shocker, Operation, 165
Shubik, Martin, 232
Shultz, George, 256, 262, 267
Sibert, William, 35, 39
Silent Spring, 238
Single Integrated Operational Plan (SIOP),
    226–27, 229, 287
smart bombs, 5, 11, 88, 252, 272–73,
    275–78, 281–84
Smith, Edgar Fahs, 39
Smyth, Henry, 142
Smyth Report, 142
Somoza, Anastasio, 278
South Vietnam, 6, 94, 236–42, 247, 249,
    251–53
Soviet bombers, 182, 220
Soviet missiles, 200, 208, 220, 226, 232,
    256, 258, 271
Soviet surface-to-air missiles, 196
Spaatz, Carl, 45, 47, 54, 76, 80, 82–86, 95,
    140, 193–94
Special Projects Division, 160
Speer, Albert, 87
Sperry, Elmer, 274
Sperry bombsight, 70–71
Sperry Corporation, 65, 68–72, 274
Sprague, Robert, 218–19
Spring Valley, 41
Springfield Armory, 244, 247
Sputnik, 206–8, 220
Stabilizing Bomb Approach Equipment
    (SBAE), 70
Stalin, Josef, 138–39, 143, 174
Stalingrad, 147, 152–53
Standard Oil Development, 94–98
Star Wars, 255, 263
Stein, Max, 34
Steinhoff, Ernest, 195
Stevenson, Adlai, 197
Stimson, Henry, 86–87, 135–37, 139–40,
    144, 151, 156, 160, 170
Stinger MANPAD, 234, 236–37

Stoner, Eugene, 244, 246
Strangelove, 7, 224–25
Strassmann, Fritz, 122
Strategic Air Command. *See* SAC
strategic bombing, 5, 48, 50, 57–59, 61, 64, 72, 75–6, 80–83, 86–88, 96, 111–13, 118, 144, 146, 200, 249
strategic bombing doctrine, 68–69, 85, 87, 108
Strategic Defense Initiative, 5, 263–64, 266–71, 289
Strategic Missiles Evaluation Committee, 199
Strauss, Lewis, 171, 173, 185–86
Strela MANPAD, 236
submarines, 5, 8, 13–16, 18, 20, 22–24, 40, 196, 221, 227, 229, 277
Suez crisis, 208
Super (hydrogen bomb), 127–29, 169, 171–74, 179–80, 187
Superfortress (B-29 bomber), 107
Symington, Stuart, 212
Szilard, Leo, 121–24, 1353–6, 170–71

Tabun, 149, 152–53, 157–58, 161–62
Talbott, Harold, 198
Tarr, Paul, 162
Taylor, Maxwell, 245
TCC (Technical Coordinating Committee), 246–48
Teller, Edward, 6, 9–10, 40
    early life, 127
    hydrogen bomb, 171–72, 174, 178–81, 183–88, 198
    later life, 289–90
    Manhattan Project, 121, 123, 126–29
    SDI (Strategic Defense Initiative), 222, 224–25, 256–69
Tesla, Nikolai, 14
Tet Offensive, 236, 251–52
Texas Instruments, 276
Thanh Hoa Bridge, 276
Thatcher, Margaret, 125, 263
theater missile defenses (TMDs), 270
Thiel, Dolph, 202

Thieu, Nguyen van, 253
Thomas, Norman, 224
Thomas, Parnell, 131
Thor missile, 201–4, 206–8, 221, 225, 227
Thorpe, Clarence, 65
Thunderclap, Operation, 85, 108
Time magazine, 156, 185
Tinian, 105, 111
Titan ICBM, 199, 202
TMD (theater missile defense), 270
Toftoy, Holger, 192, 195
Togo, Hideki, 143
Tomahawk cruise missile, 273
Travis, Robert, 178
Trenchard, Hugh, 44, 49–51, 55, 74
Trident missile, 232
Trinity test, plutonium bomb, 128, 138–39
Truman, Harry, 7, 9–10, 135, 194, 197, 213
    atomic bomb, 135–40, 144
    chemical weapons, 159, 161–62
    hydrogen bomb, 170–71, 173–76, 183–84
    incendiary bombing of Japan, 119
    Korea, 182–83
Tupolev-4, 110
Turkey, 208, 221, 230, 279
Twelfth Air Force in North Africa, 80
Twentieth Air Force, 106
Twentieth Bomber Command in China, 109–10
Twenty-First Bomber Command, 106, 112, 114

U-2 spy plane, 219, 221
UAVs (unmanned aerial vehicles, or drones), 272–84
Ulam, Stanislaw, 178–80, 184, 188
unconditional surrender, 7, 80–81, 112, 120, 136
Unification Act, 197
United States Strategic Bombing Survey, 86, 108, 120, 142
University of Chicago, 131, 133–34, 169, 287

Uranium, 122–28, 130, 132–34, 140, 177
Urey, Harold, 10, 126, 129–32, 135,
    170–72, 174, 183, 287–88
Ut, Nick, 104
Utah, USS, 58

V-1 rocket, 157, 189–90, 192, 211, 275,
    277
V-2 rocket. 11, 157, 190–92, 195
Vance, Cyrus, 246
Vandenberg, Hoyt, 178
Vanguard rocket, 207
Veracruz invasion of Mexico, 285
Verdun, 44
Veteran Affairs, Department, 242
Victor Adding Machine Company, 71
"Victory Through Air Power," 11,
    75–76
Viet Cong, 238–39, 241–43, 249–53
Vietnam, 7, 177, 233, 238–43, 245–50,
    252, 254, 272–74, 276, 283,
    287–88
Vietnam War, 6, 104, 160, 243, 251,
    286
Vietnamization ,251
Vincennes attack on Iranian airliner, 282
Von Neumann, John, 199
Vonnegut, Kurt, 108
VX nerve gas, 164–66

Wachsmann, Konrad, 96
Waddell, Alfred Moore, 17
Wade, Horace, 7
Wahl, Art, 132–33
Walbridge, Edward, 265
Wallace, George, 286–87
Wallace, Henry, 135
Wallop, 259, 263
Wargasm, 223
Warner, John, 280
Watergate, 6, 253
Watkins, James, 261–62
Weinberger, Caspar, 283

Weinberger-Powell doctrine, 283
Weissman, Samuel, 133
Westmoreland, William, 241, 243
Westover Air Force Base, 73
Wheeler, Earl, 246, 250
White Sands, 194–95
Wigner, Eugene, 121
Wilhelmshaven, 78, 81
Willoughby, 35–37
Wilmington insurrection, 17, 286
Wilson, Charles, 203, 206–8
Wilson, Ward, 143
Wilson, Woodrow, 4, 12–3, 16, 22–3, 35
Winchell, Walter, 197
"Winged Defense," 53
Wohlstetter, Albert, 9, 216, 218,
    221–23
Wolfowitz, Paul, 270
Wood, Lowell, 258, 264, 289
Woodruff, Roy, 264–66, 290
Wooldridge, Dean, 199
Wright brothers, 45
Wright Field, 176
Wyler, William, 78

X-45 UAV, 281
X-Ray laser, 256–66
    Cabra test, 263–64
    Correro test, 265
    Cottage test, 265–66
    Dauphin test 257–58
    Delamar test, 266
    Goldstone test, 266
    Romano test, 264–65
X-Ray, Project, 103

Yalu River, 249
Yokohama, 120
Yom Kippur War, 166
York, Herbert, 185
Ypres, 26–27

zeppelins, 47–48